Clicker Training
for Obedience

For clickers, videos and more about clicker training:

Sunshine Books, Inc.
49 River Street, Suite #3
Waltham, MA 02453-8345

www.clickertraining.com

1-800-47CLICK
or
781-398-0754
fax:781-398-0761

e-mail: clicker@clickertraining.com

Clicker Training for Obedience

Shaping Top Performance—
Positively

by Morgan Spector

Sunshine Books, Inc.

Photography: Morgan Spector and Karla Spitzer
Spaniels on cover, and pages 193, 226: Susan Smith
Illustrations: Concepts, Morgan Spector; design, Co-Design

First edition.
Second printing, September 1999

Designed by Compset, Beverly, MA.
Cover design by Co-Design, Jamaica Plain, MA.

Library of Congress Catalog Card Number 97-067794
ISBN 0-9624017-8-1

Foreword

In this wonderful, one-of-a-kind book, attorney Morgan Spector brings you the best current thinking about clicker training and dogs. Morgan is profoundly familiar with the questions trainers ALWAYS raise, when they first encounter operant conditioning. "Why can't I just use my voice?" What if the dog doesn't obey?" "When can I get rid of the food?" "But you can't take the clicker into the ring!" He addresses all these familiar bugaboos right away, so we can get on with the training.

And what fun training it is! From the first exercises with a baby puppy, Morgan's program is full of happy surprises. Since you aren't relying on compulsion, how about teaching that puppy a little retrieve? How about introducing the scent articles while you're at it? And if you've got a "crossover" dog, trained the old way, and mighty suspicious now, how about working on a drop at a distance while you watch TV?

This is not to say the program is casual; far from it. Morgan has your UDX and OTCh awards in mind from the first little kitchen tricks he teaches you. If you want to compete, he wants you to win. He'll show you how to use the clicker to build rock-solid precision performance at each level. If you want to settle for just getting by, that's fine; but if you want refinement and precision, he wants it too. Again and again you'll see clearly, in this book, why shaping with a conditioned reinforcer is the path to success.

Morgan is not giving you just the benefits of his own experiences or opinions. His information is backed up by scientific data and applied behavior analysis. He bases his approach on the concept of "fluencies," currently one of the hottest topics in behavioral science. Morgan is scrupulous about the use of scientific terms and principles. He explains them. He makes it clear why he uses them, what they mean, and why ordinary language won't suffice. When he says things a scientist would avoid saying (such as attributing human feelings to an animal) he explains why he's taken the liberty: "My dog Sam hated that kind of training. At least, his heeling went into the toilet along with his attitude; I call that 'hating'."

Morgan's legal skills make him a careful researcher. He is also one of the most well-read, literate people I've ever met. His wide knowledge and respect for accuracy show up in many ways. For example he is scrupulous about giving credit for every idea, method, phrase, or explanation that came originally from someone else. Over and over you will read phrases such as "In Marian Bailey's words . . ." or "Gary Wilkes originated the use of . . ." or "As Karen Pryor says in *Don't Shoot the Dog* . . ." or "B.F. Skinner wrote about this in *Science and Human Behavior*."

Morgan also identifies his more casual sources, such as Internet posts, conversations, experiences of students, and his observations of other top trainers in competition. This honesty, this honoring of his colleagues, is more than just good manners. In the tradition of scientific writing, it shows us where an idea began, and where to start digging if we want to learn more on that particular matter. In the tradition of literature, it shows us that Morgan is bringing to us more than his own thinking: He is bringing us the combined wisdom of a considerable group of people working in this field.

Morgan also has a lot of personal experience as an instructor. Clicker training, famously, does not rely on "correction," a source of much argument from outsiders. This book will clarify that dispute. Due to Morgan's pre-clicker years of teaching traditional obedience classes, he knows the ways people get into trouble in competition: the lagging heels, the crooked sits, the drop-on-recall failures, the mouthed dumbbell, the missed jump, the long sit and long down disasters. From the viewpoint of clicker training he now shows you not only how to avoid those problems (or repair them if you have to) but also why you got into them in the first place. And it wasn't because you were "too easy on the dog."

That is a mistaken assumption that even some clicker trainers buy into: Positive reinforcement is all very well for easy stuff, but if you want perfection, you have to get rough. People falsely assume that the choice is, "Either be nice to my dog, and settle for pretty good scores, or get tough and get 200's."

Morgan makes it clear that "being nice" is not the issue. The clicker can give you precision at a level most people only dream of—if you want to compete at that level. The issue is energy: yours. It's not the punishment that makes perfection: it's those miles of travel, weekends of trialing, and extra hours of concentrated thinking about how to apply the underlying principles to your daily training events.

While the *principles* of shaping and reinforcement, like the laws of gravity, are ever present, applications can vary. As I have said elsewhere, there are as many ways to shape a given behavior as there are trainers to think them up. Chapters 4 through 7 describe Morgan's meticulous methods for each obedience exercise. They work: his students are winning. But others will use other recipes, other methods. For example, Morgan uses the dog's name in training the recall. Corally Burmaster, editor of *The Clicker Journal*, prefers to omit it. Both methods

have their benefits, and both methods work. Morgan usually establishes the cue by respondent conditioning. I prefer to shape cue response as an operant, because, for me, it seems quicker. Yet both methods develop quick and reliable cue response. What you can count on, with Morgan's methods, his step-by-step instructions, is that a) the methods are sound as to the underlying principles, b) each method is free of coercion, with all that implies as to attitude and long retention, and c) these programs will work.

Writing a book of this scope is not a trivial exercise. It turned out to be more than four years' work. As Morgan's editor and publisher I was privileged to see how his methods were shaped and honed during the four years. He wrote, then taught, then came back and revised or rewrote, then taught some more. At the start of the project, Morgan and his two competition dogs were in the middle of Utility training. To make time for all this work the author had to postpone intensive competition with his own dogs. Before Morgan went back in the ring himself it would be his students, with their unusual assortment of "non-obedience" breeds, who would be finishing their UD titles and racking up the high scores.

So now you can join that lucky group. If you just want to have a hassle-free, truly enjoyable companion dog, this book will show you the way. If you want to knock off a CD and a CDX on your way to developing a herding champion or field trial dog or breed sire, then this book will do it for you, too. If you want to develop a service dog, the fundamentals can be found right here.

And most of all: If you have visions of a top-scoring obedience dog, of UDX titles, Delaney ratings, breed top tens, high in trials, big wins in the regionals, and that Obedience Training Championship— all accomplished with a happy, eager canine partner and a clear conscience—go for it! Here's your travel guide, with stopovers, scenic wonders, and good company included.

Karen Pryor

Contents

A Personal Note:

The Relationship—Or, Where This All Comes From and Where It Can Get You

Whether you are just trying to keep your dog from knocking your visitors down the front stairs or you have visions of an Obedience Trial Championship, operant conditioning can lead you to a more pleasant, productive, and rewarding training experience. I hope that this book offers some valuable "how-to" information. I hope this book also provides a coherent explanation of how operant conditioning theory works.

I came to operant conditioning not out of any academic background but from personal experience. I own Shelties. My very first Sheltie I trained with traditional "J&P" ("jerk and praise," sometimes referred to as "jerk and puke") methods. One day my wife looked at little Woody oddly and asked, "What's happened to the fur around his neck?" (Now that we are hipper we call it the "ruff," but that was then and this is now.) I looked and saw that the right side of his ruff was in a burr cut. I had unwittingly shaved him to Naval Regulations with all the "sawing" of the choke collar.

Thus began my journey. Bit by bit, step by step, I groped my way down the path of "gentling down" my methods. Woody could not hold a down stay in his early days; one morning I found myself getting angry and frustrated with him and grabbed him harshly (my wife thought I had hit him, which I did not). I took another step. I learned about "binding"

(keeping the dog close at heel) and the proper use of a pinch collar—further steps. Gentler, more attentive, more responsive handling.

Then Woody got sick. We first realized it was more than simple stomach disorder in mid-December 1991. Woody had just finished his CDX (Companion Dog Excellent, an AKC title) with a 196.5, 1st in his class and high Sheltie in trial. Ten days later we took him in for a blood panel; the lab called our vet and asked, "When did this dog die?" He had the blood of a 15-year-old dog. His thyroid was off-the-scale low; my vet could only conclude that he had virtually no thyroid tissue left. He was dying of inflammatory bowel disease (our vet called it "doggy AIDS").

We did all we could for him over the next sixteen months, and finally put him down two weeks before his fifth birthday. One Wednesday evening I took him to the park, set up an open ring with jumps one-half his normal jump height, and ran him through. Damned if he didn't work like he always had: precisely and completely willingly. Thursday morning I held his foreleg as I had done throughout his course of treatment. The vet inserted the needle and Woody went to sleep in my arms.

With all that I took a major step. I learned what heart a dog can have. I learned how much they are willing to give. And so I found myself adrift, searching for some way to train that would truly put me in tune with, instead of "at war" with, those qualities.

In March 1993, while Woody was close to death, I was seriously considering quitting obedience. My second dog, Sam, was going through (at the risk of being anthropomorphic) a major depressive episode that began during Woody's illness. I was close to retiring Sam. Not because he was too old, but because he had no enthusiasm for training or showing. I expected to get another puppy, but I didn't want to make the same mistakes I had with Sam and Woody, and I didn't know where to go or what to do. I was, in short, at a dead end.

Having nothing to lose, I found myself at a Don't Shoot the Dog seminar conducted by Karen Pryor and Gary Wilkes in Anaheim, California. In those two days all the pieces fell into place. It was a true conversion experience.

That seminar was about operant conditioning. Simply put, operant conditioning is the art and technology of developing ("shaping") behaviors. The emphasis is on shaping behaviors you want through positive reinforcement rather than eliminating behaviors you don't want through negative reinforcement or punishment.

I came out of that seminar knowing two things: (1) Nobody really knew how to use the method to train competition obedience dogs, and (2) I was going to figure out how to make it work. My first decision was to eliminate my ability to force my dog to do anything. My first step, simply, was to throw away the leash and training collar. It was at that point, I think, that I started to become a trainer.

In the time since I was first exposed to this approach I have found an interaction and relationship with my dogs—and with new dogs I meet—that I only dreamed of before. I have found the ability to "speak" to them. They can now "hear" what I am saying. A bond has formed between me and my dogs without my even really working on it as such; it has been the natural by-product of the methods and techniques I'll lay out in these chapters.

If I may say this without sounding too much like the child of the sixties that I am, this book is about love. It is about bonding. It is about real interaction between you and that alien beast that somehow controls your house without moving from his corner, or dares you to take that toy from his mouth or move him off the couch, or gives you a blank stare from across the ring when you call "Come!"

This is what training is about for me: not ribbons, trophies, or placements, but a feeling of community and "family" you can achieve in no other way.

Many people who will read this book will be into competitive obedience handling. To you, loving your dog is important, but that's not why you bought this book. You want to accomplish something in the obedience ring. If this kind of training won't get you there, who needs it? Right?

I suppose it's only fair that I state my own competition goals. I want a dog that is consistently competitive, that is, capable of challenging for placements at any given trial. I want a dog that qualifies for the Classic (which means an average score of 195 or better). I want the Utility Dog Excellent (UDX) title. I want a dog that is eager to get in the ring and performs with drive and enthusiasm. I want a dog that wants to train. I want a dog that is an ambassador for obedience training in daily life as well as in the ring.

Whatever your goals are, whether it is to achieve titles, or to compete in the Regionals or Classic, achieve a 200, or achieve an Obedience Trial Championship (OTCh), this approach to training will enable you to realize those goals.

Operant conditioning will produce a dog that is more focused on his or her work, and is therefore more attentive in the ring. It will produce a dog that works with more precision because he or she understands clearly what you expect. It will produce a dog that works with enthusiasm because the work has been reinforcing throughout the training process. And you and the dog will get there faster, and with less stress. Of course, how far you go and how fast you get there is up to you.

Structure of the book

Like almost everyone who starts in obedience I began with the usual sequence of first training Novice, then Open, then Utility. I now not only think this approach is not necessary, it can be detrimental. Many dogs that could go on at least to their CDX burn out with the repetition of Novice training. So do their handlers.

Not only do I no longer stick with that sequence, I don't train with the competition classes in mind per se. Rather, I train by first developing basic skills (fluencies), and then refining and combining those fluencies into specific exercises. That's the approach I take in this book.

So the structure of this book is different and reflects the application of operant conditioning principles. As it happens, the structure makes this book useful both for pet owners and competition handlers.

There are six chapters that follow this one. Chapter 2 is called "The Basics." This covers the outline of the method and terminology that will recur throughout the book. Many people have asked me about many of these points at training classes and on the Internet. Even if you "know the field," it will be helpful at least to scan this chapter so you will know what my terminology is and why I am using it. You may find that you prefer terms other than mine, but at least you will know what I'm talking about.

Chapter 3, "Fluencies," is, to my mind, the most important. Here I go into development of basic working skills that will apply throughout the dog's obedience career. These fluencies are not limited to competitive obedience. Some, like attention, can be applied in the conformation ring. Others, like targeting, can be applied to training service dogs. And others, like scenting or marking, can be applied in tracking or field work. If you are a pet owner, you can read this chapter and learn how to shape essential behaviors without having to cope with excessive detail about refining those behaviors into competition-level skills.

The next three chapters ("Novice—Or, Beginning Utility," "Open," and "Utility") cover the specific levels of obedience training. Each builds on the skills discussed in the "Fluencies" chapter.

The final chapter, "Who's In Charge Here?," addresses some pet behavioral issues. These are the things that my pet owner clients seem to encounter most frequently. This section can also be useful to obedience competitors. We have all encountered, at one time or another, the obedience dog who is not obedient outside the ring. You can shape obedient behavior just as you can shape obedience behavior. This section discusses the most common behavior "problems" and some approaches to solving them.

I want to make clear, however, that I am employing these categories only for convenience. It is helpful to discuss the exercises by organizing them according to the competition class in which they occur. But I do not believe that the exercises must, or even should, be taught in sequence. Many dogs respond quickly to learning retrieves, go-outs, and jumping, and can perform those behaviors quite

snappily long before heeling is in place. It is one of the ironies of the Novice class that the single thing that is hardest to train—precision heeling—counts for about forty percent of the scoring. By shaping the "advanced" exercises early in your dog's career you will not only be able to progress more rapidly through the classes, you will make training more enjoyable and reinforcing for you and your dog.

My overall training philosophy is that if the dog is physically capable of performing a given behavior, you can shape it through positive reinforcement. *Go to the dog.* Take what the dog has to give you, and build from there. Throw away your leash and collar in training. When you eliminate your ability to compel the dog to perform, I believe you will find—as I did—that you can also eliminate your felt *need* to compel the dog to perform. Then you will finally be free to work with your dog as you find him or her.

Teach the dog everything you can as early as you can. In the early stages of training it is better to introduce your dog to a broad spectrum of activities and develop a broad range of "fluencies" (see Chapter 3) than to focus on simply the Novice exercises. The more basic fluencies your dog learns early, the more things you will have to work with as you go forward. And the more your dog learns and is reinforced for learning, the more your dog will want to learn, which will make further and more advanced instruction easier.

A general caveat

Throughout this book I apply principles of shaping and changing behavior to obedience training. However, there are as many ways to shape a behavior as there are dogs to be shaped and trainers to think them up. The approaches I outline here provide a path to successful training. But the most important thing I hope you get from this book is not this or that "recipe," but a sense of how to apply operant conditioning principles creatively and develop methods suited to your particular training needs.

You are the only person who can train your dog, because you are the person who knows your dog best. You and you alone are responsible for the behavior your dog ultimately exhibits. Your dog isn't going to read this book. I have not met your dog and odds are I'm not going to. So if some particular approach I lay out here does not work with your pooch, don't just say "oh, this clicker training doesn't work."

"Principle" and "Method"

Many trainers will tell you, in essence, that "no one *method* works for all dogs." This statement is both true and false.

The statement is false insofar as it suggests that shaping through positive reinforcement may work for Shelties (for example), but not for terriers. It is a principle of training that the most effective way to teach a behavior is to shape it through positive reinforcement. *It will work with all dogs*, just as it works with chickens, monkeys, dolphins, pigs, vultures, cats, otters and cockroaches. Within the shaping principle are other principles—for example, that putting behaviors on a variable schedule of reinforcement increases the intensity of the response. These principles do not change. They express fundamental laws of learning and apply universally.

The statement is true insofar as it suggests that these basic principles have to be applied somewhat differently from breed to breed, from dog to dog, and even with the same dog from time to time. This is a matter of the *methods* used by the handler to implement the principles. To what extent do you rely on "pure" or "free" shaping? When do you "lure" the dog? How quickly do you put a behavior on a variable reinforcement schedule? How far do you extend that schedule? When do you "go back to kindergarten"?

These—and about two million others—are all questions of method. There are no recipes in this realm, no "magic bullets." This is the domain of the trainer's art.

Instead, look for another way to tackle the problem consistent with the *principles* I lay out.

In short, learn the principles and basic methods, but don't be afraid to innovate. Though the number of people subscribing to this method is growing, we are still a small family within the larger obedience community, and what we each do and learn enriches all of us.

A note on gender

Because it is awkward to keep saying "him or her," "he or she," and because I am comfortable with saying "he," I use only the masculine pronoun for dogs in the rest of this book. And I often use feminine pronouns for trainers! Please bear with this usage—it is just a convenient simplification.   M. S.

The Basics

Before you get into novice training, there are some "pre-novice" issues that you should pay attention to. Some may seem trite, even silly, but they are all of great importance.

Conditioning to physical interaction

One of the most important things you can do with any dog is to condition the dog to be comfortable with physical interaction. This means more than just enjoying a good romp in the park or some vigorous rubbing.

Your dog should be comfortable with being touched and handled all over his body. Your dog should accept having his mouth opened and his teeth and gums examined, his feet held, massaged, and rubbed, his toenails clipped, and his ears rubbed. There should be no part of his body that your dog resists having you touch, examine, or massage.

There are a couple of important reasons for this. Most obviously, your vet and groomer will need to be able to handle the dog "all over." Sometimes their handling will be invasive. You don't want your dog resisting this. These professionals are rightly concerned with dogs biting or being aggressive. Because they are deemed to "accept the risk" of dog bites in the course of their professional duties, they

have no legal recourse even in the case of the most savage attacks. If they are unsure about your dog's "manners," you may find them muzzling or even anesthetizing your dog. You will not only improve your relations with your vet and groomer, but also make your dog's experience with these professionals a more positive one, if you pursue this type of conditioning.

But there is another reason, one that we don't like to think about much. Inevitably, your dog will suffer training injuries. He will hit a jump, or land from a jump and slide, or step on a stone and cut a pad, or tear a nail. These things happen. When they do, you must be able to attend to your dog until you can get professional help. In most cases, the most important thing is to be able to quiet your dog and avoid further injury. If your dog is comfortable with handling and massage you will be able to get him under control, examine the injured area, and do basic things like ear rubs that will help alleviate his panic and let you assess the situation calmly. And knowing that you can do these things will help you respond more professionally when—not if!—accidents and injuries occur.

Another side to the injury issue is that we usually don't know that our dog is injured until the injury is really serious. Dogs are very good at hiding injury. The ethologists suggest that this is an atavistic survival mechanism: In a pack, an injured dog is subject to being abandoned or even killed. Whatever the underlying instinctual basis may be, the fact is that if you notice your dog is injured, the extent of his injury will probably surprise you. If you are consistent about massaging your dog and getting used to the normal feel of his muscles, joints, and tendons, you will be much more sensitive to even small indicators of injury (stiffness, "boardiness," slight swelling, etc.) and therefore much better able to intervene before the injury becomes drastic.

Puppies learn to accept this kind of handling fairly readily, though some will resist at first. Older dogs being introduced to this handling will be uncertain, and often "mouthy" with the handler: not really biting, but opening their mouths and putting their teeth on your skin. It is imperative to accustom the dog to being handled without responding with his mouth.

When the dog learns to accept this kind of "all-over" handling the dog will also have generally submitted to your authority and "dominance." Dominance in this sense is not a power thing. It is not something you establish by force. It is something you establish by gaining the dog's complete trust that you will handle him properly and he can therefore permit you to do so. When you have established this type of "dominance," other training becomes much easier.

General massage

Spend some quiet time with your dog every day. Use very gentle strokes around his muzzle, and bit by bit insinuate your fingers into his mouth, massaging the teeth and gums. If he resists, don't retreat but don't advance either. Stay at a particular spot until he relaxes, even if it takes a couple of days' effort to get past it. Never get into a wrestling match.

Once your dog understands the "click-and-treat" connection, you can use the clicker to soothe the dog into accepting touches. You can click and treat, and sometimes (if, for example, you have one hand in the dog's mouth at the time) just click. Treat as soon as you can. The effect will be to put the dog's mind on the reinforcer and help you communicate to the dog that the physical contact is a desirable thing. It is not necessary to click and treat in this way for long, because as the dog learns to accept the physical interaction it becomes reinforcing in and of itself.

Pay particular attention to the legs and feet. Use long, smooth strokes down the legs. Massage the toes and between the toes, separating and lifting each toe.

If the dog gets mouthy or tries to jerk his foot away, speak to him in quiet tones and reduce the level of invasiveness—but don't stop the massage altogether. Do not encourage the dog into thinking he can make you stop by biting or threatening to bite.

Massage the body with long strokes upward along the rib cage with your palm open and your fingers slightly spread. Also massage along the length of the body, against the grain of the hair.

Massage the tailset and tail, wrapping your fingers around the tail and pulling lightly.

TTouch™

TTouch (a copyrighted name) is a therapeutic technique for animals, developed by Linda Tellington-Jones. I am not a TTouch practitioner and don't pretend to be able to teach the method. I do use some of the touches on my dogs, however, and find the technique to be beneficial to them and me alike. I strongly recommend buying Linda Tellington-Jones's book and video and developing some proficiency with basic touches such as the clouded leopard, raccoon, Noah's march, python lift, butterfly, bear, and abalone. These touches give you a number of ways to intervene physically for your dog's well-being in a variety of circumstances. I often use TTouch before going into the ring to calm both me and the dog.

At certain points in the book, where a particular TTouch may help in training the exercise, I will indicate the one(s) I use and briefly describe how they work. This is not intended as any substitute for learning the material from the source.

So what does all this have to do with obedience?

If you are a pet owner, you will find that the more physical interaction you can develop with your dog, the better. You will be able to resolve problem behaviors more easily, and with any luck at all avoid many of them altogether. And you will generally find that your dog's responsiveness to you will increase.

For the competitive obedience trainer, anything and everything you can do to develop your dog's confidence in you and your comfort in handling and working with your dog will help you in the obedience ring.

For example, very often behavior that looks like fear in exercises like the stand for exam is really discomfort with being approached and handled physically. Also, many dogs are very light-footed even when standing on all fours. This is a "fight or flight" symptom. TTouches such as the python lift will help the dog "plant" more solidly. This is helpful both in the breed ring and in obedience competition. A general, overall sense of calm will also be of immeasurable aid in shaping the long sits and downs.

Physical interaction as described here will make your dog generally more comfortable and at ease, and more amenable to these exercises. Dogs that are used to rough handling will show hand-shyness while working. For example, I have seen dogs lapse into lagging because of an initial flinch away from the handler's hand during a heeling pattern.

Regular massage also makes your dog more conscious of all parts of his body. Dogs are generally not very "body-conscious." This is particularly evident with their rears. Dogs just don't think about their rear ends much (it is the sort of thing that is at work when a dog is scared and hides his head, thinking that if he can't see you, he must be invisible too). In training fronts, for example, it is not uncommon to see a dog line up perfectly with his head, and have his rump swung out. Developing your dog's body consciousness will make him more confident about his movements, particularly in heeling and jumping.

To the extent that the purpose of obedience competition is "to demonstrate the usefulness of dogs as a companion to humans" (taking slight liberties with American Kennel Club phraseology), massage has the beneficial effect of conditioning dogs to expect gentle treatment from humans generally, making the dog more tractable in the vet's office or the groomer's shop, as well as in greeting strangers on the street.

If you ever have to give your dog pills, you will be glad that the dog readily accepts you opening his jaws and handling his teeth and gums. Our dogs get sick, and they get hurt. After all the medications I had to give Woody, I taught both Sam and Dylan the cue "Take your pill," and each will open his mouth with only slight pressure from me, and let me insert my finger into his maw.

Finally, it is often surprising to me how uncomfortable obedience handlers can be with their own dogs. Their dogs will obey them in the ring, but I see many handlers who do not seem to trust that their dog will be sociable, not only with other people but with their own handlers. In part, I regard this as a by-product of the training methods. But it is also a product of physical alienation between dog and owner, and can be cured in part by overcoming that alienation through activities of the sort discussed here.

Okay. Now let's talk actual training.

Primary and conditioned reinforcers*

Reinforcement increases the likelihood that a behavior will be reproduced in the future. Put more simply, *reinforcement strengthens behavior.* Some reinforcers are "objective"; that is, they occur without anyone thinking about them as reinforcers. For example, water coming out of a fountain when you press the button reinforces the act of pressing the button. In training, reinforcers are "subjective"; that is, you as the trainer are delivering the reinforcer with the intent of causing a given behavior to be repeated in the future. Whether you know it or not, your responses are always reinforcing something that the dog is doing. Whatever behavior you have achieved in the dog, it is the product of what you have done to reinforce it. So you must always be thinking about what behavior you intend to reinforce, and how you are doing so.

Let's look at the reinforcement "tool kit."

The training "bargain"

I'll discuss this more in the section on *positive reinforcement* (+R), but I must briefly address it here. Training based on shaping through positive reinforcement rests on a training "bargain" between you and the dog. Simply stated, you say to the dog, "You give me what I want, and I'll give you what you want." The training process then becomes a dialogue between you both. The dog looks to you for direction (information about what you are asking for) and confirmation (that the dog gave it to you). It is your job to be clear, consistent and fair.

The click sound made by a hand-held clicker is the primary way that you "talk" to the dog in the training process. It works because you consistently deliver what the click promises, so the dog becomes comfortable with its unambiguous message.

---

*Throughout this book I use bold, italicized type to show words and terms that are explained in the Glossary.

The primary reinforcer (PR)

While there are different academic definitions of the term, for training purposes a *primary reinforcer* (PR) is something the dog "naturally" wants. In other words, you don't have to "condition" the dog to want it. This "something" may be food, play, or physical interaction with the handler of some sort or another (sex is also a primary reinforcer, but we'll stay away from that in this program). It is not something the dog has to be "taught" to like. Food is the easiest PR to use in training because eating is pretty basic among the primal drives and food is easy to manipulate. Play as a PR is not particularly handy (except as a "break" or as an overall reinforcer at the end of a session) because it interrupts the training session. The same is true with physical interaction (such as roughhousing or giving Ttouch or massage).

The conditioned reinforcer (CR)

A *conditioned reinforcer* (CR—sometimes also called a *secondary reinforcer*) is something the dog is "taught (conditioned) to like" by pairing it with the primary reinforcer. In theory, anything can serve as a CR: voice, a whistle, a clicker. The primary consideration is its utility to the trainer. I have heard various acronyms to summarize the necessary qualities, but I like PRIDE: The CR must be Present, Reliable, Immediate, Distinct, and Evident. Running through these qualities in a nutshell, we have:

- Present: It must be with you and easily available for use.
- Reliable. You are associating a specific sound with the primary reinforcer, so you must be able to deliver that same sound every time;
- Immediate: You must have a quick sound that you can employ very specifically in training in response to very specific actions. Saying "You were a very good dog that time, and I would appreciate it if you did it again" wouldn't do it. You must think in terms of a single-syllable word or a sound.
- Distinct: The conditioned reinforcer must be *distinctly associated* with the primary, and not "diluted" by association with anything extraneous to the training context. A word like "good" is usually not effective as a CR because you use it in so many ways outside the training context.
- Evident: The dog must be able to recognize it separate and apart from all the other sounds and stimuli that he encounters.

I use the term *conditioned reinforcer* instead of *secondary reinforcer* because it highlights a couple of small but important points. First, it is something neutral in itself that the dog is taught ("conditioned") to like. There is nothing significant about the sound of the click as such. It is association through training that makes it powerful. And second, this use avoids the implication of the term "secondary reinforcer" that it is somehow less powerful or less important than the primary reinforcer. In fact, over time, the CR becomes at least as powerful as the primary reinforcer. This is because it always precedes the primary reinforcer, and the dog comes to learn that the primary isn't coming unless he hears that "magic sound" first. The dog really comes to work for the "magic sound." That's what gives the CR its power.

Why the clicker?

The clicker is integral to the program in this book. It is the CR of choice for training purposes. Throughout this book you will see letters C/T. They stand for click/treat (or "click and treat"). You can substitute other instruments (including your voice) for the clicker, but in my experience none work as well for teaching purposes. The clicker fits all the criteria that I described earlier as essential to the CR in training. Its sound is distinct; its sound is uniquely paired with presentation of the primary reinforcer; it is immediate; it is audible over a distance; and it is neutral, that is, it is unaffected by emotion or physical factors.

Why "neutrality" is important; or, clicking isn't "praise"

Many trainers resist the concept of neutrality. They want to "praise" the dog. I don't know if this is for their benefit, or if they think there is some scientific basis for the idea that "enthusiasm" really gets the point across to the dog (so far as I know, there is no basis at all for such a theory). I am not against praise. My dogs get it early and often, in all variety of circumstances and regardless of the weather. In the learning process, though, information is more important than praise. For the dog, as with any other student, the knowledge that he is correct becomes reinforcing in and of itself.

Praise is not communication. Praise is emotional interaction with the dog. In their book *How to Be Your Dog's Best Friend*, the Monks of New Skete

*A primary reinforcer is something the dog "naturally" wants. This "something" may be food, play, or physical interaction with the handler. (**A**) Helio gets a tidbit. (**B**) Rubi's treat is a fast game of tug-o-war. (**C**) Clio loves her "bounce" cue. (**D**) Sam likes to wrestle.*

describe praise as "a physical and verbal involvement with the animal." It conveys positive *feeling,* not necessarily positive *information.*

The clicker does not convey any emotional reaction to what the dog does; it simply "marks" a correct action. It is purely informational. It provides the dog with a clear, unambiguous message: "What you just did there was right." It is almost the same as the gold star the teacher put on your spelling test in third grade. You loved it even though the teacher didn't also give you a hug. You knew you had succeeded, and that was what you needed to know.

Praise does not serve the same purpose or achieve the same result for people as does *positive reinforcement*. In high school I was terrible in the sciences, and particularly terrible in chemistry. My parents always let me know they loved me ("praise"), but that never really got me past my unhappiness with being a lunkhead in the laboratory. And though my chemistry teacher tried hard to help me learn, I never learned how to succeed in the sciences (that "left-brain" deficiency probably had a lot to do with my not pursuing a veterinary career despite my love of animals).

It's the same for the dog as with people. In training for obedience competition we are teaching dogs to perform structured behaviors and in a particular way. These behaviors don't really make natural "sense" to the dog in the way herding "makes sense" to a Border collie or tracking does to a bloodhound or pulling several hundred pounds over frozen tundra does to a malamute. The dog must not only learn the physical maneuvers; he must also learn the commands and signals that tell him when to perform these exercises. It is all rather confusing. It is therefore of paramount importance that we have a tool that gives the dog a clear, unambiguous signal that a particular, identifiable behavior was correct. By doing so we achieve clarity (or something very much like it), and increase the likelihood that the given behavior will be repeated in the future.

The limitations of using voice as a CR

Vocal sounds as a CR are generally less effective than the clicker. Measured against the PRIDE criteria, voice falls short in several ways.

For one thing, voice is not "distinct." Let's say that you use the word "good" as your CR. You probably say "good dog" to your pal 50 or 60 times a day other than in the training context. The word "good" therefore does not have an exclusive association with training. You also say that dinner is "good," and a TV show is "good," all usually within the dog's hearing. All this dilutes the specific utility of the word as a CR.

Words are also not "immediate." There are a couple of points here. First, because the clicker allows you to respond instantaneously to a behavior, you as a trainer must, and will, develop a finer sense of timing than you probably have now. In clicker training you learn how to orient to smaller pieces of behaviors, "grab" (or "capture") them, and form them into something better. Though you have the big picture always in mind, you work with details. You can literally respond to one single paw-step done in the way you want in a heeling pattern, for example. Voice does not give you that kind of refined timing.

Second, for most people, once you become used to handling the clicker it is quicker than any words you might use instead. How many times have you intended to say one thing only to have another come out? The physical reflex of pressing the clicker in response to a perceived action is easier than the process of verbalizing your positive response.

With Woody in Novice when going for our second leg, we'd had one of those fumbling "newbie" ring experiences. So by the time we got to the recall I was thoroughly rattled. After Woody did his recall the judge told me "finish," and I looked at Woody and said "finish." He looked up at me quizzically as if to say "Didn't you mean 'heel'?" and then went nicely around. The obedience trainer hasn't been born who hasn't been saved at least once by a dog who knew what was going on better than the trainer did.

As another example, I use a different word for every exercise. In Utility, the bar jump is "bar" and the high jump is "over" (as in Open). At one match I directed Sam to the bar and he missed the signal. Trying again, this time he caught the signal but I said "over." He took the bar anyway. With the clicker, you don't have to worry about the wrong word coming out at the wrong time.

Voice is also highly variable, depending on whether you are hot, tired, happy, angry, frustrated, thirsty, you name it. It is virtually impossible to deliver the same word in the same tone every time in the course of a training session. Since tone is so important to a dog, these inevitable variations mean that the same word, delivered in different tones at different times, will have different meanings. The CR is supposed to make things simple; trying to use voice in the teaching process only makes things harder.

This is not to say that verbal praise and physical interaction are not worthwhile or important. They are. I use plenty of both. But they are primary, not conditioned, reinforcers. They are things the dog is really working for; they do not signal the dog that what he is working for is coming. And they come after the behavior is completed or the work is done; they are not delivered as information while the work is in progress.

How about other sounds?

How about a whistle? It probably fits most of the criteria (assuming that the little ball doesn't get jammed), but it is not something you are going to use in an area where others are training, or indoors, and if you are right next to the dog it will be insufferably loud.

How about a squeaky toy? Useful, but not particularly "evident" at any distance.

How about a tongue cluck? This falls under "verbals." Again, there's nothing wrong with it in principle, but you will have a hard time delivering a tongue cluck with consistency. Ever try to do it when you're dry?

How about a fingersnap? Nice sound, probably inconsistent, not very evident over any distance, and hard to do immediately.

How about a Snapple cap? Fine. Makes kind of a clicking noise. Not audible over any distance, and not particularly consistent.

How about a froggie clicker? Fine. Has all the virtues of the "industrial-strength" clicker except that it doesn't have a long life.

What if your dog is deaf? Hmm. Major problem if you are relying on voice and don't have a good CR. Of course, the dog can't hear the clicker either. How about a flashlight with a flicker switch? The flash on and off is a visual "click." It's the same principle as the clicker: The flash of light is neutral. It has no significance in and of itself. But by associating it with a PR and teaching the dog its meaning, it becomes as powerful as the clicker to a dog with hearing.

"But you can't take the clicker in the ring!"

One of the objections to using the clicker in training that repeatedly comes up is, "But you can't take the clicker in the ring."

A friend of mine once told me her technique for getting her dog to give a straight front: She put a piece of bait between her knees and made the dog get the bait from between her knees. I told her that this was one reason I liked the clicker, because I could communicate what "straight" meant without a bait trick. Her response? "Yeah, but you can't take the clicker into the ring." I have yet to see her going into the ring with bait between her knees.

To the folks who object to the clicker because "you can't take it into the ring," I offer a simple challenge. Let's train using only things that you can *actually use* in the ring. Let's see. The dog can wear a buckle or slip collar, so you can use that. You can have a leash if you must, but you can't use it to make corrections of any sort because you can't make leash corrections in the ring. You get to use no toys, no food, no motivators of any kind, nothing. You can pet and praise the dog (allowed in the ring) but you cannot "correct" the dog (not allowed in the ring). You can't talk to the dog as he is working (also not allowed in the ring). Now, let's start training.

The point should be obvious. Every trainer uses tools in training that she cannot take into the ring. You couldn't train without them. The clicker is a training tool. You have to wean the dog from the clicker just as you must wean the dog from every other training device.

The clicker is a tool for communicating "Correct!" during the training process. As the dog learns what is expected, you will fade (gradually eliminate the use of) the clicker. You will also add other CRs, including verbals and "performance" reinforcements, that is, using one behavior to reinforce a preceding behavior. As a simple example, Sam loves to do a "pop" swing finish to the left. If he gives me a good front, I signal him to do the swing. If he gives me a sloppy front, I send him around to the right. I'll discuss in other sections how this approach can work in training behavior chains.

"But I want my dog to work for me!"

Another objection often voiced about using the clicker is by the handler who says, "I want the dog to work for me, not food or a sound." I notice that most of the people who say this sort of thing also are seriously committed to physical "corrections" in their training. What they do not recognize is that, given the heavy use of physical "corrections," the dog is not working "for them" at all, but rather to avoid the corrections.

More fundamentally, this attitude misses the point of what training is all about. Training is an educational process. Successful training produces a dog that is willing and happy to work, confident in what he is doing, confident about his ability to confront and overcome surprises. This is done through positive reinforcement. Positive reinforcement training is impossible without the use of a conditioned reinforcer.

The fact is, we work for ourselves and our dogs are no different. Our boss would prefer that we work out of company loyalty, but if the checks stop coming loyalty goes bye-bye. We are asking our dog to perform tasks for us. If there is nothing positive in it for the dog, why should we expect him to perform?

Some work is inherently reinforcing to a dog. A Border collie needs nothing more than a herd of sheep to push around, a bloodhound a scent to follow, a Jack Russell terrier a varmint to chase into the ground. Give a pointer a field with birds and his life is complete.

But there is no breed of dog for which obedience work is innately reinforcing. Some take to it more readily than others, but it is not "natural" to anyone, canine or human. If we want our canine partners to join with us in this activity, it is only fair to give them a good reason to do so.

"Mom's (or dad's) love" isn't enough. The dog will (or should) get that anyway. There has to be something intrinsic in the work to create the necessary motivation and consistency. That's what positive reinforcement is all about, and that's the purpose of the clicker as the conditioned reinforcer of choice.

And finally, this program does ultimately get the dog working "for you." The dog will enjoy the work, and enjoy you more as part of that. You will become more consistent and clear. The dog will be more comfortable with you, more trusting, more confident in the relationship. What more do you want?

Conditioning the sound

Most dogs don't seem to mind the sound of the clicker at all. They get the association locked in immediately. Even my sound-sensitive shelties had no problem with the sound (though I have encountered the occasional dog that gets spooked by it). Some dogs are sound sensitive and need conditioning. There are a couple of approaches.

One is to borrow a page from "gun dog" training and desensitize the dog through progression:

- Clicker in pocket.
- Clicker in hankie behind back.

- Clicker in hankie with hand in normal position.
- Clicker in hand.

If your dog is particularly sound sensitive you can even begin with a tongue cluck.

Another approach is to introduce the sound while the dog is doing something he likes, such as eating. This will do two things: It will accustom the dog to the sound, and it will establish a positive association. Steve White, a K-9 police dog trainer in Seattle, Washington, tells of doing this with nursing puppies. When the dam goes to the puppies to nurse, he clicks as the puppies take the teats (there is probably no more primal association between the click sound and a primary reinforcer than this!) In this way he easily establishes the association when the puppies are about three weeks old. They very quickly respond positively to the sound.

I find that most dogs overcome their sound sensitivity when they figure out the association between the clicker and the food reward. The fact that, as a rule, the click is not a disturbing sound to most dogs is one of the reasons you can work with a clicker around other dogs that are not clicker trained.

Timing is everything

The idea is to click exactly what you want to reinforce. This means that you must be clear in your mind as to what you are looking for. In *Lads Before the Wind*, Karen Pryor tells a story of trying to get a dolphin to swim from one tank into another. The dolphin would go through the gate, and immediately turn and swim back into the first tank before the handler had a chance to close the gate. When Karen finally got someone to observe the process, the observer noted that she was blowing her whistle just as the dolphin was starting to turn. So, instead of reinforcing the dolphin for going straight ahead, she was reinforcing the dolphin for turning. When she adjusted her timing (and we are talking about a split second here), she quickly cured the behavior "problem."

The lesson Pryor draws from this experience is that the trainer must always ask, "What am I reinforcing?" This is really a two-part question: (1) What do I intend to reinforce, and (2) What am I actually reinforcing? This requires that you plan your training sessions carefully and concentrate on what you are doing throughout.

You must focus exclusively on the dog during training so you can respond appropriately to what the dog offers. It's only fair. After all, you are asking the dog to focus exclusively on you. This is one reason Pryor notes in *Don't Shoot the Dog* that gratuitously interrupting a training session constitutes a punishment. To take your attention from the dog is to take away the possibility that the dog can achieve his goals. That defeats the whole principle of this approach.

Although the classic definition of a reinforcer includes the notion that it follows an action, this is true for the PR only. The CR must be delivered *as the action is taking place* so that it is specifically associated with the desired behavior. A common error for the beginning clicker trainer is to wait too long to click. The "click" is so immediate and specific that it always reinforces whatever is happening at the exact instant you do it. If you delay at all in delivery of the CR, it will be reinforcing something other than what you intend.

It may help you to understand this point if you think in terms of reinforcing process rather than merely reinforcing result. I want the dog to know what he is doing that is correct, not so much what he has done. How he gets there is in this sense more important than that he gets there at all. So, if I am going to make a mistake in timing, it will be to click early. That way, at least, I will catch the behavior in process. The click may cut the behavior off a bit too soon, but that is easy to remedy. I simply treat the behavior I have reinforced as a step in the right direction, and keep going forward. That is not an option I have if I click too late; in that case, I have lost the behavior altogether.

To see how this works, let's go back to the basic "sit." When reinforcing "rump on ground," I deliver the CR *as the dog is sitting*. With correct timing, the click comes out just as—or an instant before—the dog's rump hits the ground. It is possible to click much too early: If I click before the dog is "committed" to sitting, that is, before his rump has progressed down to a point where it is hard for him to stop, the click may serve to stop the behavior before there is any "sit" behavior to reinforce. It is possible to shape a "half-sit" in this way. On the other hand, if I click after the dog's rump is on the ground, I am really reinforcing the rump staying on the ground, not the act of putting it there in the first place. With proper timing I click an instant before his rump hits the ground, reinforcing the muscle action itself—as well as the result that immediately follows.

Go back to the question, "What am I reinforcing?" In almost every instance in which Fido "isn't getting it," you can trace the confusion to imprecise

timing of reinforcement. And on the other hand, precise reinforcement with the clicker can clear up confusion almost instantaneously.

Here's an example of how imprecise reinforcement can send the wrong message. One of my students didn't want to use the clicker but wanted to use voice instead. He was shaping "attention" by saying "good" and treating whenever the dog looked at him. After two or three repetitions he started to say "good." He got out the "guh," the dog looked away and "ood" followed. The trainer was visibly startled and said, "I just reinforced him for looking away." He still didn't want to use the clicker, so from that time on he used "guh" as his "click-word."

As an example of the second, I was teaching Dylan go-outs. He knew to run out, and I had separately shaped the "turn-and-sit." Now I wanted to put them together. When I called "Dylan, sit!" he turned and lay down. I did another repetition to see what was happening, and saw that as he turned his rump hit the ground and he lay down from there. So on the third try, as he turned and his rump hit the ground I clicked. He stayed sat, his eyes went wide, and his head popped up. It was a visible "Aha!" Next time out he sat, and we had no problem thereafter.

This is not to say that every problem can be solved so easily. But precise timing of the CR can generally cut through a problem more quickly than other approaches.

"Click" ends the behavior

This is one of the areas in clicker work that people find hard to grasp at first. The power of the clicker lies precisely in the way that it marks a specific, correct action. The dog learns through the early association work that when he hears the click, he has earned his goodie.

So, *it is a rule* that every time you click you are signaling to the dog that he has done what you want, and the behavior is over. And so, it is a rule also that when you click, the dog is free to stop what he is doing and get his treat.

For example, in teaching go-outs, you can click as the dog is going away from you and has gone, say, five steps in a straight line. When you click, the dog can (*and will!*) stop going forward; at that point he may (is permitted to) return for the treat. Similarly, in training the retrieve, if you are clicking for the pickup, once you click the dog is free to drop the dumbbell and come for his treat. This sounds scary:

"I don't want the dog dropping the dumbbell." True. But not to worry.

Remember one of the cardinal rules of behavior shaping: You only work on one thing at a time. In the example of the dumbbell, you are training one thing: the pickup. You have gotten and reinforced the particular behavior (picking up the dumbbell) that you are looking for. When you add "bring it to me," you will no longer click on the pickup but on the completed retrieve, a somewhat more complex behavior than simply picking an object up.

Do not use "click" to mean "keep going"

Many trainers, especially trainers who have trained in one or another of the "motivational" schools of thought—and I include myself in this group when I began clicker work—want to use the clicker as a way to mark correct behavior ("click: keep going") in the midst of a behavior chain. I think this is a residue of confusing +R with "praise" and, along with that, not really understanding how the CR works.

There are several problems with using "click" to mean "keep going."

The click means "good job, come get your reward." That's the training bargain. If I use the clicker as a "good, keep going" signal I'm no longer honoring the training bargain. I have promised something I did not deliver. Instead of maintaining the power of the clicker as a CR I am undermining it. In not too great a time the click will become just one noise among many that has a fuzzy instead of a clear meaning.

Using the click to say "keep going" will create confusion. The first time that I click as a "keep going" signal the dog will stop what he is doing. Now I have to "explain" to him that the treat isn't coming. In other words, in the interest of providing what I construe as "encouragement," I'm actually changing the rules in a way that really makes no sense to the dog, and undermines our existing "agreement."

This is a mistake that I have worked through myself. Early on in my use of the clicker I used it as a "keep going" signal. Over time I took a close look at what was going on, and I was forced to recognize that I was using the click as "encouragement" (i.e., "praise") in those portions of the exercise where the dog really lacked confidence. I had to admit to myself that the dog lacked confidence because I had not really trained that portion of the exercise well.

When I went back and trained that portion of the exercise properly, my felt need to "encourage" the dog disappeared. Now that he knew what to do, I could "click" the whole chain without worrying whether he was really sure about this or that piece of it.

Now, this is not to say that I cannot C/T a behavior in the middle of a behavior chain without completely disrupting the chain. I have a little system with my dogs. At any point that they come to a stationary position and hear the click, they hold that position until I give them a release signal (both hands lifted up and out). So, for example, on the drop on recall, I can "click" the drop. With our little system in place, I can then walk to the dog and give him a treat and return to my original position. Then I either release him or call him to front. I'm isolating a particular behavior for reinforcement without breaching our training bargain. And I'm getting an incidental side benefit as well: The dog learns to hold that down until I give him another cue. This can help make the overall exercise more stable as well.

"Click" as a "bridge"

Some of the early dolphin trainers called their *conditioned reinforcer* a "bridge" or "bridging stimulus." What they meant was that the CR allowed them to reinforce an action at a distance, and also "bridged the gap" between the moment they delivered the CR and the time they delivered the *primary reinforcer*. They gradually dropped the word "bridge," but the concept is still valid.

In training, the "goodie" doesn't always arrive immediately. For example, in training go-outs I click when Sam gets to the target stick. He will then turn and run back to me for his treat. That may take a couple of seconds. When he gets to me and gets his treat, he knows what he got it for. In this way the clicker acts as a "bridge" between the behavior and the primary reinforcer.

It is one of the powers of the clicker that you can retain this clarity, sometimes over 30 seconds or more. If my dogs start to become "chow-hounds," that is, they start pushing for the food in my hand or in the bag at my waist, I use this "bridge" concept to break the "chow-hound" behavior. I put all the treats in a container on a bench several feet from where we are working. I get the behavior I'm looking for, I click, and then we go to the bench for the treat. Clearly, this can slow down a given session and it is not something I do all the time. It is a corrective measure to teach—or remind—the dog that he is working to hear the click, and the treat only comes after that. The point is, even after we have walked the several steps to get the treat, the dog still knows what he is getting reinforced for, because the click has told him.

Basic shaping with positive reinforcement

The phrase *positive reinforcement* (+R) denotes both an *attitude* and a *method.* Both are important to the training philosophy. When I say "attitude," I don't mean an artificial happy face. I am talking about an inner quality of belief, or faith, in the dog's ability to get the job done. By proceeding carefully (employing the method), both you as the trainer and your dog will develop that faith, in yourselves and in each other.

Sports commentators often speak of a team "playing to win," as opposed to a team "playing not to lose." In both cases the team wants to win, but the approach—and therefore, often, the result—is very different.

The team that is playing to win is playing with a core confidence that it will succeed. This team is aggressive, opportunistic, resilient. The team that is "playing not to lose" is playing with a core fear that it will fail. This team is conservative, slow to respond to opportunity, easily discouraged. In the glory years of the Green Bay Packers, Vince Lombardi used to say after a defeat, "We didn't lose, we just ran out of time." Vince Lombardi knew how to play to win. Perhaps more importantly, he knew how to keep his team's attitude positive even in times of adversity.

Clicker training develops dogs that play to win. The training process teaches them that they can succeed. It teaches them that what they do—if they do it hard enough and long enough, will produce results for them. It does not produce a dog that is afraid to fail, but rather a dog that can encounter failure and keep going, knowing that continued effort will bring rewards. As the dog develops confidence, you as the handler will develop confidence in your dog. And it will show in the ring.

How does positive reinforcement help develop reliable behaviors as well as the dog's confidence in his ability to perform them?

Let's look at shaping a basic behavior: the sit. The dog gets its rump on the ground (a good thing) but flops back on its haunches (a bad thing). These qualities and others (such as speed and alignment with the handler) are *criteria,* that is, essential elements

to the proper performance of the exercise. In order to train the sit—or any exercise—properly you have to know what your criteria are, and plan how to train them.

Every exercise consists of several criteria, and there is a logical sequence for developing those criteria. There are several criteria to a good sit: (1) The dog must put its rump on the ground; (2) the dog must be balanced from front-to-rear; (3) the dog must be straight from side to side; (4) the sit must be quick; and (5) the dog must be able to hold the sit indefinitely.

You develop criteria one at a time. In the sit, you first reinforce the dog's action in putting its rump on the ground. Then you teach the dog proper "sit mechanics" so that Fido does not flop back on his haunches. This *raises the criteria*: The concept of "sit" no longer means just "put your rump on the ground," it now means "put your rump on the ground with proper mechanics." As Fido absorbs this new criterion, you will no longer reinforce floppy sits, only straight ones. In the lingo, this is *differential reinforcement (DR)*. You are not reinforcing everything the dog does, but only things of a certain type or quality.

This does not change the training "bargain." You are still giving Fido what he wants in exchange for him giving you what you want. It is just that you are raising the level of what you want. Fido now has to work a little harder and a little more consistently to get what he wants.

You can then *confirm* this proper posture by lengthening the time between the action of sitting and the C/T. Instead of clicking *as* the rump hits the ground, you extend the time by counting one second for a couple of sessions, then extending to two seconds for a couple of sessions, then three seconds, four seconds, and so on. (I don't use a watch. I count by "one-banana, two-banana," and so on.) This process not only solidifies proper posture, it also lays the groundwork for the "stay." The dog is learning that reinforcement will come; it just might take a while.

Your job is to understand the **criteria** of any given exercise and plan how to develop those criteria in a logical progression. When you do that, and build the dog's mastery of the exercise through that progression, the dog will always be confident that he knows what you want, and of his ability to give it to you. The training "technology" inevitably produces not only the behavior, but also the attitude you are looking for.

The reinforcement contingencies

In one sense, our behaviors are "reinforced" every day by the simple processes of life. You smile and wave at a friend, the friend smiles and waves back—your cordial behavior is positively reinforced. You are hungry, and you go to the refrigerator to find something to eat because you have found things to eat in the refrigerator in the past. Once Old Mother Hubbard found the cupboard was bare, she probably didn't bother looking for a bone there again. Reinforcers are an incidental part of everyday life.

The trainer employs **reinforcement** consciously. We are deliberately working to make it highly probable that the dog will produce certain behaviors on cue. Simply put, reinforcement increases the probability that a given behavior will recur in the future.

The two types of reinforcers

Reinforcement strengthens behavior. There are only two types of reinforcement: positive and negative. Both are intended to accomplish the same result, that is, increase the probability that the behavior that immediately preceded the reinforcer will recur. My training philosophy is that teaching behaviors is best accomplished through **positive reinforcement**.

A common synonym for "reinforcement" is "reward." I don't particularly object to shorthand, but it is important to be clear what the terms mean. You can receive a reward for something you have done in the past, but with no particular expectation that you are ever going to do the same thing again (such as a reward for turning in a wanted criminal). Reinforcement, however, is always intended to strengthen the behavior that triggered the reinforcer.

I don't use the terms "positive" and "negative" reinforcement in some moral or ethical or humanitarian sense, "positive" meaning "good" and "negative" meaning "bad." The terms have a purely mathematical connotation. Positive reinforcement (+R) means that you give something desirable to the dog to reinforce ("reward") the behavior that just occurred (dog sits, dog gets a biscuit). *Negative reinforcement* (−R) means that you take something undesirable away in order to reinforce the behavior that just occurred.

All leash work is based on negative reinforcement. You apply an aversive ("pop" the leash) to trigger a behavior, and then remove the aversive (release the pressure) when the dog responds cor-

rectly (moves forward at heel, sits, lies down, whatever). In all such cases, the dog's response to the particular cue (or command) arises in order to avoid the leash "pop." What −R teaches above all else is how to avoid something undesirable or punishing. As Karen Pryor puts it, −R is *something the dog will work to avoid.*

You can train behaviors through negative reinforcement, but you are always working—and contending—with aversion and avoidance. This is why "motivational" methods have become so popular. It is an effort to counteract the aversive character and consequences of negative reinforcement training. With +R, "motivation" as such becomes irrelevant; it is an integral effect of the method itself.

Positive reinforcement ("win–win")

Positive reinforcement works by giving something to the dog that, in essence, rewards the given behavior. In *Don't Shoot the Dog*, Karen Pryor defines a positive reinforcer as "something the dog will work to achieve." Skinner wrote (in *Science and Human Behavior*) that "positive reinforcement strengthens any behavior that produces it."

If Fido sits and I give him a treat, the sitting behavior is strengthened. The likelihood that Fido will sit again is *increased* because doing so produced a favorable result. Using +R is a "one-step" process: When you get the behavior you want, reinforce it.

Operant conditioning teaches the dog to "work to achieve" a reward by sitting, without any negative overtones. In other words, the trainer does not respond aversively to the dog "not sitting." The trainer simply responds positively to the sit when it occurs. At first, the sit will happen randomly. But because sitting produced something desirable for the dog, the dog is likely to do it again.

Skinner wrote that "Operant behavior is the very field of purpose and intention. By its nature it is directed toward the future: a person acts in order that something will happen, and the order is temporal." Elementary shaping teaches the dog that doing a particular thing will produce a desired result.

Over time, the dog generalizes that lesson. The dog learns that it has the power to affect what happens to it: Do the right thing and good things follow. The dog will then produce behavior on its own in order to generate the beneficial consequences it has come to expect. The behavior has now become *oper-*

ant; that is, as Skinner put it, "the behavior *operates* upon the environment to generate consequences."

This is why operant conditioning through positive reinforcement, once learned, is easier to use than training methods based on "corrections" or negative reinforcement. Training with +R harmonizes the wills of the dog and handler. This is the training "bargain" I referred to before: The handler essentially says, "Barfy, you give me what I want, and I'll give you what you want." Barfy says, "It's a deal." You develop an affirmative interaction between dog and handler. The dog learns to get what it wants by giving you what you want. Once that dynamic is created, it will carry over into every new exercise you wish to train, and as you progress training actually becomes easier.

Positive reinforcement teaches the animal not to be afraid of the new. As Murray Sidman points out in his book *Coercion and Its Fallout,* "Both positive and negative reinforcement will effectively teach what the contingencies specify, but they will also teach other things. That is where they differ. Posi-

tive reinforcement leaves us free to indulge our curiosity, to try new options. Negative reinforcement instills a narrow behavioral repertoire, leaving us fearful of novelty, afraid to explore."

The dog that is not afraid to try new options will be ready to absorb new behaviors, and will also receive "negative information" better. What do I mean by "negative information?" When the dog makes a mistake, you want to be able to communicate to the dog that he has made a mistake, but also to do so without making the dog fearful. The word "wrong," uttered in a conversational tone, is often used for this purpose. It tells the dog, "That ain't it, kid, try again." Properly developed and employed, it can stimulate the dog to rethink what it is doing.

For example, in training scent discrimination articles, if Sam picked up the wrong article I could quietly tell him "wrong" while he was still at the pile. He would drop the incorrect article, search again, and find the correct one. No stress, no fuss. In teaching the directed retrieve, if I sent him to the #3 glove and he went to #2, I could say "wrong," and

"Wrong"

Gary Wilkes popularized use of the word "wrong" in response to an undesired behavior. There has been some controversy over the purpose of the word. Some consider it a punisher (or, more accurately, a conditioned punisher). I don't agree. I regard it as an *extinction cue.*

Behaviors that are not reinforced tend to become extinct. If I present Fido with the opportunity to do something and he does something incorrect, I can extinguish the behavior simply by not offering any reinforcement. However, the extinction process is often slow and uneven, particularly with behaviors that have become at all ingrained.

The word "wrong," to me, simply serves to short-circuit the extinction process. It tells the dog, in a word, the same thing that withholding reinforcement over a period of time would: that is, "I don't want that behavior, so eliminate it from your repertoire."

While the word is useful, I tend to be leary of its use, especially in the early stages of training. The

whole point of operant conditioning is that the dog learn through experience how to select behaviors based on the history of reinforcement. Injecting the word "wrong" too readily into the process seemingly may make training smoother, but in fact it can interfere with the learning process.

It is important for dog and handler alike to get comfortable with the reinforcement contingencies. The dog has to learn how to recognize nonreinforcement when he gets it, and the handler has to learn the patience necessary to withhold reinforcement—indeed, withhold any response at all—when presented with an undesired behavior.

If you find yourself using the word "wrong" often, my view is that you are probably asking too much of the dog—that is, you are asking the dog to perform beyond his level of understanding. If you use the word before the dog understands the criteria and before the dog understands what it means for you not to respond with a positive to an offered behavior, the word is not information but only a crutch.

he would stop, consider the matter, and go to #3. So in a very real sense, training becomes a dialogue between dog and handler.

Negative information is not negative reinforcement. It only works because the positive reinforcement contingencies are in place. The dog understands that there is a correct behavior to be performed, he knows what it is, and so he can accept a *cue* that tells him that he has gone off track *as information,* process it and get back on track. *It doesn't work if the dog is afraid of the consequences of being wrong.* As Frank Herbert wrote in *Dune,* "Fear is the mind killer." In the absence of fear, the dog's mind becomes engaged and he can work through mistakes. That leads to reliable behaviors.

Negative reinforcement ("lose–lose")

Negative reinforcement, in Skinner's words, "strengthens any behavior that reduces or terminates it." Karen Pryor defines a negative reinforcer as "something the dog will work to avoid." In real life, the process is often objective: The behavior of drinking water is negatively reinforced because your thirst is quenched (goes away). In training, the process is subjective. Negative reinforcement in training has two aspects: *presentation* of an aversive, and *withdrawal* of an aversive. Put another way, the negative reinforcer accomplishes two, interrelated things: (a) it *decreases the likelihood* of a certain undesired behavior occurring in the future and (b) it *increases [by its withdrawal] the likelihood* of another, desired behavior occurring in the future.

This definition of a negative reinforcer is not entirely consistent with the language of the laboratory. I can live with that. Behaviorist theory has its vocabulary, largely developed in the laboratory, and like everyone I am a prisoner of that vocabulary. So, like Humpty-Dumpty, "When I use a word, it means just what I choose it to mean—neither more nor less." But unlike that contentious egg, I shall try to explain myself further.

Let's stick with our example of the sit. In traditional training the dog is standing by the handler's side. The handler says "Barfy, sit," and pops upward on the leash, at the same time pressing on the dog's rear end (or, in some schools, swatting the rear end lightly, or "folding" the rear legs at the hock). When the dog sits, the pressure on the leash is "released."

This is a classic use of a negative reinforcer. Standing when the handler says "sit" is an unde-

sired behavior. The "pop" upward is a "correction" (presentation of an *aversive*) intended to extinguish this undesired behavior by linking it to an aversive consequence. Similarly, the "release" of the leash reinforces the sitting action by removing the aversive when the desired behavior occurs. This method teaches the dog to "work to avoid" the leash correction by not standing when he hears "sit."

This is the training method employed traditionally employed in dog training. A skillful handler can do very effective leashwork without jerking the dog around and without causing the dog to hack or retch. But regardless of how subtle and elegant the handler's methods may be, all leashwork is rooted in negative reinforcement: The dog is working to avoid the "pop."

"Traditional" or "command-based" training is based on negative reinforcement

Traditional ("command-based") training is based on negative reinforcement. The underlying motif is that there is always an unpleasant consequence attendant on the dog failing to do what the handler wants. A current popular phrase is that the dog "has to know it has no choice but to obey." This training philosophy, regardless of how it is clothed in "motivational" or "positive" language, at bottom rests on a model of obedience as forcible domination.

I use the term "command-based" to describe traditional training because it describes how training proceeds, and denotes the distinction between traditional training and operant conditioning. In traditional training, you start by giving the dog a command (that the dog does not understand—dogs do not speak English, you know), and then do something—a leash "pop," or an ear pinch, luring with bait, or a zap from an electronic collar—to cause the dog to obey. Conceptually, the type of "correction" or degree of humaneness is immaterial. Luring and zapping are essentially opposite ends of a continuum based on a common method: Give an order and compel compliance.

Command-based training is rooted in negative reinforcement. In command-based training the "word" comes first, and you then compel the dog to "comply" (i.e., perform the behavior). It starts with confusion and tends to produce behaviors that are not particularly resistant to *extinction.*

Operant conditioning is rooted in positive reinforcement. In operant conditioning the behavior comes first. You take actions (behaviors) the dog performs on his own and shape them into a completed behavior. You do not attach the "word" (cue) to the behavior until the behavior pretty closely resembles the finished product. The dog thus learns that a certain word connects with a certain action that has always produced desirable results.

Distinguishing between "negative reinforcement" and "punishment"

The behavioral analyst would probably acknowledge the two elements in the presentation of the aversive stimulus as stated in my description of −R, but would call the leash pop *punishment* and the release *negative reinforcement.* It's not my intention here to argue academic niceties. I use the term negative reinforcement to include both the presentation of the aversive and its withdrawal, to emphasize the continuity and unity of purpose between the two actions. I also like to distinguish presentation of an aversive intended to affect an occurring behavior, and presentation of an aversive that cannot affect that behavior because it occurs too long after the behavior to do so. This last type of aversive I call *punishment.*

This distinction is important because it highlights two issues: (1) timing and (2) the necessity of presenting some desired behavior as an alternative to the undesired behavior. A dog's attention span is measured in seconds (with certain Wheaten terriers I know, in nanoseconds). So for negative reinforcement to work, the aversive must respond *immediately* to the undesired behavior. And to be fair, the negative reinforcer must present the dog with an alternative: something the dog can do—*and that the dog can perceive it can do*—to cause you to remove the aversive.

Negative reinforcement and punishment at work in the real world

In California, the California Highway Patrol uses what it calls a "white door verbal" to caution speeders. If you are going, say, 72 mph in a 65 mph zone, the patrol car will pull up next to you and the officer will look over at you. If you respond by slowing down, the officer will move on. If you don't slow down—or worse, if you speed up—the officer will pull you over and write a ticket.

The "white door verbal" is a *negative reinforcer.* The "white door verbal" presents an aversive (the presence of the patrol car and officer) together with the opportunity to eliminate the aversive (by slowing down). The withdrawal of the aversive (police car moves on to make someone else's life complete) when you slow down thus negatively reinforces that behavior.

Writing the ticket is *punishment.* If you either do not slow down, or (worse) speed up, you will get stopped; your speeding behavior is now in the past. You can't avoid the aversive. The state will gain some measure of reprisal for your refusal to follow the law (or to use common sense) by fining you, or possibly by suspending your license. Will the punishment affect your behavior in the future? People pay their fines and speed again, and our roads are filled with people driving with suspended licenses.

For several thousand years at least, animals have been trained through the centuries with negative reinforcement techniques. They work. However, negative reinforcement is not my method of choice. Those tickets and other reprisals may or may not cause one to drive within the speed limit in the future. Perhaps all they will do is motivate the purchase of a "fuzzbuster."

The "ringwise" dog

In dog training, all too often avoidance behaviors take over. It is not uncommon to see dogs "shut down" as they move up from Novice to Open to Utility. Is this because the dog is too dumb to learn the exercises? No. In many cases, it is simply because not doing anything is the easiest way to avoid the aversive consequences of doing something wrong.

When punishment is interposed in training, the subject all too easily learns simply to avoid or evade the punishment, rather than produce some desirable behavior. This is at least part of what underlies the behavior in competition called "ringwise."

The so-called "ringwise dog" is a dog that performs erratically or not at all when off-lead in the ring. Some competitors will say that such a dog is "blowing off" the handler. Some handlers respond to "ringwise" behavior by saying things like, "He's learned he can get away with disobeying when he's in the ring."

This is all nonsense. Such responses blame or attribute some devious motive to the dog, rather than focusing on the training deficiency. Everything the dog does is the result of how the dog has been trained. "Ringwise" behavior falls into one of two categories: "false positives," or avoidance.

The "false positive"

The dog that has been trained through negative reinforcement has been taught that the absence of an aversive response means that what the dog is doing is correct. In the ring, and especially when the leash is off (eliminating even the apparent possibility of being able to "correct" the dog), nothing the dog does triggers an aversive physical response. Therefore, everything the dog does in the ring is right. I call this a "false positive." The dog isn't right, but the reinforcement history tells him that he is.

Avoidance

Aversives tend to generate avoidance. When confronted with an aversive, the goal becomes simply to avoid the aversive. You do what you must, but only what you must, to "turn it off." In Murray Sidman's words, "Negative reinforcement generates escape. When we encounter a negative reinforcer, we do whatever we can do to turn it off, to get away from it. If we encounter it again, we will do what worked before." In the ring, the dog can "get away," both literally (by breaking out of the ring) and figuratively (by refusing a command). And as Sidman notes, "If we control others by negative reinforcement, we, too, become objects of aversion." This is why a dog's "ringwise" behavior is so often characterized by actions or body language indicating aversion to or fear of the handler.

Positive reinforcement is not "motivational" training

One approach to solving "the problem of the ringwise dog" lies in "motivational" techniques. I won't talk about "motivation" as such in this book. The motivational trainer has not abandoned negative reinforcement as the fundamental basis for training. The motivational trainer simply overlays the negative reinforcement regimen with toys, treats, and high-voltage praise. It's like putting whipped cream on liver. Motivational techniques often serve only to mask the underlying problem: Training based on negative reinforcement is intrinsically demotivating to dog and handler alike. Top handlers

often search long and hard to find the dog that can handle the training. And very few handlers are really able to train well with this method.

Unlike training based on negative reinforcement, training based on positive reinforcement is inherently motivating. Remember Skinner's point: "Frequent reinforcement also *builds and maintains an interest* in what a person is doing." As with a person, so with a dog. The dog works because he has learned that his own actions can generate a positive result. The dog therefore develops an intrinsic interest in generating a correct performance.

While many traditional trainers "like the way this sounds," they often come back with a question: "But what if the dog doesn't want to do what you tell him to do?" The question misses the point.

In the first place, if you have built the dog's understanding of the training "bargain" correctly, there is no reason why the dog would not perform. After all, when you give him the cue for a behavior you are really giving him the opportunity to earn reinforcement. So why wouldn't he perform? It is simply not the case that a dog won't do something unless compelled to do so.

Second, if the dog does not perform on any given occasion, is that so big a deal? Nobody is perfect. The goal of training is to get a *very high degree of reliability*. But no matter how high the degree of reliability may become, everybody—dog and human alike—misses something sometimes. It is really a matter of getting the best your dog has to offer, the maximum number of times possible. Training with positive reinforcement will get you there faster, more reliably, and with more consistent results than will training with coercion.

Superstitious behavior

Behavior shaping begins with *superstitious behavior*. In *Science and Human Behavior*, Skinner states that "If there is only an accidental connection between the response and the appearance of a reinforcer, the behavior is called 'superstitious.'" Perhaps Stevie Wonder said it more simply: Superstition is "when you believe in things you don't understand." In the context of dog training, superstitious behavior is behavior that the dog repeats because, for reasons the dog does not [yet!] understand, it produced a desirable result.

For example, sometime in the post-Jurassic period, while wild poodles still roamed the earth, I had hunted and gathered and was cutting up something meaty on the carving board. As Sam stood near my feet a piece happened to hit the floor and Sam gobbled it up. To this day, when I bring out the carving board and start hacking, Sam is there waiting. He doesn't really know "why" he got a treat when he did, that one time in the dim-and-distant, but he did, and if by chance another morsel should hit the floor from time to time (not that something always does, but I can be, um, clumsy at times), this only strengthens the likelihood that he will continue to stand in that same spot, licking his lips, whenever I'm at the cutting board.

I have probably just told you everything you need to know about shaping and maintaining behavior. But I'm writing the rest of this book anyway.

In basic operant conditioning you simply respond positively to some desired behavior offered by the dog. For example, you shape a sit initially simply by rewarding the puppy when it sits. After two or three treats the puppy will be sitting every chance it gets. I shape "sit" with every new dog I work with in exactly this way. We got our three year-old mixed-breed, Skipper, at a time when I had little or no time for training. But I did start him on "clicker awareness," and after only one session he had that sit. Whenever he thinks he's in trouble, or is just unsure of what is going on, he sits.

One of my clients had a dog that resisted the "down." No matter how I moved my hand to induce the dog to lie down, she would dip only her head, leaving her rump high in the air. I once tried to push lightly on her rear; she was too "spooky" and moved away. So I left her alone and we humans went off to discuss global politics over cappucino. A few minutes later she lay down in a corner. I clicked and tossed her a treat. A few more clicks-and-treats and I was able to introduce "down" as a *cue*. Her owner worked with her for the next week, and she was doing the down *on cue*.

You begin with what the dog gives you. You reinforce whatever part of that is in the direction you want. Raising your criteria in this regard simply means that you ask the dog to give a little more in that direction at each session.

Establishing the clicker

In this book I'm talking about clicker training, which is shorthand for "operant conditioning based primarily on positive reinforcement involving systematic use of a conditioned reinforcer." If you are going to train the way I describe here, both you and your dog have to get comfortable with using the clicker.

I talked earlier about *why* you are to use the clicker. Now, we'll talk about *how*. The first step in clicker training is to establish the clicker as your *conditioned reinforcer*. You must be certain that the dog has absorbed and accepted that "click" means "the goodie is coming."

Shaping the association

The idea is simple: Create a reflexive link between the sound ("click") and the primary reinforcer ("treat"). This is basic *respondent conditioning*. The dog learns that click = treat. Simply click and immediately treat. Repeat five times. Do this for four to five sessions. You may well feel before you have done twenty-five repetitions that the association is "in place," but carry this part through. This is so basic to everything that follows that you don't want to shortcut this step. Don't rush it.

One thing you must pay attention to right from the start is timing. At this stage you are not reinforcing any particular behavior, so you are not concerned with timing as a response to behavior. But you do want to deliver the PR as immediately as possible after the CR. This is so the dog will make an immediate association between "click" and "treat." If you dally after the click in this early conditioning, then the dog may well add other superstitious behaviors into the mix (for example, jumping up to get at your treat-holding hand). Click, and treat immediately.

I am also not a fan of letting the dog get the treats from the floor. I don't want Fido getting into the habit of sniffing around on the floor for a goodie. All treats must come from my hand. If you drop something, pick it up before Fido can grab it. Remember Sam and the cutting board.

Sometimes the dog will do nothing in particular while you are establishing the C/T association. But remember that behavior is anything a dead dog can't do, so your dog will be doing something: sit, paw at you, put his feet up on your lap, something. Any time the dog does anything that you like, or looks like something you might like if you someday developed it into a larger behavior, C/T. You'll do two things at once: establish the association, and reinforce that desired behavior.

If you like, you may even ask for tiny bits of behavior such as "all four feet on the floor." This is a good way to "countercondition" jumping-up behavior in a puppy; it will also be the start of the stand. But don't ask for too much! You may ask for "rump on the ground," but don't ask for a competition sit. It is just that the dog will be doing something, so it may as well be a very basic something that you happen to want.

If you do ask for some elemental behavior, you must be careful. You want to make sure that the dog understands that click = treat regardless of the dog's position, stance or posture. So C/T when the dog is sitting, standing, walking, lying down, whatever. In other words, randomize the C/T so that the dog *generalizes* the association and does not connect it only with one or two specific behaviors.

As an example of how this can affect the dog, beginning clicker trainers often C/T when the dog is sitting in front of them. Without realizing it, they are *conditioning* several things at once: the C/T association, the sit, and the sit in front. When they start walking with dog at left side, whenever they stop and the dog sits, the dog squirms around to the handler's front. Why? Because that's where the dog first consistently received reinforcement.

Skinner used to deliver the conditioned reinforcer when the subject was looking away from him. This was not because Skinner didn't want the subject's attention; it was simply to establish for the subject that the meaning of the CR did not depend as such on whatever it was the subject was doing when it heard the sound. Do your best to make this early association work free of any consistent connection with any particular behavior.

Testing the association

After two or three sessions, it is time to put the association to the test. There are a couple of tests to try.

- **Test #1: Dog alerts to sound.** Whatever the dog is doing, click. Watch the dog's response. If the dog has absorbed the connection you will see "expectant" body language (head cocked, ears up, eyes alert on you, etc.). If you see no tangible physical response, you know that the association is not there yet. If you get the physical response, treat.
- **Test #2: Let the dog offer a behavior.** You have clicked while the dog was standing, sitting, and lying down, but inevitably one of those positions (probably the sit) has been most common. Do nothing. Wait until the dog assumes one of the positions and C/T. Now get the dog up and moving again, and wait for the dog to offer the behavior again. It should not take long. C/T.

Your dog's responses to these tests at a point about halfway into the conditioning process will tell you how it's going. But even if your dog gets straight "A's," continue the conditioning process through to the end.

Maintaining the association

Two of the most common errors in starting out in this kind of training are to click without treating, and to treat without clicking. *The rule is: one click, one treat.* Don't click without treating (and at first, treating *immediately*), and don't treat without clicking.

Never click without treating

The click/treat association is, in a way, a conversation in which you tell the dog "When you do what I want you will get what you want, and that 'magic sound' tells you that the treat is coming." This is the training bargain. For the bargain to retain force, both of you have to live up to your part of it.

Think of every click as an "IOU." If you get in the habit of clicking without treating (for example, as a way to say "good dog" when you are not in a position to treat, or "that was good, keep going"), you will quickly go into debt. Your dog will think, "Hey, this guy doesn't deliver." This will undermine the training "bargain." The sound of the clicker will no longer have that one, clear, unequivocal meaning. If that happens, the clicker loses its power.

Never treat without clicking first

The aim is to establish the clicker as a "magic sound" that tells the dog, "That was right." So when the dog does a particular behavior correctly, he will hear the click (CR), after which he will expect the treat (PR) to follow. In other words, receiving the reinforcer *depends* on the sound. The dog learns that the treat isn't coming until he hears the sound.

So just as you can undermine the power of the clicker by not maintaining the one click/one treat ratio, you can also dilute the power of the clicker by presenting the primary reinforcer without first clicking, because you are saying, in effect, "Whether or not you hear the 'magic sound' you'll get your treat." At the beginning stages, this may not seem important. But clicker training only works because the dog is in fact *working for the sound*. This becomes clear when you are doing any advanced work. Early, consistent pairing of the conditioned and primary reinforcer makes the conditioned reinforcer powerful.

So when do I click and treat?

Timing is everything. At the start, you will click *immediately* as the dog gives you the behavior you want. As a simple example, in shaping the sit you click as Fido's rump hits the ground. This identifies the precise behavior you are seeking to reinforce.

However, it is very important early on to accustom the dog to an important principle: The reinforcer will come, but not always immediately. "Sometimes," you say, "you have to work a little harder, or a little longer, before you're going to hear that click." This does not break the training bargain. You're still reinforcing, and it's still "one click, one treat." You are simply extending time and demanding increased effort.

It is important to make the dog understand this early on. This principle underlies *variable rein-*

forcement. If your dog does not get used to this concept at the beginning you will find it hard as you go down the road to convince the dog to give you two, three, or four correct behaviors before clicking. The dog will be so accustomed to "one behavior = one click" that the absence of the click will be demotivating, where in fact the absence of the click should inspire the dog to increased effort.

So, for example, in shaping the sit, once Fido is putting his rump on the ground with regularity, start extending the time between the moment rump hits ground and the click. For a couple of sessions, count to two seconds before clicking. Then for a couple of sessions count to three, then four, five, and so on. "Release" Fido (let him up from the sit) after each click. This will confirm that "click ends the behavior."

Let's look at a couple of other things that are essential clicker training basics.

Teach Fido his name

This may sound like a stupid question, but . . . does your dog know its name? This is something so basic that we all assume that our dogs know their names. 'T ain't necessarily so.

I first noticed this with Dylan. He was so eager to do things that when I would call Sam, Dylan would come too. I then noticed in class situations that handlers would say their dog's name and get absolutely no response. And of course, the dog's lack of response only triggers anger and frustration in the handler. The simple fact is that a dog learns its name exactly the same way it learns anything else: by positive association.

When I say a dog should "know its name" I mean that the dog should respond to the sound of its name as a *cue* for a *behavior*. The behavior is that the dog stops whatever it is doing and looks at its handler.

In the early stages of puppy training I *shape* Bowser to come to me at the sound of his name with no other cue (such as "come"). This is also something I emphasize with my pet clients. This does not create any problem for the competition handler, who must be able to say the dog's name prior to giving a cue without the dog performing the cued behavior before the cue is delivered ("anticipation"). As you progress in the training it is not difficult to teach the dog to wait for the cue. However, there can be times when having the dog know to stop and come back to you merely on the sound of his name can be highly beneficial.

Here's an example. We moved to the high desert toward the end of 1995. About a month after we moved Dylan was attacked by a neighborhood stray (a Rottweiler/coyote mix, if you can imagine such a thing) and was very badly bitten. He was laid off for three months. We had two legs toward his CDX. I was finally able to enter him for his third leg toward the end of April. He was very excited to be back in the ring. After we did the Retrieve on Flat he got real excited because the jumps were coming. He bounced once or twice, did a pirouette, and bolted out of the ring. I simply said "Dylan," not even in a particularly loud voice, and he spun around and came back to me. We received a minor deduction for misbehavior; the judge told me after that he was impressed with how easily I regained control. On the other hand, I have seen numerous dogs—even dogs that had accumulated impressive scores in their career—leave the ring and defy recapture. If your dog really knows his name, you have a powerful tool to control the dog in unexpected situations.

I want the sound of the dog's name to be a completely reinforcing event to the dog, the mere sound of which makes the dog orient completely to me.

Teaching the dog his name is a form of respondent conditioning. You shape this the same way you shape anything else: Simply have five to ten sessions of five to ten reps in each session where you simply say the dog's name, click and treat (C/T). As the dog's head starts turning to you with regularity, extend the time between the response and C/T. At first, you will click immediately when the dog turns his head. Then you will silently count for one second, then two, then three before clicking. Spend a couple of days at each count before progressing.

This will cause the dog to look at you for increasingly long periods of time before receiving reinforcement. Proceeding patiently, one step at a time, you are laying the foundation for "attention" work. Developing the discipline in the dog at an early age to look at you for extended periods of time is money in the bank for all formal obedience training.

The next step is for you to remain stationary, let the dog roam a bit (in a controlled area, of course), and call his name. At first, the dog may only turn his head. Click. That will in turn motivate the dog to come to you for the treat. *This is not a recall.* The click is for the dog looking at you, not for him coming to you. The only reason you are having the dog come to you is so that the dog learns that he always has to do the work, that is, you aren't going to be chasing him here and there. This will have the incidental effect of teaching the dog that coming to you is a completely reinforcing event, but that is a mere by-product, not a goal of this training.

What if the dog doesn't respond when you say its name? Then you are not yet ready to advance to this stage. Make no aversive response. Simply move a bit closer to the dog to get the dog's attention, and click. Treat when he looks at you. Then go back to stage 1.

When the dog comes to you for his treat, now you can back away from the dog for a step or two after clicking. This will trigger even quicker movement toward you. Now the name begins to become more of a recall cue.

The goal of this training is to shape the dog's response to his name sufficiently that when you call his name in the face of distractions the dog will alert and lock onto you. This is not only a good safety mechanism for general use, it is indispensable in the ring because it is a verbal "handle" that helps you control the dog without physical contact (desirable in Novice and essential in Open and Utility).

You may think this is pie-in-the-sky, but it is not. I have mentioned Skipper already. Besides knowing how to sit, the other thing he has learned is to come at the sound of his name. I let him run loose on our property; all told he has about 15 acres including the unfenced portions of our neighbors' properties. All I have to do is call "Skip!" and he comes running, regardless of distractions (and believe me, living in horse and coyote country we have distractions).

Like every other verbal cue, the dog's name should mean the same thing every time. This means you should condition the dog to respond to it when spoken in a neutral tone. Tricking the name up with vocal flowers and perfume is counterproductive. It isn't "sweetness" that makes the connection; it is positive reinforcement.

Schedules of reinforcement

When you start reinforcing behaviors you reinforce on a one-to-one (1:1) ratio. That is, one behavior earns one click (and one treat). This is called **continuous reinforcement**. The initial purpose of this type of reinforcement is simply to establish for the dog what the desired behavior is.

Once the dog knows what the desired behavior is, you want not only to *maintain* that behavior but to *strengthen* it. "Strengthen" in this context means not only to make the behavior more powerful in the way it is presented, but to make it more resistant to extinction. There are two ways that you can accomplish this.

Continuous reinforcement

One method is to maintain a 1:1 schedule, but to progress to increasingly higher numbers of repetitions ("drill"). By using lots (and by "lots" I mean literally hundreds) of repetitions at every phase of development, you establish a very high ratio of successes to failures. This in and of itself gives you a strong likelihood that on any given occasion you will get a success. The rule of thumb in using this type of reinforcement is that you do not raise your criteria until your "success-to-failure" ratio is at least eight to one at any given level of performance.

Variable reinforcement

Another way to proceed is to put the behavior on a *variable reinforcement (VR)* schedule (or, a *variable ratio*). That is, instead of 1:1 reinforcement, you will go to 2:1, 3:1, or 4:1, or higher. Theoretically, you can extend the ratio of behaviors to reinforcement indefinitely.

I discuss later the real art of working with variable reinforcement, which is that you are always "pushing the envelope"—looking to get "more" of a behavior without suppressing or extinguishing the behavior.

Which to use, and why

Operant conditioning trainers can debate which approach to use indefinitely. In my view, it is primarily a matter of what you need to get the behavior you are working for. Certain behaviors—for example, any "problem-solving" behavior such as scent discrimination—require continuous reinforcement. The dog has to know when he is right, every time.

Other behaviors—for example, long-duration behaviors such as the long sit—can only be developed through variable reinforcement because there is simply no other way to condition the dog to hold the position or continue the activity while you withhold reinforcement for longer and longer periods of time.

In general, my preference (and it is only a preference) when training any behavior in which a precise behavior must be maintained—for example, in training fronts—is to work with continuous reinforcement and high numbers of repetitions. I generally reserve variable reinforcement for long-duration behaviors.

Extinction and how it works

When you are working with variable reinforcement you are working in the realm of reinforcement ratios that tend to extinguish behavior. So in order to understand why and how variable reinforcement works, you first have to understand *extinction.*

A basic principle of behavior shaping is that behaviors that are reinforced tend to continue, and behaviors that are not reinforced tend to disappear or undergo extinction. Extinction is useful. Sometimes, you can stop an unwanted behavior simply by not responding to (reinforcing) it.

Behaviors that are reinforced on a continuous schedule become somewhat resistant to extinction, but are fairly easily extinguished. A simple example is the behavior of writing with a ballpoint pen. If it seems to run dry you will give it a shake. If it still doesn't write you toss the pen away. Your experience with the pen until then has been one of continuous reinforcement: The pen always wrote. When the pen ran dry, you disposed of it. The behavior of using that pen was immediately extinguished.

Now say that you shake the pen and it writes again. Next time it seems to run dry you'll give it another shake. If it writes again, you'll continue to use it. Now your experience with the pen is one of variable reinforcement: The pen sometimes stops writing, but with a little encouragement it writes again. You will keep using that pen until you are absolutely certain that all the ink is gone. The behavior of using this pen is resistant to extinction.

An important corollary to the idea of extinction is the *extinction burst.* That is, a behavior that is resistant to extinction will *intensify* in the absence of reinforcement before undergoing extinction. Sticking with the example of the pen, if it has written before after a shake or two and now stops writing, you'll shake it as you did before and if it still doesn't write, you'll shake it harder. This is an extinction burst.

Another familiar example is the tantrum-throwing child. The parent tries to ignore the child, and the screams just get louder. If the parent can wait it out, the tantrum will eventually disappear (along with two or three bottles of aspirin). This intensification of the tantrum is an extinction burst.

So. On the road to extinction, a behavior that is resistant to extinction intensifies. What happens if you reinforce the behavior during the extinction burst? *You reinforce the intensified behavior,* and that behavior is then even more resistant to extinction than the preexisting behavior was.

In fully exhausting the resources of a depleted pen, I've even gone so far as to take a match and heat the point on the chance that there's some gunk that I can burn off. That's a real extinction burst. And if by chance the pen then writes, that behavior is well entrenched. In our example of the screaming child, what usually happens? The parent gives up on waiting it out and surrenders, giving the child the candy. What is the result? *The behavior of throwing a tantrum is reinforced.* And not just any tantrum, but a real wall-buster of a tantrum.

Extinction and variable reinforcement

If we stick with our example of the tantrum behavior, we can view the "surrender" response to the extinction burst as a kind of variable reinforcement of the tantrum. The parent does not reinforce the tantrum right away, but makes the child continue it for some indefinite period before achieving reinforcement. The child then learns that for the tantrum to achieve reinforcement he must intensify it both as to duration and as to power.

And that is how variable reinforcement works. Once the behavior is in place, you don't reinforce every manifestation of the desired behavior. You reinforce every second or third manifestation. And later, every fourth or fifth. The dog learns that reinforcement will come, but he is no longer exactly sure when, or what *quality* of performance will trigger it. So the dog continues to perform in the absence of reinforcement, pushing farther and harder to stimulate you to produce that "magic sound."

If you put the concepts of extinction and reinforcement together, you can see that you have to structure variable reinforcement carefully. If you don't push it far enough you won't get into the area of the extinction burst and you won't produce any qualitative advance in the behavior. If you push it too far too fast you will cause extinction. It's an art.

In discussing various particular exercises I'll lay out some VR "recipes." They are a place to start, but you will find yourself adjusting them to suit your own needs. That's fine, even essential. There are a couple of concepts that will always apply, however.

The "yo-yo" effect

In constructing any VR schedule you must get into the area of extinction burst without going so far as actually to extinguish the behavior. Mechanically, this means that you simultaneously extend the reinforcement ratio at the top end, while periodically reinforcing the behavior within the range in which the behavior is well established. I call this the "yo-yo" effect. The typical "yo-yo" program is to provide reinforcement within plus or minus fifty percent of an established "mean."

As a simple example, let's say Barfy will hold a sit for five seconds. I want to extend that to several minutes. If I simply leave Barfy on a sit indefinitely without reinforcing, I am asking for extinction (put another way, I am setting Barfy up to fail because he cannot sustain the behavior as I am asking him to). You see this all the time in beginning classes. Dogs sit for a few or several seconds, then get up to do something else. ("Correcting" the dog for leaving the sit in this situation is, to say the least, unfair. You have asked the dog to extend a behavior beyond his capacities, then delivered a punisher because he failed. Wrong.)

So, I am going to extend the sit with a *variable schedule*. Five seconds is my "mean." Plus or minus fifty percent provides a reinforcement range of two seconds to seven seconds. I will C/T at points up and down within that range. I will hit the high and low ends at least three times each. And I will toss in some "quickies," that is, reinforcement after one second. This is a "surprise" factor that prevents the dog from deciding that this only gets harder.

When the dog is reliable at five seconds, I will work at a seven-second "mean." Now my reinforcement schedule goes from three seconds to ten seconds. Then ten seconds becomes my "mean" and the schedule goes from five seconds to fifteen seconds. Then fifteen seconds is my "mean" and the schedule goes from seven seconds to twenty-two seconds. And so on.

You can extend any continuous, *long-duration behavior* (heeling is another example) in this fashion.

You can also use VR to strengthen specific behaviors, such as fronts or retrieves. By asking the dog to give you the same behavior more than once before getting reinforced you are teaching the dog to "keep plugging." In these types of behaviors the variable schedule will tend to induce slightly straighter sits, slightly faster recalls, slightly quicker pickups. Be careful here, though: Because you are asking for a specific, repeated behavior, you can get yourself in trouble if you ask for too many repetitions between reinforcements. Fido may get "inventive," and that will undo the work you have already done.

Jackpotting

With VR you are asking the dog to work harder and longer to achieve reinforcement. But there's a little hidden trap: If the payoff is always the same, you are soon going to hit a point of diminishing returns. After all, why should the dog continue to work harder if the payoff never gets any bigger? The dog will develop the same resentment and avoidance as the employee does who is made to take on increasing responsibilities with no raise in pay.

The answer lies in *jackpotting*. Think of jackpotting as a bonus—as Gary Wilkes puts it, "extras for excellence." This doesn't mean you empty the treat bag every time you get something good. But when the VR has inspired the dog to greater effort, you give two or three treats, or sometimes a handful, instead of just one. Or, give the dog something special. You might even, if the task has been difficult or the dog's effort extraordinary, end the session, play a bit, and give him a bone instead of just a treat.

Jackpotting is a powerful form of variable reinforcement, in that it can cause the intensified behavior to recur in the future. The dog learns that extra effort brings extra goodies, and that will help inspire him to give greater effort in the future.

It's easy to misuse jackpotting. You should not use it as a "motivator" in the sense of delivering it regardless of what the dog has done. Nor should you use it as a response to a poor effort (a type of "cheerleading"). This will only reinforce the poor effort, not inspire the dog to do better. Also, the jackpot should be directly related to the extra effort you are intending to reinforce. Ultimately you may be able to jackpot an entire ring sequence, but you're going to be a long time getting there. If you jackpot after a series of exercises, some of which the dog has done well and some that he has done poorly, what are you reinforcing?

So jackpotting too is a form of variable reinforcement. Using jackpotting together with a VR schedule you can extend not only the frequency but also the nature and quality of the primary reinforcer. All of this variation makes the training more exciting to the dog and will contribute greatly to improved performance.

Variable reinforcement mistakes

Command-based trainers sometimes worry: "When you are working on a VR schedule, how does the dog know if you are withholding reinforcement because he's 'right' but you 'want more,' or

because he's made a mistake?" The answer is, the dog doesn't—nor does he have to; and to a certain degree it really doesn't matter.

If I am using VR to sustain a long-duration behavior, the responsibility is mine to see to it that I do not ask for a longer behavior than the dog is capable of. If I am using VR to maintain a specific behavior by reinforcing only every third or fourth offering, the problem most likely to arise is if I ask for multiples of a behavior before the behavior is really entrenched. It is simply unlikely that I can get three, four, or five correct repetitions between reinforcers. That is one reason that I tend to stick with continuous reinforcement where I am reinforcing discrete behaviors.

But let's assume that you are working on a variable schedule, and the dog has emitted a behavior and you have not reinforced it. And let's suppose that it also happens that the dog made a mistake. What is going to happen? You will most likely see a brief extinction burst. This will take one of two forms. The dog may try the "wrong" behavior again, or he may "push" and get a more correct behavior.

If he tries the wrong behavior again, so what? Let the extinction burst play out. The incorrect behavior will disappear in short order. Why? Because you have *never* reinforced it. The dog has "tested the water" and found that this wrong behavior gets him nowhere. That behavior will not be in his repertoire for long. And then what happens? The dog will search out the behavior you want. When you get it, what do you do? *You reinforce it immediately.* This is a matter of *communication*. With the dog having made a mistake, you have to let him know that he has now worked it out correctly. After a couple of 1:1 reinforcements you can return to your variable schedule.

On the other hand, if after making a mistake the dog "demands" reinforcement and offers the correct (or at least, a "more correct") behavior, also reinforce it immediately. This process will help clarify for the dog which behavior you really want.

In this context, I say that I like my dogs to make mistakes (in training, that is, when it isn't costing me twenty dollars to enjoy the experience). The "mistake" tells me that the dog is in some way testing the parameters of the behavior. By being patient and giving the dog time and room to test and find out what those parameters are, through the reinforcement history the dog will work his way through to deciding on the correct behavior and embracing it for himself. The resulting behavior will be very reliable. To prevent the dog from making mistakes is to eliminate this learning process in training. If you do so, you can be pretty sure that you will see the mistakes come out during competition.

This brings me back to the idea of +R as "attitude." While I often dream that my dog will give me a perfect performance, the reality is that mistakes happen. Things go wrong. The question then is, how does the dog respond to the problem? If your dog has learned that errors bring *punishment*, chances are he will freeze up: It is safer to do nothing than to do something wrong. I don't want my dogs afraid to make a mistake. I want them to know, through our training experiences, that when something goes wrong they can work their way through it. I would rather have them willing to try and fail, than not willing to try at all.

When Dylan was getting ready to show in Open I had him in a match. In the retrieve over high, I threw the dumbbell and it "buried" in some tall grass. I couldn't even see it. Dylan went out, looked for the dumbbell rather cursorily, couldn't find it, and came back over the jump without it. The judge (this was a match, remember) said "He refused the dumbbell! Ear-pinch him!" I said, "No, he just didn't see it." I took him back out and marked him to the dumbbell. He picked it up and came back over the jump. We then did the exercise again.

Several months later we were at a trial. I threw the dumbbell and it buried just as it had done at the match. Dylan went out, didn't see it, came back to the jump, looked at me quizzically, then turned around, went back out, searched for and found the dumbbell and brought it back. Because he continued working, he lost no points. At that same trial, another competitor's dog froze in place when that dog's dumbbell buried, and zeroed on the exercise; that competitor is strong on "corrections."

I am convinced that had I ear-pinched Dylan at the match (I never use the ear-pinch, by the way, but more on that later) he would not have been confident about what to do when he couldn't find the dumbbell at the trial. Instead, he could be confident about trying again because he had nothing to fear if he made a "mistake."

"Whisper" commands

Although the AKC does not permit deaf dogs to compete, there must be a lot of them entered in obedience because so many handlers bellow their commands, even when heeling. Strangely, this is rarely cause for points to be deducted, although the Regulations* address the matter in no uncertain terms. The fourth paragraph of Chapter 2, Section 20 states:

> Loud commands by handlers to their dogs create a poor impression of obedience and should be avoided. Shouting is not necessary even in a noisy place if the dog is properly trained to respond to a normal tone of voice. Commands which in the judge's opinion are excessively loud will be substantially penalized.

While I can't vouch for the accuracy of that last sentence, it is a simple fact that there's no need to yell at a dog that's never more than about forty-five feet away. A dog's hearing is about twelve times as acute as that of a human. How immediately do your dogs respond when they hear a cellophane bag opening? A dog can hear a sound at a quarter mile that we cannot hear past 100 yards. Shepherds in Scotland, Wales, and New Zealand have been known to control their dogs with whistled commands up to distances of two miles.

Give all training cues in a conversational tone. Remember, this is all about communication. You are *talking* to your dog. So . . . talk. Don't yell. This will have several benefits.

Your training sessions will become calmer. You will feel more relaxed. Your dog will, too. For the dog, loud noise from another is usually a sign of stress or anger. If your dog perceives you to be stressed or angry, he will respond to that rather than focusing on the work at hand. You may be surprised to see how your dog's work in training improves if you "quiet it down."

Your work in the ring will improve. By working quietly, your dog becomes conditioned to paying attention with his ears as well as his eyes. He learns to listen for quiet cues, even when there is ambient noise. Put another way, he learns to tune distracting noise out. By keeping your voice audible but quiet, you put the burden on him to do so. I once had a judge in Open tell me that I could easily cheat in Utility, because he could barely hear my cues even when standing a couple of feet away from me. My dog never missed a one.

---

*While there are several dog registries that provide formats for dog obedience competition, it is well beyond the scope of this book to cover all the variations among them. For simplicity's sake if for no other reason, the discussions in this book are directed to the exercises and rules as set forth by the American Kennel Club in its Obedience Regulations.

Putting behaviors on cue

Before you can put a behavior *on cue,* that is, expect the dog to produce the behavior reliably in response to a specific word or signal, the behavior must be an operant—that is, a behavior the dog emits voluntarily in order to trigger reinforcement. Only then can you introduce the further *contingency* that the behavior will be reinforced only when produced in the presence of a given *stimulus (cue).*

First, we have to understand what a cue is.

Discriminative stimulus (DS)

A cue is a *stimulus* for a behavior, that is, something that causes the behavior to occur at a particular time. *Stimulus* is not the same as *reinforcement.* A *stimulus effects* (causes, or triggers) a behavior; *reinforcement strengthens* the behavior. Sticking with our old example, thirst is a stimulus for me to go to the water fountain and press the button to get water. When the water comes out, that reinforces my pressing the button.

We learn to recognize stimuli that cause a behavior to occur, as well as stimuli that cause a behavior not to occur. Both are called *discriminative stimuli.* Stimuli that cause a behavior to occur are called S^D. Stimuli that cause a behavior to disappear are called S^Δ (S "delta"). Remember the word "wrong?" That is an S^Δ.

An S^D for one behavior may also be S^Δ for another. For example, the cue "sit," given while the dog is standing, is S^D for the dog to sit, and S^Δ for the dog to stand. A particular cue, then, tells the dog that a certain behavior and no other is called for in the presence of that cue. I'll talk about this more in the section on *stimulus control.* For now, this should clarify why you do not put a given behavior on cue until the behavior is relatively complete: The dog will not clearly understand what the cue means because the associated behavior is too unformed.

If you say "sit" when all you are looking for is "rump on ground," then continue to say "sit" while you ask for a certain posture and then add to that a particular alignment at your front and side, then you have effectively told the dog that "sit" corresponds to several related (but qualitatively different) behaviors. And it is probable that while you have added criteria in the course of training you have not also successfully suppressed already established—but no longer desired—behaviors as well. You are working against yourself at all times.

You are not giving the dog clear information as to how to discriminate among various behaviors, all of which you have called "sit."

A "real-world" example may help to clarify how much information we have to process in even the simplest of situations in order to discriminate among signals and select a correct behavior. Let's say that you are driving your car and approaching an intersection controlled by a traffic light. As you approach, you see a red light. The red light is a *discriminative stimulus.* As S^D, it is a cue to engage in a certain behavior, namely, to stop. As S^Δ, it is an extinguishing stimulus for other behavior, that is, continuing forward.

You also learn that "red light = stop until green light, then go." But that is not always true. If you come to a *flashing* red light it's a "stop and go when clear" signal. That is another, related S^D/S^Δ. Of course, if the flashing red lights are on the rear of a school bus, you must stop until the flashing stops.

Nor do all red lights mean "stop." The red brake light of a car pulled over at the curb tells you that *that* car has stopped, but does not necessarily mean that you must stop (of course, you will know to stop if the red brake lights are directly in front of you; you will be aided in making this determination because the rear of the car in front will loom large in your vision).

All these things are discriminative stimuli. We first learn a basic meaning for the red light, and over time learn all the variations. We govern our behavior in the presence of the red light based on these learned distinctions. But if you are suddenly confronted with a variation you have not encountered before (for example, a light showing red and orange), you would be required (a) to perceive the unfamiliar stimulus, (b) to grasp its meaning, and (c) to choose an appropriate response. The chances are you will respond to it uncertainly, if not incorrectly.

The same thing applies in training. A cue is a discriminative stimulus. It gives the dog information as to what behavior among the many in its repertoire is appropriate, that is, what behavior will trigger reinforcement in a given circumstance. Typically, when you begin training a behavior, you do it in a relatively distraction-free environment. This enables you and the dog to isolate the behavior and related cues from other phenomena. When you add distractions, you must teach the dog that the same discrimination applies, that is, that the cue means the same thing in the presence of the distraction as it did "in the laboratory."

The degree of difficulty in discrimination increases as you progress through the classes. One of the problems is that in Novice and Open most handlers rely on verbal commands, while in Utility you make considerable use of signals. So the dog has to learn that a certain hand motion cue is a discriminative stimulus corresponding to a certain already learned verbal cue. Also, because there are several different signals and only two hands to deliver them with, the dog has to learn to distinguish between different motions delivered with the same hand. Here the burden is on the handler to make sure that all the signals are distinct and "clean."

In training we all too often accompany a cue with varying tones of voice, hand movements, body language, leash pops, etc. Much of this is unconscious. When I was training Woody for the Novice ring I was being tutored by one of our experienced club members. One night as we were practicing the finish, she watched us do one and then told me to freeze my right hand against my thigh and simply say "heel." I did so, and Woody didn't move. From all the months of popping the leash to the right, however lightly, I had built a reflexive twitch into my right hand that had become an integral part of the cue that Woody perceived to go around to heel. In a way, this was the "dark side" of stimulus control. He knew the cue ("heel" + hand waggle) and he wasn't going to move until he got them both. Good dog; sloppy trainer.

An awful lot of the time spent in training is really time spent in eliminating extraneous discriminative stimuli. Perhaps the clearest example is in the transition from on-lead to off-lead heeling. I will discuss this in greater detail later, but for now let me make just a simple point: There should be no problem with the "transition" if the dog really understands that "heel" means "move forward with me and stay in the fully articulated heel position."

If when off-lead the dog does not move forward immediately as you say "heel," or does not maintain proper heel position, this tells you that (among other things) the dog has come to associate any number of discriminative stimuli with the command to "heel," including everything from the mere presence of the leash, to the pops (forward, in, out, and back), to the different feel of a prong collar if you use one, and so forth. It is not "disobedience" but the process of fading these additional discriminative stimuli that makes the "transition" so difficult.

This is why it is important to limit extraneous stimuli in the initial training process. For example,

the presentation of the dumbbell should be a sufficient S^D to trigger the "fetch." When you get to that point, it is relatively simple to add the cue ("take it," "fetch," "find it," whatever). Now you have two discriminative stimuli working together, both of which the dog understands. If you introduce the cue before establishing the stimulus of the dumbbell as such, you are back to trying to teach two things at once: (a) the fetching behavior, and (b) the cue—for a behavior that the dog does not yet understand.

All this is complicated by the fact that dogs perceive so much more than we do. Because as a human one cannot know what a dog sees, smells, or hears, much less how he processes all that information, one can never really know what stimuli a dog is associating with a given behavior. All we can really know is the *behavior*. In order to isolate the behavior from incidental, extraneous stimuli, we have to neutralize those stimuli as much as possible.

Let's return to the earlier step of *shaping* the sit. When you start, the dog will often be in front of you. Now let's say you add the cue "sit" without reinforcing the sit as such from every imaginable position. To you, that is of no importance. Sit means "rump on ground," dog has rump on ground, that's all there is to it. But to the dog, the place in which he is sitting it is part of the *topography* of the exercise. When you try to get a sit-at-heel, the dog will want to swing around to your front. Why? Because being in front of you is part of what the dog has learned the word "sit" to mean.

As an extreme example, one of my Internet buddies was training her poodle in the finish in her basement. Without really thinking about it, she always faced the same way when practicing. There was a picture on the far wall. One day she faced in another direction, and the dog continued to move around until he could see the picture. Being able to see the picture was part of the exercise to him.

This also helps explain why, if you regularly train in one certain place or environment, behaviors "fall apart" when you go to other places or environments. All of the normal environmental factors are to some extent part of the discriminative stimuli that the dog associates with obedience work. So *generalization* consists to a large extent of universalizing all those extraneous stimuli, educating the dog that "sit" always means "sit" whether you are in a building, a playground, or a mountain trail.

Among its other benefits, shaping behaviors through operant conditioning minimizes (indeed, comes close to eliminating) this difficulty. You work from behaviors the dog offers, and you reinforce and refine them. You do little or no inducing. You do not add a cue until you have reinforced the behavior in a variety of situations and from a variety of positions, and the behavior is pretty much what you want it to be. So when you add the cue stimulus ("sit," "stand," etc.), you have "prefaded" extraneous stimuli, and are only putting one discriminative stimulus (the specific cue) into the mix.

Stimulus control

We say a behavior is "under *stimulus control*" when Fido will produce it reliably "on cue." In the terms of the preceding discussion, you have stimulus control when Fido recognizes a particular cue as S^D for a particular behavior and S$^\Delta$ for all other behaviors. The aim of all training is to establish stimulus control over all the necessary behaviors. There are several aspects to this.

The "three-part contingency"

For a behavior to be "on cue," there are three elements that must be in place: (1) a *stimulus*, (2) a *behavior* and (3) a *reinforcer*.

We are dealing with operant behaviors, which means that we are conditioning the dog to offer behaviors in the expectation of reinforcement. By reinforcing certain behaviors, we increase the probability that those behaviors, and not others, will occur. By adding the cue and reinforcing the behavior when it occurs in the presence of the cue, we increase the probability that the behavior will occur specifically in response to the cue.

As an example, let's say there's an object on the floor. Fido walks over and noses it out of curiosity. This is an offered behavior. With a dog it occurs instinctively, and also because, sometime in the past, investigating something new has led to pleasant consequences. If you were now to reinforce (C/T) Fido for touching the object, he would soon touch that object with greater frequency. If you then said the word "touch" as he touched the object and just before you delivered the CR, the probability would soon become very great that when Fido heard the word "touch" he would touch that object. If it suited your purposes you could then *generalize* the cue by putting more and more objects on the floor and reinforcing Fido for touching each one, so that "touch" would come to mean "touch whatever is on the ground."

This is one more reason why we establish the behavior before we put the name (cue) to it. Doing so provides the maximum likelihood of success, because we are increasing the probability of an already highly probable behavior.

Now both the object and the cue have become discriminative stimuli. If you are teaching targeting, you can transfer the "touch" command from the target stick to any other appropriate target (for example, a coffee can lid taped to a door to teach the dog to close a door, or a string of bells attached to a doorknob to teach the dog to ring the bells when he wants to go outside).

If you are teaching a retrieve, the *operant discriminative stimulus* is the dumbbell. If you start with a wooden dumbbell, you will transfer that stimulus to the leather and metal articles. You ultimately want all three to mean the same thing to the dog: "Pick me up." Then, in Utility, you have to associate different cue stimuli (i.e., scent) to help explain to the dog which of the leather or metal articles among several in a pile you want the dog to pick up.

But no matter how complicated it becomes, all these behaviors rest on the same three-part contingency.

The "four-part test"

The other aspect to stimulus control is reliability. This can be measured with four criteria, three of which flow directly from establishing the "three-part contingency." These three are:

1. Fido does X when you say "X" (sits when you say "sit").
2. Fido does not do Y when you say "X" (does not lie down when you say "sit").
3. Fido does not do X when you say "Y" (does not sit when you say "down").

When these three elements are in place, you know that the cue "sit" is S^D for that behavior *and no other*. Put another way, you have successfully extinguished all behaviors other than sitting when the stimulus of the "sit" cue is present.

You can get (1) and (2) very early on if you are doing nothing but shaping the sit. The dog will do things other than sit, but if you only deliver reinforcement when the dog is sitting, soon he will sit instead of doing anything else. You can then attach the cue and you will have a reliable sit.

The third criterion comes into play when you are shaping additional behaviors. In our example here, you are shaping both the Sit and the Down. In order for both behaviors to be under stimulus control, the dog must be able to discriminate between the stimulus for the one and the stimulus for the other. And of course, in order to make that discrimination, the dog must have some grasp of the significance of these particular cue words. This is why you don't try to put a lot of behaviors on cue all at once. As the dog "learns to learn," it becomes increasingly easy to add cues because the dog understands the correlation between word and deed.

There is a fourth criterion, which is usually the one that causes all the trouble:

4. The dog does not do X except on cue.

Errors occur when the dog offers the behavior before the cue is given. Competition trainers will recognize this as the "anticipation" problem. On the recall, you may see this in various ways. Bowser doesn't wait where you left him until you call. Or, he comes to front, and before you can give the cue to "finish" he bounces around to heel. Or, worse, he goes directly to the heel position without even stopping in front.

Just to be clear, this last criterion only applies when the dog is working. If the dog is on his own time, I don't care if he sits, lies down, perches in a tree, or bounces back and forth among the three. But when he's working, he is to do what he is told, but only when he is told to do it.

Getting this fourth criterion in place requires that you have established the first three elements of stimulus control over each part of the exercise. This is why I focus so much on "pieces" of the exercises. Maintaining the fourth criterion also requires that, once the whole exercise is "in place," you periodically isolate and reinforce the various elements so that the dog does not blend them into one indistinguishable whole. I discuss this in the context of particular exercises in later sections.

In addition to the four elements listed, you may add a fifth: Stimulus control means that the dog will produce the given behavior under any conditions. This involves what traditional trainers call "proofing," and what I refer to here as *generalization*. I later discuss this issue more fully (see pages 34–35).

Latency and the "limited hold"

Another critical element of stimulus control is that the exercises be performed *immediately* as the cue is given. While training, you sometimes want to give the dog time to figure things out. When performing, however, you want the dog always to do the job as quickly as possible.

Latency refers to the gap between cue and behavior. Ideally, the latency period on each exercise is "0," that is, no gap at all. As shorthand, I call this ideal *zero latency*.

On the drop on recall, the dog has zero latency when he is hitting the brakes as *the handler's hand is rising* into the down signal. In heeling, the dog has zero latency when the dog is moving as *your left leg flexes and your left foot comes off the ground*. On directed jumping, the dog has zero latency when the dog starts heading for the jump *as the handler's hand thrusts* in the direction of the jump. And so on.

It is all too easy to create problems for yourself by giving your dog too much time to respond. A slow recall can lead to slow sits, hesitation on jumps, and so forth.

In thinking about response time, don't let yourself be gulled by myths about a given breed's "nature" as having any effect on latency. True, a basset is not going to career around like a Border collie. But that does not mean that a basset need work slowly. The "slower moving" dog can still respond immediately to a command and perform the behavior without delay. That is all latency involves.

If you have not "*preconditioned*" your dog to responding immediately and working quickly, you can "*recondition*" your dog to do so through latency training.

Limited hold is one way to quicken the latency period. You will use reinforcement to reduce progressively the time between the time you present a cue (or, before you add the cue, any stimulus to act) and the time the dog acts on the cue or stimulus. For example, in shaping the retrieve, you will present the dumbbell to the dog's mouth. At first, it may take the dog (say) ten seconds to open his mouth and take it. You reinforce the take at that time span. Over a succession of repetitions, he will start to take the dumbbell more quickly—say, in eight seconds. Now, you only reinforce "takes" that are done in eight seconds. Soon, he will take the dumbbell in a shorter time yet. Then you only reinforce those even quicker "takes." And so on.

What if you have a certain time established for the "take," and the dog does not take it in that time? Then, you simply remove the dumbbell for a moment and then present it again. By removing it, you are in effect saying to the dog that he cannot earn reinforcement by "taking" slowly. You don't use any words in this part of the process.

Latency as "habit"

An important aspect of latency is that by insisting on immediate performance in one area you will tend to get quicker performances in other areas. Latency is a habit. "Habit" is just a way of saying that one usually does that which one usually tends to do. If you always work quickly, and make it your habit always to reinforce the quickest responses from the dog, the dog will get used to working quickly and you will find that you do not have to place any particular emphasis on his doing so as training progresses. Your dog will always tend to work quickly simply because it has become habit: That is how you and the dog always work.

Energy will "spill over" into other exercises just as laziness will. For this reason, be sure that you reinforce the quickest responses in all behaviors. Even if you are not working on a specific schedule to reduce the latency period, by your consistently reinforcing the quickest performances, the dog will begin to produce those quicker performances more consistently, and across the whole spectrum of behaviors.

Without pretending to know exactly what goes on inside a dog's head, one can at least say that working quickly becomes a habit for a dog, in the sense of an acquired, learned behavior just as a straight sit is an acquired, learned behavior.

Latency and anticipation

As you improve the dog's latency and move it closer to zero in general, you are likely to encounter the problem of *anticipation*. That is, the dog will be so geared to go that he will begin the exercise before the cue. In the universe of obedience problems I would rather have to slow down anticipation than speed up delayed responses. But still, anticipation can cause a failure just as surely as the dog not responding at all.

You have a fine line to walk in addressing this problem. On the one hand, you want to cure the anticipation. On the other hand, you don't want to increase the latency period unduly. You are back to the fourth element in stimulus control: The dog must not perform behavior X except on cue.

To solve an anticipation problem, you must analyze the source of the problem. Marian Breland Bailey presents a simple ABC formula for this sort of analysis:

Antecedent
Behavior
Consequence

This formula illuminates what I have previously described as the "three-part contingency." It requires the trainer to ask (a) what has caused the behavior, (b) what exactly is the behavior I am trying to change, and (c) how has that behavior been reinforced?

To analyze the antecedent, you might look for any extraneous cues that you may be giving. The experience I had with Woody and my twitching right hand on finishes is an example. Or, look for cues that you may be giving sloppily. For example, in the directed retrieve one student "marked" by bending at the knees and bringing her hand all the way down in the full forward position. When she adjusted her hand movement to bring her hand down by the dog's head and then thrust forward the dog was still taking off on the flex of her knees. All these sorts of things can be cured. You just have to be able to identify the problem.

You may also look at *consequence*, which is another way of examining the history of reinforcement. Has your timing of the clicker been accurate? Have you inadvertently reinforced something that now, in its fullest form, you see you don't want?

Assuming your cues are clean and free of extraneous stimuli, and assuming that you are delivering the CR timely, one way you can generally solve anticipation without diminishing speedy response is by reinforcing stimulus control. In the example of the directed retrieve, you can reestablish stimulus control by C/Ting the dog for looking at your hand while it is next to his head. Once you have that pause in place, C/T for the dog proceeding immediately upon your hand thrusting forward. In other words, it is a form of **selective reinforcement**. When the dog watches your hand and goes on cue, you can put the exercise back together.

Wherever "speeding up" the particular exercise is an issue in later sections, I discuss latency and limited hold and how to apply the concepts in context. For now, it's enough to say that the theme is always "quick, quick, quick." This will have collateral benefits. Your practice sessions will be crisper. As you progress, your dog will tend to work more quickly as a rule, shortening the training process generally. When you are in the ring you will work more quickly, which will keep both you and your dog focused and will help diminish the effect of distractions.

Generalization ("proofing")

I am often asked, "What if you get the dog into a new situation and he does not perform? If you don't physically 'correct' the dog, what do you do?" This raises the question of "proofing," or what is correctly called *generalization*. This is an area in which you can readily see essential differences between "command-based" and clicker training.

It is essential to all training that the dog learn to perform known behaviors under all circumstances. The goal of training is **stimulus control**, which means that a given cue acts as a stimulus for the same given behavior no matter what. To know that a given behavior is truly learned, you must expose the dog to the cue in a wide variety of circumstances.

In "command-based" training, the trainer "proofs" the behavior by putting the dog in a situation where he is likely to make a mistake, and "correcting" him for making the mistake. For example, if Rover will hold a one-minute sit in your back yard, you take him out to a public place and put him on a sit. You expect, perhaps even hope, that he will "break" the stay. If he does, you "get in a good correction." The purpose is to teach Rover that the same rules apply everywhere: "Do as I say, or else."

I don't use the word "proofing" in part because I don't think it is precise, and in part because the term "proofing" has a profound negative connotation. Generally speaking, it involves "setting the dog up to fail." I use the term *generalization* or *generalizing* instead. This is to emphasize that the purpose of this part of training is to teach Fido how to take what he knows "on the road," that is, to teach him how to perform under a wide variety of conditions. But the point of "proofing" should not be to "set the dog up to fail." Remember, our goal is to teach the dog that he can succeed. So, the goal of "proofing"The point is not to "set the dog up to fail," but to set the dog up to succeed.

Karen Pryor cites as a cardinal rule of shaping that whenever you introduce a new criterion, you must temporarily relax existing criteria. Simply put, any time you add something new, you must expect already-learned behaviors to decline somewhat as the new element is absorbed. Once the new element is absorbed, already-existing behaviors come back up to established standards.

*A new environment is a new **criterion**.* Pryor uses the example of dress rehearsal for an opera: The chorus and singers know their marks and cues when not costumed and on a full set, but when they don full costume and are performing on a complete set, their performance seems to fall apart while they figure out what they're supposed to be doing with their heavy props in hand and with stairways where stepladders used to be.

When you introduce Rover to a new and unfamiliar environment, you can expect that he will not maintain whatever level of performance he attained while "in the laboratory." This is inevitable. The question is, how do you deal with it?

If you regard the decline in the quality of the behavior as a "mistake" and "correct" Rover for it, you will go in the wrong direction. This will not make Rover comfortable with performing in strange conditions. Furthermore you cannot possibly expect to expose him to all the possible variables that you will encounter in the course of a competition career. What you are really working for is to get him comfortable with unfamiliar surroundings generally. Physical "corrections" are a crude instrument, at best, for getting there. At worst, they are destructive to the purpose.

When you take Rover to a strange place, you must "go back to kindergarten" as Pryor puts it, in terms of the behavior you ask from him. If he holds a sit for one minute at home, ask him for ten seconds in the new place, and rebuild from there. If he heels for thirty feet in a straight line, start with five feet, and rebuild from there. If he does fifty-foot go-outs, ask him for ten feet, or even five, and rebuild from there. And so on.

You are using the new environment as a teaching opportunity. You are telling Rover, in essence, "You can do the same thing here as you do at home." This accomplishes several things at once.

First, you do not burden the dog with unrealistic expectations. You are asking him only to do things which are easy for him given the level of work he has achieved in familiar territory. This makes the initial training sessions generally unstressful.

Second, you confirm the behavior in the dog's mind as you retrace the original learning curve. You are not asking the dog for anything new, simply that he do what he already knows how to do.

Third, you build the dog's trust in you. He learns that as he goes into new situations you will be there, asking him to do things that he can do easily, not things that are risky or uncertain. This is leadership.

Fourth, you build the dog's confidence in his ability to perform in new situations. As you expose the dog to additional distractions and unfamiliar places, he will start to generalize through his experience. He may not have seen these particular children playing soccer before, but he has done a long sit with other children playing soccer nearby. He may not have seen this particular park before, but he has now worked the same exercise in ten other parks. With time, it becomes a matter of "been there, done that."

The generalization process tests your flexibility, imagination, and sensitivity as a trainer far more than it tests your dog's knowledge of the exercise in question. You know that learned behaviors will "fall apart" when he is confronted with new situations and distractions until Rover becomes generally de-

sensitized to these things. That is a given. The real question is: How are you going to respond?

So the answer to the question, "What if you have your dog in a strange situation and he fails to perform the exercise?" is simply this: "When you go to a strange situation, relax your expectations to the point where the dog can still succeed. Then retrace the learning curve from there." You are unlikely to encounter failure if you do not ask more from the dog than he is able to give. Be attuned to what your dog is able to give in new and unfamiliar situations, and you will be able to use generalization as yet one more way to build on success.

The behavior chain

A *behavior chain* is an exercise consisting of a series of distinct, identifiable behaviors that must be performed in a certain sequence, usually involving more than one cue (though there may be "mini-chains" within a larger chain that are performed on a single cue, such as the dog going out, picking up the dumbbell, and returning to front, all of which, while initially shaped as pieces of a chain, are performed on the single cue "Take it").

A behavior chain may be one uninterrupted sequence of behaviors, or a series of linked behaviors, or a combination of the two. The unvarying characteristic is that the behaviors must be performed in a given sequence from start to finish, and each behavior must be *on cue* and fully under *stimulus control*.

In Novice, the only true behavior chain is the recall. It consists of a sit, "stay," recall, front, and finish. In this exercise, each "link" in the chain is performed on its own cue. It is a scoreable error and possibly a failure in the exercise if the dog "anticipates" (that is, performs before the cue is given) any behavior in the chain.

In Open and Utility, all the "performance exercises" are behavior chains. There are four in Open (drop on recall, retrieve on flat, retrieve over high, and broad jump) and seven in Utility (signals, two articles, directed retrieve, moving stand, and two directed jumping).

Shaping the behavior chain
Backchaining

In performing a behavior chain the dog moves from one behavior to another. The critical element is that the dog feel confident with the progression. The best way to accomplish this is by *backchaining*, that is, shaping the chain "backward," training the final behavior first and working back to the first behavior. In this way, the dog is continually going from something new to something familiar. This allows the dog to approach the new behavior with confidence.

Another essential element in backchaining is that before you put the new behavior "link" in place, it must be on cue (which means that the dog fully understands the cue) and under stimulus control. If I am adding a behavior to a chain, it must be a behavior that stands on its own outside the chain. Otherwise I will be in the position of training the behavior as such, as well as in its relationship to the chain, and that only creates confusion (in the preceding section, I referred to Karen Pryor's dictum that you train only one criterion at a time; here is another application of that rule).

When the behavior is in place, its relationship to other behaviors takes on a reinforcing quality as well. I call this *repertoire reinforcement*. The idea is that, within a chain, each succeeding behavior works to reinforce the behavior that precedes it. The other side of this is *repertoire cuing*: Within a chain, one behavior can be a cue for a succeeding behavior. Here's how this works.

Repertoire reinforcement

Let's say you have a chain of behaviors A, B, and C. *Repertoire reinforcement* means simply that the cue (or stimulus if other than an express cue) to perform behavior B is a reinforcer for proper performance of behavior A. A very good example of this is in Utility go-outs (directed jumping). In training, the dog gets to take a jump if he does a proper go-out. If he does the go-out incorrectly, I call him back and start again. As the dog learns the connection between the two pieces of the chain, the opportunity to jump directly reinforces the go-outs. Similarly, denying him the opportunity to jump tells Rover something was "wrong" with the go-out. (For these purposes, it doesn't really matter what that something "wrong" was; that's for me to identify and solve in the actual training process. The point is that if *anything* is wrong with behavior A, behavior B doesn't happen.)

In "equation" form, a simple reinforcement sequence looks like this:

Cue A → Behavior A = C/T.
Cue B → Behavior B = C/T.

In this construct, reinforcement follows every behavior delivered "on cue." But when you put behaviors A and B together, it looks like this:

Cue A → Behavior A → Stimulus B →
    Behavior B = C/T.

Now reinforcement follows only behavior B. Behavior A is not reinforced with a click. The only thing that reinforces behavior A is the cue (or stimulus) to perform behavior B. Giving Rover the cue or stimulus to perform behavior B becomes a way of saying "right" as to behavior A. This is repertoire reinforcement.

Repertoire cuing

Repertoire cuing occurs whenever Rover must perform more than one behavior on a single cue. A clear example of this is the retrieve. On the single cue "take it" ("fetch," whatever) Rover must leave your side, go to the dumbbell, pick it up, return to you, and sit in front (holding the dumbbell until you take it from him is a continuing behavior). There are five behaviors in this chain, but only one explicit cue. Following the same formula as earlier, it looks like this:

Cue A → Behavior A → Behavior B . . . →
    Behavior E = C/T.

You have taught Rover each behavior and put it on cue, but when the behaviors are linked for performance purposes you cannot give him separate cues. So, what tells Rover what he is supposed to do, and when? In essence, *each behavior is the cue for the behavior that follows it*. Going away from your side is the cue to find the dumbbell. Finding the dumbbell is the cue to pick it up. Picking the dumbbell up is the cue to return it to you. And so on.

Repertoire cuing is what allows you to construct new behavior chains without having to reteach every element. Regardless of what the dog is retrieving, every pickup is a cue to return to you, which is a cue to sit in front. The dog learns these cues and applies them in all new retrieve situations.

Avoiding extinction of intermediate behaviors

I call an "intermediate" behavior any behavior in a chain that is not directly reinforced. For example, the sit at the beginning of the recall is an intermediate behavior. In training you typically don't reinforce the sit, but the dog coming to front. A not uncommon problem for the new novice trainer is that the dog "breaks" the sit and comes to the handler before the handler gives the recall cue. Why is the sit "breaking down?" What can you do to fix it?

"Three Is A Lifestyle"

When I see a problem with any behavior arise, I apply my "Rule of Three": Once is a mistake, twice is a trend, three is a lifestyle.

Dylan and I are practicing the drop on recall. I give the signal to drop; Dylan keeps coming in. There may be all kinds of reasons why Dylan didn't drop. The bottom line is he didn't drop, and so he doesn't get to complete the exercise, but that doesn't solve my problem. I have to pay attention ("once is a mistake"—and mistakes happen). It may be that the simple act of stopping the exercise and making him start over will get him back on track.

If we repeat the exercise and he misses the signal again, we have a problem ("twice is a trend"). Perhaps I am giving the signal differently from the way he is used to. Perhaps he is distracted. Whatever, I need to address the problem now ("three is a lifestyle"—if I simply give him the opportunity to repeat the mistake again I am risking allowing the mistake to become entrenched).

I will now isolate and reinforce the drop in four steps. (1) Put him on a stand, walk ten to fifteen feet away, give him the down signal. If he drops, C/T. (2) Repeat. If he drops the second time, I put it back into the recall, in stages. (3) Leave him on a sit, call him, cue the drop. If he drops *on cue* while coming toward me, C/T! (4) Leave him, call him, and drop him. If he drops this time, I reinforce by calling him to front and C/T.

In the first two repetitions I address extinction by isolating and reinforcing the behavior that has become a problem. With the third repetition I address stimulus control by putting the drop back into the recall, but reinforcing it separately from the second recall. This reminds him that once he is dropped, he is to stay dropped (if bouncing up is the problem, I would extend the time between the drop and the C/T to rebuild the "stay"). And with the fourth repetition I reintroduce repertoire reinforcement by reinforcing again, but only after the successfully completed second recall.

Three principal components to understanding the problem are *repertoire reinforcement, stimulus control, and extinction*. It is a simple, observable fact that when you put a series of behaviors together in a chain and only explicitly reinforce the ultimate behavior in that chain, the intermediate behaviors tend to disappear. In competition circles this is often addressed in general terms as "anticipation." Rover does not go all the way down on the drop on recall, or pops back up immediately as he goes down. Or, Rover fails to give you a front on the recall or bounces into the finish before your cue or signal. What is happening here?

The intermediate behavior is undergoing *extinction*. This is because you have not paid attention to reinforcing it properly. You only reinforce the front, so the drop tends to disappear. You only reinforce the finish, so the front tends to disappear. In each case, the behavior goes away not because the dog does not know that he is supposed to perform it, but because it is not reinforced.

Stimulus control is also breaking down. Incorporating stimulus control, "sit" means "Put your rump on the ground and keep it there until I tell you to do something else." When the dog comes to you before you give the recall cue, you have lost this stimulus control. Why? Because the dog is perceiving a repertoire cue. You have left and gone to the other side of the ring, and the dog sees that as a cue to come to you. The dog's perception is reinforced by the fact that he gets the C/T when he gets to you, not for staying where you left him.

Using repertoire reinforcement

One way to address this problem is with *repertoire reinforcement*. Simply, you require that each behavior be properly performed before you give the cue for the next behavior. I often see trainers muddle this badly. The dog comes in for the drop on recall and does not drop. The trainer goes to the dog, "pops" him down, then returns to her original position and calls the dog to front. What happens? The "correction" notwithstanding, the trainer is actually undermining the drop because the trainer is permitting the dog to complete the exercise—and thereby earn reinforcement!—even though the dog performed the drop improperly.

For repertoire reinforcement to work, you must insist that each element in the chain be correct. So, if Fido does not drop properly, you "break the exercise off" and start again. He does not get to complete the exercise by coming to you unless and until that drop is correct.

There is an element of "punishment" here, in that you are deliberately withholding a reinforcer (coming to you) that you have conditioned the dog to expect. But as punishment goes, it is of relatively low toxicity. The purpose, as in withholding any reinforcer, is to trigger an extinction burst. You want Rover to focus on the behavior required to cause reinforcement, and to improve that behavior.

Using selective reinforcement

The other way to address this problem is to use *selective reinforcement*. That is, you isolate and reinforce the problem behavior, then put it back into the chain. Were I using repertoire reinforcement, I would simply not allow Rover to go to behavior B unless he performed behavior A correctly. With selective reinforcement I go a step further and address behavior A in isolation.

Actually, in my training I routinely use both, and I try to use them before I see a problem arising. I employ repertoire reinforcement constantly; behavior A does not necessarily have to be off by much for me to have the dog "Do it again, and this time do it right." I also selectively reinforce frequently, isolating and reinforcing intermediate behaviors at random to remind the dog that they are there and must be given full value. As a practical matter, the two intersect. The question of which I use, and when, is primarily a question of tactics.

Fading the clicker

As I mentioned earlier, a favorite barb tossed at the clicker trainer is, "But you can't take the clicker into the ring." Of course you can't. Nor can you take food, or toys, or a prong collar. Regardless of your training approach, an essential and inevitable aspect of the training process is *fading*—gradually eliminating—the tools you use in training.

Anyone who has struggled with fading toys or food from the training process is likely to be very leery about the process of fading the clicker. Fading the training tool is not a minor consideration. I saw one very experienced handler hiding a squeaky toy under her arm as she prepared to go into the ring. She had a friend stand behind her and remove the toy from under her arm so her dog wouldn't see it being done. And this was someone who has more

than one OTCh to her credit! The good news is that, unlike toys and food and other "motivators," it is not hard to fade the clicker out of the performance picture.

The fading process is built into the system in several ways. (1) It is one of the by-products of variable reinforcement. Through VR the dog learns to work longer and harder to achieve reinforcement. (2) In training behavior chains, successive cues replace clicks, as do repertoire cues. (3) When a behavior is part of a larger repertoire (say, a chain in which several behaviors are performed on a single cue), repertoire reinforcement replaces clicks. (4) You pair other conditioned reinforcers with the click during the training process. You can add verbal reinforcers such as "good" or "right," and (5) you provide other *primary reinforcers* than food in training. For example, you can use petting and playful physical actions like letting the dog jump straight up into the air or putting his paws on your extended forearm for a quick pet.

But what really makes it possible to fade the clicker is the power of the clicker itself. The clicker is an "event marker" that tells the dog unambiguously when he has done something correct. During the training process, this unambiguous information gives the dog increasing confidence. He comes to know that he is right even when you don't tell him. And to the dog, the "click" becomes something he is making you do. If you don't click every time, then the dog just learns to work a little harder.

Once the dog knows the behavior—and through using the clicker you can be more sure of what the dog knows than with traditional methods—you neither have to practice it over and over nor reinforce it every time the dog does it. As an example, consider learning basic math. At first, you learn addition and subtraction, and you are graded on how well you add and subtract. Then you progress to multiplication. You no longer get a separate grade for how well you add; you are graded on how you do the whole problem. In fact, if the teacher were to write "Great Addition!" on your problem you'd probably feel embarrassed. Maybe even insulted. "Of course," you'd say. "I know how to do that already!"

The same is true for the dog. You don't have to reinforce every sit. The dog knows how and when to sit. The dog gradually becomes reinforced by the bigger picture—the entire behavior chain, the entire ring sequence. But you only get there because you have built up to it by training from success to success.

Crossover dog, crossover trainer

Perhaps you have never trained a dog to do so much as do his business outside. If so, great. In that case, the methods outlined in this book will probably seem clear and straightforward to you. But I expect that many, if not most, people reading this book will have some background in traditional training methods. Throughout this introductory chapter a recurring theme has been a comparison between operant conditioning and so-called "traditional" training. This continues throughout this book. For myself, and so many people I know and work with—*and their previously trained dogs*—taking up operant conditioning is a "crossover" experience.

The "crossover" trainer is a trainer who has learned the traditional, "command-based" way of training. "I am Alpha, hear me roar." In the program of operant conditioning I outline in this book, you are going to work off-lead (or at least, "hands free") at all times. You are *never* going to have the means to *compel* the dog to perform. You are going to have to teach the behaviors you want by other means. It is going to be a bit disorienting for both of you. I know it was for me. But it is enlightening as well.

The crossover dog

The "crossover dog" has already been trained, but by traditional methods. This dog has learned a certain set of "rules" through that training process. Now those rules are about to change.

Think about how you have trained so far. To teach the dog to sit you say "Fido, sit" and pop up on the leash while pushing down on the dog's rump (or fold his rear legs, whatever). The command comes first, and you then enforce it. Essentially, the dog learns "sit" as a way to avoid certain unpleasant actions that you are ready to impose on him. And as you went along you followed the same pattern: command, compulsion (or inducement), behavior.

So how has the dog learned what is "correct?" Command-based training is rooted in **negative reinforcement**. That is, the behavior is reinforced by the withdrawal of something aversive. In essence, "right" becomes equated with the absence of the set of responses that say "wrong." Principally, this means the *absence* of a leash correction though it can also mean the absence of an ear pinch, or of a verbal "NO!," or an electric "stimulation."

With clicker training, we're turning this on its head. Now you are going to teach the dog "right" by *reinforcing desired behavior*. And rather than "commanding" the dog, you will teach the dog *cues* that tell it what behavior will generate reinforcement at any given time.

The most common thing I encounter with crossover dogs—and the extent of it depends above all on how far along in the training the dog is—is that seemingly at random throughout the training process the dog becomes hesitant and uncertain for some period of time. For example, I have had many students who have gone through twenty or more weeks of standard beginning classes. When they come to me, one of the first exercises I have them do is to wrap the leash around their waist, take their hands off the leash, say "heel" and step forward. Ninety some-odd percent of the time, the dog does nothing. Or, if the dog moves forward, he does so in a very tentative manner.

The dog has not really learned the exercise. He has not learned to move forward, on cue, with the handler. Instead, he has learned only how to avoid the *aversive*. Take the leash off, and the dog does not really know what to do. He has already avoided the aversive. What else is there?

The dog is also confused, because the handler has eliminated all the signals and cues that the dog has become accustomed to. "Heel" does not mean "walk forward," it means "Hear word, get popped, move forward." Now there is no more "pop."

You are also seeing something more insidious. Command-based training creates a dog that is conditioned to do nothing except on command. The dog trained in operant conditioning knows that when in doubt he is free to do *something*, because he has been conditioned to know that if he does the right thing—whether because he worked it out or merely by happenstance—reinforcement will follow. What is the worst that will happen? No reinforcement will follow.

The traditionally trained dog, however, has learned the opposite lesson: when in doubt, do nothing (or, most commonly, sit still). The reluctance of the traditionally trained dog is, at bottom, an expression of his understanding that the penalty for a mistake outweighs the chance of reinforcement for trying to do something. This dog is conservative.

When you start the "crossover" process, you will see a fall-off in the dog's level of performance, pretty much across the board. This fall-off is inevitable, and ultimately positive. It happens simply because of what I have already described. Your dog has learned to work to avoid aversives; you are no longer delivering aversives. The dog has to unlearn the lesson that "absence of aversive means you're right," and learn instead that it is the presence or absence of *reinforcement* that matters. In working through this period the dog will learn what is truly expected, and will learn to give it willingly. This is not to say that the crossover dog can't cross over, but simply that it will take some time.

Having worked with many crossover dogs, I have come to the conclusion that the shortest route lies in proceeding on the premise that the dog knows nothing about any of the exercises. Force yourself to start from scratch, as you would with an untrained dog. This won't be easy. But it is the best way to let the *behaviors* re-form as *operants*. In the long run, the training will go a lot faster and will produce far more reliable results than the command-based methods you used the first time around.

No more "learning plateau"

A final point about the crossover dog is the so-called "learning plateau." It is something I experienced often in traditional training, and encounter hardly at all in operant conditioning. The theory of the learning plateau is that there are points in the learning process where learning seems to stop (hits a "plateau"). This period may last a day or two or as long as a week or more.

I think that the learning plateau occurs simply because, in traditional training, you are often trying to "teach" the dog too many things at the same time. Quite naturally, there will be periods when the mind needs to stop receiving new input and tries to make sense out of everything it has received up until then.

As I say, I have not encountered any "learning plateaus" when working with operant conditioning. I think the reason for this is that shaping demands that you proceed in careful increments. You are constrained by the method itself from ever giving the dog more than it can handle, because you are always working within the "envelope" of behaviors that the dog has to offer. The dog is thus able to absorb—and retain!—each lesson and go forward in a consistent fashion.

The crossover trainer

The rules have changed for you as the trainer, also. You, too, have to learn something new. And this is not a system that you can successfully "cut and paste" into what you are already doing, whatever that may be.

We are all conditioned to "mix and match." Go to all the seminars, read all the books, buy all the videos, take a little from column A and a little from column B. I doubt that I am the only obedience trainer whose equipment bag bears silent witness to trying everything on for size, at least once. But that approach won't work with this system. You have to give yourself over to this strange new game. The training techniques are not hard. Indeed, most people find them much simpler than what they have been doing so far. The real challenge is mental.

The most important step is *to get rid of the leash.* The "leather crutch" is almost as addicting as nicotine. Handlers get used to moving their dog around instead of demanding that the dog do it himself. Handlers get into ruts where they "pop" almost reflexively, regardless of what the dog is doing. Because the handler can compel a behavior with the leash, the handler often deludes him- or herself into thinking that the behavior is in place when it is not. If you don't train with a leash, you never fall into this trap. You will always see exactly what the dog does—and does not—know.

Get rid of the leash —and the prong collar, and the choke collar, and the ear pinch. You can no longer compel the dog to perform. Now you have to learn to *communicate* what you want to the dog in a way that the dog will understand and respond to. You have to "go to the dog." You have to accept that when the dog does not perform an exercise properly it is because the dog does not understand what is required. In turn, you can accept your responsibility to teach the dog.

You can't trust your dog off lead in a public area? Then do your homework in a secure area and don't expose your dog to higher levels of distraction until he is ready.

Your dog heels for twenty minutes on-lead but will only go a few steps off-lead? Those few steps represent what the dog really can do. Accept reality and start from there. You are not sure how to tell the dog what you want if you cannot use one or another method of compulsion? Well, that's what this book is for.

A word about "compulsion"

Many trainers who dip their toes into the waters of operant conditioning still reserve for themselves the option of "making" the dog do an exercise at some point in the training process. The theory, expressed in different ways, boils down to the notion that "obedience isn't optional; the dog must know that it doesn't have any choice but to obey when I give X command." In response, I pose two questions:

1. Are you, yourself, more likely to do something you *want* to do, or something that you *have* to do? (Bet your dog would give you the same answer.)
2. If you are doing something you *want* to do, are you more or less likely to be motivated and enthusiastic about doing it? (Bet your dog would give you the same answer there as well.)

Operant conditioning works on the principle that the dog does what *you* want because the dog learns that by doing so the dog will get what *the dog* wants. The dog comes to want to do what you want it to do. Reliability is almost "built in" if the training is done properly.

The dog always has a choice

But what if the dog thinks it has a "choice" whether to obey or not? Anyone who thinks they can avoid "choice" on the dog's part is deluding himself. What is the delusion? It is the belief that negative reinforcement ("compulsion") can eliminate choice. The dog *always* chooses whether or not to perform. Remember the "ringwise dog?" If a dog *truly refuses* to perform an exercise, you are seeing *avoidance*. "You can't make me, so I won't do it." That's choice, like it or not.

We've all seen dogs that have made this choice. They get their CD (Companion Dog, an AKC title), and are too burned out to go on for their CDX (Companion Dog Excellent) or UD (Utility Dog). Traditional instructors training competition students avoid these dogs because they perceive their likelihood of ever doing very well as being low. The dogs are castigated as not being a "good obedience breed," or having low "drive" of one sort or another, or being stubborn, or simply too stupid to learn. But more often than not the truth is far simpler: the dog has not found obedience work to be reinforcing, so he has "opted out." The problem is in the training method, not in the dog.

There are top competitors who search high and low for the "right" puppy. What they want is a dog that won't buckle under stress and punishment. Those qualities have to be inborn in the dog, because the training method will not develop them. A few years ago Bernie Brown, a well-known competitor and judge from the Midwest, wrote a series of columns in *Front & Finish* about a new puppy he was working with, a Belgian Tervuren named Raisin. Brown said, in the first of these columns, that he hoped to show people what he looked for in a "keeper." As it happened, he didn't keep Raisin. The puppy couldn't tolerate the stresses of Brown's training style, and Brown placed the dog with a family on a farm somewhere.

Training with compulsion produces "narrow and ultimately unsatisfactory results"? Compulsion creates a dog that works out of fear of force, rather than a dog that works in active partnership with the handler. Once more let me quote scientist Murray Sidman, author of *Coercion and Its Fallout*. He writes that negative reinforcement, "particularly if intense and continous, can narrowly restrict our interests, even causing a kind of 'tunnel vision' that keeps us from attending to anything except the stress we are currently being subjected to. We may handle set routines very well, although perhaps in a stereotyped, mechanical, or compulsive fashion."

Sound familiar? This is the so-called "pattern-trained" dog, a dog that does it all well so long as the pattern is not disrupted. But when called upon to solve a problem or respond to the unexpected, the normally "reliable" behaviors fall apart. What's worse, the dog does not have the resources to work through the unexpected problem. Why? Because, again, the dog has been conditioned to passivity in the face of uncertainty. For this dog, it is better not to make a mistake than it is to try something and fail. This dog may not "have a choice"; this dog also does not have vitality.

Train to do your best, not to be perfect

Does this mean that shaping through positive reinforcement will produce a dog that will never make mistakes or fail? No. Nobody is perfect. We are talking about *maximizing the likelihood* of correct performance at any given time.

In watching the gymnastics at the 1996 Olympics I was struck again and again by the delusion of perfection. Here were young, powerful athletes, in their prime, who devote hours a day, six and seven days a week, to their sport. Most of them train more in a month than most obedience trainers train in a year. And all of this for one objective: an Olympic medal.

And what happens? A world champion's hand slips through the ring. Another world champion steps out of bounds in the floor exercise. A national women's champion falls off the balance beam. Two or three others fall off the bars. And these are people who have dedicated themselves to mastery of their art, putting far more into their training than we ever do with our dogs. "Perfection," whatever that is supposed to mean, cannot be your only gauge of success.

What can we really expect from our dogs? Only that they will give us their best when we ask them to. Training through positive reinforcement optimizes the chance that this will happen.

The need for compulsion arises from trainer error

In most cases where a trainer feels the necessity to resort to compulsion, the trainer has overreached. Put another way, the trainer has asked more from the dog than the dog is able to give at that stage in the training process, has asked for too much behavior, too soon. The trainer takes dog to a strange environment, says "Watch," dog doesn't "watch," trainer pops leash. Has the dog disobeyed? Well, the dog didn't respond to the command. But this may be for a couple of reasons, neither of which has anything to do with disobedience.

Perhaps the dog is exposed to an unusually high level of distraction, has not yet been reinforced for that behavior in these circumstances, and the trainer has not reduced her expectations accordingly. Compulsion in such a case is not only not called for, it is counterproductive and unfair. It is *punishing* the dog for not knowing how to do something in a strange situation. Do you want your dog to be fearful of punishment when confronted with a strange situation in the ring?

Or, perhaps, the dog is trying to send a message to the handler. Turid Rugaas, a canine ethologist from Norway, has written a book called *On Speaking Terms With Dogs: Calming Signals*. She has identified thirty or so "calming signals," which she says dogs who perceive another dog in stress send to that dog in order to calm the other dog down. One such signal is for the dog to turn its head away. So, just for fun, let's assume for a moment that Ms. Rugaas is onto something. Let's also assume that the handler is somewhat tense—perhaps because her instructor

is looking on and ready to pounce at any sign that the dog is not working as it should. In that case, could it be that the dog is turning its head not in disobedience, but in an effort to send a calming signal to its handler? Maybe. Maybe not. But it is certainly possible. And if that is any part of what is going on, what good would it possibly do for the handler to respond to the calming signal by using force? All this is going to do is cause the dog to try harder to calm the situation down—and thus do other things that the handler may perceive as even worse (such as moving slightly away from the handler). Is there a "command-based" trainer out there who hasn't experienced this progression—or something very much like it?

I am not an ethologist, and I can't assess the validity of Ms. Rugaas' theories from a scientific standpoint, but they "resonate" with me. They seem to have more than a grain of truth to them. If we admit that we are not very good at "reading" our dogs, and if she is right about this one type of communication, isn't it the wisest course to find a way to train that does not trigger innate canine behaviors that work against specific behaviors (such as attention) that we are trying to teach?

Forget the word "correction"

As often as I have heard trainers use the word "correction," I am not sure that any of them know what the term is supposed to mean. Indeed, its application is too vague to be considered even remotely scientific. I have seen trainers "hang" a dog that has been aggressive and call it a "correction." The trainer is not giving the dog the chance to produce any nonaggressive behavior, so the action is purely punitive. I have seen trainers "pop" a dog that was too slow to sit. This gives the dog the chance to perform the desired behavior, so the leash action is something like negative reinforcement except that the trainer released the leash before the dog performed the behavior, so I'm not at all sure what this "correction" is supposed to be or how it is supposed to work.

I offer for your consideration this simple rule: If at any time in your training you must resort to force of any kind to achieve the behavior you want, you—and not the dog!—are doing something wrong. Be honest and fair. Take a break, sit down, and figure it out before starting to work again.

For all these reasons, you will not find any "corrections" discussed in this book. Instead, I write time and again about careful, incremental development of the exercise so you never put yourself in a position where you are asking the dog to do something that you have not conditioned the dog to do, and therefore you are never in a position where you have to compel behavior. You will build toward success by building on success, one step at a time.

Let's go to work.

Fluencies 3

Begin at the beginning: Building fluencies

Before you and your dog are ready to do all the serious work involved in getting ready to show, you want to lay the groundwork for the training to come by giving the dog a broad range of *fluencies.* A fluency is a basic, learned behavior that you can incorporate into other, more complex behaviors and into behavior chains. If you can learn to think in terms of fluencies, then when you confront problems in a performance (a sit is slow, a front is crooked) you can think of the problem as a fluency issue and identify more accurately what the problem is, and what you must (or can) do to rectify it.

Whether you are starting with a puppy, an older "green" dog, or working a "crossover" dog, the same approach applies. Put the fluencies in place first. The basic fluencies for obedience work are:

- Targeting
- Attention (focus)
- Rear-end consciousness
- Sit
- Down
- Stand
- Hold the position (stay)
- Left-side walking
- Informal recall
- Informal retrieve
- Jumping
- Marking
- Distance targeting (go-out)
- "Find the one that smells like me"

Except for jumping, you can begin work on all these fluencies, and in the above sequence, with a ten-week-old puppy. Puppies respond readily to this training. They are little "sponges," and are ready to absorb anything positive that comes their way. Fluency work is not particularly demanding or stressful. It is a way to train the puppy without overload.

If it sounds strange to you to work on such things as retrieving, marking, and scent discrimination before getting serious about heeling (which, after all, is the single most significant exercise in the Novice class), consider this. All these fluencies are either native to the dog, or use native talents. It is far easier for dogs to learn the basics of the skills required in Utility than it is to learn (or should I say "tolerate"?) Novice heeling.

Fluency work allows you to put the basic skills required for the advanced obedience classes in place and maintain them until you are ready to formalize them as "exercises." When all these fluencies are in place you have the foundation for shaping every obedience exercise, as well as behaviors applicable to other sports such as Agility and even some service dog behaviors.

Fluency work is also valuable for the pet owner. It gives you a lot of "games" to play with your dog, all of which will make your dog more responsive to you generally.

I talk about each of these fluencies in the sequence just listed.

Shaping with the target stick

The target stick is perhaps the most versatile training tool in your "kit," and next to the clicker one of the most indispensable. You can use it to teach any exercise in which targeting is an element, or in which targeting can clarify a concept in the dog's mind. It is also an excellent "starter" tool for both the crossover and the new trainer, as well as the dog. It introduces the trainer to how operant behaviors work, and lets you learn timing of reinforcement. It introduces the dog to how the new rules work.

I can comfortably say that with a target stick and a clicker you have all the training equipment you need (except for things like dumbbells, jumps and Utility articles) to teach every Obedience and Agility exercise there is.

Shaping to the target stick is an essential fluency for shaping the obedience exercises. When you have completed the foundation work the dog will touch the stick with his nose while stationary, and will follow a moving stick to touch it. Once these responses are established, you are set to use the stick in training other exercises.

You can use the stick as a target on fronts, to locate the finish (either left or right), as a focus point in heeling, to lead the dog over jumps, and as a target for the broad jump or the Utility turn-and-sit. The target stick is invaluable in Agility for teaching

A   B

*The target stick and clicker are all the equipment you need for shaping most obedience exercises. Here Dylan follows the target stick while heeling (**A**), and sits in the location indicated by the stick (**B**).*

the dog to take direction from a distance and to hit contact points. In short, the target stick can be used in shaping every exercise in which position is an element—and there is a "position" or "target" element in every exercise. It is therefore very useful to take the time to establish the target stick as a tool, *before* beginning training specific exercises.

There are commercially available target sticks. Usually they have a glittery, hologram-type design on one end that apparently is easily visible to the dog. The commercial target stick also folds in half or in quarters, making the stick easy to carry and store and versatile in use.

Actually, however, any three-foot dowel will do for most purposes. Just paint or tape one end with a three-inch yellow stripe (yellow and blue seem to be colors dogs can easily recognize). If you have a tall dog you will probably want to have two dowels, one full length for general targeting and a shorter one that you can use for heeling or other close-in work.

The shaping mechanics

You have already established the clicker as a conditioned reinforcer. You will now use the clicker to condition the dog to the target stick. The goal is for the dog to touch the stick with his nose.

Though you may start with the dog on a sit, I find it preferable that the dog be standing because you can get motion more easily from a stand than from a sit. Don't make an issue of this, though. Start where the dog is and see where it goes.

Present the target end of the stick directly in front of or slightly above the dog's nose, no more than an inch away. The dog should make some show of interest, if only inclining his head slightly forward. C/T *any movement of the head toward the stick.* Most dogs will "nose" the stick immediately, if only out of curiosity. This exercise takes advantage of the dog's primal instinct to acquaint itself with something new by sniffing it. Some dogs, however, will be leery of it.

Dogs that readily respond to the stick may start to mouth it fairly quickly. You want the dog to touch the stick, not chew it, but you have to be careful. Later you may use the target stick to introduce the dog to the retrieve, so don't give any aversive response to this.

Solve mouthing by being very clear about reinforcing contact only. Usually, this is just a problem of timing. People who find their dogs mouthing the stick have waited too long after the initial contact to click. As I discussed in Chapter 2, if you are going to mis-time the click at all, be early. Here is an example of how that works, and how correct timing "makes or breaks" the shaping process.

If you click early (i.e., while the dog is moving his head toward the stick, but before the dog has touched it), what will you reinforce? Movement of the dog's head toward the stick. This is fine. You are reinforcing progress toward the goal. "Click" ends the behavior, so you won't get a complete touch. Is that a problem? No. You can wait a little longer before clicking the next time. Remember, you have reinforced progress, and the dog has not mouthed the stick. It will not take long for you to capture an actual touch. And because you are clicking early, you will be likely to get a touch without any mouthing.

If you click late, on the other hand, you are going to have one of two undesired results. Either the dog will start mouthing the stick, or the dog will be pulling his head away from the stick when you click. In the first case, you will find yourself reinforcing chewing the stick. In the second, you will find yourself reinforcing the dog for pulling away from, rather than going to, the stick. Remember Karen Pryor's story about trying to get the dolphin to swim from one tank to another? You will be doing the same thing here. You don't want the dog to "peck" at the stick; you want a firm, at times even a sustained touch.

A problem sometimes arises because of the placement of the stick relative to the dog's head. The dog may be mouthing because you have the stick nearer his mouth than his nose. If you are holding the stick in front of the dog's nose, hold it so it is slightly above the dog's nose.

For a dog that is leery:

- First, C/T the dog merely for looking at the stick. The stick will begin to attain the status of a conditioned stimulus.
- Second, *reinforce any motion of the head* toward the stick. You may *induce* motion by holding the stick slightly to one side or the other. If your dog has been sitting, this may also be a good time to get the dog on his feet. He may be more likely to move his head if his body is in a mobile position.
- Third (escalating your criteria as a good trainer should), *reinforce only more and more significant motion* toward the stick.

As you reinforce the dog for moving his head toward the stick, he will continue to do so and will eventually touch the stick, even if only accidentally. C/T. This initial success is a good opportunity to introduce the *jackpot.*

Getting multiple touches

The target stick is a great device for introducing VR to the dog, simply because it is such a basic fluency for the dog to learn, and for some reason most dogs get excited about it pretty quickly. If you spend a few minutes twice a day with the dog and target stick, in two or three days the dog will likely be touching the stick four or five times in a row, within a few seconds of having it presented, on a *continuous reinforcement* schedule.

Now you introduce VR. When the dog touches the stick the first time, do nothing but leave the stick in position. Your dog will probably show some surprise at not being clicked. Wait. Within a few seconds, the dog will probably touch the stick again. C/T. You have gotten your first "two-for-one" behavior. Not as exciting as other firsts in your life, perhaps, but significant nonetheless. The dog has faced his first chance to abandon a behavior that has hitherto been continuously reinforced, and he didn't do so. The "touch" behavior is now a little more resistant to extinction than it was before. For two or three sessions now, randomize the C/T between a 1 : 1 and 2 : 1 ratio.

From here you can go to a 3 : 1 and then a 4 : 1 ratio. When you do this, though, always remember to throw in some 1 : 1s as well as some jackpots.

When you are adding the VR you will see some interesting little things come out. The dog may become more assertive about touching the stick. He may start moving toward it, or shoving it with his nose. These are good signs. When you get anything along this line, you can start to introduce *differential reinforcement* (reinforce only the strongest touches).

This is probably your first VR experiment, so "play" with it a little and become comfortable with how it works. Give the dog a little time to absorb the new rules. This will not only help entrench the touch behavior, it will be money in the bank when you apply VR in other, more complex situations.

Adding the cue

When you have consistent touches (whether you are still on a continuous or variable schedule of reinforcement), you can add the *cue.* The cue for the tar-

get stick is "touch." You add the cue by making it part of the reinforcement sequence. In a sense, you are *describing* for the dog what it is he is being reinforced for by adding a unique word to the event. You are *not commanding* the dog to "touch," you are informing him that that is what he is doing.

In this way the dog associates the cue with the behavior, and the two together with the reinforcement. In short order the dog will touch the stick when he hears the cue, not because he "must" but because he recognizes it as an *opportunity to earn reinforcement.*

The sequence is: behavior → "touch" → click/ treat. Say "touch" *just as* the dog is about to make contact with his nose, click as he makes contact, and treat after he stops the "touch" action.

Transferring the "touch"

I discuss this more fully in the section on the retrieve, but the idea is simply to use the stick to guide the dog to other targets. With a service dog, for example, you can transfer the touch to a coffee-can lid. If you then tape the lid to a door that simply swings open or shut, you can shape the dog to open or close the door, as the case may be. This is also a nifty little trick for the pet owner.

In this phase of the training it is not particularly important what you transfer the "touch" behavior and cue to. If you can think of something that might be useful to you, do that. Try to find as many different things as possible so that the dog *generalizes* that when anything is presented to him with the word "touch," he is to touch it.

The transfer process is simple. Simply place the stick so that the touch end is at or on the new target. Give the "touch" cue. As the dog is about to touch the stick, move it slightly so that he makes contact with the new target instead of the stick. C/T. In short order you will be able to present the new target without involving the target stick at all.

Touching the stick in motion

Once you have consistent touches and the touch is on cue, you can introduce motion. But first you will have to work through a small but illuminating problem. If the dog has regularly done the "touch" from a sit, guess what? The sit has become part of the exercise. It has become a *superstitious* association with the "touch" behavior. Before you can ask the dog to make any significant movement toward the stick, you have to "explain" to him that "sit" is not part of the behavior. One helpful thing is to have the dog both sit and stand during the early stages. But there is also a simple trick you can shape at this point to get the message across.

Hold the stick three to four inches above the dog's nose, just high enough that the dog cannot reach it simply by craning his neck. The dog will now have to rear up on his hind legs to touch the stick. Sometimes the dog will look up at the stick but see he cannot touch it from the sit position, and because of the superstitious association between "sit" and "touch" he won't know what to do.

First, C/T as he looks at the stick. Do this a couple of times to communicate that this is a stick-oriented event. After a couple (perhaps a few) of these you will see the dog edging toward some actual motion. C/T the first time. The second time, say "touch" as a cue when he starts to move. Chances are he will rear up the slight distance necessary to touch the stick. C/T and *jackpot.* After a few repetitions the dog will understand that it's OK to move to the stick. If you are feeling adventurous at this point you can shape this further into a "stand up tall" ("Yee-hah!" or "Hi-Yo, Silver") trick.

Now you can introduce motion on the ground. Your first goal is to have the dog move both left and right to touch the stick. As in every exercise in which you direct the dog toward a target, you will *always* have him work in both directions at all times. The reason for this is that dogs are left- and right-pawed, just as humans are left- and right-handed. Observe your dog approaching an object: He will tend to approach from one side or another. Observe your dog turning: He will tend to turn in one direction or another. Often while working, your dog will have to turn against the direction he naturally tends to favor. You want him to be comfortable if he has to do so. To get there, train your dog to be ambidextrous right from the start.

This is also helpful for the Agility competitor. One of the difficulties in moving a dog from Obedience to Agility is that the dog is strongly conditioned always to be on the handler's left side. In Agility, however, the dog often has to be on the handler's right side. By always working "left/right/left/right," you will get the dog comfortable in both places. This will not undermine "left-side" position for Obedience because you will have definite cues to put—and keep—the dog on your left side when required. But it will give you the flexibility required for other sports.

Ethel has taught her miniature pinscher, Angel, to touch the end of the target stick. Now, while she shapes the behavior of following the moving stick, she may relax her criteria temporarily and click for a good "follow," even though the dog is heading for the middle of the stick instead of the end.

To teach movement, have Fido standing in front of you (exact position does not matter). Hold the stick in the usual position and let him touch it. C/T. Now move the stick to a position about three inches ahead of the dog's nose, and step back from Fido with your left foot. This backward step is intended to trigger some movement in the dog. At first you may expect that the dog will take but a single step with one foot to reach the stick. That's fine. Build from there. Do not ask the dog to move too far, too fast. Until the dog gets used to the idea of following the stick to touch it, he will easily lose it as you move it away.

As soon as the dog has taken one step to your left to touch the stick, have him take one step to your right. Go back and forth a few times. With each touch Fido will become more sure of what you are asking. You will quickly find him moving several steps to touch the stick.

Gradually extend the motion until the dog will move in a complete circle around you in both directions to touch the stick. As you extend the range of motion, intersperse long with short moves as a variety of variable reinforcement.

You can use a target stick to teach movement in any direction—useful in obedience and especially handy in agility training.

Some useful (or just plain fun) variations:

"Left" and "right" turns

Once you have the dog moving both ways, use the stick to shape turning in place. It is easiest to start while the dog is in motion because momentum is on your side. As the dog moves to your right, circle the stick in a counterclockwise direction away from your body and outside the dog. As he starts to follow the stick around, C/T. When he will make a full 180-degree turn following the stick, add the cue "left."

You can then add the turn in the other direction. As the dog is moving to your left, circle the stick in a clockwise direction away from your body and outside the dog. When he will make a full 180-degree turn following the stick in that direction, add the cue "right."

You can then add the cue "turn around" to direct the dog to make the 180-degree turn. I suggest *fading* the "left" or "right" cue depending on which is the most natural for the dog. If Fido naturally turns to his right, then fade the "left" cue and put the full turn to the left on "turn around." This will not only strengthen the behavior but will help keep Fido working ambidextrously.

These turning movements will be handy in various ways. In teaching heeling you can use "left" and "right" to help cue the dog through learning turns. You can also use these cues when pivoting in place for the Utility exercises, as well as in having cues available for bringing your dog into heel position between exercises. "Turn around" is very helpful when grooming the dog or if you get yourself in a clumsy position (say, stuck in a doorway with groceries in your arms) with the dog at your feet and you need to maneuver him so he can move away from you.

And again, if you are feeling adventurous, you can extend one or both of the 180 degree turns into a full circle, adding the cue "spin" or "twist." I can't think of any particular use for this in the obedience ring, but it can be fun and sometimes that is its own reward. If the dog really enjoys pirouetting then you can use this as a PR between exercises or at the end of a full performance. (If you are going to use it between exercises, though, be very sure that you have it under complete stimulus control.)

Distance targeting (go-outs and marking)

The next step is to train the dog to go to the stick at a distance. This gives you the basis for go-outs and the directed retrieve.

Go-outs

In the Utility go-out the dog must go away from the handler (on cue) to a distance of at least thirty feet and then stop, turn, and sit on cue. One of the difficulties in training the exercise is that until you get to go-outs, the only reason the dog has ever left your side is in Open, and then it was in order to retrieve something. Now the dog is going away in order to get into position to do something else. As a

fluency, the task is to shape the dog to accept the idea of going away from you on cue.

Begin by sticking one end of the target stick in the ground. Now it is a stationary target. Stand a couple of feet away from it with the dog at your side. The dog is already fluent in touching the stick, and knows the cue. Often, the dog will go to the stick on his own. If he seems hesitant, indicate or tap the stick with your hand and say "touch." C/T when the dog touches the stick. After one or two repetitions, Bowser will go to the stick readily after each reinforcement.

When I did this with Dylan, he quickly created his own little circuit. He'd run to the stick, touch, hear the click, come back for his treat, circle around me, and head right back out to the stick. It became a fine game.

When your dog is returning to the stick repeatedly with no additional cues from you, you can insert the cue "away." Say the word just as Rover is about to touch the stick. Rover hears "away" as a cue synonymous with "touch." While later it has to become more than that, this is a fine place to start. Each time Rover heads toward the stick, say "away" a little earlier in his progress until you are saying "away" before he starts.

Now start adding distance. I like to sneak the distance in by stepping back one step as Fido is running out to the stick. Then when he returns I am one step further away from the target. Since this is a very comfortable routine for the dog, you can add three steps per session in this phase.

Extend the distance over many sessions until you are at least sixty feet from the target. If you can build up to eighty or one hundred feet, so much the better. Before you start formalizing the exercise in any way or adding distracting obstacles you want the "away" cue clearly defined in the dog's mind to mean "Fido, you keep going until I tell you to stop."

If your dog starts to arc (this is particularly common with the herding breeds), then shorten the distance until you are nearer than where the arc starts, and rebuild from there. What you want to do here is reinforce *muscle memory*. The dog cannot understand "straight" as a geometrical proposition, but he can, bit by bit, remember what it *feels* like to go in the proper direction.

When you are reinforcing "straight" as such (as opposed to touching the stick, which is a slightly different issue), C/T at first after the dog has taken a few steps in the right direction, then extend the distance that you let him go, a couple of steps at a time, before clicking. *When you click, the dog will stop his forward progress and return to you.* This is OK. Remember, "click ends the behavior." You are reinforcing "straight," not distance. When you have gotten "straight" for a few steps and you "end the behavior," you are simply laying the foundation for getting "straight" over greater and greater distances.

Marking

There are two Utility exercises in which **marking** plays a role: the directed retrieve (gloves) and the go-outs. Marking simply means that you are using a hand signal to give the dog a directional cue. With the dog at your left side you bring your hand down to the dog's head level, palm toward you and open, fingers together. You then thrust your hand forward in the desired direction. The dog follows the path of your hand as he moves away from you; from there, "muscle memory" takes over as he continues along that path toward the target.

The cue to go forward is not you placing your hand by the dog's head, but the action of thrusting your hand forward, combined with the verbal cue. This is a fine point of stimulus control. The dog will quickly learn that when you bring your hand down by his head you are going to send him out, so he will tend to anticipate the thrust of your hand. As with most cases of anticipation, this is a good thing. It tells you that the dog understands the sequence of events. Nonetheless, the dog must also learn to wait for each cue.

The first step is for the dog to pay attention to your hand when you bring it to the side of his head. C/T for the dog cocking his head at all in the direction of your hand. Some people use the cue "mark" for this behavior, but I prefer not to introduce a cue here. I don't think it serves much of a purpose in training, and you will simply have to eliminate it for ring work. The only stimulus for the dog to "mark" your hand should be the act of you placing your hand by his head.

The second step is for the dog to move forward with the movement of your hand. Stand two or three steps from the touchstick in the ground. Have Fido on a sit. Present the mark. Now thrust your hand toward the target and say "away." Fido should go to the target. When he gets up and moves a step toward the stick, C/T.

When the dog is (a) waiting for your hand to thrust forward and (b) moving forward when you thrust and say "away," let him go all the way to the target, click when he touches it, and treat when he returns. Build distance as before.

By the way, you won't have to use any cue such as "come" after Fido touches the target stick. He'll be heading back toward you in expectation of the reinforcer. The act of touching has by now become a repertoire cue; that is, it prompts Fido to return to you. This is useful for the directed retrieve; for the go-outs you will insert another cue ("sit"), which will interrupt the "go-out-and-return" sequence.

Don't concern yourself with adding distractors or obstacles at this point. The fluency here is for the dog to go all the way to the stick, up to a distance of 60 to 80 feet.

Adding variable reinforcement

Variable reinforcement in this exercise works a little differently than usual. We have discussed VR as giving one reinforcement for multiple behaviors. But the go-out or long-distance marking is somewhat analogous to a long-duration behavior. The critical element is that the dog keep doing one thing (go away) until told to stop.

In varying your reinforcement pattern, vary the distance you have the dog go away until stopping him with the click. You can click him at one step, twenty steps, or eighty steps. I have found that this works best if you approach it as **random reinforcement** rather than with a structured VR schedule. That is, click at various distances, but don't set any particular pattern. The dog will get accustomed enough to stopping at a set distance when actually competing in the Utility ring. There's no benefit in introducing that to your dog too early.

Attention

There is no question that successful obedience work requires that the dog have his full attention on you at all times while you are in the ring. I prefer to think of this in terms of *focus*. By focus I mean the quality of the dog *actually being involved in what he is doing*. The mere fact that the dog is looking at you does not mean that the dog is really tuned in. The expression "The lights are on but nobody's home" applies as much to dogs in the ring as it does to humans wherever they may be.

"Focus" develops spontaneously, intrinsically, over time, through the shaping process. The dog becomes increasingly wrapped up in the work because of the various reinforcement contingencies you have established. And as the dog develops focus, you are also going to get the physical manifestations of "attention." So to some extent, the "watch me" effect will develop in the dog even without you working for it as such. Nonetheless, you can also shape the dog to keep its eyes on you.

This is simply done. All you need to do is C/T whenever the dog looks at you. If you start this at home or in another quiet place that is familiar to the dog it will be relatively easy to start. The dog will be undistracted and you will be the most interesting thing in that bland environment. The dog should look at you readily.

Do not do anything to induce the dog to look at you. This is "pure" shaping. If you start trying to induce the dog to look at you, all you are going to do is build extraneous cues into the behavior that you are going to have to weed out later. The idea is not for the dog to look at you when you are waving food around, clucking your tongue, telling the dog to look at you, making smoochie noises, or giving "motivational pops" on the leash. The idea is for the dog simply to look at you.

We are not starting "heel position" in fluency training, but we are going to do "left-side walking." So early on you must randomize the dog's position in relation to you. In other words, don't always have the dog in the same place in front of you when you C/T for watching. Do it when the dog is across the room, by your left side, somewhere on your right side, in front of you, sitting, standing, lying down, wherever the dog is and whatever posture the dog is in. In this way, "eyes on me" becomes the sole constant. Regardless of any other behavior in which the dog is engaged, looking at you triggers reinforcement.

Extending the "watch"

You don't want the dog simply to look at you and then turn his head away. You want the dog to watch you at all times. The randomizing of position and posture I discussed in the previous section will contribute to this. But you also need to put in some effort extending the *length of time* that the dog looks at you.

This helps you solve a problem that often arises in early attention work. The dog looks away, then looks at you, and you C/T. What you end up reinforcing is not the "look at me" behavior, but the "chained" behavior of "look away/look at me." [This is one example among many you will encounter of a dog being quite adept at constructing his own behavior chains, attaching extraneous (usually undesired) behaviors to desired ones.]

Think of attention as a *long-duration behavior.* First, extend the period in which the dog holds his eyes on you first by *lengthening the time* between the moment the dog looks at you and the C/T. By adding a one-second count every couple of days you can build this time up to about fifteen seconds. Then, put the behavior on a *variable schedule.*

Remember that in planning your variable schedule you are going to work plus or minus 50% around the mean, which in this case is fifteen seconds. So at the start your low end will be seven seconds and your high end twenty-two. Refer back to the "Basics" (Chapter 2) for a fuller discussion of how you do this. Your ultimate goal is that the dog hold his attention on you for ten minutes at a time. This will take you well beyond anything you have to do in the ring.

Finally, this is a good behavior to shape informally. When you are just sitting around doing nothing in particular, C/T the dog for looking at you accidentally. In the early shaping phase with any dog I have cans of Pounce strategically located around the house together with a clicker, so that I can do this sort of informal training in all the places where I tend to spend any time or where I have use of it (for example, at the front door).

After a little bit of all this, be prepared for your dog to be boring holes in your skull with his eyes. It can be startling, but there are worse fates.

Don't put the behavior on cue

This is one behavior that I do not put on cue. I never want to have to call for it. The stimulus for the dog to pay attention to me is the fact that we are working. If I have to call on the dog to watch me, then the dog is not really engaged in the work.

"But," you probably are asking, "what if I lose the dog's attention in the ring?" This happens. When Dylan was attacked he was injured seriously enough that he could not train for almost three months or show for four. Seven months later, when we went through a string of shows, I realized that due to the attack he had become very jumpy about loud noises outside the ring. Before the attack, he was oblivious to everything. You could set off a bomb outside the ring, and he would not have cared. But now he had become hypersensitive. He would get distracted and fail an exercise.

How did I get his attention back? I did two things. One, I remembered to use his name frequently while in the ring between exercises. As I have discussed, your dog's name is the single most powerful cue in your "tool kit." And two, I "worked" him more consistently between exercises. I talked to him a lot, kept him focused on me during the transitions from one exercise to the next, and kept moving quickly. Keeping him involved in what he was doing helped to get past his newfound hypersensitivity. I don't think a "watch me" cue would have made any difference at all. If anything, it may well have become an additional source of stress.

Generally, you are going to have to solve the problem of "focus" by training. This is a prime purpose of *generalization* work. If you carefully teach the dog that he can perform what he knows regardless of the circumstances in which you ask him to do it, it will be increasingly easy for him to focus on the work at hand regardless of anything else that may be going on around you.

Expose the dog to increasingly distracting situations and retrace the shaping curve in their presence. It is also helpful to set up situations where you walk away from the dog when he gets involved in something else. Do this either in a closed area where there are no risks or with a helper who can keep an eye on the dog.

If you are in a room, you can leave the room and hide behind a door or set up a screen and hide behind it. If you are outside, just start walking away. Do not call the dog or show any concern for what the dog is doing. Put the burden on the dog to realize that he has "lost" you and needs to find you. These exercises will make the dog conscious of watching you all the time simply because he cannot be sure what you are going to do if he directs his attention elsewhere. After a few of these sessions the dog may turn his head momentarily, but he will not really let you out of his sight.

When you are training particular exercises, C/T for attention from time to time. This will keep the dog mindful that attention is a constant feature of all work that he is doing with you.

Do not "shape" attention with aversives

There are "attention-training" programs that involve such things as "mo-tivational pops" (whatever that is supposed to be) to get the dog to look back at you in the event the dog looks away. I think that any use of aversives in shaping attention is bound to be counterproductive.

Remember always that the point of all this is that the dog be focused on his work. Remember too not to confuse "looking at me" with "focus." In some circumstances there is no real harm in Fido taking a moment to look around, as long as his mind is back on the job when you need it to be. And if Fido happens to be looking away when you need him to be looking at you, aversives won't help much. Use other cues or maneuvers (e.g., cue him to maneuver into position again) to get his mind back on his work.

We may also think a moment about Turid Rugaas's theory of calming signals. Is it possible that Fido is looking away because he perceives that you are stressed, and he wants you to relax? *It is possible.* If so, use of aversives will only intensify the stress he perceives, and will only serve to intensify the "calming signal" behavior—which will take him farther and farther away from where you want him to be.

"Ready"

"Ready" is a type of cue that you can use at the start of every exercise. This is an acceptable cue (as long as you say it in a neutral, conversational tone, neither wheedling nor commanding) because it responds directly to the judge's question, "Are you ready?" However, I do not really think of it as an attention cue. Rather, I think of it simply as a reminder to the dog that we are about to start an exercise.

Conformation: The conditioned "watch"

For people showing in conformation, it is very useful to have a *conditioned stimulus* to catch the dog's attention when stacking, free stacking, or when the judge is going over the dog. A very handy conditioned stimulus is the index finger held up and in front of you.

You can shape the dog to watch your finger in a couple of ways. A simple way is to hold your finger up, and C/T the dog for any glance toward it. This will take advantage of the work you have done with the target stick in that the dog is already used to looking at (targeting) something held in front of him.

You can use the target stick more directly by transferring the target stick to your finger. Hold the target stick in your palm so that the stick runs along the underside of your finger, and the target end extends just past the tip of your index finger. The dog will respond to the target stick. C/T for the look. Bring the target end down so that it is coextensive with your finger, then eliminate it from the picture. Now the dog is looking at your finger.

Whichever way you approach it, you can use your finger as a target when gaiting, stacking, or when the dog is being examined.

Head position when at your left side

This is one of those stylistic matters that I consider extraneous to shaping the exercise as such. Many trainers put a lot of effort during their heel position training into getting the dog to adopt a posture with the head up and turned toward the trainer's body. This posture produces a "dancin', prancin' " gait. In terms of scoring it is irrelevant, in that a dog that walks in a stylized manner should not score any better than a dog that walks normally, as long as both otherwise completely conform to the requirements for heel position (though it can cause problems, which I discuss in the heeling section in the next chapter). Nor is it essential to the dog being able to keep his eye on you.

Dogs have great peripheral vision. Humans at best see about a 180-degree field. Dogs see a field to the side of about 240 degrees. Their vision also allows them to see things above and behind their head. So the dog can see you quite well even if his head is not turned completely toward you; and even if his head is turned completely toward you he can see things to the side and be distracted by them. This is another reason for my emphasis on *focus* rather than the mere physical posture of "attention."

When you add motion to attention, that is, put it together with the dog walking at your left side, your *criteria* should simply be that the dog's head (1) is cocked toward you and (2) is at least parallel with the ground.

By "cocked toward you," I mean that, if you visualize your left foot as being at the center of a clock and 12:00 is directly ahead, the dog's head is pointed at least toward 1:00. That is sufficient for your body to occupy the majority of the dog's field of vision.

"Head parallel to the ground" should require no physical description. The purpose of this criterion is

to help avoid sniffing. You don't want the dog orienting to the ground at all except when performing one of the retrieve-related exercises. Otherwise, in all circumstances when working, the dog's head should be up.

If you have a dog that walks with his head down for any reason, shape "head up" the same way you would any other behavior: Catch the moment when his head is up and C/T. Again, it is best not to induce this because you don't want to have this behavior reliant on extraneous cues. Like everything else, you want to be part of the dog's operant repertoire.

Teaching the dog to work his rear end

Perhaps the hardest element in teaching a dog to work precisely is teaching the dog how to work his rear end. I don't really know why it's so hard for a dog to be aware of what his hind end is doing. Nor is this phenomenon necessarily peculiar to dogs. Ever see a cat "hide" by sticking its head and forequarters under a chair, leaving its rear end exposed for all the world to see?

Whatever the basis for this quirk, the dog must learn to be conscious of his rear in order to align it properly with the handler, whether in motion, sitting, or standing at heel or at front.

(In using the word "conscious" I know that I am engaging in a bit of anthropomorphism, that is, attributing human qualities to a nonhuman subject. Dogs do process the information they receive, but I don't really know how. So I am hesitant to use a word like "conscious" that suggests qualities that attach to the human thought processes. It would probably be more precise to frame the point in terms of *behaviors;* however the dog will be learning several different rear-end behaviors. Here, I am talking about a *fluency* fundamental to all of them— the dog learning to be aware of, and purposefully to control the movement of, his rear end. Needing some way to name that learned awareness, and in recognition of the fact that some sort of mental process exists and takes place, I'm calling it "consciousness." Apologies all around.)

Preliminary to being able to develop any particular rear-end behavior (such as aligning the rear with the head on a sit-in-front), the dog must learn that the rear end is back there and doing something whenever his front end is doing something. This does not come naturally. There are several methods for accomplishing this.

The TTouch™ body wrap

Use a three-inch-wide Ace bandage wrapped in a figure-eight around the withers and chest at one end and around the rear legs at the other, connected along the back with a cross-tie. Wrap it just tightly enough that the dog will be aware of the pressure at both front and rear. With the dog wrapped, do some left-side walking and recalls. Spend about twenty minutes on movement, but don't worry about accuracy. Just let the dog move in some controlled fashion with the body wrap on. Then remove the wrap and do nothing more with the dog that day. Let the dog sleep on it (the "lesson," that is, not the wrap itself).

With one "second chance" dog I helped rehabilitate at the Pasadena Humane Society we noticed a marked difference in the dog after only one session. She was not only moving much more freely, her general attitude changed. She was more confident and outgoing. She had been very shy. The morning after the body-wrap experience, when one of the staff approached her run she trotted to the door and gave the staffer a "play-bow." She became very gregarious in socialization sessions, both with people and with other dogs, and we placed her two weeks later. Gina Arons, the TTeam practitioner there, said, "For whatever reason, the body wrap makes dogs smarter."

I don't know that you will have that sort of result, but after two or three of these sessions the dog will almost certainly show greater awareness of his rear end movement. You will notice the dog stepping with his rear feet instead of "hopping" with them. And as the dog sits, you will notice the dog starting to adjust his rear spontaneously.

The obstacle walk

Walk the dog over and around low obstacles. You can set the obstacles in a series, or in various pat-

Ethel targets her miniature pinscher, Angel, over the cavalettis, a series of low obstacles. The varying obstacles teach the dog to lift her hind feet as well as her front feet, and the target, as opposed to a leash, gives her the freedom to find her own balance and stride.

terns. This is a variant on the horse-trainer's cavaletti technique. You do not want obstacles high enough to cause the dog to jump them, but just high enough that the dog has to be aware of lifting his feet—especially his rear feet—to clear them.

Stair stepping

A variation on the obstacle walk is to have the dog step his way up some stairs. Most dogs going up stairs will push off with both back feet as they reach forward with their front feet. You want the dog to step with his back feet just as he does with his front feet.

Here you will use the target stick. Hold it closely in front of the dog's nose as you lead him to the step. *Click as* he steps up with his front foot and treat. Keep the target stick close in front of his nose but lead him slightly and slowly. Watch the back foot. C/T any movement of a single back foot toward the stair. C/T a single back foot stepping onto the stair. C/T the second back foot moving toward and onto the stair. If at any point the dog starts to "hop" upward on the stairs, simply do not reinforce, return the dog to the bottom and start over.

If your dog is too small to take normal stairs without jumping, you would have to find low obstacles like a curb, or build a small stairway with lower risers.

The plastic dowel

For quite a while I used a Plexiglas dowel to help the dog keep his rear end "in" while heeling, and to help him find front. I don't do that anymore. The plastic dowel is not "punitive," nor is it an "aversive," and to the extent it "compels" any behavior it is pretty darned nontoxic. Simply, I don't find it necessary in most situations, and, like most lures and props, if you don't use it now, you won't have to fade it out later.

In heeling, assuming that your dog is structurally sound, if you maintain a pace that is correct for the dog then you will not tend to have a problem with the dog's rear end swinging out ("crabbing"). If you do, a plastic dowel probably won't help much. If the dog learns to push against it, you may find yourself with kind of a "rebound" effect when you remove it. One of my students encountered this with her miniature pinscher. When starting heeling off-lead, the dog would swing out twenty-four to thirty inches away from her, and after a few steps return to

heel position. It seemed to me that this was sort of a learned behavior related to resisting the leash "pop" at the start to keep her in position. We went to targeting for heel position, and in about three weeks had virtually eliminated the problem.

On fronts, the plastic dowel can be helpful but *only if* you have done the work to teach Fido how to move his rear end consciously. The key lies in teaching Fido exactly where front is, and building the level of difficulty in very careful increments, with continuous reinforcement and very high numbers of repetitions at each level. If you use the body wrap and the obstacles and such to teach the dog how to work his rear end, he will shortly figure out how to maneuver to get into proper front position. Once Fido is working his rear end without the dowel, you may find it helpful to introduce the dowel as a purely passive obstacle, just to "spark" the thought processes a bit.

If you do use such a tool, remember that the purpose of the tool is transitory only. Use the tool because you *must* in order to get the behavior, reinforce the behavior, and get rid of the tool as quickly as possible.

My tendency away from using this sort of tool has a twofold basis. One, I am always working toward finding the "straight line" between point A and point Z. Everything that I add into the training process I ultimately have to take out, and that creates a whole new learning curve to traverse. It is a matter of "simplify, simplify, simplify." And two, I am increasingly of the view that I want to let the dog do the work of figuring out what I want for himself as much as possible through careful shaping. You can get to where you want to be with careful development of criteria and accurate scheduling and delivery of reinforcement.

Shaping the sit

For the formal Obedience competitor, the sit is *the* fundamental obedience behavior. It occurs multiple times in every exercise in every class. The dog must be able to do it at your left side, in front of you, and across the ring from you. He must be able to sit without a verbal cue in the course of a heeling pattern (often after having just changed pace or executed a turn), at the end of a recall (having come running across the ring to you), and at your side (at the start of every exercise). And he must be able to maintain the sit position for up to three minutes in the Open ring. All this involves criteria of proper posture, alignment, and quickness. For the Obedience competitor, the sit is a behavior in which Rover must be completely fluent.

The sit is also helpful for the Agility competitor at the start of the run. If you have that control you can help your dog get "collected" and "focused" on the run to come. And if your dog goes off course, it can be helpful in getting your dog under control and back on course.

For the pet owner, "sit" is the most commonly used command, and the handiest behavior for controlling the dog. As I discuss more fully in the last section of this book, "sit" can be very useful in eliminating unwanted behaviors, such as jumping up on people or door-dashing, because the dog cannot jump up on someone or charge out the door if he is sitting. And when you are out walking on the street, knowing that your dog will sit when you halt gives you a comfortable level of control in traffic or on a crowded sidewalk.

You may encounter any one of several problems with the sit. If your dog is a puppy you may have to teach him to sit from scratch. If your dog is somewhat older he may know how to sit but may not respond reliably to the "sit" cue in the presence of distractions (such as greeting strangers). If your dog is already competition trained you may want to improve his posture or get him to sit more quickly.

Regardless of your purposes, or the age or previous experience of your dog, sit starts with one simple concept: "Put your rump on the ground."

Begin at the beginning

Whether you are faced with training the sit from the beginning or improving the sit that your dog already does, start with the assumption that the dog doesn't understand what "sit" means. This is obvious with a puppy. It is somewhat obvious with a dog that "sort of" responds to the command.

In my discussion of the **crossover dog** I said that in training a crossover dog the best approach is simply to begin as though the dog does not know any of the obedience behaviors. If you have trained your dog through at least a Novice title you probably said, "OK, that makes some sense," but mentally reserved retraining behaviors like the sit because they are so fundamental and so well ingrained. Wrong. Yes, your dog knows to sit, and he will offer it frequently even when confused, because if he has learned nothing else he has learned that sit never gets him in trouble. But you still must remove the element of force. Respond to the sit so offered as an *operant behavior,* and reinforce and shape it accordingly, just as if it were brand new. Most importantly, you must eliminate the cue for the time being.

Even if your dog is "trained" for competition, if the sits are crooked or slow or slumped, the dog's concept of "sit" as a command includes all those flaws. Without intending to, you have trained these flaws into the dog just as surely as you have the concept of "rump on ground." Since you intend the cue "sit" to mean a perfect, not a flawed, sit, the fact that you have these flaws when you deliver the cue means that for all practical purposes the dog does not understand what "sit" means any more than the pinhead puppy does. Put another way, Fido understands that "sit" at least means "rump on ground." As to the rest, he's not so clear.

So with the crossover dog (especially if you are trying to get rid of ingrained faults) you have to think not in terms of "polishing" the sit, but of teaching a new exercise. You will almost certainly ultimately use the same cue, but by the time you reintroduce that cue it will have an entirely different meaning.

The shaping mechanics

With the **green dog**, you will start with what the dog gives you. You can be in your living room or in your backyard, wherever, doing whatever. If you are outside, walk around with the dog in a completely informal fashion, then stop. Say nothing, do nothing. Let the dog be doggy.

At some point Lassie will sit, if only for lack of anything better to do. C/T. What happens with Lassie? A **superstitious response.** At the risk of putting human language in the dog's mind: "Hmm. That was nice. Wonder why that happened?" Get the dog moving again, stop again. Lassie will sit a little more readily this time. C/T. Repeat.

Lassie will shortly be sitting at every opportunity. *You are not worried about the dog's position relative to you, nor even posture;* you are concerned only with whether the dog is putting her rump on the ground.

Now something interesting happens. In a very short while Lassie will sit in such a way (body language, eye expression) as to appear to be demanding the reward that you have conditioned her to expect. This is a major step forward. *Do not disappoint her.* You have told her that if she performs this act, she will trigger a goodie. This *insistence* tells you that she has figured the game out and *wants to play to win.*

C/T with a *jackpot.* Make sure she wins!

As I discussed earlier, you may find yourself shaping a sit at the same time as you are conditioning the dog to the clicker. There's nothing wrong with this (after all, the dog is not dead, so she will be doing something). Just be sure that you randomize the C/T association. The "game" will still work. I have conditioned many dogs to the clicker in the process of shaping the sit (or shaped the sit in the process of conditioning the dog to the clicker, depending on your point of view). The dog may not yet understand that "click" = "treat," but she certainly knows what the treat is, and if that odd sound happens to come with it, that's okay too.

This sit is the product of "pure" *shaping.* You not only have *not induced* the sit in any way, and you have *not compelled* her to sit with the threat of any *punisher* should she fail to do so. There is no *aversive,* no *coercive force,* connected with the activity. You are not pulling up on a leash or pushing down on or slapping her rump, or any such thing. The sit is freely offered with no aversive baggage. The dog is sitting for one reason and one reason only: Doing so triggers reinforcement.

The crossover dog

Shaping can be difficult with the crossover dog because the idea of "offering" behavior is contrary to everything you have taught him. The crossover dog is conditioned to do things "on command." The crossover dog has been **conditioned** to want to avoid making mistakes (that is, after all, the fundamental effect on any subject of using aversives). So, in the absence of any direction from you, the crossover dog is most likely to do nothing. If you encounter this, you must be alert to reinforce even very tiny behaviors. You may find yourself working at first with nothing more than the dog licking its lips or raising a paw slightly.

I had an interesting example of this with Sam at a Don't Shoot the Dog seminar in Guelph, Ontario, in 1996. I "loaned" him to a group of five for a free-shaping session. I did not participate in the group. They were not to give any cues. I did not give Sam any cues, but just turned him over to the group. And for the better part of twenty minutes, he just sat. I have since heard of many other crossover dogs who manifest the same type of behavior.

Fortunately for this exercise, sit is kind of a "default" action for the crossover dog: "When in doubt, sit." It's hard to get in trouble that way. The sit is probably the easiest behavior to get the dog to "offer." It is also a good exercise to reshape, simply because it is such a basic part of the dog's overall *repertoire.*

What you are likely to encounter with the crossover dog is that he will tend to maneuver so as to sit either in front of you or at your left side. This is *superstition* at work: placement is irrelevant to the sit behavior as such, but due to all the early training Fido knows that he always sits in one of two places: in front of you or at heel. Sit as a *fluency* simply means that wherever Fido finds himself, wherever you are in relation to him, and whatever he happens to be doing, he plops that rump on the ground.

So it is important in this shaping process that you randomize the *place* where he sits. When you get to Utility the dog is going to have to sit on cue while all the way across the ring from you, and there may be other circumstances when training or showing (or simply being out with your dog in public) in which you want the dog to sit exactly where he is, and not come to you in order to sit. C/T the dog for sitting wherever, whenever. Not only will this help you identify the specific behavior you are looking for, it will free up the dog from some of the overly structured approach to working that you have already conditioned in him.

As I mentioned earlier, with the crossover dog you want to get rid of the "sit" cue for some period of time. (Since dog trainers are notoriously impatient, I will say "a couple of months" just to emphasize the point, though the actual time may be less.) *Slow down!* It's taken you a while to create whatever mess you find yourself in, so give yourself some time to clean it up. It will help you, in doing so, to start in what would otherwise be an informal, non-training setting, such as in your living room while watching TV.

Inducing the sit: Some help for the pet owner

The pet owner may well find circumstances where you may have to induce the sit. For example, if you have a big galoot of a hound, you may have a significant safety problem if, for example, he likes to use your frail grandmother's shoulders as an armrest or if, in his enthusiasm, he bounces your 6-year-old niece off the nearest wall.

I do not recommend that the competition trainer induce fundamental behaviors. You have time to allow the raw behaviors to emerge and shape them as operants. And even for the pet owner, unless you are faced with an exigency (for example, my client's Rottweiler, who in his bliss knocked a neighbor's child into a glass door), I far prefer shaping to inducement. The only reason that I bring this discussion up at all is that sometimes the pet owner needs to go for immediate control. The sit is a great way to get control, and inducing the sit works in that situation. We will shape using inducement and reinforcement.

Mechanics of inducing the sit

To induce the sit you have the dog on his feet and stand in front of the dog. Hold the bait in your *left* hand with your palm facing the dog. Bring the bait directly over the dog's nose and s-l-o-w-l-y move it back toward the rear of his skull. You may also step forward a half step with your right foot so that you are on a slight angle as you move toward the dog. This nonconfrontational posture will help avoid triggering any "dominance/submission" quarrels.

The dog's initial impulse will be to rise up to get the bait. This is usually caused by having the bait too high above the dog's head. *Do not respond with any negative acts.* If you feel you must vocalize, a soft "ah-ah" will suffice. Simply lower the bait and "push" it slightly further back toward the dog's back skull.

The dog may also respond by backing up. In this case you are probably moving the bait backward too fast or are holding it a little too low over his head. Raise your bait hand slightly and move it more slowly. What you should see if you are doing this properly is that the dog is rising up slightly in front while folding his rear end toward the ground. The dog is on his way to sitting. If the dog is continues to back up, move him around so that his rump is against a wall. Now he'll have to cooperate.

As the dog's rear is folding, lower the bait toward the back of the dog's skull. This will cause the dog to complete the sit. If you are getting a partial motion toward the ground, click the downward motion of Fido's rear end. This will quickly progress into a complete sit. Once Fido is moving his rear end consistently toward the ground, there will come a point in his momentum where he cannot readily stop his progress. Now, click *just as the dog's rump is hitting the ground.* When inducing the sit (as in any exercise) you not only have to reinforce the finished product, you have to "mark" the muscular action that gets the dog there. There is a "sticking point" where the dog is half to two-thirds of the way down, but has not fully committed to the sit. Watch the dog a couple of times and you will see that point. When the dog passes that point, click.

Although "click ends the behavior," don't worry that clicking as the dog is about to sit completely will stop the sit. As long as the dog has passed that sticking point, his momentum will carry him the rest of the way down.

Treat when the dog is fully sitting. You'll notice there is a gap of a second or so between C and T. No big deal. Remember, the "click" acts as a *bridge* between the behavior and presentation of the PR. You have told the dog (C) that he did right. The dog now expects the treat, so the fact that there is a lag of a second or two is of no real consequence.

Repeat this process until the sit is smooth from start to finish. As long as the dog hesitates at all, you are not ready to go forward.

Your hand motion becomes the cue

Dogs are primarily nonverbal communicators. I say this despite the fact that I have Shelties. (How many Shelties does it take to change a light bulb? Only one—if he barks at it long enough it will change itself. Why do Shelties bark? So many molecules in motion, so little time.) The greatest part of communication between dogs occurs through body language. Even if you are not sure about Turid Rugaas's theories, take some time to watch two or more dogs relating to each other. Body language is everything. For this reason, dogs are readily attuned to human body language. In fact, next to sleeping and scenting, reading body language is probably what dogs do best.

Even when you are using verbal cues, you may accidentally establish incidental physical cues. One student was working to put sit on cue. She was holding bait in her left hand, and when she said "sit," her dog would jump up slightly for the bait. Not to let him get the bait without sitting, she would lift her left hand to her left shoulder. The movement of her hand quickly became part of the sit cue. It was not hard to get rid of it; I merely note how remarkably dogs associate things that to us are entirely unrelated. This is also one illustration of why it is worthwhile to use a video camera when training, even if you have a training partner.

But I digress. In all the shaping to this point you have not used the word "sit." However, you have been conditioning a cue. Every time, just before the dog has sat, he has seen your left hand moving toward him, palm open. With repetition, that hand motion becomes a cue for the sit just as surely as the word "sit" would.

If you are a pet owner, being able to use your hand as a signal for the sit makes a nice conversation piece. It's always impressive to see a dog respond to a signal given in silence rather than to a bellowed command.

If you are a competition trainer, this process will lay the foundation for the dog learning to respond to hand signals instead of verbal cues. This will improve the dog's attention because he will learn that he cannot rely on *hearing* you tell him what he is supposed to do. And it will lay the foundation for the signals work in Utility.

Reinforcing the sit: Shifting the motivation

You will use a food treat early on to reinforce the sit. What else can reinforce the sit? I'll answer by asking another question: Why does the dog jump up on people? Usually, to get attention. So receiving attention from a human is reinforcing to the dog. If, then, you can make human contact contingent on the dog sitting, the human contact will itself reinforce the sit.

Begin with family. When you come home, have the dog sit before you greet the dog. Don't let him jump up. When you are passing by, have the dog sit and then pet him. After you have petted him and while he is still sitting, C/T. The C/T will reinforce the entire repertoire of "sit and accept petting."

When the dog will sit reliably in order to be petted by family members, introduce strangers. Tell the stranger what you are doing. Have the dog sit before the stranger approaches. Remind the dog to sit, and *C/T frequently* for him doing so as the stranger approaches. At first, it may be all the dog can do to hold the sit while the stranger nears. If so, let the stranger approach, greet the dog vocally, and walk off. When you think the dog is reasonably likely to hold the sit, let the stranger pet the dog.

With repeated exposures, the dog will generalize and decide that sitting when someone approaches is the best thing to do, because that gets rewarded and all other behavior does not.

From inducement to "offering"

Even when I start with inducement, I want to move as quickly as possible to getting the dog to *offer* the behavior before I put it on cue. You will know the dog is offering because he will appear to expect a positive response from you when he does it. It doesn't take much perceptivity about canine body language to recognize this: You can see this in his eyes, the set of his ears and head, etc. Fido is offering the sit, perhaps even getting downright obnoxious about it. (I never thought I would use the words "assertive" and "sit" together until I worked with a boxer who gave me precisely that. He was sitting, and by golly you better come through with the goodies!)

The reason to wait for offering before putting the sit on cue is simple: When the dog offers the behavior, the dog demonstrates that he understands that that behavior triggers reinforcement. It has now become part of his conscious and willing repertoire. Now you can put it on cue with confidence that the dog will respond.

One final note. At this point, Fido does not understand that there is any difference between "training time" and the "real world." He will offer the sit any time, anywhere. *So always be prepared to reinforce the sit!* It isn't any big deal to keep a clicker near at hand, and you can easily get to a biscuit or some other little treat after you click (remember all my little Pounce cans stashed in various corners of the house).

Proper posture

This is not a major consideration for the pet owner. You don't really care whether the dog is sitting up straight or flopped on his haunches as long as he can maintain the sit reliably. It is true that the better the posture, the better the dog will hold the sit, but it is not a major issue.

For the competition trainer, the dog's sit posture is critical. There are no points for proper sit posture as such, but posture will affect such things as straightness, and even the dog's ability to stay still on a long sit, particularly the 3-minute sit in Open. Good sit posture means that the dog is balanced from front to back and from side to side.

The "puppy sit"

In the "puppy sit" the dog is unbalanced to the rear. He flops back on his haunches, and typically his rear feet are splayed out to the side or even off the ground, his weight on the hock joint. Viewed from the side, this produces a "rock-back" sit that will put the dog out of heel position at any halt while heeling. Viewed from the front, this produces a sit that is not straight but skewed to one side or another.

Mace shows a nice "tuck" sit.

At first you will find the dog lifting his leg in response to the upward pressure. Relax the upward pressure slightly, let the leg sink back toward the ground, and try again. C/T when you feel some slight responding pressure downward from the dog. Your aim is to shape the behavior of the dog putting some weight on those front feet (the dog tends to resist this because the dog is innately prepared to be ready to move those front feet and run). A few of these sessions will stabilize the sit immensely.

"East–west" balance

Once the dog has proper front-to-back ("north–south") balance, you have to help him find proper side-to-side ("east–west") balance. This is fairly

Harpo is quite well balanced from side to side (but his tongue could throw him off).

You may use inducement to shape the puppy sit into a proper sit. As the dog sits, hold the bait in front of and very slightly above the dog's nose so that the dog will stretch slightly toward the bait as he lowers his rump to the ground. This will cause the dog to bring his rump forward, "tucking" it under his body. The dog's weight will now be more evenly distributed from front to rear. If anything the dog will have slightly more weight on his front paws than on his rear paws.

In a long-legged dog this sit will look fairly vertical. In a more square-bodied dog this sit will look more balanced, almost a right triangle.

When you have the tuck position you can help the dog settle his weight on the front feet by using TTouches such as the python lift. In the python lift you circle the dog's leg with your entire hand and lift gently upward, applying just enough pressure to move the skin and muscle. Hold the "lift" for about 4 seconds and slowly return the skin to the starting point. Move your hand a little bit along the length of the dog's leg and repeat. Do this three or four times up and down the leg.

easy. The dog's feet should be about at shoulder width apart. With some dogs, the natural balance point is even a bit wider. For a very few, it is narrower. You want to help your dog find that balance point for himself.

While the dog is sitting, place your hand on the dog's shoulder blades. Gently, but with enough pressure to cause the dog to move, push the dog's shoulders back and forth from right to left a couple of times. If the dog is off-balance he will adjust one or both feet due to this rocking motion. C/T when you feel the dog stabilize under your hand.

Establishing the verbal cue

Now you want to put the behavior in context. For example, you want Fido to sit when greeting someone at the front door. Though you have (to a greater or lesser degree) established the hand signal, you may not be able to deliver the hand signal in this situation—especially if Fido is looking at the door and not you.

You establish the verbal cue for "sit" the same way you do for every other behavior. Once the dog is reliably offering the sit, simply say "sit" *as the dog is moving into the sit*, just before you C/T. In other words, you "catch" the behavior and add the cue while the behavior is in process. Bit by bit, "back it up" until you are saying the word "sit" at the *beginning* of the sit motion, and then *before* the dog has begun to sit at all.

Eliminate "off-cue" sits (stimulus control)

When the dog will sit in response to you saying "sit" *before* he has begun to sit at all, then "sit" is on cue. Now, you will change the rules a bit. In training, you will no longer reinforce sits offered at random. For the sit to be under *stimulus control,* Fido must sit *only* when given the cue to do so. As with all rule changes, this will cause some momentary confusion. Fido will offer a sit, expecting reinforcement, and won't get it. You may see some *extinction burst* behavior. The boxer I referred to earlier will "throw" sits at me all the time. When I don't C/T, he bounces up and down in place and "whuffs" (I don't know what else to call it) at me. It is very important now that you stick to your guns and reinforce only those sits that are in response to the cue.

Why is this important? On general principle, this establishes the discipline necessary for an obedient dog. But for the obedience competitor, think about the Utility go-out. You send the dog away, and he must keep going until you tell him "Sit." What is one of the more common problems for new Utility dogs? They decide to stop on their own. This is an issue of stimulus control. By insisting, very early in the game, that the dog only do X on command X, you will have a good "leg up" in solving this problem if it crops up in this (or any other) exercise.

"Ah-ha!" I hear someone say. "But what about the 'automatic sit' when you come to a halt while heeling? You aren't giving a cue there, the dog just has to sit when you halt." Yes, you are. But what kind of cue? Go back to the discussion on *repertoire cues.* Your heeling training establishes the halt as a cue for the sit. In other words, *the sit is on cue* (the cue being "I've come to a halt"); it is just that the cue is a physical part of the exercise, not delivered separately by you. You can see this better if you think about putting the "stand at heel" on cue for Utility signals and the moving stand. You have a lot of work to do to get that behavior precisely because the sit-at-heel-when-halting has become such a powerful repertoire cue.

No "corrections"

What do you do if Bowser doesn't sit when you say "sit?" *Nothing.* You may think of his failure to sit as "disobedience" if you like, but categorizing it as such doesn't help in what we are doing. If you call it "disobedience," then Bowser is a "bad dog," and you really leave yourself with no alternative but to respond with punishment of some sort. What is the point?

Let us try to perceive the matter differently. By failing to sit in the presence of the cue to sit, Bowser has *missed an opportunity to earn reinforcement.* And you immediately know something: The behavior is not yet strongly enough associated with the cue to allow you reasonably to expect that the behavior can be produced predictably in response to the cue. *This is trainer error!* If this is indeed the problem, you have to return to the mechanics of establishing the cue before going further.

Assuming that the cue is established and Bowser has simply "missed it," break the exercise off (you may say "wrong" if you really cannot control your own urge to growl, or, better yet, simply take a step or two away from Bowser and then turn back to him), give it a few seconds so there is no continuity between the first cue and the next, and give the cue again. Reinforce only when he sits in response to the cue. Bit by bit, his responses will become more consistent.

Do not attempt to incorporate the sit into any other exercise (such as walking) until Bowser is sitting consistently in response to the "sit" cue.

Latency

However you imagine using the sit in real life, it will be important that the dog sit quickly when told to do so. If, for example, you are using the sit to prevent jumping or door-dashing, it is particularly important because you will rely on the latency "habit" to overcome the stimulus to jump up on someone or bolt through the door. The same is true if you want the dog to sit when you come to a curb and have to stop. You don't want the dog wandering into the street before he decides to park it.

If you are a competition trainer, an immediate sit is paramount, whether the dog is sitting when coming to a halt while heeling, sitting at front, or doing a go-out. Slow sits while heeling can cost you valuable points. In the front, a slow sit is apt to become a no-sit, which can becomes an "automatic" (anticipated) finish. In the case of a Utility go-out, a slow sit easily becomes a no-sit, and a no-sit easily becomes a failure to stop altogether—and a failure in the exercise. None of this is desirable.

If you add the cue carefully you will incorporate **zero latency** into the exercise because you will not put the cue at the start of the behavior right away. The dog will get used to sitting as he hears the word "sit" (a) through your continuous association of the word with the action of plopping his rump on the ground in a certain way, and (b) extinguishing off-cue sits. When Rover understands the "off-cue = no click" rule, it will intensify his on-cue responses. If you are in a hurry to add the cue, however, you will end up working against yourself. You will get slow (or no) responses to the cue, and this will undermine latency over the long run. As grandmother always said, "Haste makes waste."

When you are giving the cue before the dog is making any movement toward sitting, do not give the dog more than a one-second count to respond. Here is a place where the word "wrong" can be useful (though it may well be unnecessary if you have been careful in your shaping progression so far). You say "sit" and silently count "one-banana" (this count makes for one second and gives you syllables to chop off if you want to reduce the time even further). If the dog is not sat, say "wrong" and release

the dog. Give it a moment to break any continuity between events, and repeat the cue.

If the dog is not fairly quickly sitting within the one-second time frame, the odds are that you have tried to put the behavior on cue too quickly and the dog is still uncertain as to the cue's meaning. The word "wrong" is not going to solve that problem. Go back to kindergarten for a bit, make sure that the dog understands what he is being reinforced for, and reincorporate the cue as described, only a bit more patiently.

Sustaining the sit (sit/stay)

Now the sit is reliable and stable when the dog is stationary, it is on cue, and it is fluent in that the dog will sit on cue, wherever he is in relation to you and whatever he is doing. The next step is to extend the time that the dog will sit before getting up. This is essential to using the sit as a control behavior and for the *long sits* in competiton. Remember, the sit is (once the rump is on the ground) a **long-duration behavior**. You extend time by the two-step process of first simply lengthening the gap between behavior and reinforcer, and then putting the behavior on a variable schedule of reinforcement.

At first, you are clicking when Fido's rump hits the ground. Now, after his rump hits the ground wait for a count of one second before you C/T. Release and repeat four to five times. After a couple of sessions, wait for a count of two seconds before you C/T. Then go to three seconds, four, five, and so on up to about fifteen seconds. Be sure always to release the dog from the sit after each C/T.

When you are at fifteen seconds, put the behavior on a variable schedule of reinforcement, using the same formula discussed in Chapter 2. At fifteen seconds you will reinforce at intervals between seven and twenty-two seconds. When the dog is reliable at twenty-two seconds you will make that your new "mean" and reinforce at intervals between eleven and thirty-three seconds. And so on.

The pet owner should get the dog to hold the sit for a period of three minutes. This will give you adequate control in public. This means that you work up to a variable schedule based on a two-minute "mean." Go for a longer duration if you want to.

The competition trainer should get the dog to hold the sit for a period of ten to fifteen minutes. You don't have to get to that point to have the sit established as a fluency, but it is your ultimate goal in training. For a ten-minute sit, this means that you work up to a variable schedule based on a seven-minute "mean." For a fifteen-minute sit, the "mean" becomes ten minutes.

You may think that ten minutes (to say nothing of fifteen!) is excessive. It is not. You will find situations in competition where you are waiting outside the ring for the *group exercises* for a few minutes before going in. You don't want your dog to socialize during that time, so chances are he will be sitting or lying down. Then when you get into the ring, you may find a delay before the exercises actually start. If you haven't done the long sit yet, you do not want to have your dog lying down in the ring because that may well induce him to lie down once the exercise starts. So your dog may well be sitting for a total of seven to ten minutes during this entire period, and you don't want him to feel burdened by the experience.

As a general point, it is wise to *overtrain* your dog, that is, to condition the dog in training to perform at a level that he will never be asked to perform at in competition. That way, whatever happens in competition, it is not likely to be something he is not well prepared for. This is true in all exercises and activities.

Do not use a "stay" cue

This is going to be controversial (as is everything else in this book that is not conventional wisdom). I do not recommend that you use a "stay" cue.

"Stay" is not a behavior. The behavior is "sit." The "stay" element of the sit is simply a matter of the dog continuing the sit until you release him or tell him to do something different. Put in terms of the stimulus control "formula," the dog is doing behavior X (sitting) on cue X ("sit"), he is not doing behavior Y (lying down, whatever) on cue X, and he is not doing anything else in the absence of another cue.

So in conditioning the "continue the sit" behavior, you are not going to use a "stay" cue. This should be sounding fairly familiar by now. You are simply conditioning the behavior of putting rump on ground and keeping it there until released. There is no reason to add a "stay" cue at all.

I am increasingly convinced that the verbal "stay" cue is not for the dog's benefit, but for the handler's. We are uncertain of what our dog will do, and so we have added another word to the training lexicon, even though the word "stay" adds nothing to the cue we have already given.

True enough, the "sit" does not occur in a vacuum. You may find yourself in a turbulent situation, whether on the street or in the obedience ring. You want a cue that allows you to immobilize the dog if necessary. *However, the cue to "sit" or "down" is and should be sufficient for the purpose.* "Stay" is completely extraneous. Put another way, if Bowser will not hold a sit or down indefinitely without a "stay" cue, the "stay" cue will add nothing. Your task is to establish stimulus control over the behavior, not "trick up" the situation by adding excess verbiage.

In my ring work, when leaving my dog (whether for a recall, or on a long sit) I simply use the cue "sit," while bringing my hand down in front of the dog's face. I don't use a verbal "stay" cue at all. The hand signal simply serves to put a visual "wall" in front of the dog's face. I'm working on eliminating that as well. I found with both Sam and Dylan that when I started leaving them on the Open long sit with a "sit" command instead of a "stay" command, their long sits became more reliable.

I think that part of the reason for lack of reliability in the group exercises is that we attach the same cue ("stay") to three different behaviors (sit, stand, and down) to mean the same thing, that is, "stay where you are." So it is not entirely surprising that the dog will tend to blend the behaviors. This is not the dog's fault; the fault arises because "stay" as a cue attaching to all three behaviors muddies the issue as to any one of them. If "sit" = "stay," and "down" = "stay," and "stand" = "stay," and "stay" always means "don't leave the spot where you are," then how is the dog supposed to distinguish between this "stay" being a "sit-and-don't-leave" and that "stay" being a "down-and-don't-leave?" You are simply asking for trouble.

Make sure your dog understands that when you have given a "sit" cue he must continue to sit until you release him. No other cue is necessary, or even helpful, and may in fact be destructive to the overall purpose.

The sit-in-motion

Now you have a reliable stationary sit. At the risk of repeating myself: It is fluent because the dog will sit at any place that you tell him to, he will sit on cue (hand signal or verbal cue), and he will remain in the sit until you have either released him or given him a cue to do something else.

The next step is to establish the sit-in-motion. For the pet owner, this will allow you to have the dog sit when you come to a halt at an intersection or to look in a store window. For the competition trainer, this is the first step toward the formal sit-at-halt during heeling.

You will do most of the work establishing the sit-in-motion once you have reliable "left-side walking," discussed later in this chapter. But you can start simply by moving with the dog. At random, and while the dog is reasonably close to you, give the dog the "sit" cue.

"Motion" is a new criterion, so you are going to relax your other criteria for a bit. Your only concern at this juncture will be that the dog put his rump on the ground when cued to do so. The dog may move a step or two toward you; that is not desirable over the long run, but you can live with it for the moment. You will even sacrifice a bit of latency at the beginning. Don't give the dog an indefinite time in which to respond, but if he takes three to five seconds at first, that's acceptable.

When the dog is sitting consistently, put the sit on limited hold to reduce the time you allow the dog to perform the behavior. Reduce the latency period again to zero. This is one application of *differential reinforcement.* You do not punish slow sits, you simply do not reinforce them. If you are consistent with this, the dog will select out those behaviors that trigger reinforcement (i.e., the fastest sits) from those that do not (i.e., slower sits). The end result is that the dog performs at the highest level not because he is afraid not to, but because he learns that doing so is what triggers reinforcement.

Once Fido is putting his rump on the ground with zero latency, you will add the criterion of "stop-and-sit." For the pet owner, this is important for general control. For the competition trainer, this is important in exercises like the Utility go-out.

This won't be as hard as it sounds, because if you have zero latency Fido can no longer be moving between the moment you say "sit" and the behavior. *In other words, "stop-and-sit" has become part of the package simply as a by-product of latency training.* So you are not going to compel a "stop." Rather, you are simply going to make it a defined part of the criteria. From now on, if Fido moves at all after you say "sit" he has missed the opportunity for reinforcement.

The down

The down is the second essential basic behavior after the sit. The down is very important for the pet owner because it gives you a powerful control be-havior. You can use it, for example, to stop such behaviors as door-dashing or jumping up on people. For the obedience competitor the down is not only a stationary exercise in Novice and Open, but a moving exercise in Open and Utility.

Shaping the down is deceptively simple (or, simply deceptive?). It is an easy behavior to capture and shape, simply because dogs lie down all the time. Some trainers will say that dogs "do not like" the down. I don't agree. Dogs love to lie down. They are world-class experts on the subject. Lying down is the most common resting posture among wild canids, far more common than sitting. In the obedience ring, dogs are good at lying down even (especially?) when you don't want them to.

If dogs don't like the down *as an exercise* it is because as an exercise it is taught improperly, with heavy reliance on aversives. When I taught public classes for a club using "traditional" methods, two of the three times I was bitten occurred while helping a handler force a down. Why the down is trained so harshly is beyond me. Of all the exercises that do not require force to train, the down heads the list.

The down is deceptive, however, because even as a pet owner you ultimately want two types of "lie-down" behavior. And one of them takes some work.

Basic shaping

It is true with all behaviors, but it is especially obvious with the down, that you are not teaching the dog to do the behavior as such. In other words, you are not teaching the dog how to lie down. He already knows that. You are just teaching the dog to lie down in a certain way, at a certain time.

I remind you of this because as I have noted, in most beginning classes I have taught and observed, "teaching the down" is a needlessly traumatic and punishing experience. In a typical sequence, the student starts by sweeping the dog's front legs forward and lowering him to the ground while saying "Dooowwwwn." If after a week the dog is not lying down "on command," the next step is to stand next to the dog and pop the leash sideward (this defeats the dog's efforts to "lock" his forelegs) and down. If he still resists, the student is told to put his foot on the leash and step down while pulling up on the leash. Fun for all concerned. And at last, when the dog is still resisting and you're wiped out and have quit for the day the dog just goes off and lies down in a corner somewhere.

This method is harsh and aversive for all concerned. Dogs not uncommonly snap at their own owners in the process. One of the nastiest bites I got as an instructor was when a German shepherd mix "came up the leash" at me when I was showing the handler how to stand on the leash to keep the dog's head down. It tells me a lot about what I used to do as opposed to what I do now that I was bitten by students' dogs three times when I taught in the traditional manner. I have not been so much as snapped at since I went to operant conditioning. *Vox cani, vox dei.*

Dogs lie down quite nicely on their own. So the basic shaping approach is a simple one: When the dog lies down, C/T. Don't worry about *how* he got from "stand" or "sit" to "down," just *reinforce* him for having done so. You are concerned with one thing and one thing only: The dog is lying down. And so, at first, you are simply reinforcing the position (just as, with the sit, you first reinforced the rump being on the ground at all). You will start working on reinforcing the muscular process of getting into the down once the dog knows that the position itself is a good place to be.

You will find the dog soon offering the down just as he offered the sit. Often, in an early shaping session, when the dog gets a little tired from sitting and bouncing around, he will lie down as a matter of course. Click and treat, and you will find the down coming around quite nicely.

The "resting" down—A natural posture

As a rule, the position that the dog will offer on his own will be lying down, rolled on one hip. This is the "resting" down, as opposed to the "ready" down that you find in competitive Obedience ring exercises such as the drop on recall. For the pet owner, the "resting" down is the one you are most likely to find your dog giving you, and it is the position you want to establish. When the dog is in the "resting" position it takes more effort to move, so it gives you maximum control if you are using the behavior to counter undesired behaviors.

Since this is the position the dog will tend to offer on his own, it takes no particular shaping to achieve it. Just C/T when you get it; the rest will take care of itself.

Adding the cue

When the dog is lying down, say "down" immediately before you click and treat. Release the dog from the down (that is, get him back on his feet) after each reinforcement.

After a few repetitions, say the cue, click as the dog is dropping to the ground, and treat when the down is complete. This connects both the cue and the CR to the physical action of going into the down. Bit by bit, say the cue earlier and earlier until you can say the cue before the dog has done anything at all, and the dog lies down as a response to the cue.

During this entire sequence you are reinforcing continuously, that is, one reinforcer for each behavior. There is no need nor any purpose to variable reinforcement at this time. Typically it does not take long for the dog to "get" the cue and lie down on cue.

The "accordion drop" ("ready" position)

If the dog is sitting and "slides" his front feet forward into the down, he will end up in the "resting down" posture. This posture is not conducive to the dog getting up immediately and moving. Also, it is a slow process for the dog. In order to teach the dog the drop in motion and get a quick response, you must first teach the "accordion" or "fold-back" down, which produces a "Sphinx" posture when the dog is fully on the ground.

In the "fold-back" down the dog stops all forward momentum and "folds back" into the down, settling onto his haunches. His front end touches the ground first, then his rear. The motion is smooth and continuous.

This down stops all forward momentum. If Rover is moving, he comes to a complete halt. If he is standing still, he does not move forward at all while going into the down.

While this is primarily of interest to the obedience competitor, it has value for the pet owner as well. You may be in a position where your dog is off-lead, and you want your dog to drop at a distance. For example, you may be playing in a park and your dog starts to head for the parking lot. If you have taught your dog to go down this way, he will respond immediately to your command and drop "right now."

When Sam was about a year old we lived on a busy street in Pasadena, California. I opened the front door one morning to get the paper. A boy rode by on a bike and Sam (tenacious little herder that he is) bolted after him. We had about six feet of "lawn" and a sidewalk before he got to the street. I had already taught Sam the drop in motion, including the accordion down. Without really thinking about it, I

Linda is teaching Mace the "accordion" or fold-back down. The dog stops all forward momentum and folds back. His front touches the ground first, then his rear; the motion is smooth and continuous. The result is a "Sphinx" down, with legs balanced on each side. With practice the dog can "down" in this manner almost instantly from any gait.

yelled (yes, I yelled—surprise will do that for you) "Sam, down!" He dropped right where he was, about two feet from the street. Goooood dog.

Training this behavior takes a little more effort, but the more you teach your dog the more he will know, and the more likely it will be that he will respond to your cues in those rare moments when you really need them.

Teaching the fold-back down takes two steps. First, teach the dog to "get back." Then, have him drop.

Shaping the "get-back"

The "get-back" is useful for a lot of things, including being able to have your dog back away from you if you need him to get out of your way. A simple way to teach this is to stand in front of the dog, with the dog standing, and walk into him. Just as you are about to make contact, the dog will startle and back up. C/T at the first movement backward.

One step at a time (literally), shape the "get-back until Fido will move backward five or six steps. Add the cue "Get back" when Fido is taking several steps.

This technique is not only simple, it "looks like" what Fido will actually see if he is ever in front of you and you need him to move backward away from you.

The get-back is one behavior I don't necessarily mind *inducing* to some extent. This is because (a) walking straight into the dog does not always produce the desired response, and (b) dogs do not tend to move backward comfortably on their own (i.e., they are unlikely to offer the behavior).

You can use the *target stick* to get Fido to move backward. The first step is to bring it to his nose, and then move it slowly back between his eyes. Move toward him slightly as you give him the "touch" cue. He will move backward just enough to enable him to touch the stick. Click *as he moves*. Treat after the touch. Step by step, increase distance. As described earlier, add the cue "Get back" when he is taking a couple of steps.

When Fido is moving backward five to six steps, you next want to get him in position to go down with his front end going to the ground first, then his rear. To do this, move the target stick from over Fido's head to beneath his head and in toward his chest. Fido is already comfortable with moving backward; now you are going to get him to drop his head while he does so.

In this part of the training, hold the target stick so the back of your hand is facing the dog. As you move the target stick into him, the back of your hand will "waggle" back and forth toward the dog. This can become a hand cue for the "get-back."

Retrace your steps until he will go five to six steps backward with his head down.

Now, you can add the cue "down." He will lie down, his front end going down first.

You can use *bait* instead of the target stick if you are so inclined. My preference is for the target stick. I think it is easier to control. Also, by using the target stick you continue the program along a single track rather than introducing something that is pure inducement and that you will only have to fade later. But if your preference is otherwise, so be it. Follow the same sequence as with the target stick.

The drop in motion

While this is primarily useful for the obedience exhibitor, it is an invaluable safety net for the pet owner as well.

One of the biggest bugaboos in competition obedience training is the drop on recall. Handlers work night and day to get a "bullet" recall for Novice. Boy, does Fido love to come to papa. Then they start training for Open, and darkness descends in the form of the drop on recall (DOR). I talk in detail about the DOR in Chapter 5. The only point to make here is that teaching your dog to drop while moving need not be related to how fast your dog moves. It is a matter of stimulus control and requires above all clarity of cuing from the handler.

How do you get the dog to be alert to drop without losing speed on the recall? How do you keep speed on the recall without losing the drop? It is the stuff of which murky legends, rumor, and innuendo are made. One top handler is reputed to hit his dog with his hat. Some handlers use a throw chain. Some now advocate using an electronic collar. The grain of reality in all this is that the drop on recall is probably the most common cause of failure in the Open A ring.

I suggest a simple answer: Treat "drop-in-motion" as a *fluency*. Let the dog learn that you may require him to drop while moving any time, anywhere. *To do this, of course, the down first has to be established as a fluency.* This may sound too obvious to bear stating, but you cannot train the drop-in-motion unless you have the drop in place. Many new Open trainers find themselves in a mess precisely because they have not really taught the down

A

B

C

D

The "get-back" can be shaped one step at a time, with a target stick or a food lure. While not required in obedience trials, it is a useful behavior if you need the dog to step out of your way or to back up from a door that opens inward. Here Morgan uses the "get-back" to correct a forged sit.

except as a stationary (stay) exercise, and at a close distance. Since the down is not fluent, it cannot be added into any more complex exercise.

There are myriad ways to shape drop-in-motion. Much will depend on the resources available to you. One friend of mine took advantage of the physical layout of her house. Her puppy could do laps through the living room, down the hallway, around into the dining room, and back into the living room. Being a puppy the dog would really fly, and my friend would stimulate her by stamping her foot. Then suddenly, in the middle of one of these "zooms," she would say "Down!" Click! Treat! Her dog developed a really reliable—and fast—drop on recall.

If you have a couple of training partners, do round-robin recalls between you, and add the down into it. Have each person give the "down" cue, in random order, not having the dog go down on every recall, but every time the "down" cue is given. If you don't have people to play the "circle game" with, set yourself up in a small enclosed area. Use a ball or toy to get the dog moving. As he retrieves the toy and brings it to you, say "down." Click the drop. You then have two alternatives: You can either treat where the dog is down, or release the dog and let him come to you. I find it is good to mix them up; theoretically it doesn't (or shouldn't) matter where the dog is when you treat, but I find that treating in position helps to confirm the desired position.

You can also add the "drop" with the dog walking at your left side. As you are walking, say "down" and pivot directly in front of the dog. Don't stand right over him or he will be likely to sit instead. Give him a step or two of room. Be ready with the target stick to remind him what he is supposed to do if necessary. C/T the drop. The reason to pivot directly in front of the dog is to stop forward motion. You want the drop to be "in place," and immediate.

When the dog is reliably dropping while moving in a small area, expand the area and ultimately get him outside.

You have two *primary reinforcers* with the drop-in-motion: the treat, and the game of the dog jumping up on cue and running to or after you. This exercise allows for a lot of play, so give the dog plenty of it here. Remember always that the PR is for the down, not for coming to you afterward. When you want to add that element, do not click for the down but for the secondary recall.

The "down/stay"

As with the sit, I do not use a "stay" cue. The "down" command, properly trained, serves the purpose completely.

With the down, the concept of "hold the position" has two separate aspects. One is the "stay" as part of the "resting down" on the group exercises. The second is the "stay" after having been dropped while in motion. Both involve *stimulus control,* but the considerations are a little different.

The long ("resting) down

You train this the same as you do the long sit. Extend the time that the dog will remain down without moving to about fifteen seconds, then put it on a variable schedule. Because the dog will lie down almost any time that he has nothing better to do, you can work on this long down in all sorts of informal conditions. Put the dog on the stay while you are cooking, watching TV, or eating dinner. The dog will enjoy the company, and would probably stay near you anyway even if not compelled to do so.

Stay after drop in motion

The second situation in which you need the dog to stay is after the drop in motion. As a rule, this is not going to last long, but it could. For example, if you have dropped the dog while at play it may last only a few seconds—or longer if you have to go to where the dog is to get him for some reason (for example, he's across a street or driveway, there's traffic, and you don't want him to come across to you). And while none of the exercises in the obedience ring that involve a drop followed by a recall will have the dog down for long, it is essential that the dog remain down until you call him. So get Fido used to dropping and holding the drop position for up to twenty seconds.

As I discussed earlier, this is an issue of stimulus control. "Down" means "lie down and stay there until I tell you to do something else." It is a matter of teaching your dog to be responsive, but patient. You establish control over the release from the drop in motion simply by the timing of your click. Initially, you will C/T for the drop as such. Once the drop is consistent, start to delay the click. Start with a "one-banana" count, and build up to five. Now go onto a variable schedule and build the high end up to twenty seconds. Once you are at twenty seconds, go to a *random schedule of reinforcement.* Now the dog will never have any idea of when the reinforcer—whether the C/T or the release—is coming.

We'll come back to refining this "stay" behavior in the drop on recall and the signals down in the discussions in later sections.

The stand

For the pet owner, the stand is highly useful. Your veterinarian and groomer will both be delighted with a dog that will stand up on command and accept handling. For the Obedience competitor the stand is essential. It appears once in Novice (the stand for exam) and twice in Utility (signals stand and moving stand). As with the sit and down, it is one thing to reinforce the posture; it is quite another to get the stand done the way you want it.

Basic shaping

When the dog is standing, click and treat. It's that simple. Well, pretty much. I think that one of the difficult things about shaping the stand is that the dog is probably not aware that he is doing anything in particular when he is standing. He's just standing. You click and treat, and the dog may not have even a hint of a clue as to what you did that for. Without meaning to get too much into what the dog's mental processes may or may not be, I tend to think that because standing is so "normal," it takes a long time for the dog to figure out that it is the stand, and not whatever else it might happen to be that he was doing at the time, that earned the reinforcement.

With both the sit and down, we were not only concerned with the basic posture (rump or full body on ground) but with some specific posture points. In the stand, "posture" is not a concern unless you are showing in the conformation ("breed") ring.

Unlike the conformation ring with its peculiar and specific "stacking" requirements, in the Obedience ring there is no particular explicit or implicit requirement as to *how* the dog stands. The only logical point must be that the dog stand in a way that is comfortable and that will not induce him to move.

Look at your dog when he is standing still. Make a mental photograph of his posture in your mind. You will see his front legs directly under his chest, his feet just about at body width. Unless he is one of those breeds like the German shepherd that stands with one hind foot forward and one back, his back legs will be at or just slightly behind his tailset. His weight is balanced front to back and side to side. He

Mace and Angel both have comfortable, natural stands.

can hold that posture indefinitely. That's how you want the dog to stand: natural, comfortable, balanced, relaxed. So, when you are lolling around the house with nothing better to do, click and treat the dog when you see him standing naturally.

Shaping the stand

It could happen that you don't get that "natural, comfortable, balanced, relaxed" stand spontaneously. This is unlikely. It is more likely that you get it but are not in a position to reinforce it except when you are in training. If that's the case, then you will probably need to be able to induce and shape the stand.

Yes, the stand usually requires some inducing, and often some interaction from you. This may seem unnecessary if you are a pet owner. After all, if the dog is standing he is standing, and what more do you need? But bear in mind that you will often be asking the dog to stand when he is in a stressful situation. He will be at the vet, or at the groomer, and he will not be comfortable. If you discipline him to take and hold a nice, solid stand, it will give you an additional tool to work with to keep Fido under control. Put another way, the discipline of the stand is incompatible with squirreling around while the vet is examining him. So develop the stand and use it.

Shaping the front feet

Work on one end at a time, starting with the front feet. Bowser is most likely to move if the front feet are unbalanced, because he will not be stable. At the least, he will move his feet to get them balanced. No big deal unless you are in the obedience ring. At worst, he will feel free to move away. That can be a problem if he's standing on the vet's exam table. The front feet should be squarely under the shoulders, about shoulder width apart and in line with each other. This is a balanced position.

If your dog's front feet are unbalanced, you can easily get them into the balanced position by placing your hands behind the front legs at the rib cage, lifting his front end about one inch off the ground, and immediately returning them to the ground. Presto! They are balanced. However, this is not necessary and, if you are an obedience competitor, I don't recommend it. If you are a competitor you want the dog to move into the stand on his own; you don't want to be wrestling with him. We'll discuss that more in the Novice stand section.

So how do you get the dog's front feet into correct position without physically moving him? Remember, if the feet are not in a balanced position already, *Fido will move them into a balanced position himself.* He won't stand all cock-a-hoop forever. So all you need is . . . patience, and a clicker and treats ready to hand. You can do this yourself. It is sometimes easier if you have a training partner who can click for you.

If you are by yourself, stand slightly to the side so you can see what Fido is doing with his front feet. If they are in proper position naturally, click and treat, have him move a bit, and let him stand again. If he stands with feet askew, you are ready to shape. *Simply wait* until Fido moves one of his feet to the proper position and C/T when his feet are properly placed. Once he is completely, properly balanced, release and repeat. If he is still unbalanced, continue to wait until he moves a front foot again for balance. C/T.

A caveat: *You don't want Fido walking forward.* What you want is for him to shift his feet without moving ahead. At first, he will tend to move forward in order to get his balance. Try it for a few sessions to see if this goes away on its own. If it does not, use the target stick. Hold the stick directly in front of Fido's nose; this will "hold" him in position. Now as he shifts his feet he should not move forward.

"Planting" the front feet

Check your dog's front feet again. Just touch them lightly and see how easily they come off the ground. I call this "fairy-foot" (as in Tinkerbell). While standing, the dog's weight is not ordinarily evenly distributed front and rear. He naturally tends to put very little weight on his front feet. Why? Because his motive power comes from his rear feet. If he decides to move, the front feet have to respond to what the rear feet do. And if he is "goosey" and uncertain about whether to move or not, the front feet are going to "dance" before he takes any decisive action. To get a firm stand you have to get those front feet planted. There are two ways to do this, and I recommend you do them in sequence.

First, push lightly down at the dog's withers (if you are unfamiliar with dog anatomy, this is the shoulder area, about where the neck and backbone meet). At first, this might cause him to shift his feet slightly. Do and say nothing. You wanted him to remain where he was and he didn't, so simply withhold reinforcement. Stand him again and repeat. After a couple of repetitions you will feel an answering pressure from the front feet. C/T any response of this nature. You are halfway home.

Second, once you are getting that answering pressure, employ a TTouch. Here I use the python lift. Wrap your hand lightly around the dog's leg, one leg at a time. Lift upward lightly. At first, the dog will lift his paw in response. Simply reposition the leg and lift again. Be sure you are not using too much pressure. Place your fingers on your forearm, and put just enough pressure on so that you can move your own skin. That is all the pressure you need for this. When the dog does not lift his leg in response, C/T. In short order you will feel the dog pushing down when you do the lift. Repeat with the other leg.

If the python lift is a little too much at first, do the butterfly touch. Wrap both hands lightly around his leg; use your thumbs to make a movement upward and outward along the leg, using about the same pressure you would to move the skin over your eyelid without bothering your eye. When Fido becomes comfortable with this touch, progress to the python lift.

The rear legs

Here is where a real difference between conformation "stacking" and the Obedience stand is obvious. Many breeds have highly stylized stacking postures. The posture for the German shepherd, for example, is to carry one leg well behind the other. Conformation handlers also have to pay a lot of attention to things like the tail being up, the topline, and so forth. All this is irrelevant in Obedience.

The major concern regarding the rear legs is that they be sufficiently planted to keep the rear end still—especially if the judge presses down on it at all. You don't want any "jelly-butt." If the rear feet are slightly behind the tailbone they are far enough back for this purpose. Again, you can shape this by reinforcing the dog's natural standing posture. In most cases, the dog's own stand will show the hind feet just about that far back.

If your dog does not stand with his rear feet sufficiently far back, induce a slight amount of movement—about a half-step worth if you can. Now that he is conscious of his front legs, he will get them properly under him and the rear feet will remain more or less still as he stretches his rear legs slightly forward. C/T.

I used to use a "toe-tap" technique to get the dog to move his rear feet backward, but I no longer think that is necessary. Work with the stand that Fido gives you and you will do quite well. You can use the butterfly and python lift to stabilize the rear legs once they are generally in the position you want. You may also press down on the rear, lightly at first and later increasing the pressure. C/T any resistance or "pushing up" offered by the dog.

The "stand" cue

The verbal cue "stand" is obvious. You add it in the same way that you do any other. If you are training for competition, you will likely want to establish a hand signal as well. It makes quite an impression in the Novice stand for examination, and shows real control and teamwork, if your dog stands smartly with a single signal. Plus, you *must* have a stand signal in Utility for the signals exercise and the moving stand, so you may as well get Fido used to it from the beginning.

The hand signal I like to use is to bring the right hand with palm open up to shoulder height, then across the body (turning slightly to permit the movement) and then down over the dog's head. Introduce Fido to it when he is already standing. You can show it to him instead of the verbal signal if the verbal is not yet in place, or together with the verbal if you have already established the verbal.

After you have established the stand cue, you want Fido to stand from two positions: from a sit, and at a halt after moving with you. The latter requires that you have a very clear signal; you must have the stand-at-halt under stimulus control because you do not want Fido standing instead of sitting if you have not given the signal. I'll talk about the stand-at-halt in detail in the Utility signals section in Chapter 6.

With Fido on a sit or down, present your stand cue. In all probability, Fido will stand straight up. This is what you want. You do not want him walking forward. You may see some uncertainty in his response. If so, click for partial responses—in other words, shape the response to the cue. He will quickly get the message and start producing a nifty "straight-up" stand.

The "kick-back" stand (stand from a sit)

The stand is a good exercise to look at to see how damaging the "command-based" trainer's practice of first giving a command and then compelling or inducing compliance can be. The "command-based" trainer gives the command "stand," and then moves the dog into position; a typical technique is to pull the dog forward and up using the collar. Some simply say "Well, in Novice it doesn't matter what you do to get him to stand," and so they literally lift the dog into position. In either case, the one thing the dog does not learn for himself is what the stand means and requires. One of my students had to teach her dog to stand on cue for the first time when he was in Utility.

If you have taught Barfy to stand by pulling him forward into position, you have taught him that stand is a forward-moving exercise. In Novice, this can lead to a dog that starts to move and keeps moving while you are trying to get him set in position. I once watched a Newfie move into the stand—and keep moving forward a step at a time, not unlike a diesel truck moving forward in low-low. It was all the handler could do to keep her feet, much less stop the dog. In Utility, this leads to a dog that has a great deal of difficulty learning to stop stock still when you give the stand signal.

Before I got into operant conditioning and shaping, and even for quite a while as I was learning and absorbing the process, I embraced a method of training the stand called the "kick-back stand." In this method, with the dog on a sit you give the "stand" cue and slide your left foot back to "tap-tap" the dog's rear paw. You do not touch his paw with any force; you are merely "pestering" it. Dogs are very touchy about their feet, and in most cases the dog will immediately move his foot back, causing his rear end to rise, which causes him to stand. Using a clicker, you click as the rear end comes up. (You see, you can [mis]use a clicker to reinforce behaviors even using command-based methods. You get the benefit of being able to send the dog a clear message of "correct" but, as in this example, it is a far cry from free operant conditioning.)

None of this is required with dogs whose stand is shaped as described earlier. For such a dog, the stand is always immobile because you have never reinforced the stand except when he is standing completely still, and you have not induced or compelled the stand with forward movement. If you watch a dog rise into a stand from a lying-down or sitting position, you will see him quite naturally rise straight up. If you are using the clicker casually around the house to "capture" and reinforce desired behaviors other than in a formal training session, you can use it to considerable advantage here.

Left-side walking

Respectfully submitted for your consideration: One of the biggest mistakes obedience trainers make with their dogs is to try to teach the dog to "heel" at too young an age. And by "heel," I mean walking with the trainer complete with all the formalities required of a correctly heeling dog.

"Heeling," considered as a whole, requires the greatest overall discipline of any of the competition Obedience exercises. The dog must hold the heel position for a long duration, through changes of pace and turns. It is an elaborate and at times exquisite dance. Trying to teach a dog new to training to "heel" is like teaching a beginning dance student the Lindy hop. It can be done only by the most expert of trainers, and even then only rarely and with the most gifted of students. Trainers try to impose far too much precision on their dogs at an early age (or, in the case of an untrained older dog, at too early a stage in the overall training process). The all-too-predictable (and common) result is a demotivated dog—to say nothing of a demotivated handler.

Typical heeling training is a mess. The handler gives the "heel" cue before the dog has any idea that its simplest meaning is "Walk with me on my left side." And most of the time the handler is trying to shape several things at once: attention, alignment of the dog with the handler's left hip, correct distance from the handler, etc. We dump so many things on the dog at once, it is a wonder that they learn to heel at all. If there is any one exercise that "command-based" training typically turns into a pig's breakfast, it is heeling.

It is even worse for pet owners who have no thoughts at all of ever requiring their dog to maintain competition heel position. At almost any "traditional" pet class I have taught or observed I see the owners walking around in a circle for fifteen or twenty minutes, hauling this way and that on their dogs' leashes while the dogs drag, lunge, fight the leash, and so forth. And all the time the trainer's patter is more or less like this: "Give them a good pop forward as you say 'heel.' Jerk them back when you can see their shoulder. Don't let them go after another dog. If the person in front of you is too slow, move around them. I want to hear a good 'zip' on that collar when you correct! When the dog is right, praise!" And so on. How do we expect anyone, dog or human, to learn anything that way?

And so it goes. That's how it's always been done. Tradition is truth. Wrong.

For the pet owner as well as the competition handler, it is an absolute mistake to start this process by demanding "heel position." For the pet owner, most of what constitutes heel position for competition purposes is simply irrelevant. For the competition handler, heel position is such a complex thing that you *must* work toward it in careful stages, always being careful to keep the work reinforcing. What is the single most common complaint about heeling? "It's boring." If it is boring, it will also be non-reinforcing. If it is non-reinforcing, it will also be unreliable, as well as uninteresting to judges and spectators. Also submitted for your consideration: Heeling is boring because we make it so. It does not have to be that way.

"Left-side walking": The fluency for heeling

Historically, heeling began with hunting. The hunter carried his rifle or shotgun in the crook of his right arm, barrel pointed toward the ground. The dog walked—literally—"at heel," that is, to the handler's left and directly behind the handler's left foot. If the rifle accidentally discharged the cartridge or shot would fire at the ground ahead, and neither hunter nor dog would be in danger.

It was to the advantage of hunter and dog for the "heel hound" to be slightly behind the hunter. Today we call this "lagging," and it does not serve either the pet owner or the competition handler well. If we competitive types are going to have our dogs out of position while heeling, we want a "forging" dog (that is, a dog that moves ahead of us). But training should start with establishing an informal, comfortable position that handler and dog can sustain indefinitely while walking. This is the *fluency* I call "left-side walking."

The "left-side walking" position

As my name for this fluency suggests, the dog is on the handler's left side. While we don't have the hunter's considerations, left side is of course essential for the competition handler. It is also a useful convention for the pet owner. For one thing, you always know where the dog is. For another, since it is the common position for a dog walking with its owner to be in, it makes life predictable and a bit more manageable. If two people meet on the street and each has his dog on his left side, the people will form a barrier of sorts between the dogs. If there is any hint of dog aggression, the people can easily intercept it. On the other hand, if one dog is on the right and the other on the left, there is absolutely nothing that stands between the dogs should they have the urge to "get into it." There may be other considerations you could toss into the pot as well, but the idea is clear: There is good reason for the left-side position even if you never intend to take your Austrobavarian Lunchenhund into the competition ring.

The "control area"

The dog is on your left side. Where in relation to you should the dog be? For the competition handler this is ultimately defined by the AKC Regulations (all other registries impose the same criteria). But what about when the competition handler is walking the dog on the street? Surely you are not going to insist on strictly defined heel position throughout.

For purposes of this fluency, I define a "control area" within which it is permissible for the dog to be

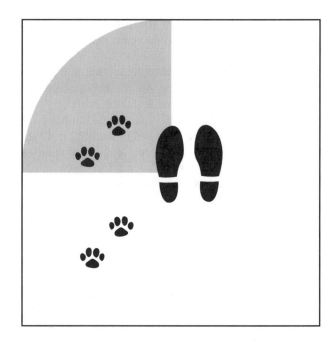

In left-side walking, the dog may be anywhere within the "control area," beside or slightly ahead of the handler, and up to eighteen inches away.

at any given time. If you visualize your left foot as the center of a clock, with you facing toward 12:00, the "control area" is the arc between 9:00 and 12:00, with roughly an 18-inch radius from your foot to the numbers. It looks like the shaded area in the illustration above.

The shaded area represents the "control area." The dog's front end may be anywhere in that space. The control area gives the dog a certain amount of freedom. He can be slightly wide of you, and slightly ahead of you. But at no time will he be more than eighteen inches away from you in any direction. If you are working with a very small dog, you will reduce the eighteen inches appropriately to the size of your dog. If you are working with a very large dog, you may enlarge it slightly (but not too much).

For the pet handler, this is a relaxed area to maintain. For the competition handler, this position allows the dog to forge slightly. For casual walking, this is not only not a problem, it is desirable so long as it is within limits. It is easier to keep your eye on the slightly forged dog. The dog will be used to being at your side or slightly ahead of you. And when you move toward stricter competition training you will not have to struggle to overcome a lag. (Ask anyone who has tried: It is far easier to bring a forging dog "back" than it is to bring a lagging dog "forward.")

You can shape the dog to work as close to your side and as little forged as you like. I strongly urge that in the early stages you not be excessively demanding. The idea is that the dog become comfortable walking with you long distances in this controlled manner. The competition trainer should perceive an *evolution* from this left-side walking to competition heeling. Shaping to the "control area" gives you a comfortable place to start, and you can

bring the dog into the specific alignment required by the Regulations through simple escalation of criteria.

Training "hands-free"

I said in the first section that my first act upon switching from "traditional" training to clicker training was to get rid of the leash; I did this to force myself to abandon all notions of physically compelling the dog to perform any exercise. You should do the same thing. Here is the time and place for

One way to break your own old leash-popping habits is to tie the leash around your waist. The dog is safely restrained but the handler must work on heeling exercises with reinforcement instead of automatic "corrections."

you to do it. You are going to shape, not compel, behavior.

If you are a competition trainer and your dog is already accustomed to working off-lead, do all your left-side walking training completely off-lead. If you have not done any off-lead work, then work off-lead when you are at home or in an enclosed area. If you are a pet owner or a competition trainer whose dog is not yet reliable off-lead, work "hands-free." Hands-free simply means that you do not have your hands on the leash. The simplest way to do this is to attach the leash to your waist; this makes it a passive restraint.

If you have a short leash (up to thirty-six inches), you can loop it through one of your belt loops. If you have a longer leash, loop it around your waist, running the snap end through the handle. Regardless of the arrangement, you are removing the leash from your hands. No "corrections." No "motivational pops." No hands at all. You are not going to compel the dog to walk with you, nor are you going to compel the dog to walk within the control area. Through shaping, you are going to allow the dog to make his own decision to do these things. And the dog will make the right decision.

Dylan has been trained off-lead from the very first day. I don't think it is any accident that he is the most reliable, enthusiastic and consistent dog I have. Sam—a crossover dog—has been trained off-lead since April 1993. He has gone through major swings in the level of his performance, but he is generally more relaxed in training. Skipper, who is an adult and green, I work with hands-free.

How long should your leash be? Abraham Lincoln was once asked, "How long should a man's legs be?" He answered, "Long enough to reach the ground." Following his wisdom, your leash should be long enough to reach the dog, allowing him room to move freely within the "control area" but tightening naturally when he gets to that area's boundaries. Since the "control area" is only eighteen inches in any direction, you should be working with no more than a thirty-six-inch leash, depending on the size of the dog.

Have the dog on a buckle collar. There is no need for a slip (or "choke") collar of any kind in this training. People who have taken to using a pinch collar for "power steering" can discard it. Trainers who use the pinch for fine-tuning can also put it on the shelf. Shaping and careful use of differential reinforcement will get the job done.

The buckle collar provides a barrier for the dog when he hits the end of the leash, without any really punishing effects. The dog can wear the buckle collar all the time, so there is no big deal involved in putting the "training collar" on. Any time you go walking, whether to the market or into the obedience ring, you expect him to behave the same way.

I discuss next some methods for extinguishing the "pulling" behavior. If it is really a problem and you need to do something *now,* you might consider using a Gentle Leader. This is a head halter that fits around the dog's muzzle, just behind the lips. The dog can breathe and it is not uncomfortable or restrictive to the mouth. I prefer the Gentle Leader to the Halti because the Gentle Leader has a little screwlock that keeps the muzzle from slipping, making it a completely passive restraint. *When using this device, your hands must be completely still!* The Gentle Leader acts on its own to restrain the head; if you put any hand motion into it at all you risk wrenching the dog's neck.

If you are using this device, when the dog stops pulling forward or away due to the passive restraint, click and treat. As with all extraneous pieces of equipment, the idea is to get rid of it as quickly as possible. Do what you must to get the desired behavior, reinforce it, and let the behavior take over. So, use the Gentle Leader to *communicate,* not merely to restrain.

If you are training for competition and have worked your dog through basic Novice instruction with a lot of leash work, I suggest a little test at this point as an eye-opener. Take your dog completely off-lead, get the dog to sit at your left side, look straight ahead, give the "heel" cue, and step forward. The odds are you are going to get a surprise: The dog won't move or, if he does move, he will move very tentatively. Why? Haven't you just spent between ten and twenty weeks teaching him what "heel" means?

No. You have taught the dog what "heel + forward pop + happy talk" means—and only incompletely at that. Remove the pop, remove the hand action, remove the happy talk, and the dog hasn't a clue. All these things have become part of the cue to the dog for the activity—and he still isn't sure exactly what the activity is.

So when you go hands-free (or, better yet, off-lead altogether), the first thing you find out is what your dog really understands. There is no room here for illusions on the subject. If you give the "heel" cue, step forward, and your dog remains sitting with a puzzled look on his face—or is out of control—you know he doesn't know what you want of him.

Don't feel badly. There is a reason that the transition from on-lead heeling to off-lead heeling gives conventionally taught up-and-coming competition trainers fits: Heeling is taught incorrectly. As I go into in more detail in the Novice section on heeling, there is no such thing as "on-lead" as opposed to "off-lead" heeling. That is an artifice imposed by the AKC for purposes of showing in Novice. There is only heeling. The AKC compels your dog to wear a leash part of the time you are in the Novice ring, but it is a mere decoration and is at best irrelevant to the performance of the exercise (at worst the presence of the leash can cost you points if it goes tight, or if you inadvertently give a little tug). The dog has to do exactly the same thing off-lead as on. So why train it as though it were two different exercises?

For present purposes, whether you are a competition handler or a pet owner, the best way to teach the dog what you want when it comes to the dog walking with you is to shape the behavior without compulsion from the very beginning. You will always see very clearly exactly what the dog's level of understanding is, and you will have no alternative but to build your criteria in careful increments. The pet owner will end up with a dog you can comfortably take anywhere that dogs are allowed. The competition handler will end up with a highly charged heeling dog.

First criterion: "Left-side" position

The first criterion is that the dog be on your left side. If you have a crossover dog, this is not an issue. That dog knows darned good and well not to be anywhere else. What follows is for the owner of the untrained dog. Do not worry about starting with the dog on a sit or any other formal starting position. In fact, it is usually best if the dog is on his feet. Simply start to walk.

Since you are not going to coerce the dog into this position, you may find yourself doing some maneuvering at first. Go ahead and do it. All the dog knows right now is that you and he are both in motion. He has no idea at all that he is supposed to be in a particular place in relationship to you.

C/T timing is critical! All you are concerned about at this point is that the dog be on your left. C/T for the first step that you get with the dog in that place. It does not matter what you have to do by way of maneuvering to get the dog on your left side. If he is on your right, pivot so that he is on your left, if only for an instant. Don't be "proud," be inventive. Do what you must to get the behavior, then reinforce it.

Nor does it matter if the dog is lagging, at your side or forged. He may even bound ahead of you (though if you are "hands-free" he won't get far!). Click *immediately as* he takes a *single step* on your left. Your task is to "catch" him in a proper position even if he is there for only an instant on his way to somewhere else. So you must be quick with the click.

The first few time you click the dog for "left side" you will surprise him. Remember, this is pretty much an unconscious activity for Rover. He's just moving. He is not thinking about where you are, much less where he is. He will recognize the click as a "that was good" message, but he won't know what he did that was good at first. Was it being over here? Was it charging forward? What?

Rover will experiment with you. He'll be on your left and hang back. C/T. He'll be on your left, hang back and lunge forward. C/T. At each point, you will click when you get the left side. Bit by bit, the "left-side" factor will be the only constant that triggers the click, and this awareness will sink in.

You are getting one step before you click. What do you do if you get that one step, you click, and then he lunges to the end of the leash? Treat. Remember! You are reinforcing the event you clicked for, not whatever it is that the dog does afterward ("click" ends the behavior).

That said, remember to deliver the treat as quickly as possible. You do not want Rover to develop superstitious behaviors associated with reinforcement. In other words, if for example you click and Rover then always dances away from you, and you then always treat as he does so, this can easily become part of the repertoire that he associates with reinforcement. You can end up with some very weird control problems. However, do not try to solve this problem by responding aversively to unwanted post-click behaviors. It is first and foremost your responsibility to deliver the treat in a timely way.

Stopping the charging dog

What do you do physically about the fact that the dog hits the end of the leash? In a sense, nothing. Do not fight the dog. The leash is at your waist, which brings your body and not just your hands into play. Say nothing. Simply stop. If you have a large dog, shift your weight slightly back. Make yourself immobile. Become a tree. A post. Your inertia will stop the dog's movement.

When the dog stops, wait a moment. The dog will relax his pressure against the collar, even if only slightly. Make sure that the dog is completely stopped for a couple of seconds. Now, move away from the dog, back and to the right. If you can visualize the face of a clock, you are facing towards 12:00. Your movement away will be toward 4:00. The reason for this is that the dog's musculoskeletal structure gives him good resistance front-to-back, but poor resistance side-to-side. He will readily move with you.

The other key to this movement is that you turn completely in the direction you are going, so that your back is to Fido as you move. This sends the message "I am going and you are following;" if you face him as you move away your body language is less decisive and the message therefore less clear.

The nice secondary benefit to this maneuver is that because Fido cannot resist at all, he quickly gets the notion that when you move, he cannot fight you. And so you will quickly see that as you start to move, he is "anticipating" your movement and catching up to you right away. It is a very nontoxic way to let him know who is in charge.

Now, as you move and he moves toward you, click as Rover again gets to your left side and deliver the treat immediately. In a sense, even before Rover learns that "left-side" triggers reinforcement, he has to learn that this is an event in which he has the same power to trigger reinforcement as, for example, he does when he sits.

In other words, a principal feature of this early training is expanding Rover's sense of his own power. Successful shaping of any behavior depends above all on the dog understanding that *reinforcement depends on what he does*. From this point of view, as you introduce new behaviors to him, you are essentially expanding the repertoire of behaviors he has at his disposal to trigger reinforcement. In the early stages, this lesson takes time. "Learning to learn" is in this sense the process by which the dog generalizes the lesson of his power over the reinforcer from new behavior to new behavior. Every one gets easier. You will find after a while that when you introduce the dog to something new the dog will increasingly offer behaviors or look to you for direction as to what you expect. A real, though nonverbal, dialogue develops.

Establishing the "control area"

There is so much variation from dog to dog that it is impossible to say how long it will take to get the left-side notion in place with your dog. But even the most impervious of subjects should get the basic idea after two or three sessions. Now you must start to establish the "control area." This will require you to take more than one step, perhaps as many as five to seven. In many cases, when the dog gets the left-side notion he will start walking more closely to you. That's fine. Don't discourage this. It's only natural: Rover knows the goodies come from you, and he's going to want to be as close to them as he can get. But try to randomize your clicking so that you are reinforcing for left-side *and* the control area. Let the dog know that he has a little freedom to work with, as well as what the limits of that freedom are.

As you move forward, *do not click* as the dog is moving away from you. This would only reinforce that action. C/T if the dog is near you. If he moves away a bit, C/T if you get one step with him in a stable position within the control area.

Extending distance

With the two essential criteria in place, you now have to develop the dog's willingness to sustain that position over an indefinite distance. *This is why I start with a loose "control area."* The real discipline in heeling is not establishing the proper *physical* positions as such, but the *mental discipline* required to sustain that position. You increase the physical demands of the *position* aspect of the exercise as Fido's mental maturity increases.

Mental maturity will develop as you extend distance. The longer Fido has to hold the general position, the better he will be able to do so. For the competition trainer, this brings you to the point of refining the control area into what the Regulations define as "heel position." For the pet owner, the process of extending distance means that you can be increasingly reliant on your dog doing what he is supposed to do when out in public.

The base for variable reinforcement

Building one step at a time, work your way up to a distance of twelve to fifteen feet. Add a step every couple of days. Do five to seven repetitions each session. If Rover seems to be "out of it" on any given day, shorten the distance for a couple of repetitions to get him interested, then go the full distance scheduled for the day.

On days when Rover is being contentious, it may also help to start with things like a couple of informal recalls or a series of sits. It's well to remember not to conduct every training session exactly the same way. *Don't always start with the "walking" exercise.* Sometimes the dog needs to run off a little steam, sometimes he needs to get his juices flowing, sometimes you need to do something else to get him focused.

Variable reinforcement

Once you are up to fifteen feet, extend distance from there using *variable reinforcement* (VR). Like heeling, left-side walking is a long-duration behavior. Use the approach outlined in Appendix A. In theory, and especially for the pet owner who may walk her dog five miles on city streets, there is no limit to the distance that you may build up to. For most practical purposes, a distance of about sixty feet (more or less thirty steps) is a good target distance. The dog that will hold the left-side walking position for that distance will be pretty reliable for longer distances.

People who intend to take long exercise walks with their dogs may want to develop tolerance for distance beyond sixty feet systematically. I suggest that you convert your VR schedule to *time* rather than number of steps. The structural mechanics will be the same, but it will be easier to work with time rather than counting steps after that point. Time yourself walking sixty feet and use that as your starting mean.

Variations on a theme

There are other ways to introduce some elements of surprise into the activity and keep the dog involved. In this regard you are limited only by your imagination. (If you are looking toward competition heeling, see the discussion of proofing in the section on heeling in Novice ring exercises in Chapter 4.)

One basic maneuver that can be very helpful is *"get back."* I covered this in the section on teaching the fold-back down. The dog learns to move backward. You can incorporate this into left-side walking, by saying "get-back" and taking a couple of steps backward. If you are interested in bringing the dog closer to you, this is a good way to do it. Say "get-back," take a couple of steps backward with the dog, and then *step slightly toward* the dog and take a couple of steps forward. C/T. In this way you will have maneuvered yourself into a closer position and then reinforced the dog for being there.

"Walkaways" are also useful. If you find your dog persistently getting distracted and moving away from you at or slightly past the boundaries of the control area, you can surprise him by turning suddenly toward 4:00 (as described earlier), and moving off in that direction. Quicken your pace slightly, or perhaps even jog for a step or two. C/T when Fido catches up to you. In short order the dog will start looking around after taking a step away from you, anticipating the walkaway. Don't disappoint him. The walkaway will not only *discourage* him from wandering, it will improve attention.

As I have said before, you do not need worry about training for "attention." Bowser will learn to keep an eye on you as a matter of self-preservation: He never quite knows what you are going to do next, so he watches you all the time.

Extinction at work: The obstinately pulling dog

I thank Lana Mitchell for this method, with one caveat. I am not sure that what I outline here is what she teaches, so if our approaches differ, don't ask her to explain what I'm doing, and if there are any errors in what I lay out here, the responsibility for them is entirely mine.

The obstinately pulling dog is so highly attracted by something that he will forget all about walking in the control position and just pull to get where he wants to go. Here is a "set-up" to stop this behavior, using some of the techniques discussed earlier. Start by putting a chunk of food (a piece of bagel, or chunk of hot dog) on the ground about fifteen to twenty feet away. Make sure Rover sees it. His only task now is to traverse the distance between you and the food. He will have to do it on your terms.

Keep Rover on a short leash, and start forward. Immediately as he lunges or pulls forward, withdraw all reinforcement by stopping completely. "Become a tree." Be sure that you break his forward momentum entirely by waiting a couple of seconds before moving away from him.

Now, move decisively away from the dog, back and to the right as previously discussed. This reestablishes your power over the dog's movement. Return to your starting point, even if it is several feet before the place where Rover started pulling (though at first it may be only a step or two). You are telling him that he must cover the entire distance under control before he can get to the treat.

Now, start to move again toward the distractor. Continue forward until Rover starts pulling or lunging forward again. At that point stop, and repeat the steps as before.

Rover gets the goody when he walks by your side under control all the way to it. Make sure that he walks with you *all the way;* that is, do not let him lunge the last couple of steps.

Typically, this exercise takes about ten minutes to complete successfully. Repeat it over a few days until the dog will readily walk toward the goody under control without you having to stop once. You then *generalize* by practicing the exercise in public places.

I don't know if Lana clicks during this process or not. I don't until we have reached the goody with Bowser under control. Were I to click at any other point I would have to treat, and it seems to me that this would break the dynamic of the exercise. The point of the exercise is that Rover only gets to get the goody *if he stays under control at all times.* Each step forward is a "click and treat" (a kind of repertoire reinforcement), that is, the opportunity to continue toward the goody on the ground. When you allow the dog to gobble up the goody, that's a *jackpot* for a job well done.

Let's take a quick look at what is happening in this process. First, you are *extinguishing the undesired behavior* (pulling) by not giving the dog any reinforcement for it. You are stopping, and you are moving the dog away from the desirable something that is causing him to pull. Second, you are *shifting the motivation* by allowing the dog to move toward the desirable something, but only as long as he remains under control. Third, and this is a corollary to the second, you are *reinforcing desired behavior* by allowing the dog to move toward that desirable something as long as he remains under control.

The earlier in the course of training that you introduce Fido to this discipline, the easier it will be to encounter new distractors when you are outside. The first time you "become a tree" and then walk away, you will trigger that memory of what this all means and you will find his sense of self-control quickly reemerging.

Turns and maneuvers

Regardless of your purpose in training, there will come times, during left-side walking practice, when you have to change direction. You want to be able to do so in reasonable comfort. At the same time, this is not military "close-order drill." You want to be able to maneuver as you will have to in ordinary situations. This necessarily precedes the refinement and tightening involved in training competition turns, just as ordinary walking precedes any sort of fancy footwork.

Since few city planners design streets and sidewalks so that dogs and handlers can walk unimpeded, you also need to be able to move around and among people and obstacles. There are three essential turns: the right about, the right turn, and the left turn. (The left about or U-turn is not a maneuver you are ever likely to make. You may have to in an emergency, but our own conditioning is such that when we reverse direction we usually do it to the right, not to the left. We use the left-about-turn in competition training primarily to refine other heeling points such as forging, or in helping the dog learn to work its rear end in close to the handler on the left turn.)

Arcing

All turns and maneuvers begin with arcing, whether to left or right. When arcing to the right, the dog has to move faster in order to stay in the control area; when arcing to the left, the dog has to move a little slower. As always, you want the dog to take responsibility for his position. As you refine the arcs into turns, you will increase the demand on the dog. That is, he will have to move faster (to the right) or slow his pace sharply (to the left) in order to maintain position.

This is a place in traditional training where leash work is paramount. The trainer is popping and releasing continuously as she trains the turns. Many advanced trainers go to a pinch collar at this point because the fast action allows for very quick and accurate "corrections." Some even use two leashes—one around the dog's hindquarters—to induce proper turning action on the left turn.

You will accomplish the same goal without all that leashwork. You have some fluencies to work with already: targeting, and the dog's conscious rear-end movement. Now it is a matter of application.

The arc should resemble one-half of a football. The midline of the arc should be about thirty steps. As your dog becomes more fluent you will shorten the arc into more like half of a basketball, then increasingly smaller (shortening the midline accordingly). As you steepen the arc you will increase the working demand on the dog. Ultimately your turning radius will be a hairpin. For the pet owner it will not ordinarily be necessary to get the dog to turn that sharply, but it cannot hurt to extend the dog's skills as far as possible.

On the arc to the right, hold the target stick slightly ahead of you to bring the dog forward. Take a few steps forward along the path of the arc, let the dog drive to the stick and "touch," C/T. Gradually extend your line of travel.

So that you never ask the dog to go so far to touch the stick that he will lose interest, develop distance on the arc the same way you do on a straight line. When the dog will take about ten or twelve steps before touching, introduce VR. Because the arcing demands a little more of the dog, start your VR schedule at five or six steps and build from there.

On the arc to the left, the challenge for the dog is to slow down enough to retain the desired position. The dog may also have to back up a little bit as your motion will be carrying you into, rather than away from, the dog.

At first you will find you and your dog attempting to occupy the same space as you arc to your left. Your dog is trying to go straight ahead at the same time as you are turning into him. If you are training with negative reinforcers you might use your knee to bump the dog out of your way. Some trainers do such things as strapping a wire bristle brush to their left thigh to induce the dog to move away. We won't do that.

Use the target stick. Instead of holding the stick out in front to induce a "charge" as you did on the rightward arc, bring it closer to your hip so that the dog has to "tread water" in order to watch it or make contact. Be sure that the stick is slightly above the dog's head so that you get the dog to move backward slightly.

Does this sound familiar? It is the *"get-back"* maneuver that you used to work on the accordion down (and possibly refined a bit as discussed earlier), now put into motion. If you like, you can use "get-back" as a verbal cue at this point.

Spiraling

Spiraling simply takes the arc you have worked on and reduces it to tighter and tighter circles until you are virtually turning in place to the right and left. Start with a circle about ten feet in diameter. With each orbit, reduce the diameter until, after four or five circuits, you are at the center and spinning there with the dog. Watch out for vertigo.

Obstacles

When you have good tight spirals to the right and left, introduce obstacles. If you can invest in eight to ten tall cones, do so. This allows you to set up a "slalom" course in which Fido will have to arc first right and then left. Otherwise, use chairs, trash cans, and so forth. The only real requirement is that the obstacle be obvious and large enough to require avoiding.

In going around an obstacle to your left, give Fido plenty of room at first. You want him to get used to the maneuver; also, you do not want him going around the obstacle, putting it between the two of you. Gradually close the distance between you and the obstacle so that he has to work a little harder to get around it while maintaining the control position.

Another good variation is to set up a "jumble" of obstacles, that is, a number of obstacles strewed around randomly. This will force you to make maneuvers with varying degrees of sharpness and degrees of difficulty for the dog.

The ultimate test, of course, is for Fido to be able to move freely among people. If you don't have several training partners to do this with, take Fido to a place where there are people just going about their business. Walk him through the crowd, clicking and treating as you go. Avoid the temptation to put your hands back on the leash; Fido must maintain his own self-discipline throughout. Remember too, the presence of strangers and the density of the crowd are all new criteria, so adjust your expectations (downward) and reinforcements (upward—jackpots are appropriate here) accordingly.

The informal recall

The goal of the informal recall is for the dog to come to you when called. You want the dog come to a position in front of you and wait there, not running past you or toward and then away from you. You are not concerned with the dog coming to a sit in front of you. The dog coming up in front of you and waiting there (whether standing, sitting, or lying down) is an important safety skill. It also lays the essential foundation for the competition front. Get the dog used to it from the very first day.

Shaping the recall is simple. This is especially true with a puppy, but you can get an enthusiastic recall out of virtually any dog. Skipper was three and a half when I got him, and totally untrained. The very first thing he learned was to come at the call of his name. Even out on our large, unfenced property, when he hears "Skip!" he comes, wherever he is and whatever he is doing.

To start training the recall, as Fido is coming to you or even moving somewhat in your direction, click. Fido already knows the click/treat connection, so when he hears the click he most likely will come all the way to you to get his treat. When he gets to you, treat.

It's important, especially with a crossover dog, that you not attach any cues to the process at this point. The recall is an exercise that seems to become possessed with myriad demons throughout the training process. There are a couple of common mistakes that cause this. One is to put a lot of hooplah and "cheerleading" into this training, most of which is misdirected and possibly even destructive to the desired end of an enthusiastic recall. (There is a common myth that when the dog shows any reluctance, you should respond by showing "enthusiasm." However, given that dogs generally tend to respond to noise by shying away, this is probably not helpful.) The other mistake is to make the recall aversive by using lots of long-line "corrections." This triggers resistance in the dog at the very moment you want the dog coming to you unreservedly.

It is vital that you maintain a relaxed atmosphere in this early shaping phase. Let Fido learn that coming to you—whenever, wherever, whyever—is simply the most reinforcing event on the planet. The more comfortable he becomes with that simple lesson, the more enthusiastic his recalls will become.

This is an excellent situation in which to shape informally; having clickers and packets or canisters of dried treats stashed around the house will serve you well. As with the down, you may get some of your best results in an unstructured situation. Simply C/T when the dog is coming in your direction in *any* context around the house. Start with continuous reinforcement until you are *certain* that Fido is eager to move in your direction. Then you can go to a 2 : 1 ratio.

This is a very good thing to do with the crossover dog. You have not given him a cue, but you are rewarding a behavior that he is emitting spontaneously. Better yet, you are reinforcing something he is doing that is not in a formal training context. This sort of spontaneous reinforcement will help you convey the message to him that it is his behavior as such (and not simply behavior in response to a command) that is important in generating reinforcement.

Vary the primary reinforcer

The recall exercise will ultimately have a lot of energy in it. As the dog becomes more reliable and you extend distance the dog should and will come to you at high speed. If you are working with a puppy, speed will be an almost immediate by-product of the reinforcer. An older dog may take a little longer to get the idea, but as a rule recalls will be high-energy.

So this is a good time to use *primary reinforcers* other than—or in addition to—a food treat. Your dog may enjoy some roughhousing, chasing a ball or toy, jumping, or a good roughing-up of his coat or ruff. Doing these things will add to the dog's enjoyment and may in fact prove to be more reinforcing than a food treat. Sam is eight and a half as I write this, and a bit of rasslin' is still one of the things he loves most. *You still click as the dog is coming to you;* you are using different primary reinforcers, not eliminating the conditioned reinforcer.

Keep your dog leashed in public

This is a cautionary note, and this is as good a place as any I can think of to bring it up. This training program is off-lead. We all like to have our dogs off-lead. I know some folks who like to "show off" their well-trained dogs by having their dogs off-lead even in crowded places.

Let me state this as simply as I know how: *When you are in a public place, unless you are training in a safe area, your dog must be on leash.* Most cities and towns have laws that require it. If obeying the law is not a sufficient inducement, consider your dog's safety. If an emergency arises and your dog is off-lead, you have no immediate way to gain control over the dog physically. You have to rely on your dog's responsiveness to a cue, and that may not be good enough. It only takes an instant for disaster to strike.

One friend of mine had a UD (Utility Dog, an AKC title) dog entered in a Classic. The night before the show the dog was in the "exercise" area at the motel where they were staying. The dog was doing its business off-lead across the driveway. There were no cars in sight. When the dog finished it started back to its owner, who was standing about twenty feet away. In that moment a car came around the corner and struck and killed the dog.

One of my students had a one-year-old whippet that loved to play Frisbee. While playing in a park the Frisbee got away and skipped toward the parking lot. The dog chased it (and when a whippet chases something, it chases it fast!) and was struck and killed. The stories are legion. So, unless you have a specific reason for letting your dog off-lead in a public place (for example, for training purposes), keep the dog on-lead. Otherwise, you might spend a lifetime in remorse for having indulged a single thoughtless moment.

The need for a reliable recall is brought into sharp focus by the recent advent of "dog parks." These are areas designated by a municipality where dogs can run free. In theory, it sounds fine. We love to let our dogs be doggy. But there is a major problem. Many owners who bring their dogs to these parks are not responsible owners. Their dogs are not trained. Not a few are dog-aggressive. I know several people whose dogs been badly injured by other peoples' dogs in these parks. Sometimes that other person has paid the vet bill, but that is hardly the most important consideration. If you are in an area such as this—or any public area where dogs are running around off-lead (with the blessing of the powers that be or not)—you are going to have to be able to bring your dog back to you with a very high degree of reliability. When I train in one of the public parks that allows off-lead training I am frequently forced to call my dog off a distance exercise and get him back to me because some heedless owner is allowing his dog to run uncontrolled. And as we all know, the size of the dog is immaterial to the danger.

'Nuff said.

Adding the cue ("here")

With the recall I like to add the cue after the dog is showing some reliability coming to me in the presence of low-level distractions. This tells me that the dog is willing to let the recall overcome other things of interest. The cue I use for the informal recall is "here." I save "come" for the more formal exercise (it takes no major effort to add that cue—in fact, when you get to using signals you will have several cues, including various verbal ones, for the same exercise). "Here" means "come over to me and stick with me." Again, as a cue it is distinguished from "come" in that it involves *coming to my front*, but does not involve the sit in front. Add the cue as

you do any other: Say "here" *as Fido is coming to you*, immediately before you click. Say the word in a conversational tone. Treat when he gets to you.

Many trainers get used to bellowing this command. It is not necessary. *Dogs don't "refuse the recall" because they did not hear the cue.* First, dogs have excellent hearing. Their hearing is about ten to twelve times as acute as ours; how many times do your dogs set up a racket because they have heard something that you can't hear even when you try? If Fido "refuses the recall" it is not because because he has not heard you, but because you have not put the recall fully under stimulus control, or because you have burdened the recall with aversive baggage. In either case, pumping up the volume will not bring the dog any closer to you.

If you accustom Fido to responding to cues delivered in an ordinary, conversational tone, you will find that you can work quietly even in rather noisy environments. It is another element in teaching Fido to concentrate on you and the cues you are delivering. Some people seem to think that raising the volume communicates "I really mean it" to the dog. This is a false premise. The fact that you have given the cue is all the dog needs to hear to know that you "really mean it."

Trying to get the dog to come on cue before you are sure the dog has learned to associate "here" with the act of coming to you will undermine the cue and destroy the exercise. On the other hand, your recall cues are something the dog learns very readily once you have made the recall a powerfully reinforcing event.

"Command-based" trainers have a motto: "Never give a command you are not in a position to enforce." Shapers have a related but different motto: "Never present a cue you are not certain the dog understands." The dog comes to understand the cue because you associate it carefully with a strongly conditioned behavior. Ask the dog to respond to a cue before the behavior is fully in place, and you are asking for failure.

Generalization ("proofing")

Although this is an *informal* and not a formal recall, *generalization* ("proofing") is important. The dog should *always* come to you when called. While you are at home this will normally not be a problem. But away from home, it may be.

As with any other exercise, generalization is a process of incrementally raising the level of difficulty while keeping the new critieria within the dog's ability to perform. It is *not* an opportunity for you to get in a punisher. Remember, shaping is a two-way street. From our point of view, we are training the dog to perform various behaviors. From the dog's point of view, he is learning ways to make us C/T. Don't change the rules of the game just because you have moved to a new ballpark. You want the dog to learn that he can still play the game and win.

Take the dog to a new place. Have him on a long line that is clipped to your belt. Give him only a maximum of six feet at first. Move around just enough to get him up and moving. Let him be doggy. Do not call him or attempt to make him come to you using any kind of physical compulsion or luring. At some point Fido will look at you. C/T. You are not clicking for attention as such, but you are reinforcing him orienting to you. At some point he will start to move toward you, if only accidentally. C/T. In fairly short order he will make a connection: This has happened before; if I go to boss, boss gives me a goody. You have reaffirmed the game. Fido learns that he can do what it takes to make you C/T in this new place just as he did at home.

With a crossover dog, I find it especially helpful to go through this pure shaping for an extended period. The crossover dog already "knows" the recall, but it probably has a lot of coercive "baggage" attached to it. As a crossover trainer you have popped on the leash; you may have had someone toss a throw-chain at the dog, or used a "chaser" stick of some sort or other. All this undermines the recall. The recall becomes an aversive rather than a reinforcing experience.

By going all the way back down the learning curve and reinforcing the dog for the simple act of coming to you, you can fairly quickly discard those old associations. Make the experience purely reinforcing; that is why you do not use any cue for a while. It is a good exercise to convey to the dog that his behavior is what is important, not just his responsiveness to your commands.

Do not worry that this temporary detour will undermine your apparently already reliable recall. It will only help. Chances are, your recall is not really reliable. The dog may come like a bullet in the ring but slow down as he gets to you, or consistently sit just a bit—and almost too—far away. Or, he may respond to your cue a bit slowly. Or, the dog may be steady in the ring but impervious if off-lead in a nontraining situation. This is either avoidance behavior or lack of stimulus control.

Closeness

In formal Obedience competition, the dog is supposed to be close enough in front that you could bend at the waist, let your arms hang straight down, and touch him. As a rule of thumb, the dog should be within three to six inches of your feet. So "closeness" is an important *criterion* and you want to be thinking about it from the start. However, and this will sound contradictory, it is not something you should try to induce. Once Bowser is coming to you reliably, simply click for closer arrivals and step back and ask again if he stops too far away.

"But what if my dog doesn't come?"

I have not encountered this problem with my dogs after going through this program. My dogs have the run of a several-acre property at home, most of which is unfenced. If I were going to encounter this problem, I would see it here.

As I write this Skipper, a three-year-old golden retriever/Tervuren mix that we rescued in December 1996, is essentially untrained. Skipper is very active and disappears often. He chases ground squirrels and quail. He knows all the neighbor dogs and several of the coyotes, and loves to herd our neighbors' horses. But when I call his name (most times I do not even need to say "here"), he comes running. Why? Because I was careful to make responding to his name and to the "here" cue a completely magnificent opportunity for reinforcement.

I can also say that none my students who have either started with this program or crossed over to it have encountered the problem of their dog refusing to come when called since. But it might arise. The world is a large and interesting place. Lots of delicious scents and little fuzzies to chase. So . . . we also need distance control.

Distance control

A prime issue in the perfected recall is "distance control." The dog that is very reliable at, say, ten feet may be unreliable at twenty or thirty feet. I find this to be especially true with crossover dogs. Crossover dogs often have learned that there is a range at which their trainer cannot compel them to perform. The handler trains the recall to a distance of forty feet using a long line, which gives "reliability" in the ring situation—*and to a distance of about forty feet when not in the ring!* If the dog gets significantly beyond forty feet, he is outside the range of effective control established by the handler. So the recall "breaks down."

Bill Koehler sought to address this problem in his basic book on dog obedience by having the student extend the distance of the long line up to one hundred feet, and then gradually fade it. However, most people are not this diligent. And regardless, as with any training based on compulsion, if you give the command—whether in the competition ring or in training—even once and are unable to "enforce" it, you have lost your "edge."

If your dog is working to avoid an aversive, then the aversive must always be present if the dog fails to perform. You cannot maintain behavior with a variable schedule of aversives. At best, you will only succeed in making your dog thoroughly neurotic.

Since clicker training is based on **contingencies of reinforcement,** not compulsion, you should not encounter this problem. There really is no "effective range of reinforcement," that is, no distance at which the dog cannot earn and you cannot deliver a reinforcer. If you build it, he will come. If you are shaping the recall and find that the dog does not come when past a certain distance away, recognize that you simply have not done the work to establish the reinforcement contingencies at that distance.

"Okay, okay, I get it. He'll always come. But what if my dog doesn't come?"

You have carefully shaped the informal recall. You have generalized it conscientiously. You have been careful about establishing the cue. And . . . you call your dog and he does not come. What do you do?

First, locate the dog. If you cannot see the dog you cannot know what is going on. The dog may be caught in a fallen tree branch. Or he may be cornered by another dog or animal. Your first concern is always your animal's well-being. In her book *Playtraining Your Dog*, Patricia Burnham tells of one of her greyhounds out on a lure course. The lure line failed, and as her dog was coming back to her it appeared that the dog had tangled her leg in the line. Burnham told her dog "down" repeatedly, and each time the dog started to go down but refused to go all the way. After Burnham untangled the line and got her dog back to the car she noticed a network of line burns high on her dog's belly; somehow the line

had ridden up high and cut her every time she tried to drop. How would you feel if you repeatedly called your dog and he did not come—and the reason was that his collar was caught on a branch and he was choking himself increasingly with every effort to respond?

You have to trust your dog—believe that he will respond if he is able—and you have to be fair. I will always remember, years ago, watching a "flower child" mother calling her child. Her child was in a wrestling match with another boy, and was pinned. The boy he was wrestling with took a certain malicious glee in keeping him pinned as his mother called. After she had called him several times, with increasing vehemence, he managed to break away and run to her. She spanked him in a spasm of rage. Aside from delivering exactly the wrong message in terms of reinforcement, it was completely unfair. The child's failure to come when called was not willful.

A second possibility is that your dog may have found something that is highly reinforcing to him. This may give you something new with which to work on generalizing the recall. If the dog is safe but simply not coming (probably because his interest is absorbed by whatever he has found or is doing), *calmly go toward the dog. Do not* go storming up to him as if you are conducting a narcotics raid. *Do not continue calling "here."* Sometimes reducing distance restores a measure of control. As you approach the dog, simply say his name. If he looks at you, click. If he stops what he is doing and comes to you, treat. Even if he does not come to you, the click ought to have the effect of stopping his activity. As you approach, he ought to show that he expects a reinforcer. Treat when you get to him.

Now you might think this counterproductive. After all, are you not rewarding the dog for not coming? No. You have to be very specific about what is going on at any given time. Although the dog's failure to come when called is very much on your mind, *to the dog* the event of not coming is in the past. *To the dog* you are now into a new round of behaviors. This is why I say not to continue calling "here." Doing so only keeps the dog's failure to respond in the present and confuses the situation. What matters at this juncture is that you have called the dog's name and he has alerted to you. You *must* reinforce that.

If the dog has been eating something undesirable (such as the carcass of some dead animal), get him away from it immediately, although not in a panicky fashion. If you have a "leave it" cue in place, use it here. Put the dog on a sit, and throw the thing away. Hold the dog's collar if necessary in order to prevent him from retrieving it. Check your dog's mouth to see if there is anything obnoxious in it, and sweep it with your forefinger if necessary. If you have to go into his throat to get it out, do it. *Again, make sure your dog is safe!* If the thing he was eating seemed especially putrid, plan on an immediate trip to the vet.

Now, you have to reestablish your control. The dog is on a sit. Take a couple of steps and say "Rover, here." If he comes, C/T. Now walk him out of the area and back to where you were to begin with. You may do some short-distance, informal recalls along the way.

The "scruff-shake"

If you are in a situation where you can see the dog and the dog seems simply to be ignoring you, then a little physical intervention may be appropriate. Again, approach the dog in a calm, nonthreatening manner. If the dog sees you approaching and starts to come to you, *do not* click and treat. This would only reinforce the dynamic of the dog ignoring you as long as possible. It could also lead you into a game where the dog first ignores you, and then invites play (dogs are very good at constructing their own "behavior chains"). Let the dog establish his own reinforcement contingencies and you will very quickly lose all trace of stimulus control. Do nothing to encourage this sort of development.

So if the dog moves toward you, keep walking calmly toward the dog. This will communicate to him that he is not performing an ordinary recall. When Fido gets to you (or vice versa), get hold of his collar, crouch or kneel so that your face is level with his, take a firm hold of his scruff, give it a terse shake and give him a talking-to in a low, growly voice. It doesn't really matter what you say. This is a typical dressing-down, done in "dog talk." I would say something like: "Listen, you. When I say 'here,' you come to me. No messing around." *Remember to keep your voice low.* Someone standing a couple of feet away should be able to hear your voice but not make out your words. After growling, continue to hold his scruff and stare directly into his eyes. You have prevailed when he casts his eyes down and licks his lips slightly. The whole process takes less than a minute.

Having asserted your authority, you now have to reestablish the positive relationship. Stand up, back up a couple of steps and say, "Rover, here." He will come to you. C/T and play a little. Now walk him back to where you were when all this started. Do several short-distance informal recalls along the way and when you get there, reinforcing continuously.

This "ruff-shake-and-growl" is not clicker training as such. It derives from ethology, not behavior analysis. It is a moderate aversive, to be employed only rarely in cases of serious disobedience, and then very briefly. It is easy to take this sort of thing too far; I am not an advocate of the so-called "Alpha roll" (flipping the dog on his back) advocated by the Monks of New Skete. To me, that has always seemed a good invitation to get a face full of canine teeth. However, a mild dose of "facing the dog down" in this way, on his terms, can be productive *if* you are sufficiently assertive *and* you use it sparingly. In my entire training history I have used this perhaps five times.

The "time-out"

If you are not interested in trying to communicate with Rover in this way, then another approach—more in the behaviorist than the ethological mode—would simply be a "time out." Put the dog on leash and walk him to someplace really boring. If your car is nearby and Rover's crate is in it, this is ideal. Otherwise, you may find a bench somewhere and put him up for a bit. Walk him away from the scene in a neutral manner. Do not let him get interested in anything along the way, do not interact with him, and when you put him away do not embellish the moment with any verbal remonstrations. Keep it clinical and dispassionate.

If I am working two dogs, a "time-out" is a great opportunity to send a message to the recalcitrant one. I'll put the one up on a bench or in a crate, and work the second right there in front of the first (or, at least, within immediate hearing range). This invariably has the effect of sharpening the first dog's responses when I bring him back out.

After you have put Fido up for about ten minutes, bring him back out and do some short practice, either of the "failed" behavior or something else. If you work on the "failed" behavior, be sure to set it up so that you get a successful performance. Close the day on a success, and quit.

The play "deliver:" Beginning the retrieve

Most of my personal experience with teaching the retrieve is in teaching it to Shelties. Shelties have their charms, to be sure, but retrieving is not one of them. Shelties are generally reluctant retrievers. I have no idea why this is so; I cannot lay it off to their being a herding breed, since other herding breeds do not necessarily show the same attitude. But every Sheltie I have had or have worked with starts out by looking at the dumbbell as if to say, "How do I know where that thing has been?"

This method has worked well with my Shelties. And by now I have also used this method to teach the retrieve to many other breeds, so I can say with certainty that it works even with dogs that enjoy retrieving.

In *Webster's New World Dictionary,* the word "retrieve" is "said of dogs" to mean "to find and bring back." So the essence of the exercise is to return the found article to the handler. All too often, trainers teach the retrieve such that the focus becomes the dog getting the article. And often, one of two things happens. The dog is reluctant to bring it back to the handler, or the dog is reluctant to release it.

Therefore, although it may seem like an unnecessary nuance, I have found it best to orient to the retrieve as early as possible not so much as a "take it" but as a "deliver it" exercise. If the dog learns from the beginning that *the point is the delivery to me,* rather than just getting the object, it is relatively easy to train the variations.

Introduction: Pure play

Get Bowser used to bringing things to you in order to play as early as possible. Most puppies, regardless of breed "predisposition," love to chase and catch things. So it is usually easy to get a puppy into retrieving soft toy objects. The "game" is simple: Get it and bring it back.

At first, play the game at a very short distance. Don't toss the toy any farther than you can reach. Sitting or kneeling on the floor, let the toy hit the floor, grab it while it is in the puppy's mouth, and reinforce him for releasing it to you. At first, the primary reinforcer can be food. But very quickly, the reinforcer will become getting to play the "get it" game again.

If the puppy refuses to release the toy, keep hold of it (do not let the puppy "win" a tug of war) but stop tugging. Sometimes, this makes the "game" boring enough that the puppy just lets go. If not, then use a piece of food to bait the puppy to release it. Take the bait and put it at and barely above the tip of puppy's nose. Draw it slowly back toward his eyes. This will cause him to open his mouth to get the food, releasing the toy. Click as his mouth opens and give him the treat.

Putting the release on cue ("thank you")

You can put the release on cue very quickly. As he starts to follow the bait and open his mouth, say your cue. For the formal retrieves I say "Thank you" (always a gentleman, no matter what temporary disadvantages I may struggle under), so I introduce it here.

"Leave it"

Another handy cue to use at this stage is "leave it." I will actually establish both, and they serve different purposes. "Leave it" is a good cue to have in place to stop the dog from picking up trash, lizards, or skunks. Fully trained, it is a recall. The dog is to abandon what he is going after and come to you.

At this stage, saying "leave it" simply acts as a cue for Fido to abandon his grip on the toy. A little later on you can add the recall element to it ("leave it" . . . "come" or "here"). It then becomes a little behavior chain: "Leave it" cues the dog to abandon the object and run to you. (Perhaps the most spectacular demonstration of "leave it" I have ever seen was by Janice DiMello, who is not a clicker trainer, at a seminar in 1993. She sent her dog Jeep rocketing across the ring to retrieve a dumbbell. Just as he was about to grab it from the floor she said "Leave it," and he jerked his head back, whipped around, and raced back to her.)

Establishing the "deliver"

If you throw the toy too far too early (and barely just out of reach can be too far because your movement can trigger a chase), you risk undoing the connection that makes the reinforcement work. If the dog gets away from you with the toy, *do not* chase him or demand that he bring it back. Simply, wait. Don't "play." In most cases, he will return to you in order to get the game going again. If he completely fails to return, simply stop the game and go do something else. Let several minutes pass, then try again. If Fido has the toy and sort of starts in your direction but does not come all the way, C/T for the starting step. Then, shape him to come all the way back.

When he comes back to you, *do not* reach to him to get the toy. That will start the chase again. Hold your hand at your lap, palm up. Have the patience to make him come to you. Bring your hand up easily to take hold of the toy. When you have hold of the toy, go to your "release" cue. It does not normally take long to get the dog into the "game" of getting the object *and bringing it back.* That is the basis of the retrieve. What remains is to formalize the retrieve as a *fluency.*

Start with metal

Most dogs do not have a problem either with wood or leather articles. They are organic and "chewable." Some dogs have a problem with metal articles. Dylan was convinced that the metal article was an alien plot to eliminate all Shelties from the planet. He was reliable with wood, leather, and cloth, but resisted metal mightily. Through that experience I learned the value of exposing the puppy to metal very early.

Obviously, you do not want the puppy teeth chewing on a metal article. That is not the point. Simply, get the puppy used to having metal in his mouth and carrying the metal thing around. If you start fluency work with a wooden or leather dumbbell because it is easiest, make sure that as soon as the dog is taking that dumbbell readily you introduce metal. Once the dog will readily take a metal object such as a spoon, he will take anything.

From target stick to dumbbell

Your initial target stick work will start to pay its way now. Fido is used to touching an object held in front of him, so it will be fairly easy to transfer that behavior to the bar of the dumbbell. The sequence then is to shape the "touching" into a "taking." Throughout this entire part of the process, use no cues.

And just a note: This process is aimed at the reluctant retriever and with variations and "skips" will apply for the most part to most dogs. But all dogs are different. Your dog may leap past every stage and immediately grab the dumbbell. Well and good. But try to track the sequence, even if you only

make a "pit stop" at each stage, simply to be sure that the retrieve is really shaped completely.

Touch with nose

Hold the dumbbell immediately in front of the dog's muzzle and C/T any touching by the dog with his nose. This is a familiar thing for the dog and should not take long. When you are getting touches at a 3 : 1 ratio (3 touches between C/T), work on *latency.* Put the contact on *limited hold.* Give the dog no more than five seconds to touch the dowel. If Bowser doesn't do it in that time, remove it for a few seconds and then present it again.

Touch with lips

This is where the dog starts moving to actually taking the bell. If your dog is an innate retriever, you may find yourself getting lip touches fairly quickly. You may also find this if you have played retrieve and tug-of-war games with the dog in his puppyhood. If your dog is an adult and you have not done a lot of play retrieve with him, don't be too surprised if he is reluctant at first to take the dumbbell from you. Part of this "resistance" is the dog's natural reluctance to take something from the Alpha. Also, *to the dog,* once he has taken this thing from you, it makes little or no sense at all to give it back to you. These are specific new rules that we have to impose on him.

If your dog does not readily start moving his lips toward the bit, you may have to manipulate the object somewhat so as to "make" him touch it with his lips. This is OK. Just *be very quick with your C/T* so that you catch even the tiniest correct touches.

If your dog rolls his head away from the dumbbell, do not try to follow his head with the dumbbell. This will not help. Whatever the aversion is that is causing Fido to turn his head away from the dumbbell, "chasing" him with the dumbbell will not overcome it. The answer lies in simple *incremental reinforcement.* Simply remove the dumbbell for a moment or two, "hiding" it behind your back or raising it to your shoulder, then re-present it to him. Now you will C/T for the dog not moving his head away. Then you can get him showing some movement toward the dumbbell, touching the dumbbell, and so on.

Removing and re-presenting the dumbbell in this fashion will become a familiar pattern when you put the "take" on limited hold (discussed later). It serves to terminate the exercise for a moment. It is a silent "That ain't it, kid." It deprives the dog of the chance to "win" the game, if only momentarily. Once the dog knows what the game is, it is a powerful if low-key "corrective."

Touch with teeth

When the dog will (a) touch the bit with his lips on a count of "one" and (b) do so on a 3 : 1 ratio, you can again raise your criteria. Withhold reinforcement until you feel the dog's teeth on the dowel. Again, once you start feeling the teeth at all, put the "teeth-touch" on limited hold (you are always working on latency).

Taking the dumbbell

When you get a quick touch with the teeth and that touch is on a 3 : 1 ratio, withhold reinforcement until the dog opens its jaws. Now, the dog will typically do one of two things. Innate retrievers will more or less quickly go from opening their jaws to closing them on the bit. Less-than-motivated retrievers will take some time to go from opening their jaws to moving their head forward enough to get the dumbbell into their mouth, and some are even loath to close their jaws on the dumbbell even when they are in position to do so.

Again, I think it important to remember that you are to some extent using shaping to overcome innate behaviors. It is unusual among dogs for one dog to "give" another a present. I have watched many dogs tease another dog with some object, not intending to give it to them at all but in sort of a "nyah, nyah" fashion. I read it as sort of an Alpha game. So it may take some work to get the dog really comfortable with the idea that you want him to take the dumbbell from you and that it is not some sort of challenge. This is one reason I do not like to use the ear pinch: It does not address what I think is behind early reluctance to retrieve.

If you have a reluctant retriever, you may advance the process by moving the dumbbell slightly forward into the dog's mouth. Be sure to keep it in contact with the dog's teeth. C/T as soon as you feel the jaws close on the bit. This is only a transition! Do not make it a habit. Remember! The dog must do the work here. When you have reinforced the dog's action of closing teeth on the bit once or twice, you should immediately stop moving the dumbbell into the dog's mouth, and start requiring of the dog that he move his head forward over the bit to take it.

Using a dowel to transition from target stick to dumbbell

Some dogs may show no response at all to the dumbbell, or may get obsessed with getting their mouths on the ends rather than the bit. With these dogs, it sometimes helps to use a wooden dowel to provide a transition from the target stick. Use a dowel about twelve inches long, the same thickness as the bit you are going to use on your dumbbell. Start by holding one end of the dowel in your fist. C/T first touching with the nose, then the lips, then teeth, all as before. When Bowser is touching the dowel with his teeth, put both fists on the ends of the dumbbell so that the dog has about four inches to work with. Now you want the dog to take the dumbbell from between your hands. The hands roughly approximate the "look" of the ends of the dumbbell (no, it is not necessary to wear white gloves).

Gradually narrow the space between your fists until the space between them is about one-half inch wider than the dog's muzzle. This conditions the dog to focussing on the bar rather than on the ends of the dumbbell. When the dog is taking the dowel consistently, you can switch to the dumbbell. When you present the dog with the dumbbell, it's going to look an awful lot like the dowel. By now you have conditioned the dog always to take the dowel, so the dog should readily take the dumbbell by the bit.

Still, because the dumbbell is a new thing, you can expect that the dog will not take it immediately. So you are going to retrace the learning curve. The good news is that it won't take anything like the time it took the first time. Essentially, you are teaching the dog that he can take the dumbbell the same way that he took the dowel.

"Hold"

Once the dog is taking the dumbbell, the dog must hold it in his mouth until you take it from him. Some dogs have a "hard mouth" (very strong bite); some have a "soft mouth" (gentle bite). I have not found either of these tendencies to follow either breed lines or retrieving aptitude greatly. Most Shelties I know are "snappers" when it comes to bait (a Sheltie-owning friend of mine had a vanity license plate that read "PIRANAS"), but "soft-mouthed" on the dumbbell (they don't want to keep that thing in their mouth any longer than absolutely necessary). Many Goldens are also "soft-mouthed," though tenacious retrievers. And while Pit Bulls have a strong bite, Border Collies are among the most tenacious at holding on the dumbbell once they have it. At one competition I watched a handler literally lift her Border Collie off the ground trying to wrest the dumbbell from the dog's mouth.

"Hard-mouthed" dogs will be unlikely to drop the dumbbell, but will tend to resist giving the dumbbell up. "Soft-mouthed" dogs will tend to give the dumbbell up readily, but are susceptible to dropping the dumbbell while returning to the handler (particularly when jumping). Both "hard"- and "soft-mouthed" dogs can have problems "mouthing" the dumbbell. The "hard-mouthed" dog will chomp it; the "soft-mouthed" dog will roll it around. To some extent "mouthing" of any type may be caused by the material the dumbbell is made of (plastic or wood), or by an improperly fitting bit. Ultimately, it is a behavior that you can address through shaping.

Shaping the hold

After the dog is taking the dumbbell, extend the time between the "take" and the "give." (You don't need a "give" cue at first. "Click ends the behavior," so the only essential is that you have your hand in position to receive the dumbbell when the dog drops it when you click so that the dumbbell does not hit the ground.)

Let me inject a reminder here: It is OK if the dog drops the dumbbell when you click. Remember, "click" marks the behavior that you are reinforcing. And, "Click ends the behavior." So, if you "click," Fido drops the dumbbell, and you then treat, you are not reinforcing him for dropping the dumbbell. "Click" marked the spot, so to speak. He knows that he is getting the treat for doing what he was doing when you clicked, and not for what he was doing when you gave him the food.

The dog's jaw must remain immobile. A "soft-mouthed" dog will tend to hold the dumbbell loosely. You must induce a tighter grip. One way to do this is with physical pressure. You may (a) lightly cage the dog's jaw, (b) use your hand under the jaw to put pressure upwards, or (c) lightly tap the ends of the dumbbell (this will cause the dog to tighten his jaws reflexively). If I am going to use any of the three, I prefer (c). One collateral benefit of this little maneuver is that, when your hands approach the dumbbell to take it, the dog will tighten his grip slightly instead of loosening it. This will help you avoid the dog dropping the dumbbell as you reach for it.

If you use this tactic, remember that the point is to reinforce the resulting behavior and eliminate the stimulus as quickly as possible. So you tap the ends, then click immediately as you see the jaws tighten. Now, extend the time between the moment the jaws tighten and the click.

The more elegant approach is to rely on shaping. You may need a partner. The trick is timing. I was working with a Flatcoat Retriever who mouthed the dumbbell vigorously. His owner put him on a bench and I watched from the side, clicker in hand. As his lower jaw came up to close, I clicked. He released the dumbbell and took his treat. Within five minutes he was holding the dumbbell for ten seconds. I did the same thing with a German Shorthaired Pointer.

This is an example of why we say the clicker is magic! The clicker allowed me to deliver a very immediate response to a very specific, identifiable act: closing the lower jaw on the dumbbell. We were able to distinguish that particular move from everything else the dog was doing with the dumbbell at that moment. Each dog caught on quickly to what we were asking for.

Adding the cue

When the dog will keep the dumbbell in his mouth for five to seven seconds without mouthing it, go back to one or two seconds. Add the "hold" cue by saying "Hold" just before you C/T. Gradually, extend the time between the word "hold" and the C/T. In this way a stationary behavior—holding the dumbbell quietly—will follow the cue. Once the cue is established, you can use it as information. If the dog has brought the dumbbell to you but his jaws are not tight around the bit, say "Hold" and watch for the jaws to tighten. C/T when the dog tightens his grip on the bit.

Establishing range of motion

Adding distance to the "take-and-deliver" goes relatively easily. First, increase the distance *forward* that the dog must move to take the dumbbell until the dog must take a step to do so. Hold the dumbbell. When Bowser will take one step to get the dumbbell, make him take two steps, then three. I also like to have the dog move both to his left and to his right to get the dumbbell at this stage. This way, he does not become accustomed to picking the dumbbell up from one direction only. (As a rule, whenever I am training a "motion" exercise—for example, jumping—I always have the dog go right and left in practice. This gives you a greater likelihood of direct pickups rather than arcs toward the dumbbell when he has to go out some distance to pick it up.)

Fido will take a step to take the dumbbell from your hand. When he takes it, let go of the dumbbell, take a step back, and call him to you with an informal recall ("here"). He only has to move a step or two back in your direction to return it to you. When he gets to you, give your release cue. Click when he releases the dumbbell, and treat. In this way, you are establishing the essential elements of every chain: "Get the thing and bring it to me." It is the delivery to you that triggers the reinforcer.

For trainers who have trouble, especially in Utility, with a slow return on the retrieve, doing this kind of practice will help you to solve the problem. If you teach the dog that it is the delivery to you that triggers reinforcement, then in all likelihood the return to you will become more "enthusiastic" because the dog knows that this is what he has to do to get the goodies.

When the dog is consistent at three steps, start to lower the dumbbell toward the ground, three to six inches at a time. At first, C/T for the dog taking the dumbbell at each lower stage. Then, at each stage, add the "step back/recall" element back in. In this way, at each stage, you are reaffirming that the *delivery* is what really counts.

You may also find, as you move the dumbbell right and left and have the dog moving toward it, that the transition toward the ground goes relatively easily if you lower the dumbbell while also moving it forward, instead of simply holding the dumbbell stationary and lowering it. Do what you must to get the behavior. Every change may cause some new uncertainty for Fido, so keep the overall dynamics as familiar as possible.

You will probably also find that with this type of motion established, it will be fairly easy to transfer the "take" to the ground, because dropping it to the ground will be a natural development. If you get the dumbbell on the ground and Fido seems uncertain what to do, keep the limited hold in place (three to five seconds, maximum) and remove the dumbbell. Don't give him an eternity to consider his options.

You may find it helpful to leave your hand near the dumbbell at first. Or, you may have to C/T progress toward the dumbbell on the ground. This is, again, in the realm of the trainer's art. By now you should know your dog well enough to know what it will take to get him over this little hump.

Once the dog is taking the dumbbell from the ground, you can start adding distance by tossing it a short way. In this phase it is best not to make it formal, but treat it more like play. Don't require a sit-at-heel before you throw it, and ask only that the dog bring the dumbbell all the way back to you and deliver it to hand (no front and finish). These other elements are all fluencies that you will train separately. It will be no real problem to add them in once the "go-out-pick-it-up-and-return" behavior is firmly in place.

What to do when the dog comes to you

You don't have the "front" shaped yet, and you do not want your dog to get into the habit of returning to a sloppy front position. On the other hand, the dog does have to return to you. Let the dog bring the dumbbell back to you in "play mode." You can raise your hands to induce the dog to jump up on you, if you like. Or, simply C/T for the dog coming anywhere to the front of you.

This will not disrupt formal retrieve training. When you start working fronts, you stand in a very specific posture: straight up, feet slightly apart, hands at your sides. All else aside, this posture will quickly become a visual cue to the dog that he is to come to front and sit. Nothing you are doing at this stage will corrupt the meaning of that cue.

Carrying the dumbbell

Before you can expect Bowser to fully understand "go-out-and-take-it," you need to build motion into the exercise. The reason for this is based on **back-chaining**. You are telling the dog that the ultimate purpose is for him to bring this object to you. This will help him understand the "fetch," which obviously comes before he brings it back.

First, have Fido take the dumbbell; then have him walk with you informally for a few steps, pivot into the dog, and take the dumbbell from in front. When that is reliable, have Fido take the dumbbell, leave him on a sit or stand, and have him bring the dumbbell to front, holding it until you take it from him. Start at about six feet and build to about twenty feet.

The formal "front" position is standardized for the handler as well as the dog. Developing your own correct position as a habit now will help your dog understand it as a cue, later on.

I have found it helpful to do a couple of these "in motion" exercises early in the session, then work on the "take it," concluding with an "in motion" repetition.

Some variations

This brings me into the field of "the trainer's art." There are infinite ways in which dogs will respond to the shaping process and in what it may take to trigger a "breakthrough." Here are some ideas that

have helped in some cases, and *may* help in yours. The real point here is to encourage you to use your imagination.

Let the dog figure it out

Once the dog is taking the dumbbell from your hand and moving forward one step, you can "let him work it out for himself." Just pick a time when you can be at home in one place for an open-ended period of time, do a couple of retrieves from hand, and then put the dumbbell on the floor a few feet away from you . . . and wait. The dog will not pick the dumbbell right away. The dog may not even pick it up the first time you try this. If after fifteen or twenty minutes the dog has not picked it up, take the dumbbell from the floor and try again tomorrow.

This approach works, but my bias against it is that it tends to work against short latency periods. It gives the dog a lot of time to pick the dumbbell up, after which you will give a reinforcer. You then might have to work on the limited hold. On the other hand, some trainers I know who have used this method tell me that they have not encountered this problem. So, I leave it to you.

The "chase" game

It is sometimes possible to take advantage of the dog's innate tendency to chase and grab ("prey" drive). With Dylan, once he was taking the dumbbell and moving with it, tossing it and letting him just chase after it got us over the hurdle of fetching from a distance. If the dog already chases and fetches toys, you can intersperse the toy with the dumbbell, associating the two activities for the dog.

When to add the cue

The "traditional" approach, as with all exercises, is to introduce the cue at the first step. So, for example, in Koehler's approach you say "Joe, fetch" at the very first time you press the dumbbell against the dog's lips. As I discussed earlier, a major problem with this is that the cue becomes associated with a lot of garbage that you then have to extinguish. At first, it attaches to a delayed behavior, so you are building in an obstacle to latency. Another problem is, if you say "fetch" and pinch the ear, the ear pinch becomes as much a part of the cue to take the dumbbell as does the word "fetch" (and the word "fetch" becomes associated with the ear-pinch as much as it does with taking the dumbbell). I have known more than one dog that simply would not retrieve until he had been ear-pinched. Yes, this is probably the product of sloppy training; on the other hand, it is a problem that is built into too-early presentation of the cue.

Add the cue when Rover will go out to a distance of four to six feet, pick the dumbbell up off the ground, and bring the dumbbell back to you. It is only at that point that you can say with reasonable certainty that the dog knows what he is doing and the behavior is reliable.

Say the cue as the dog is closing his jaws on the dumbbell. This associates the phrase immediately with the action. Then "back it up" as discussed before until it becomes directive. As always, don't push it. You never want to be in the position of having given the cue without also getting the corresponding action.

Delivery to hand ("give")

The dog cannot drop the dumbbell (or carried object) in any competitive (Obedience or Field) situation. The dog must deliver it to your hand. It is a substantial deduction (at least three points) in all retrieve exercises if the dog drops the object before delivering it to the handler's hand. Fluency in the retrieve means that the dog *never* drops the dumbbell but *always* delivers it to hand.

In the initial training stages, when you are allowing the dog to "drop" the dumbbell when you click, make sure that your hand is *always* in position to receive the dumbbell so that it never hits the ground. At this point you cannot expect the dog to pick the dumbbell up himself, and you cannot afford to give the dog any idea that it is acceptable for you to pick up the dumbbell from the ground if he drops it. So be exceedingly attentive on this point.

Putting the release on cue

When you have established the "hold" cue, the click will still end the behavior. Now you need to teach the dog to release the dumbbell *on cue*. The dog already knows that he is to deliver the dumbbell to hand, so you can readily put the delivery (or release) on cue. How do you do it?

The dog is holding the dumbbell for fifteen to twenty seconds before you C/T. Now, put your hands in position to receive the dumbbell. It is a good idea from very early on to receive the dumbbell by the ends rather than just letting it fall into your hands. Give your verbal release cue *immedi-*

ately before you C/T. The "drop" will then be almost immediately correlated to the verbal cue. The sequence is actually "give"/C/drop/T. It typically takes only a few repetitions before the dog is releasing the dumbbell in response to the release cue; C/T after the release. It doesn't really matter what verbal cue you use. I like to use "thank you," mostly because it's a nice little bit of theater. Also, it avoids some aural confusion: my retrieve cue is "get it." If I used the word "give" as my release cue, the start of both words would be the same (a hard "guh"). It would be a little much for me to expect the dog to distinguish between two one-syllable words that start with the exact same sound.

Problem: Dog resists release

It is a substantial deduction if the dog shows "reluctance or refusal to release the dumbbell to the handler" (C4, S9). This problem won't arise so long as the dog is letting go of the dumbbell in response to the click. "Click" ends the behavior of holding the dumbbell, and the "drop" is natural. However, once the release is on cue, if you have a manic retriever or a dog with strong "prey drive," you may find the dog resisting the release. There are a couple of approaches to solving this.

Inducing release with bait

I alluded to this one earlier. If the dog resists releasing the dumbbell, simply take a piece of bait and bring it directly over the dog's nose and move it slowly toward the stop. It takes a mighty dedicated gripper to refuse to open his mouth, drop the dumbbell, and go for the bait. As the dog opens and the dumbbell comes loose, give your verbal cue, receive the dumbbell, and click. Get the click in at the release, not when the dog takes the bait. This way you are reinforcing the release of the dumbbell and you can soon fade this tactic.

Pressuring the jaw with the dumbbell

It may happen that the dog decides to play "tug-of-war" in the ring. This can happen even with a very reliable dog if the dog is particularly jazzed. I mentioned earlier the handler who virtually lifted her dog off the ground trying to get him to release his grip on the dumbbell. Wrong move.

Instead of pulling *up* on the dumbbell, press *down* and roll it toward you. It is much easier for the dog to maintain pressure with its upper jaw than its lower, so this motion will work away from the dog's natural strength. It's a good idea to do this in practice so that (a) the dog does not get the idea that it can resist the release, and (b) you get fluent with the motion so that if you ever do need it in the ring you can do it without calling undue attention to yourself.

Teaching tenacity: "Search and find"

This is especially important for those of us who show outdoors. You have to spend time—not necessarily a lot of time, but you have to do what you have to do—teaching Fido to be tenacious about looking for the dumbbell. Why? Because you are inevitably going to show at a trial where the grass is not cut as short as it is supposed to be, and the dumbbell will "bury," that is, be hidden from sight. The smaller the dog, the bigger the problem; but it can happen to large dogs as well.

One simple piece of advice, which has nothing to do with shaping, is, always to use a dumbbell with white ends. That way, there is at least something that will stand out against the green and brown background (actually, shades of gray to the dog). I have seen many dogs miss an unpainted wooden dumbbell that had landed on a patch of brown grass. Don't make your life unnecessarily difficult.

The idea of "search and find" is that the dog understand that the dumbbell is always "out there," even if he cannot see it. Simply, practice retrieves where you place the dumbbell in taller and taller grass, even burying it a bit sometimes with leaves. At first, let Fido see where you are putting it (even though he can't see the dumbbell once you have placed it). Keep the distances short at first; when you have worked up to about twenty feet, increase the difficulty of the "find," reduce the distance, and work through it all again. This is actually fun for the dog.

If Fido looks around and does not find the dumbbell, "mark" him to it using your hand (if you have done basic marking) or the target stick. His failure to find the dumbbell is not a "refusal"; he simply does not yet understand that the dumbbell is actually there even though he cannot see it, and that he can find it if he keeps looking. You have full fluency and a tenacious retriever when he goes out on cue and keeps searching for the dumbbell until he finds it.

Jumping

Most books on obedience training advise you to train jumping by taking the dog over a solid jump at a low height, and building from there. The dog won't learn much about jumping this way, and may never develop consistent mechanics. Before you can introduce the dog to the particular disciplines of the jumping exercises, the dog should be fluent in jumping generally.

There are a couple of good books out on jumping, and I'm not even going to try to cover ground that those books cover so well. The first manual I read and used for training jumping was Suzanne Clothier's *Natural Jumping Method*. Chris Zink and Julie Daniels have a relatively new book titled *Jumping From A to Z*. Zink and Daniels's book has a wealth of information about dogs' body structure and how it relates to jumping, as well as a lot of imaginative approaches to cavaletti training. I recommend you read both books and—to the extent the systems differ—make your own choices.

Most if not all dogs love to jump over, onto, or off things, and most dogs have a natural jumping rhythm. You don't need to teach your dog to jump. You do need to give Spot time to develop his natural rhythm, including adjusting that rhythm to variations in height as well as distance in which to take the jump. For your dog to become a confident jumper you must expose him to a planned, carefully escalated series of jump obstacles. It is a learning progression, just like everything else.

Zink and Daniels's approach involves ground-pole work for the puppy, and three stages of skill training in jumping. In the early stages in particular, the emphasis is on letting your dog get comfortable with simply clearing the obstacles. I introduce my dogs to jumping with the jumps set at a height just sufficient to cause the dog to jump to clear it. For many dogs, eight inches is sufficient. For the larger breeds, you may need to go to ten or twelve inches. In any event, in the early stages height is not the issue; clearing the obstacle is the issue. You will have plenty of time to get your dog to full height later, and if you spend the time letting the dog become comfortable at low heights, the progression to full height will go much more easily, and you will significantly minimize the risk of injury.

Jumping injuries are pernicious. One cause is that puppies enjoy jumping around so much that they jump more than they should (this is especially so with very athletic breeds such as boxers). Both the front shoulder assembly and the spine are readily susceptible to puppy-age injury. These injuries can easily become chronic, plaguing your dog throughout his jumping career. It will be difficult with a highly active puppy, but you have to do everything you can think of to avoid letting the puppy jump over, onto, or off anything over eight to ten inches high. Given that your average puppy is fifty pounds of *joie de vivre* in a five-pound sack, with all the judgment of a bag of rocks, you are not going to be consistently successful in this endeavor. Do your best.

Avoiding injury

Dogs are really good at hiding injury. Muscular or tendon injuries often are not apparent until they have become quite serious, by which time you may be looking at several months (at least!) of recuperation. Pay close attention to even slight signs of distress. The problem will typically be greater than the dog is letting you see.

As I discussed earlier, get into the habit of massaging your dog on a regular basis. Even very gentle probing of an injured area will often get a response telling you of an injury you would not otherwise be aware of. Be alert in particular to areas that feel "hot" as compared to the rest of the dog's surface temperature, or "boardy" (stiff rather than elastic). The more consistently you put your hands on your dog, the more sensitive you will be to these indicators.

Keep your working dog lean. Dogs tend to eat too much, and for most of us even our "working" dogs do not get a whole lot of exercise. The overweight dog, even if a small breed, is at greater risk of injury than is the lean dog. Additional poundage means just that much more stress on the rear end in taking off for the jump, and for the front end upon landing. Since proper jump training involves repeated jumping, even at low heights, the overweight dog is at risk. A rule of thumb is that you should feel some subcutaneous fat over the ribs, but you should be able to feel the ribs. Sam weighs as much at eight and a half years as he did when he was two.

Rear-end injuries; dysplasia

We are very familiar with rear-end injury problems, if only because we all know the fearful words "hip dysplasia." But even mildly dysplastic dogs can be good jumpers if you train them properly. The dog's rear end is put together with joints, muscles, and tendons; weaknesses in the joints can be compensated for by strengthening the muscular structure around them. Lee Pulis, an Obedience and Schutzhund trainer in northern California, competed with a dysplastic giant schnauzer in both

sports for several years. She gave the dog plenty of running exercise to keep the rear-end musculoskeletal structure sound.

If your dog is dysplastic, your exercise program should be monitored by a vet conscious of canine "sports medicine." Even if you do not expect to be able to jump the dog competitively, it may well be that a carefully modulated program of low-set cavalettis (discussed later, page 101) would be beneficial for his general health. And you never know how the dog's strength will develop. Be careful, give it time.

Now that AKC jump heights have been lowered to the nearest multiple of two inches of the dog's shoulder height, it may be easier for mildly dysplastic dogs to compete in the future. This is good, but it puts an even greater responsibility on the trainer to train the dog thoroughly so as not to let the lower jump heights be an invitation to greater injury.

Front-end injuries

In the dog's front end, the appendages are linked to the body by muscle and tendons, not joints. You don't jump a young puppy because you need to give all that connective tissue the time it needs to form properly. Muscle tears are not uncommon, and if you do not find them early they can be debilitating throughout his lifetime.

Once your dog is jumping at full height, do not jump him regularly at full height in practice. My Shelties are oversize and both jump twenty-two inches in competition. When we are in the "off-season," they jump sixteen inches in training. When we do cavalettis, they jump between eight and fourteen inches. When we are showing, I jump them only occasionally between shows at full height. At other times I run them through cavalettis rather than repetitive jumping of standard obstacles. There is no good purpose served, and potentially serious harm can be done, by jumping the dog repeatedly at full height once the dog is comfortable jumping at full height.

"Overtraining" jump heights

Should you jump your dog at more than full height? *Overtraining* in this regard is in the realm of "pushing the envelope," and you should not do it unless you are experienced, or have a good instructor. The reason to overtrain height is to be prepared for the unexpected. Sam, for example, is a tad under eighteen and a half inches at the shoulder. Under the old jump heights I entered him at twenty inches, and that is what he usually measures out at in the ring. However, he could measure at or just a hair over eighteen and a half inches, and in that case he would have to jump twenty-four inches. If he has to, he could do it. (This discussion may be moot now that jump heights are so much lower; under the new Regulations I can set Sam's jumps at eighteen inches, which is a cakewalk for him.)

You also overtrain height so that the dog will not be thrown if he approaches a jump on uneven ground or if, as sometimes happens, the "twenty-two inches" at a particular show is a tad higher than the "twenty-two inches" your dog jumps in practice. I overtrain only to a height two inches over their standard jump height. I have the dog at that height only rarely, and only during a time when we are doing a lot of practice jumping.

There is a theory of "overtraining" that you want the dog to clear the jump by a wide margin, so you "overtrain" the dog to jump much higher than necessary. Some people try to accomplish this by running a thin wire across the jump, two inches or so above the top board. I am not an enthusiast of this practice. A dog's natural jumping trajectory will tend to be a flat arc, allowing him enough air to clear the jump while landing without putting undue stress on his front end. There is no reason to ask the dog to build more air into the jump than that. Forcing the dog to take an unnatural arc over the jump can lead to injury on landing because the dog will be coming down too sharply on his front legs. If your dog is not jumping his normal height cleanly, you have progressed too far, too fast.

The crossover dog

You have to be honest with yourself: Is your dog a confident jumper or not? The easiest way to tell is if the dog "stutter-steps" or if his pace is uneven approaching the jump. The dog's jumping gait should be a smooth canter. If your dog does not approach the jump at a smooth pace, accelerating slightly as he prepares for take-off, you are seeing a lack of confidence. Even if you think your dog is confident, if you have not gone through a progressive cavaletti program your dog would probably benefit from it. Certainly, it will "do no harm."

The puppy

Don't jump your puppy at all until he is physically mature. Depending on the breed and size of dog, physical maturity will come somewhere between six months and a year. Give your puppy plenty of exercise, keep him away from situations where he is "invited" to jump in play or on a chase, and do a lot of groundwork. This will strengthen him physically and give him confidence that will carry over into the jumping program.

Initial training: Ground work

The first goal is to teach the dog to think about all four feet. You have already done some of this with the "rear-end" work. But jump training takes you a little bit further. In jumping the dog may have to turn (for example, in Agility or after the broad jump or directed jump), or to set himself up for the jump on an angle or from irregular distances. In all these situations, although the front legs will lead, the rear legs will come into play. The rear legs "drive" the jump, so the dog must be confident about using them.

"Step obstacles"

I use a line of six to eight PVC poles for this, initially set very close together, so that the dog has to cross one with his front feet while he is crossing another with his back feet. Start with half-inch pipe, and work up to one-inch pipe.

You can use the target stick to lead the dog across the obstacles. At first, C/T as he *steps over* the first obstacle. You don't want any sort of jump or hop. Pay particular attention to the rear feet. The green dog will typically step with his front feet, but "hop" with his rear feet. If you need a training partner to see your dog's rear feet, recruit one. Once you get accustomed to watching your dog, you will be able to tell by the motion of his rump whether he is stepping or hopping.

Here is a situation where the clicker really earns its keep. When you are working on one step-obstacle at a time you can click the back feet as they step over the obstacle. By not reinforcing the "hops" and clicking the steps, you can quickly extinguish the hops because the dog will recognize which actions get reinforced and which do not. I work with a miniature pinscher who regularly "hopped" the poles at first. With accurate clicking, her owner eliminated 90% of the hops in about ten minutes.

Don't go to the second obstacle until you are getting a *stepping* motion over the first. If you go to a second obstacle too quickly, it is probable that you will not communicate to the dog what you are looking for. As an example, he may step over the first and hop over the second. You have clicked the first but not the second, and you must now deliver the food even though part of what the dog did was a mistake. When you have two step-obstacles in place you will click after he clears the second one, but only if he has stepped over both. Therefore, the "stepover" motion for the first must be consistent.

This is not jumping; this is body awareness training. Work your way up, one pipe at a time, until the dog can go through the whole line, stepping all the way. It is generally not necessary to add a cue for this. The dog will see the poles and walk them readily. If you want a cue, use the word "step."

The next step is to spread the poles more so that the dog will take one full stride between each pole. This will go a lot faster than the first series, but because the poles are spread apart you may find the dog going faster and again "hopping" them. You don't mind the speed, but you want to be consistent about reinforcing only a stepping motion. When Rover is consistently stepping over the spaced poles, next space the poles randomly, some at the original distance, some at the second distance. In this segment the dog will have to adjust his stride slightly and think about different things as he goes through.

Next, angle the poles so that the approach to each one looks slightly different to the dog than the one before. You still want the dog to go in a straight line, but confronting and crossing unevenly placed obstacles. By this time it may seem that your dog could care less. In that case, increase the size of the pole. You don't want him jumping yet, but you do want him thinking about the stepping movement. You can get PVC pipe or conduit up to 6 inches if you need it, though two-inch pipe is usually sufficient to get the attention of even large-ish puppies.

An alternative to simply increasing the size of the poles is to set them so that one end is higher than the other (for example, place a brick under one end). It is simply a matter of using your imagination to find ways to change the "look" of the puzzle within the dog's level of ability. Get your dog used to seeing "unusual" obstacles early; it will make it easier when he sees really unusual things later on.

You have reinforced the act of stepping over each pole. As his distance increases, reinforce only at the end of the progression. You don't need to worry about the early stepovers becoming "demotivating"

somehow. The dog will quickly learn to enjoy the game as a whole. The chance to do more is probably the single most reinforcing part of it all.

Work in both directions

Always work your dog in both directions through the poles, so that he is now working on your left, now on your right, now to his left, now to his right. Dogs are right- and left-handed the same as people, and you will find as you progress that your dog will tend to be more comfortable approaching the jump from one direction or the other. By working back and forth from the very beginning you will build your dog's fluency for working from either direction. This helps even in obedience jumping.

Using the target stick to start the dog jumping

In "traditional" training you would start the dog jumping with leash work, either standing next to the dog and popping him toward the jump, or standing across the jump from the dog and popping him toward you on a long line. Neither is necessary, nor particularly helpful. Thanks to your target stick training, the dog will follow the target stick in motion. This not only allows you to get the dog to circle left and right around you and walk on your left side, it gives you a ready tool to lead the dog across the jumps.

Set up two jumps, one bar jump and one solid jump, each at eight inches. Even with a big dog, this is just enough to get him to hop over. If you have a very small dog, set the height lower. The purpose here is not to do any serious jumping work, but to lead the dog into jumping and to put the cue in place.

Move toward the jump with target stick in hand. Do not ask the dog to be on your left side; if he goes there, you may even pivot so you are facing him. All jumping should be free of any superstitious insistence by the dog on being at your left side. As you get to the jump, move the target stick so that it is slightly past the jump, in the middle. Make sure that the dog moves steadily toward the obstacle. You can say "touch" if the dog seems a little unclear on the concept. Typically, the dog will readily jump over the obstacle to get to the stick. Click as the dog clears the jump. Continue walking in a straight line

A

B

C

Following the target stick from Morgan's left to right, Dylan (a) goes over a low jump and (b) learns to continue straight ahead after landing. The exercise is repeated (c) from right to left. Most dogs prefer one side to the other, and need to learn confidence in both directions.

for a few steps past the jump, let the dog get to the stick and touch it, and treat.

Notice here that you are not treating immediately after you click; the clicker works here as a **bridging stimulus.** Despite the brief passage of time, the dog will still know what the click meant, and will still associate the treat with the click.

Always work back and forth on the jumps. In this introductory phase, once Fido has taken the jump from one side, turn back and have Fido take the same jump from the other side. If he was on your left side at first, he will now be on your right. You are likely to see early on that Fido is more confident jumping from one side or the other. Work back and forth consistently until he shows equal confidence from both sides. This is especially important for Agility competitors, but it will benefit you in the Obedience ring as well. Confidence is its own reward.

A   B

Cavalettis help the dog develop a rhythmic, balanced stride for take-offs and landings. Dylan loves a good run at the cavalettis; the behavior can be used as a reinforcer for other tasks he finds less interesting.

Step two: Cavalettis

Anyone who has worked horses knows about this. I've never worked horses, so I was a slow learner. But I'm catching on. Cavalettis are a series of low jumps, set in various patterns. You start with the jumps set at a single height, in a straight line, spaced to allow for the dog's normal jumping stride. There are formulas for determining this stride in the books I mentioned earlier. Once the dog is jumping fluently along this line you can vary the sequence by (a) setting different jump heights, (b) setting different jump patterns (figure-eights, zig-zags, etc.), (c) adjusting the distance between jumps so that the dog has to adjust his stride, and (d) combining these variations. I also like to use bars, solid obstacles, and broad-jump boards so that the dog gets used to seeing and working with all of them.

The click and the cue

The "jump" cue

This is one of those areas of personal preference. I use different cues for each jump: "bar" for the bar jump, "over" for the high jump, and "jump," for the broad jump. I think it helps the dog to associate a particular cue with a particular behavior, and I don't have a lot of trouble remembering which is which. In Utility, having the separate cues will help you help the dog in taking the directed jumps. The dog may not catch your hand signal, but the specific cue will help him go in the right direction. You add the cue for jumping the same way you do in every other exercise, immediately before the click. So the question is, when do you click?

Timing the click

Click *as the dog is clearing the jump.* Don't wait until the dog has touched down, because then you are reinforcing the landing, not the jump. Try to click as close to take-off as possible, but make sure that the dog is into the air when you click.

When you are doing the cavaletti progressions you can click at every jump if you wish. Although as a general rule you don't use the click to mean "keep going," in this situation where the dog knows he is going to keep going anyway in order to complete the exercise, clicking every jump poses a minimal risk of diluting the effect of the click. You will probably find, though, that it is not necessary to do this. As the dog becomes more confident with the jumping, the jumping itself becomes a reinforcer.

This is a type of *repertoire reinforcement:* Each succeeding jump reinforces the preceding jump. You can also see *repertoire cuing* at work: Each preceding jump is the cue to take the next one. Let this sink in and take hold; especially if you plan to do Agility, it will condition the dog from the very beginning to come off of each obstacle looking for the next one.

Nor do you necessarily have to deliver the jump cue every time. Once the dog learns that there is a sequence of five, six, or seven jumps, you will quite possibly find him running the sequence with no cue at all other than the cue to start. Indeed, many dogs become so enthusiastic about the cavalettis that they will take off for the jumps with no cue from you at all. This is a good thing (it shows that the dog is enthusiastic about the training and knows what to do). Don't worry about it unless you have progressed to the point where you have put the jumping on cue and want to extinguish all off-cue jumping.

Adding the cue

This should be becoming familiar territory. Deliver the cue *while the dog is performing the behavior,* immediately before you click. With the bar jump, for example, say "bar" as the dog is launching into the jump, and click almost simultaneously.

From cavalettis to regular jumps

When Rover is comfortable and confident with the cavalettis, you can start increasing height on the bar and solid jumps. Do not increase the height for the cavalettis; you do not want Rover jumping a series of high obstacles. You will now have him take a single jump at progressively greater heights. Raise the height in increments of one to two inches at a time. Give Rover at least five sessions at each height, working back and forth from left to right as always. Intersperse this with cavaletti training so as not to diminish his confidence.

In the course of your cavaletti work, you will have spaced the jumps at various distances, beginning with a distance that allows the dog to take two strides between each jump. By now, you should have a good idea of what that distance is. In setting up for single jumping, make sure that you are at or slightly beyond that distance. You won't always be able to control the distance the the dog has to cover to get to the jump when coming back to you (dumbbells have a way of bouncing crazily), but you can always control where you are when you start. You will have to rely on your dog's ability to do problem solving while jumping when he returns the dumbbell over the jump in Open exercises.

In the initial single-jump training you will be calling Rover to you over the jump. Sit him the appropriate distance away from the jump, go to the other side, and call him to you. Your jumping cue should be enough. Having worked back and forth and led him through the jumps, he should have no trouble grasping the concept of jumping to come to you. Work with all three kinds of jumps.

Applied targeting: Jumping for the retrieve

In the retrieve over high, on a single cue Bowser has to go away from you, take the jump, pick up the dumbbell, and take the jump coming back. Though you may not have a retrieve in place yet, you can begin to implant this concept using the target stick.

Set the target stick in the ground about 12 feet to the far side of the jump. Keep the jump low so that Bowser can easily see the stick. You have the cues "over" and "touch" to work with. Start with him at your side and give the "over" command. If he seems uncertain, lead him to the jump. When he takes the jump, say "touch." He should readily go to the stick. Repeat until he will go away from you, take the jump, and touch the stick on the single cue "over." As a rule, this does not take long because of Bowser's understanding—and enjoyment—of target work. You can gradually raise the height again. Don't go over shoulder height.

You also want Bowser to come back to you. Guess what? This is to some extent built into what you are already doing. You will click when he touches the stick. It is probable that Bowser is going to come back over the jump to get his treat. He may start to go around the jump, but you can easily avoid this by saying "over" when he turns from the target stick and starts to head back toward you. Most dogs quickly get the idea that whenever they *go out* over a jump, they are to *return* over that jump.

To make this informal chain complete, stop clicking when he touches the stick and instead give the "here" command. You may supplement it with "over" if Bowser seems at all confused as to what to do to get back to you. You now have a three-part *behavior chain:* over (and out), touch, over (and back). Since you are treating when he gets back to you, the danger is that the "touch" element will start to extinguish. Be careful about this. If necessary, move the stick farther away. Make sure that he goes all the way to the stick and touches it before coming back to you. As a fluency, the concept is that whatever task Fido is to complete before he comes back, he must be sure to complete it. You will find this discipline invaluable when you transition to formal retrieve training.

Although Rover will only encounter the bar jump once in Obedience in the Utility directed jumping exercise, there is no harm in going through this same routine with the bar jump. Indeed, there is a benefit in that Rover's jumping discipline becomes fully rounded.

Applied targeting: Broad jump

I discuss details of broad jump training in the Open chapter, Chapter 5. However, for fluency purposes, you want to instill one thing: Rover must learn to extend his line of travel well past the end of the broad jump boards. If you implant this as part of the jumping fluency, then when you add the front for competition purposes you will get a nice arc rather than a tight turn. Aside from maintaining consistency, you will help avoid injuries to Rover's front end caused by him turning too quickly after he lands to get to you (or, worse yet, turning in the air so that he lands on an angle).

To do this, use the same approach described earlier. Set the target stick in front of Rover on the left one-third of the jumps, about twelve feet past the last board. Leave Rover in position and walk to a place somewhere between the last board and the target stick. Cue him to take the jump and cue him to touch the stick. Click and treat.

Fade the "touch" cue so that Fido takes the jump and touches the stick on the single "jump" cue (this is a small behavior chain). When he is touching the stick regularly, add the informal recall. After he touches the stick, say "here," click, and treat when he comes to you. Bit by bit, fade the "here" cue.

Now, just as with the high jump, you have a three-part behavior chain: jump, touch, informal recall. Rover will perform the sequence on a single cue ("jump"). As before, make sure that the touch element does not disappear. The other important element for fluency purposes is that you move around. Starting somewhere between the last board and the target stick, move from one side of the boards to the other (while staying in that same general area), to various positions past the target stick, and to positions to either side of the boards between the first and last boards. In this way, Rover will become completely comfortable with going all the

way to the stick and coming back to you, wherever you are. This will make it relatively easy to formalize the position for competition purposes.

Jumping mishaps

No matter how much foundation work you do, mishaps can happen. A jump may be against a confusing background and Fido may crash into it. He may misjudge distance or height, and hit the jump. He may slip and fall on landing if the grass is wet or if he hits a slick spot. These things happen. An unexpected mishap, especially one that causes any physical shock, will be upsetting to the dog. You cannot allow yourself to become upset as well. Your job is to remain calm so that you can calm your dog. Do not act "happy"; that is mindless. Your dog has a right to expect your concern, and you have a right to be concerned.

The first thing to do is to get physical control of the dog and check for any injuries. Do this even if you are in the ring and you have to take hold of the dog's collar. If the judge decides to excuse you for handling your dog in the ring, so be it. Your dog's safety and well-being come first. Then check for any injuries. Look to see if there is any damage to the pads or nails on his feet. Gently massage his legs and chest to see if there is any sign of muscular strain or pain. If you are in any doubt, leave the ring or stop the practice session and tend to him.

The old adage about getting back on the horse after being thrown is true, and it holds good here as well. If you are in the ring and see no signs of real injury, you may decide to continue, even if it requires Spot to jump again. I generally don't recommend this because there is a good chance that Spot will refuse the next jump, and you may end up causing yourself even greater problems. Until February 1998 there was no way to resolve this problem while at a trial. Your only choice was to continue, or leave the ring with no immediate remedial measures available. Now that the AKC allows "training" on the grounds you can leave the ring, set up a low jump well away from the rings, and let Fido take a pass or two. Then pack up and let him rest.

If you are in training, walk Fido around a bit at first. Check his gait and stride for any signs of limping or uneasiness. If he seems completely comfortable walking, trot him a little bit, keeping an eye on how he is moving at all times. If you decide to let him jump again that day, lower the jump height four to six inches first. Get a couple of clean jumps in, and quit. This way you end on a positive note and Fido has conquered the obstacle. The only time not to do this is if you see real signs of injury.

If your dog is injured sufficiently seriously to require a break in your jumping program, you will have to take a few steps backward when you start again to rebuild his confidence and stamina. Don't rush it. The very worst thing that could happen would be to push a reintroduction to jumping too fast, and have a second mishap. That can create a repair job that could last a lifetime.

Always be ready to go back to kindergarten

Don't think of your cavaletti training as something you do early on and then forget about. As you progress through the heights and add distractions, you may find that Fido suffers temporary lapses of confidence. To some extent this is inherent in the learning process, and his confidence will return as he becomes comfortable with the new situation. But be watchful. If you start to think that any lessening of confidence is other than transitory, take him back to the cavalettis for a few sessions and let him get comfortable again.

Be especially ready to do this if you have any jumping mishaps that have led to injury. If your dog lays off jumping for a while after having been injured, it is quite possible that his confidence will suffer when you begin again. Going all the way back to what he knows best—the cavalettis—will be indispensable to restoring his mechanics and rebuilding his confidence.

Any healthy dog can learn to jump well. A confident, smooth-jumping dog is a joy to work with and to watch. Take your time, be consistent, patient, and fair, and you can get the most out of whatever breed you have.

"Find the one that smells the most like me"

This fluency is the basis for scent discrimination. You can introduce this after Fido is working comfortably with the target stick. It is not necessary that you have a retrieve in place, though if you do the game will go farther, faster.

Doing what comes naturally

Before going further, a simple point. There is no time, ever, in any of your training, at which you will be teaching Fido "how to scent." Dogs have an extraordinary ability to identify scent. Next to sleeping, scenting is what dogs do best. The problem, I submit, is not that Fido cannot distinguish your scent from others, nor easily learn that you want him to find the article that smells like you. The problem is ours: We humans have a lot of trouble trusting that the dog is really doing what we hope he's doing. This is because the dog's sense of smell is so extraordinary that we have nothing human that even remotely compares to it.

In his book *Tracking Dog,* Glen Johnson tells of training dogs to detect gas leaks in buried commercial gas pipelines. The initial training consisted of having the dogs find wooden pins saturated with butyl mercaptan (the additive that gives gas its smell). After the dogs had been working the actual pipeline, they would also locate wooden pins that had been thrown away weeks before. Johnson sent the pins to a laboratory to determine the concentration of mercaptan on them at that point. The laboratory reported that there was no detectable mercaptan on the pegs; the dogs had to be able to detect the mercaptan *at better than one part per trillion*—at distances of over forty feet.

Ian Dunbar writes that "In the dog it has been estimated that there are some 200 million olfactory cells compared with about five million in humans. However, the canine sense of smell is much more than forty times better than that of humans" (*Dog Behavior,* 1979). The difference is, as they say, geometric rather than arithmetic. Along with the ability to detect minute traces of scent, the dog's olfactory cells give the dog a processing mechanism that cannot be compared to that encompassed in any sensory organ that we humans have. The strongest single sensory organ we humans have is eyesight, but even our sense of sight (particularly our ability to distinguish color) is nowhere near as refined as the dog's sense of smell. I can, for example, discern hair color: "Heather is blonde." But if I am at a distance, or Heather's back is turned, I may well not be able to distinguish Heather from another blonde. A dog, on the other hand, can immediately identify Heather by her scent, whether she is alone or in a crowd, whenever she is close enough for her scent to carry, even in the dark.

We tend to trust the evidence of our own senses. Conversely, what our own senses don't tell us, we don't trust. Let me step away from scenting for a moment. You could condition an infant to select a green-colored object from a pile of variously colored objects, even before the infant knew conceptually what "green" was, by reinforcing the infant every time she selected the green-colored object. And you would know that the infant was "right" because you could verify her choice of "green" through your own senses: You know what "green" looks like, and you know that the infant's eyes are seeing what you are seeing.

It is not the same with dogs and their sense of smell. Simply, we have no idea what the dog is really perceiving with his nose; I can impart my scent to a leather article for 5 minutes, and it will still smell like leather to me. As Glen Johnson writes, "In scent work the dogs are asked to perform something which the trainer cannot see, hear or feel and whether the dog is actually performing correctly or not cannot be accurately deduced since the vagaries of scent are, as yet, a mystery. One correction applied when the dog is actually performing correctly could have a lasting detrimental effect."

In light of all that, allow me to suggest that we complicate our scent discrimination training *not because the dog needs it, but because we do.* If, however, we can take a leap of faith and decide simply to trust the dog to do what he knows how to do best, scent discrimination "training" need not be difficult at all.

As I said at the start, you are not teaching the dog "how to scent." Rather, you are teaching the dog what to search for and what to do when he finds the scent he is looking for. Johnson writes, "What a dog smells, or how scent behaves, or just what scent is, should not even enter the novice's mind when attempting to train a dog in tracking. The only important thing is the type of behavior desired in the finished product of a handler-dog team." What is true in tracking training is equally true in scent discrimination training. You want a certain behavior. A human really has no business interfering in the sensory processes that get the dog to the point at which that behavior appears.

Training scent discrimination simply means educating the dog as to *which article* out of several you want him to retrieve. The dog can easily tell the difference between a scented and an "unscented" article (I put "unscented" in quotes because there is always a scent on a given object, including some of your scent; it is simply not the scent we want the dog to identify). The dog can also easily tell the difference between your scent and that of anyone—or anything—else. Given that, establishing the scent discrimination fluency is simply a matter of communication: I want Rover to choose the one that *smells the most like me,* not the ones that smell like anything (or anyone) else.

Step one: Choose from one of two articles in hand

You are teaching the dog to select the object that bears your scent. The other objects may be "cold" (i.e., the scent is old) or may bear some other scent (that of another person, or just whatever scents attach to it in the ordinary course of day-to-day life). I know people who put the "unscented" articles in the refrigerator overnight, literally making them "cold." This is unnecessary, and in my opinion is simply another expression of human distrust of the dog's scent discrimination abilities.

Start with a leather article. Grip it tightly in your fist for three to five seconds. Do not "rub" it or spin it between your palms. *Your dog can pick up your scent!* You do not need to "heat it up." With Fido standing or sitting in front of you, present the article holding it by the end piece ("bell"). Let him put his nose to it (you are getting the benefit of your target and retrieve work here), and C/T (you will need a moment to get the treat, but that's okay; remember the *bridge* concept). You are not asking for a retrieve at this point; you are simply asking him to indicate the article. Right now you want his nose to work, not his jaws. Click and treat.

This introduction is purely informational; you have not Fido to make any choices yet. After a few repetitions, re-scent the first article and pick up a second ("unscented") article, so you are now hold-

With a little practice you can hold your clicker and scent article (or retrieving article, or target stick, or whatever) in one hand and still click when you need to.

ing one article in your left and one in your right hand. Hold the clicker between your thumb and the bell, as shown in the accompanying picture. There is no danger that holding both articles will confuse Spot. One article has your "fresh" scent on the bar, and one has no fresh scent there at all. Among other things, dogs are very adept at locating the *source* of a scent. Spot can readily distinguish between scent coming from your hand at the article's end, and scent on the bar. Now Spot has to make a simple choice: he has two he can indicate, but only one is correct. At first, he will indicate to each. C/T when he indicates the scented article. Repeat several times until each time you present the two articles he is going directly to the scented one.

Now, there is a chance of a certain **superstitious** association developing here. That is, the dog is not only indicating the article with your scent, he is indicating the article in your right hand. So you need to eliminate that association. Switch the scented article to your left hand. In every case when I have taken this step, Fido has gone immediately to the scented article. Why? Because scent is a very powerful source of information for the dog. Now that he knows what scent you want him to look for, that is where he is going to go. So while you need to make sure that you do not implant any superstitious association here, when you test it you are likely to see that there was no such association at all or, if there was any, it was very weak. After several repetitions of Fido touching the scented article in your left hand, switch the article back and forth between hands.

So far you have been relying exclusively on *offered behavior,* that is, Spot is "nosing" the article simply because it is there. Now that he is consistently indicating the correct article you are ready to add the cue. As Fido noses the correct article, say "find it" (or "find mine," whatever—I like "find it" because the two words come out crisply), click and treat. Repeat until the "nosing" behavior is on cue; that is, he does it in response to the cue and not otherwise.

Step two: Articles on floor

When Fido is (a) consistently indicating the correct article in hand, (b) on cue, you are ready to put the articles on the floor. Start with the same two articles. Place them about three feet away from where you are with your dog, and about twelve inches apart. Send Fido to the articles with the "find it"

As Morgan kneels in front of the sitting dog, Dylan indicates the scented article. Identifying an article that "smells like my owner," anywhere, any time, is a basic fluency that can be taught early in training.

cue. At first, you are still primarily concerned that he locate the correct article, so click when he indicates the correct article. If he has the retrieve impulse and picks it up, well and good. But remember that this is fluency training: The retrieve is not essential to what you are doing here. If Fido does pick the article up, you click, and he drops it, that is acceptable. Remember, "click ends the behavior." When you come to adding a full-blown retrieve into the exercise you will no longer click when he picks the article up, but when he returns it to you.

When Fido is consistently going to the correct article, move the two articles around in relationship to each other. Continue sending him out until he consistently goes to the scented article regardless of its position relative to the "unscented" article. Rescent the desired article from time to time to keep it "fresh." Remember, both articles bear your scent to some extent. You are always really asking Fido to find the one that "smells *most* like me," that is, the one with the *freshest* scent.

The next step is to vary the distance between the articles. On some repetitions put the two close together, perhaps even touching. On others, spread them two, three or four feet apart. Having the articles close together will tax Fido's ability to perform precise location. Spreading the articles far apart will develop his ability to keep looking. When you are satisfied that he is strong on both counts, add a third article. Retrace the sequence you did with two articles. Then add a fourth article, a fifth, and so on.

Step three: Vary the articles

Since this is fluency training and not specific training for the Utility scent discrimination exercise, you want to expand the dog's cognitive ability as far as possible. So, once Fido is reliable in selecting the scented article from among four articles of the same type (you can then be confident that the basic fluency is in place), add different sorts of articles. Put a spoon, or a toy, or a chewy on the ground. These are things that will really attract him for reasons other than scent. Keep the other articles there as well at first, so he will get the idea that the new things on the floor are somehow related to what he has been doing already. This teaches him that when he is "on the scent" he is to disregard everything and anything other than the source of the scent.

Step four: Hide the scented article

Now you will increase the level of difficulty by hiding the scented article. Don't make it too hard at first. Put it under a cloth or paper towel. Put it under an unscented article. Put it under a table, then under a chair (obviously, one that he can reach under with his nose). If you have drapes, put it under the drapes. The idea of this type of training is to teach Fido that the scented article is "out there," and that he must continue searching until he finds it. Escalate your level of difficulty as Fido becomes more tenacious.

When should I add the retrieve?

I add the retrieve element once Fido is picking the correct article off the floor out of a pile of three. This assumes, of course, that you have shaped the retrieve independently. If you have not, do not try to introduce it here. On the other hand, if your dog is an enthusiastic "play" retriever, let him play. Just make sure that Fido always brings the article to you. If you find him grabbing the article and taking off, you will have to spend time working on the retrieve ("deliver to me") fluency before going any farther with scent work. Don't let Fido get into the habit of treating scent work as an opportunity to play keep-away with you.

Novice—Or, Beginning Utility

To the person starting in competitive obedience, "Utility" has something of the same aura as a haunted house. You know it is there, you know there is something human about it, but it is awesome if not frightening to behold.

Utility is difficult. But in many ways it is a bigger leap from Novice to Open than from Open to Utility. In Novice the dog is always working at your side or coming to you. The big leap in Open is that there are three exercises (retrieve on flat, retrieve over high, and broad jump) in which the dog must work away from you. Once the dog learns to do so, you have crossed a major training obstacle. Everything you do in Utility has its roots in what you do in Novice and Open.

So I call Novice "Beginning Utility." Novice is not a distinct class with its own laws and rules. It is merely the first step down the long—and rewarding!—trail to the UD (Utility Dog), the UDX (Utility Dog Excellent), and (why not, if you are so inclined) the OTCh (Obedience Trial Championship).

The problem, I submit, is not so much that the advanced training is so hard, but that insufficient care is taken in the beginning training to establish proper fundamentals. All too many new handlers (myself included) find that after they have completed their first CD (Companion Dog) they have to "retrain" everything in order to go on to Open. Why? Poor fundamentals. You can squeak by and get a CD with weak fundamentals (I can no longer count the dogs I have seen get a CD who haven't a clue as to what "heel" means), but you cannot move into advanced training without them. The task is to shape the novice exercises in a way that gives you a solid foundation from which to move on to advanced work.

Here is a "flow chart" of the exercises as you progress through Novice, Open, and Utility. This flow chart illustrates the continuity between the classes, and the importance of what you train at the Novice ("Beginning Utility") level as foundation for everything that comes after.

Novice	Open	Utility
Heel on lead	Heel off lead	Signals
Figure-eight	Figure-eight	Moving stand
Heel off lead		
Stand for exam		Moving stand
Recall/front	Drop on recall	Signals recall
and finish	Retrieve on flat	Articles (2)
	Retrieve over	Directed retrieve
	Jump	Directed jumping (2)
	Broad jump	[Moving stand]
1-minute sit	3-minute sit	Sit on go-out
		Signals sit
3-minute down	5-minute down	Signals down

Let's look at the distribution of exercises more closely. The *sit* is everywhere. Every exercise except the long down *begins* with the dog sitting at heel, and every exercise in every class except the Novice stand for examination and the long down in Novice and Open *ends* with the dog sitting at heel.

The *stand* disappears in Open and reappears in Utility. The problem in Utility is that in both the signals exercise and the moving stand, the dog must "nail" an immobile stand in the heel position after heeling forward. For this reason, I include stopping and standing still in teaching the Novice stand. Both the Utility and Novice stand for examination should pose no problem for a dog that is well conditioned to being touched and handled.

The *down* appears once in Novice (long down), twice in Open (drop on recall and long down), and once in Utility (signals down). Nonetheless, in one way and another it is one of the most troublesome of exercises and accounts for a lot of failures in all classes.

Heeling is a constant through all classes. In Open and Utility, all heeling is off lead. Novice has both an on- and off-lead component, but in reality there is only heeling. The dog that is not reliable off-lead will not be reliable on lead. Many problems arise in going from Novice to Open because the dog's heeling seemingly "falls apart" in Open. But in fact the heeling was not reliable in the first place. The program laid out here has you training heeling off lead from the first day.

The *recall/front and finish* appears once in Novice, four times in Open, and six times in Utility (not counting the "call to heel" on the moving stand). Novice is therefore the place to establish all the necessary elements, most particularly a clear conception of "front," a "brisk" finish, and "heel position." These elements, plus a fast recall, are *fluencies* that if properly developed in early training will carry over nicely into advanced work. That is, once the dog is on its way back to the handler, it should know what to do: Get there quickly, line up in front, go on cue to the heel position. These elements should not have to be retaught with every exercise.

The *retrieve* is added in Open. It reappears in Utility in the scent discrimination (articles) and directed retrieve (gloves) exercises. You can also use the retrieve to teach go-outs for the directed jumping. Puppy and Novice training should incorporate play retrieves to make the dog comfortable early with the notion of "going away and coming back."

So with the exception of the formalized retrieve and jumping, the Novice exercises lay the foundation for everything else that is done in Open and Utility. Therefore, assuming physical soundness and a dedicated trainer, *any dog properly trained to a CD can progress to a UD.*

With that "can-do" spirit in mind, let's begin.

Heeling

"Heeling" is something handlers struggle with throughout their obedience careers. However, though it can be demanding to develop and maintain a well-heeling dog, you need not be intimidated by the prospect. Let's start with a comforting thought: If you have done your fluency work, you really do not have much to worry about.

Assuming you have done your fluency work, you have already accustomed Fido to left-side walking. Now, if you are interested in competition, you must progress to formal heeling. Don't be intimidated. If your dog indeed walks reliably and consistently at your left side, you will have no problem qualifying for your Novice title. Rover is at your left side, reasonably close, and if he is out of position from front to back at all, he is slightly forged. If he maintains that position throughout the heeling pattern, you will qualify in the heeling exercise.

But is not perfection required? No, not to qualify for a title. The AKC Regulations provide that: "In deciding whether a faulty performance of a particular exercise by a particular dog warrants a Qualifying score, the Judge shall consider whether the awarding of an obedience title would be justified if all dogs in the class performed the exercise in a similar manner" (C2, S3).

Yes, you will lose points to the extent that the dog's position is not exactly as described in the AKC Regulations, but you can and will qualify. Indeed, if your only interest is in attaining titles, "left-side walking" would probably carry you through all three classes. None of which means that there is nothing of interest for you in this chapter. You need to learn how to make consistent turns and changes of pace, and there are a few other nuggets you may benefit from. Simply say, don't approach heeling with a sense of dread.

Considerations for competition

Heeling is seemingly a simple thing: The dog and handler walk together, with the dog staying at the handler's left side. You don't have to think about what you are going to do next or choreograph anything in advance, because the pattern is called by the judge and there are only certain things you can be required to do. How tough can it be?

Tough enough that it can take up to two years to develop a reliable heeling dog (developing a

AKC Regulations

If you are going to compete, you have to know the rules that govern your conduct as a competitor. The AKC Regulations define the manner in which the exercises are to be performed, and also govern what a handler may and may not do in the ring and on the grounds of a trial. You owe it to yourself and to the sport of competitive obedience to know the Regulations and to comply with them.

All registries have their own Regulations, and if you are going to compete in other registries you must, of course, know what their Regulations are. It is, however, well beyond the scope of this book to attempt to cover all the variations between registries. So, when I talk about "the Regulations," I am talking about AKC Regulations. If I quote from the Regulations, I will cite the place quoted from with C# (for chapter) followed by S# (for section). So, for example, the accompanying quotation about qualifying scores is cited from Chapter 2, Section 3 (C2, S3).

The Regulations change from time to time. In February 1998 the AKC made a number of changes, most notably to allow a certain amount of "training" on the trial grounds and to lower the jump heights. You may now also put a festive collar on your dog if you like. Rumor has it that there will be an Advisory Committee selected to consider even further changes in 1999 or 2000. None of these changes affect the fundamentals of what I lay out in this book.

reliable heeling handler may take longer). When new teams progress from Novice to Open, the thing that falls apart most quickly is heeling—even though that was what they worked on most while training for the Novice ring. You will work throughout your dog's competitive career to keep the heeling reliable.

Teamwork is paramount

The AKC Regulations shed some light on the issue. The introductory section ("Purpose") states that "The performances of dog and handler in the ring must be accurate and correct and must conform to the requirements of these Regulations. However, *it is also essential that the dog demonstrate willingness and enjoyment of its work.*"

At C2, S2 ("Standard of Perfection"), the obedience judge is instructed to judge each dog and handler against that judge's "mental picture of the theoretically performance in each exercise." That standard "shall combine the *utmost in willingness, enjoyment and precision* on the part of the dog, and *naturalness, gentleness, and smoothness* in handling."

At C3, S5 ("Heel on Leash & Figure Eight") the Regulations state, "The principal feature of this exercise is the ability of the dog and handler to work as a team."

Absorb the significance of these passages. Read together, these sections emphasize one concept over everything else: *Teamwork is paramount.* So what is "teamwork"? The *American Heritage Dictionary* (3d ed.) defines "teamwork" as "cooperative effort by the members of a group or team to achieve a common goal." In order to have true teamwork, the dog must work with the "utmost in willingness and enjoyment." The dog that does not truly find its work reinforcing is not going to be a team player. On the other hand, in order to have "naturalness, gentleness, and smoothness in handling" the handler must have established true communication and understanding with the dog.

At C3, S6, the Regulations specify a number of heeling faults that may cause the team to fail, or to suffer substantial or minor deductions. But these are all components of the "principal feature" of the exercise: "the ability of the dog and handler to work as a team." They are the trees in the forest, so to speak. Returning to the point with which I began this chapter, if your dog will walk consistently with you while maintaining the "left-side walking" position, this is more than enough "teamwork" to constitute a qualifying performance in heeling in any class.

The essence of the heeling exercise is "cooperative effort" by the dog and handler "to achieve a common goal." There are several obstacles to achieving this ideal, not least of which is the lack of a common language (dogs don't speak English). So establishing a line of communication is essential. The task of the handler is manyfold. The handler must to know what she wants, be able to communicate that to the dog, and bring the dog to where the dog wants to work for what the handler wants.

Teamwork begins with the handler. The handler must "go to the dog" in order to build teamwork, because the dog has no independent concept of what this is all about. Scores, placements, titles,

First-and-Foremost and Schuman rankings, Top Gun, and the Cycle Tournaments, the AKC Invitational (see Appendix B), and all the other things we humans aspire to in this sport are unknown to the dog. The best the handler can do is make the dog "want" to please the handler by performing the heeling exercises in a certain way.

But we are talking about "cooperative effort," which means that along the way the dog must also develop some concept of his own responsibility in the act. As a rule, when a team fails heeling it is because the dog has not developed this sense. And this brings us back to the handler. Proper training, that is, operant conditioning, will engage the dog in earning reinforcers, and stimulate the dog to take some initiative in its performance. The goal of training heeling, then, is to bring the dog and handler into harmony as a team.

The fallacy of traditional training

I have discussed some of this already. But I ask that you indulge me a bit once more. If there is any exercise where traditional methods interfere with the learning, it is heeling. Therefore, the topic deserves special attention.

Traditional training methods are not really geared to accomplishing teamwork. Traditional training methods are derived from early military training techniques, in which "willingness and enjoyment" were not issues. The only issue was whether the dog performed or not. Traditional training methods pose training as a "contest of wills" between dog and handler, a contest that the handler must win. The principal technique for winning the contest is the consistent use of *aversives*, convincing the dog (in the case of heeling) that the "best" place to be is by the handler's side because the consequences of being elsewhere are so undesirable.

I am not going to comment on how dogs performed twenty or thirty years ago using these methods, because I was not involved in the sport then and cannot speak from personal experience. I can only say that in my experience of showing and teaching, I have found that the traditional methods fall short.

Almost every new dog first encounters heeling as ten weeks of unmitigated hell. In the very first week of public basic obedience class the dogs are on a choke chain and the handlers are stepping forward saying "Heel!", "popping" (usually with gusto),

"releasing," (occasionally—how many times do you hear the instructor say "Let those leashes go loose"?), and generally dragging the dog around in circles while the dog sniffs, lunges at other dogs, and every once in a while actually moves its feet in the same direction that the handler is moving. What does the word "heel" mean to the dog? "Oh, good. Now I get to be choked and dragged around while Boss walks away from me."

When that new handler decides to go forward into Novice competition, "heeling" has become a very unpleasant experience for dog and handler alike. Small wonder that so many Novice dogs do not truly demonstrate "willingness and enjoyment," heel poorly (but just well enough to earn that CD), and "fall apart" in Open.

Even handlers who work with "motivational" methods may find themselves resorting back to aversive methods in training heeling, on the theory that the dog has to learn that "it doesn't have a choice." Even assuming for the moment that the dog does in fact learn such a thing, conceptually it goes completely against the grain of what we are working to achieve. To say that one does not have a "choice" is to say that the action is compelled *against the will* of the actor. So how, then, do you produce a dog that works with "willingness and enjoyment" by a method that denies the dog the opportunity to choose his actions? To say that one does not have a "choice" is to say that one is performing without any sense of purpose. How do you develop "teamwork" with a partner that has no purpose of his own?

And of course, given the opportunity, the dog always "chooses" what he is and is not going to do. Compel the dog all you will when he's on lead, once that lead comes off something other than compulsion must be at work in order for the dog to perform. *The dog must "choose" to heel* (my apologies to Dawn Jecs and her book by that title, no infringement intended)—or you don't have a dog that will heel. Go to any trial you want and you will see the dog who "sparkles" on lead and disappears when off lead: lagging, sniffing, stopping dead in his tracks, and so forth.

You may often hear the term "ringwise" applied to such a dog. But that is an excuse, not an explanation. Why does this happen? Perhaps the simple answer is deceptive, but I think it true: *It happens because the dog is not willing to heel.* And you cannot develop "willingness" through compulsion.

AKC Titles

The titles mentioned in this book are the obedience titles awarded by the AKC. The first three titles you can attain are:

- Companion Dog (CD—Novice)
- Companion Dog Excellent (CDX—Open)
- Utility Dog (UD—Utility)

To *qualify* for each of these titles you must attain a score of at least 170 *and* at least 50% of the available points in each exercise, in three trials (called "legs") under three different judges. If you have never shown a dog to an AKC obedience title or co-owned a dog that has been shown to an AKC obedience title, you may first compete in Novice A. Once you have your first CD, you will start your next dog in Novice B. Open A and Utility A are for *dogs* that do not have their CDX or UD, unless they are owned by an obedience judge or a person who has put an OTCh on any dog. In order to compete for the CDX you must have your CD. In order to compete for the UD, you must have your CDX.

Once you have attained the UD you may compete for

- Utility Dog Excellent (UDX)
- Obedience Trial Champion (OTCh)

This UDX was first established in 1994. To attain it you must *qualify* in both Open B and Utility B at the same trial ten times. Placements are irrelevant. In my humble opinion, this is a true test of the consistent working dog.

To win the Obedience Training Champion Title, or OTCh, you must attain at least 100 points, which you earn by placing first or second in Open B or Utility B. The points are calculated based on the number of dogs actually competing in the class. You must also have at least one first place in both Open B and Utility B, as well as another first place in either. You are not required to show in both classes at any given trial. Typically, only between eighty and ninety OTCh titles are awarded annually.

There are other registries awarding titles, such as the Canadian Kennel Club (CKC) and the United Kennel Club (UKC, which now also includes the American Mixed-Breed Origin Registry [AMBOR]). The title structure in these other registries tracks the AKC system through the UD. Some do and some do not have an Obedience Trial Championship or equivalent. One quirk among the various registries is that if you have an AKC title in a given class, all other registries will require you to compete in the B class when going for that same title; however, the AKC does not recognize titles from other registries, so you could have Novice titles on your first dog from three non-AKC registries, and when you entered an AKC trial you would still be showing in Novice A.

Shaping heeling as a long-duration behavior

A side-step here. Heeling is a *long-duration behavior*. I distinguish it from behavior chains in that, although there are a number of maneuvers that must be performed, they are not performed in any given sequence or pattern, or in response to a series of cues. Heeling is a single behavior maintained over time and distance. And while there are certain basic patterns that most judges use (Appendix C), it is disadvantageous to "anticipate" the pattern. I have seen many judges adjust the pattern slightly here and there throughout the day to catch the handlers who have memorized it. You do best in the ring when you "go with the flow."

The one and only constant in heeling is that the dog must maintain heel position, whatever the handler is doing: whether the handler is moving at a fast, normal, or slow pace, turning, or coming to a halt. If we treat heeling as a long-duration behavior, the training task is to develop the dog's "willingness" (and ability) to maintain heel position throughout all these variations.

"Look ma, no hands . . ."

It is my view that, in competition, there is no such thing as "off-lead" as opposed to "on-lead" heeling. There is only heeling. You need a leash in the

Novice obedience ring because the AKC says that the first round of heeling is to be done on lead. But on or off lead, the dog has the exact same job to do. And if the dog cannot heel properly without compulsion, it will not heel properly with leash attached.

The leash is a decoration that the AKC requires the Novice team to wear part of the time they are in the ring. It is otherwise useless at best, because you cannot use it to make any leash "corrections." Doing so can cost you points, and possibly cause you to fail the exercise (C3, S6: "If a dog is unmanageable, or if its handler constantly controls its performance by tugging on the leash . . . the dog must be scored zero"). Though the language of the Regulations scores *the dog* zero, in reality it is the handler who fails. If you must "constantly control its performance by tugging on the leash," then you have not trained your dog properly.

So drop the "leather crutch" while training. Teach your dog to heel off lead from the beginning, and teach heeling only once. Your training will develop through true communication. You won't get deluded into believing the dog "understands" what is required when in fact the dog is only responding to the leash. You will always know exactly what the dog can really do.

As I go through all the following discussions you will get the distinct impression that I am very conscious of footwork. You will be correct. For most of us, when we go in the ring our minds go blank. Tension and concentration overwhelm thought. As you begin to compete you will do things in the ring that will astound you by their stupidity. But that's why God invented laughter. In 1997 Dylan was in Top Dog, a southern California competition to choose a team to compete against other teams in a multistate competition. We had made it into the runoff round in Open. We started off fine, but then I was sure I heard the judge say "left turn." I started to turn left, and realized I was walking into the broad jumps. "Snap!" went my steel-trap mind: The judge obviously had not called for the left turn. So I did a little sidestep and got back going straight, made the about turn when the judge called for it, stepped into a pothole, and started stumbling toward the center of the ring. I righted myself at the halt, and somehow managed to get through the rest of the pattern without causing harm to myself or others.

Okay, I was a klutz. All I could do was laugh. But the amazing thing was that all throughout Dylan did his darnedest to hold heel position. That's a dog

---

It's Always Something

Dylan was the first dog that I trained completely with the methods I describe in this book. He has never had a "leash correction" in his life. I have trained him in every exercise in every class off-lead. He learned left-side walking, and that was all I insisted on during his first year of life. In his second year I began shaping more precise heel position. When he turned 2, I entered him in his first match.

The week before the match, it suddenly dawned on me that he had never had a leash on him while working, and that it might be a good idea to introduce him to the leash in practice. He was deeply offended. He reacted like a wild horse on a halter for the first time. Seemed to me he went out of his way to get tangled up in the darned thing. It took about three sessions before he would tolerate the leash, and it took much longer than that before he stopped giving me a disgusted look.

It's always something. . . .

---

that knows what he has to do, and is willing to do it. We missed making the team by one point.

Experienced handlers "go into a zone" where they are so focused on the dog that a bomb could go off outside the ring and they probably wouldn't hear it. When I am really focused on my dog all that exists in the world is me, my dog, a wall of white noise, and a disembodied voice telling me where to go, and when. In that "zone" I am not thinking about anything; I am on automatic pilot.

So, develop your mechanics to such a point that they are automatic. *You don't want to have to think about what you are doing when you are in the ring.* The time to think is when you are practicing. When you are competing, repetition and muscle memory should take over.

Work out and practice your footwork *without the dog,* until *you* perform each maneuver the same way every time. Then, when you add the dog, you can put your attention on what the dog is doing without having to worry about what you are doing. The dog can learn the routine with confidence because he will learn that each maneuver takes place in its own, consistent way. Being able to go on "automatic pilot" can be a real life-saver in the ring when the un-expected happens—and it usually does.

The "heel" cue

Throughout the shaping program that follows you will *never* tell the dog to "heel." The goal of the program is to condition the dog to regarding heel position as completely reinforcing and the best possible place in the world to be (unless he's in front position, but that's another story). The dog *chooses* to be there because it is reinforcing. He *wants* to maintain heel position because it is a completely positive experience.

But don't you have to use the "heel" command in the ring? No. There are two sections in the Regulations that apply (C2, S20, and C3, S5). The pertinent parts read as follows:

C2, S20: Moving forward at the heel without any command or signal other than the natural forward movement of the handler's body shall not be considered as anticipation.

C3, S5: [On the judge's order "Forward"] The handler *may give a command or signal to Heel,* and shall walk briskly and in a natural manner with his dog on a loose leash. . . . *It is permissible* after each Halt, before moving again, for the handler to give a command or signal to Heel (italics added).

So a verbal command (cue) to "heel" is not required. It is a matter of **stimulus control.** What does stimulus control mean in this context? It means that the dog becomes conditioned always to move with you when you move (and sit when you stop) *unless* you tell him otherwise. Put another way, *movement* is the "default." "Stay where you are" is the exception. There is nothing more "natural" in the world than that a dog should walk by the side of his owner. All we are going to do is bring that so completely natural event into the formalized presentation required for the Obedience ring.

Getting started

If you are working a "green" dog (that is, a puppy or a dog that has had no prior obedience training), you will work your way up to heeling through a sequence of increasingly formal training steps. If your dog has already been exposed to heeling, then you are simply going to "go back to kindergarten."

Before getting to specifics, let's take a minute to review what is meant by "heel position." The AKC Regulations (C2, S18) give a complete definition:

The Heel position as used in these Regulations, whether the dog is sitting, standing, lying down, or moving at heel, means that the dog shall be *straight in line* with the direction in which the handler is facing, *at the handler's left side,* and *as close as practicable* to the handler's left leg *without crowding,* permitting the handler freedom of motion at all times. The area *from the dog's head to shoulder* shall be in line with the *handler's left hip.* [all italics added]

All of the italicized portions of this description constitute the *criteria* for "heel position." These criteria are expanded on in the Regulations somewhat at C3, S5 and C3, S6. The one additional criterion in this section is that "At each order to Halt, the handler will stop and his dog *shall sit straight and promptly in the Heel position* without command or signal, and shall not move until the handler again moves forward on order from the judge" [italics added]. There are additional elements of "naturalness" that apply to the handler, but these issues are not really the subject of this book. I will discuss them "on the side" at various places throughout.

Remembering that you only train for one criterion at a time, in training "heel," in this program you train the criteria in this sequence:

(1) Dog at left side.
(2) Closeness to left side without crowding.
(3) Facing straight in line with same direction as handler.
(4) Area between dog's head and shoulder in line with handler's left hip.
(5) Sit at heel (a) promptly and (b) straight.

In this sequence, each element most naturally builds on the one(s) preceding it.

Now you may find that with any given dog some of the elements seem to come together more naturally if done in a slightly different sequence. I have found that the sequence listed will produce the most reliable results, but if your "feel" for your own dog leads you to alter it in some particular, that's OK. As Karen Pryor says, "There are as many ways to shape a behavior as there are trainers to think them up." So if you want to improvise, do it. If it works, great. If it doesn't, at least you have had a relatively harmless learning and training experience. If you do shuffle things around somewhat, think about it ahead of time. Plan the changes and have a clear reason in your mind for doing it the way you are going to do it. Your feel for your dog may lead you in a certain direction, but if you cannot articulate a clear plan and rationale, you are better off sticking with the "recipe" until you can do so. The only real "mistake" in this context is to proceed without thinking.

Don't worry about "attention"

In discussing *fluencies*, I did not list "attention" as a fluency for obedience. And although I said that I am not worried about "attention" as much as I am about "focus," no doubt you expect that at some point I will talk about "how to get attention." I am not going to do so. "Attention," meaning that the dog watches you closely, is a product of "focus," that is, the dog's involvement in the work. In turn, the dog's involvement in the work is a product of reinforcement. Though people who see Dylan frequently remark that "He is always watching you!," the reality is that we have not spent so much as a minute on "attention training" as such. Attention comes from the dog's willing involvement in what he is doing.

Nothing in the Regulations requires that the dog appear to be "paying attention" to the handler while heeling. It is true that if the dog is not paying attention he will not heel well, but I believe this is better understood as mental "focus." If the dog's mind is on his work, he will be focused, and in order to maintain focus the dog will keep an eye on you. That is all you really require. You may expect, even "demand" focus. But true focus will develop organically in the dog as the dog becomes aware, step by step, of what is required to maintain heel position and, more generally, to perform his work properly.

A while ago, here in southern California, there was a great competitive Irish setter named Daisy. She rarely lost more than half a point on heeling and was odds-on to win High Combined in any trial that she entered. Her head carriage was natural, not "eyes-up." Her gait was natural, not "dancin' and prancin'." But she never lost position. She knew what she had to do, she was a willing worker, and she performed consistently well. She was always a joy to watch.

If you watch any Obedience competition, however, you will see any number of dogs with a stylized, "heads-up" attention posture, head cranked to the right and up looking directly at the handler's face. This head position is not necessary in order to produce good heeling, nor is it anything that a judge can score you on (and admit it). The posture does produce a "dancin', prancin' " gait, which can at least make it look as if the dog is performing with "willingness and enjoyment," but a dog can certainly demonstrate those qualities without it.

Head position as such is mere artifice. I have only two concerns: that the head be at least parallel with the ground (prevents sniffing), and that the head be cocked toward my leg (if you picture yourself on a "clock," you are facing 12:00; any "cocking" toward 1:00 is acceptable). Otherwise, let the dog choose the position that is most natural and comfortable for him. Woody watched my calf. Sam watches anywhere from my knee to my hip. Dylan has his head up (of course, this doesn't prevent him from forging, it only makes him swivel his head in an almost supernatural fashion when he does so). Each chose the position most comfortable for him.

There was and is only one constant: When sitting at heel, each dog's head is up, watching me. My instant cue that things are "off" in the ring is when the dog looks away. The dog that is not looking at the handler while sitting at heel is either distracted, disinterested, or avoiding the situation. None of these things are the dog's fault. If the dog is consistently distracted the handler has failed to make the work the most reinforcing thing for the dog to do. The same goes if the dog is disinterested. And if the dog is avoiding the situation, the handler has somehow made the process distasteful or unpleasant for the dog. So why "correct" the dog's gaze? Tend to your job of making the obedience work the most reinforcing event in the dog's universe and you will see your dog develop focus while "attention" problems melt away.

Think about yourself in grade school. It's spring. A balmy breeze is blowing. Yesterday was Sunday and you were playing in the park, riding the merry-go-round, having some fried chicken, maybe napping under a tree. Ah, bliss. But today is Monday and Miss Crabtree is trying to teach you long division. Do her demands that you "pay attention, young man!" gain her any more of your attention than she already had? Perhaps for a moment, but all she is really getting is the appearance of attention. You look at her, so you look as if you are paying attention. But your mind's on baseball. The light's on, but nobody's home.

It's the same for your dog. If you are "losing" your dog, reexamine what you are doing. Why is the dog not interested? Answer that question! Find, in Ian Dunbar's words, the way to make the work "relevant" to the dog. That is how you'll "get your dog back." Leash "pops" are not the answer. They will only add aversion to the "mix." They will not bring you a flea-hop closer to real involvement and communication.

A word of caution about "perfection"

In recent years a trend has emerged of handlers learning under highly demanding instructors. There are instructors who decide for their students when they are "ready to show." I have seen cliques of such students at trials be upset because one of their number came out of the ring with "only" a 198.5. This creates a lot of pressure on the handlers, and has introduced an artificial degree of competitiveness into even the Novice A classes. Don't get sucked in. Competitive obedience should be reinforcing to you as well as to the dog; it won't be if you impose artificial expectations on yourself.

You can *shape* very consistent, precise performance through careful escalation of your *criteria*, combined with a clear sense of what you are looking for. If you want to be a highly competitive exhibitor, then you must watch the exhibitors who are highly competitive now and see what they and their dogs look like in the ring. Form your own "mental image of perfection."

But there is another side to it. You get to choose your own poison. You can participate in Obedience competition for a long time and accomplish a great deal without pressuring yourself to be "perfect" (which, in competition Obedience, means only that you did nothing that warranted a half-point deduction). If you do not want to put this kind of pressure on yourself, don't. You have to find a perspective that makes the sport reinforcing for you.

Part of this requires that you define your goals in a way that suits your temperament, your abilities, and the time you have to put into your training. The other part is to be reasonable in your expectations. As a rule, in *operant conditioning* you get the be-

havior you shape for. You will not attain that for which you do not strive. There's nothing wrong with being satisfied with heeling deductions of one or two points (a perfect score on each heeling exercise in Novice is forty points; when a handler says "we have one-point heeling" she means "we never get deductions of more than one point"). Yes, perfect heeling means zero deductions. But if you are working for one- to two-point heeling, and that is what you get, do not fret because your heeling is not "perfect." It is not what you are training for. In short, do not waste your time and energy envying those who do better. You can join them if it is worth it to you to put in the time and effort required. Be clear with yourself about what you want from yourself and your dog, work for it and rejoice when you get it—whatever it is.

Criterion 1: Dog at left side

If you have a "crossover" dog, you may think this is already a given. Don't kid yourself. I have seen too many dogs lose left-side heel position, even in top national competitions, to believe that this is something one can assume is established.

Begin informally. Simply walk with the dog. Because you are off-lead, begin in an area that poses no potential risks for the dog, such as your backyard or a fenced-in area like a tennis court. Get the dog moving, and as the dog moves toward and with you, maneuver easily so that the dog is on your left side. When the dog is at your left, C/T, and start walking again.

A note here: "Click ends the behavior." So when you click, if Fido bounces out of position to get his treat, do not worry about it.

If you are off lead, the dog will at some point wander away from you. Safety is not a concern at this point because you are working in a safe area. Right? OK. What do you do? Essentially, nothing. If you have the room, walk away from the dog in an ambling manner. If you don't have the room, just wait until the dog looks back at you, then start walking away from the dog. The dog will gallumph over to catch you. As soon as the dog is at your left side and has taken a couple of steps (only enough to confirm the position!), C/T and release.

No commands! No cheerleading!

It is vitally important that you *do not* introduce any verbal commands or "inducements" or "cheerleading" to get the dog at your left side. This sort of silliness will only confuse the issue. Reinforcement must flow from one thing and one thing only: the dog assuming the correct left-side position. Let the dog grasp and absorb that connection through simple shaping tactics on your part. Walk, maneuver if you must to get the dog on your left side, C/T. Rover will quickly grasp your point. Then he will start to "offer" left-side position. Now, heel position is something he has chosen for himself. From now on, it will be more and more reliable.

Variable reinforcement (VR)

I discussed in Chapter 2 the differences between *variable* and *continuous reinforcement* schedules. Heeling is the sort of behavior that must be developed through a variable reinforcement schedule. So you are going to build the dog's tolerance for walking in the left-side position incrementally. Start with one step, then three, then five. Once you are at five steps, go to VR schedule 1 (Appendix A). Proceed through Level 3. You must get Fido walking at least sixty feet in a straight line, maintaining constant heel position, before you can add turns or changes of pace.

Remember! You can only train for one criterion at a time. So don't worry about anything other than the dog staying on your left side. Don't make being close to you a contingency for reinforcement at this point. You'll get to that later. Similarly, don't worry about forging (if you did "left-side walking" you conditioned a certain amount of forging into the position already, so if you are still getting it now, accept it), "straight in line," or even quick (or any) sits. You are working for one thing and one thing only: covering long distances with Fido reliably walking at your left side.

Criterion 2: Close to left side without crowding

If your experience is typical of most people I work with, you will find that left-side work also brings the dog in closer simply because that's where the reinforcement centers. Nonetheless, you want to make sure the dog understands that "close" is part of the equation.

This is the type of thing trainers who revert to compulsion are talking about when they say the dog must understand it "doesn't have a choice." In learning "left side," the dog "chooses" to move closer to you. But even if the dog weren't particu-larly close, so long as you were shaping only "left side" you would still deliver the reinforcement. "Close" is a happy by-product. But it cannot be *only* a happy by-product. The dog *must* maintain a position "as close as practicable to the handler without crowding" throughout the heel pattern.

But to say that Fido must maintain a "close-in" position does *not* mean that he must be *physically forced* to assume a "close-in" position. Once you are getting "close," begin to reinforce it specifically. Now, reinforcement will become conditional on the dog not only being on your left side, but being as close as the Regulations require. This is sufficient to establish and "enforce" this criterion. From the dog's point of view, though, this isn't too hard. As I said, in many cases the process of shaping "left side" will bring the dog in close. Indeed you may find more of a problem with crowding than with going wide away from you.

If you have trouble establishing "closeness" with straightforward shaping, you may use the target stick here to establish the desired position. Hold the stick across the front of your body so that the target end is just a few inches past your left side. Now, to touch the stick the dog must get closer to you. Start with a single step, C/T, and increase distance as Fido becomes consistent.

Don't have Fido follow the target stick indefinitely. Once you have reinforced the "close-in" position, *fade* the target stick by holding it at your right side and only bringing it across for Fido to touch occasionally. You can give the "touch" cue if you find it necessary; very often the dog responds to the sight of the stick by seeking to touch it without the need for any cue.

You are now adding a new criterion ("close in"), so you must relax existing criteria, of which there are two: left side, and distance. You will still be insisting on left side, so you must relax distance. Therefore, do not start at VR Level 3, but go back to the beginning. One step, then three, then five, then go to VR as before.

Criterion 3: Dog faces in the same direction as the handler

This may sound almost superfluous. "Same direction" has come to be construed not simply to mean that the dog and handler are walking along the same line of travel, but that the dog's body is parallel to the handler's body. This is not always easy to attain. Many dogs "crab out" (rear end

Improving heeling with the target stick: Angel is a little wide (a) so Ethel uses the target stick to bring her in a little closer (b) and gets a nice, close sit-at-halt (c). Click!

pushes out to the dog's left). You will often see this with dogs that have poor front-end structure, limiting their ability to "drive" with their front legs. You also see it in younger dogs with good structure who simply have not yet fully learned to match the power of their rear legs with their front legs.

Properly understood, crabbing is not necessarily a bad thing. Crabbing is often a result of drive and enthusiasm. Lagging dogs don't crab, and crabbing dogs don't lag, and if there is anything you don't want, it's a lagging dog. So while the dog must learn not to "crab out," that is, must learn to work its front and rear together, crabbing is definitely not something you want to "correct." Help the dog develop the necessary physical discipline and the problem will resolve itself in good time.

Crabbing happens while moving for various reasons. As always, first look to yourself. Three common handler training errors contribute to crabbing: slow pace, use of food to lure the dog into heel position, and use of food to teach the dog an artificial "focus point."

As an example of the latter, many handlers teach their dog to focus on their left hand, which they carry at their belt buckle. Some trainers train their dogs to "push" for the food, driving at the handler's left hand. When that "push" is combined with the hand position, it forces the dog to "wrap" its head around the handler's left leg. This can cause forging and crowding, and it also causes the dog's rear end to swing out to the left.

Changing the "focus point" doesn't really address the problem. To do so requires a lot of retraining, and the handler will first have to establish and then eliminate artificial "focus points." The simplest way to avoid the problem is not to create it in the first place. Teach the dog what proper heel position is, let the dog choose his own "focus point," and be consistent with your own mechanics.

Pick up the pace

In competition, the handler must maintain a "brisk pace," which the Regulations define as "keenly alive, alert, energetic." Very often, crabbing results from the handler walking too slowly. Judges are not very consistent about enforcing "brisk pace," but if you do not maintain a brisk pace you will cause other heeling faults that the Judge will dock you for. These include forging and not being straight in line with you, and may also include crooked or forged sits. As with tugging on the leash, the errors are attributed to the dog on the scoresheet, but they are faults caused by the handler.

Now, most of us don't walk at a brisk pace unless we are going somewhere with a purpose. We stroll, we amble, we may even mosey, but we don't maintain a "brisk pace" very often, much less indefinitely. So you must consciously develop a "brisk pace." One good way to do this is to use a metronome. A good pace is at about 120 steps per minute, or two steps per second. Depending on your size, length of stride, and the size of your dog, you may go slightly up or down from there.

Most Novice handlers move too slowly. This is partly because most Novice handlers are not certain of what they are doing. This tendency is magnified by the related tendency to worry about what the dog is doing. This leads the Novice handler to stare at the dog. If the dog then starts to lag, the handler starts slowing down (usually inadvertently) to match the dog's pace. I've seen some that look as if they're going into reverse. Any noticeable adaptation of handler's pace to that of the dog is scoreable and could cause a failure (C3, S6: "if [the dog's] handler . . . adapts pace to that of the dog, the dog *must be scored zero*"). *The best cure for moving too slowly during heeling is for the handler to practice footwork and pace until all the movements are automatic.*

The best cure for the lagging dog is to pick up the pace, not slow down. There's a bit of role reversal at work here: The dog that gets the handler to slow down for the dog has done a nice job of shaping on the handler. Practice at a brisk pace, and do not reinforce laggardly work by the dog. Then maintain that same briskness at all times in the ring. I even like to have my dogs trot or run between exercises to the next starting point. This is a variation on the theme of working for *zero latency*. Work quickly at all times.

Arcing to the right

Along with picking up the pace, you can solve crabbing by walking in a long arc to your right. Visualize the arc as half of a football. Start with a diameter of about twenty feet and work up to a diameter of about one hundred feet. The dog will have to reach with his front legs in order to maintain position. As you see the dog starting to reach with his front legs, C/T to reinforce that specific muscular action. If you cannot see what your dog is doing, use a "spotter." Have a training partner stand out to your left and watch the dog. When your spotter sees the dog reaching, the spotter will C and you will T. When you give the treat in this manner, be sure to give it forward from the dog so the dog continues to reach as he gets the treat.

These methods, combined with the "rear-end consciousness" work you have already done in developing fluencies, will resolve virtually all of the "crab-out" problems you may have. Early on in my shaping work I used a clear plastic dowel riding on the dog's left flank to help "remind" him to keep his rear end in, but I no longer find it necessary. The fewer tools I can use in training, the better. Accurate reinforcement does the trick.

Arcing to left

As you progress in keeping the dog's flank in while moving on a straight line, you can intensify the lesson by moving in arcs to the left. In order to maintain heel position, the dog must consciously work his rear end "in."

When you were arcing to the right you began with a short arc and extended it. This is because you were building the dog's "reach" with the front legs. In this exercise, you do the reverse. Begin with a hundred-foot arc, and gradually close it. In this way you will incrementally the dog's ability to work his rear end "in." This will lay a foundation for the left turn.

Criterion 4: Area from dog's head to shoulder in line with your left hip

This is a description in the Regulations that is often confusing. The Regulations do not require that the dog's *head* be in line with your left hip. Rather, it is "the area from the dog's head to shoulder" that must be aligned. This covers a bit more territory. The dog's head begins at the tip of the nose. The "shoulder" is where the neck joins the body (the "withers"). As long as any part of the area spanned by those two points is in line with your left hip, the dog is in proper "heel position."

As a practical matter, the judges aren't that generous. Why? The judge has three responsibilities: (1) to qualify the dogs that should qualify, (2) not to qualify the dogs that should not qualify, and (3) to correctly place the top four dogs (for placements). The first two are relatively easy. But with the highly refined skills of so many handlers, the judges cannot accurately identify and separate the top four dogs without being very picky about small details. In many ways, scoring focuses heavily on heel position and straight sits.

For this reason, you can expect that if the dog's nose is in line with your left hip you will be nicked for a lag. Similarly, if the dog's shoulder is in line with your left hip, you can expect to be nicked for a forge. These will be half-point deductions only, but

During heeling and other at-heel exercises, it is not the dog's head that should be in line with your left hip, but "the area from the dog's head to shoulder."

those half-point "hits" add up in a hurry. Remember, too, in Novice you have to do the heel pattern twice (once on lead, once off). Double the pleasure, double the fun, double the deductions. You must also be aware that small faults can become big ones in a hurry. A slight forge can become a big forge on the "slow," or lead to crowding and bumping in left turns or the figure-eight. A slight lag can lead to a large lag on the "fast," or heeling wide or lagging on right or about turns.

There is another issue. The amount of "fail room" you have in this regard will vary greatly depending on the size of your dog. The person heeling an Irish wolfhound has a lot more room to work with than the person heeling a miniature pinscher. On the other hand, if a large dog is out of position it is *really* noticeable. The safest thing to do is shape the dog to maintain a position in the middle of the "head to shoulder" span. The easiest target point for you to use in identifying this position for yourself is the dog's ears.

Once you know what it looks like for the dog to be properly aligned with your hip, you have to teach the dog how to identify that position. This is easily done as a "targeting" exercise. Use the target stick to establish the desired position, just as you did with "close-in."

So it's back to one step at a time. Have the dog sitting at heel—(1) at your left side, (2) as close as practicable without crowding, (3) facing in the same direction you are, (4) with the area between the dog's head and shoulder in line with your left hip). Hold the target stick so that the dog can touch it without moving from heel position. You will probably see the dog "nosing" at the touchstick while sitting. If so, C/T. This will confirm the association with the touchstick in this new context.

Now take one step forward. *No command!* All your shaping to date has reinforced the dog for moving when you do, so the dog should move with you. As the dog moves forward, move the target stick forward so that it is directly in front of the dog's nose. If he touches the stick spontaneously, C/T. If you perceive any uncertainty either in the dog moving off with you or in touching the stick when moving, say "touch" as you step forward. This duplicates your initial shaping with the target stick and should make almost instant sense to the dog.

Build distance as you did before, using the VR schedule in Appendix A. This is now very familiar ground to the dog, so you will find it progressively easier to work with the schedule.

What to do about existing criteria

Your only concern here is the dog's alignment with your hip. You are not going to worry about the other, existing criteria. You will likely find that, with the possible exception of "straight in line," those criteria will hold together pretty well, if only because they are integral to the dog developing an understanding on this one. "Left side" goes without saying by now. Proper positioning of the target stick will maintain the "close" criterion. You may find the dog crabbing again as he drives for the touchstick, but if you are not inducing this by moving the touchstick too far forward and you are maintaining proper pace, any crabbing should disappear by itself.

Criterion 5: Sit at halt

At C3, S5 of the Regulations it states that:

At each order to Halt, the handler will stop and his dog *shall sit straight and promptly* in the Heel position without command or signal, and shall not move until the handler again moves forward on order from the Judge [emphasis added].

We know what "straight" means. The Glossary defines "prompt" as "without hesitation, immediate, quick." In other words, there should be no hesitation in the dog's sit. The instant you are halted, the dog is "sat."

When the dog doesn't sit immediately as the handler halts, it's the handler's fault. There are several things that can cause a slow sit or a no-sit, and the handler is responsible for each one. *"Focus"* is one of them. And again, I don't mean some "focus posture" or "focus point," but actual mental engagement of the dog in the work. *Pace* is important as well. The dog must be able to distinguish between the transition into a "slow" and the transition to a halt. It is not uncommon to see Novice dogs sit on the "slow" because the handler's pace causes the dog to misread the action. Consistent footwork is critical; the dog should be so clear about what is happening that he is sitting *just* as you come to a halt.

A note on scoring

The sit is not a "principal part" of the heeling exercise. In other words, you aren't going to fail if the dog doesn't sit at halt. All scoring is done on the basis of minor and substantial deductions. A "minor" deduction consists of up to two and a half points; a "substantial" deduction is any deduction of three points or more, all the way up to a failure for the exercise. If your dog fails completely to sit, this will usually earn you a three-point deduction. The typical pattern will have at least two and often three halts, so a failure to sit at each halt would mean six to nine points off. A slow sit will usually earn you a half to one point, depending on the degree of slowness. Again assuming three halts, this is one and a half to three points off.

The greater problem arises with crooked sits, because they can cause multiple deductions. For example, the dog can be (a) wide, (b) not straight, and (c) lagged or forged, each of which would be worth half a point. If the dog also skews around in front of you so that he is in your way when you start up again, then the dog is (d) substantially out of heel position and (e) has interfered with the handler's freedom of motion. These too should be penalized.

In training, the key is *latency.* Throughout your training, reinforce only the quickest sits. Do not give Fido extended amounts of time to decide whether to sit or not. If your footwork cues are consistent, Fido should be settling into the sit just as you are coming to a halt.

I train on the principle that a quick sit will be a correct sit. The more time Rover takes to "think" about what he's going to do, the greater the likelihood is that what he does will be wrong. The sit should be automatic. When developing this with Dylan he was so conditioned to sitting that he would even sit on the about turn if I gave him any footwork that looked like a "halt" cue. I discuss how to differentiate the sit from turns and the "slow" pace later on.

Footwork for the sit

The goal is for the dog to sit *as you complete your halt.* You now must introduce some formality into your footwork. I find the quickest sits come with a two-step halt; that is what I will describe here. If you prefer a three-step halt, fine. As always, the only real issue is the reasoning behind your choice.

I always used a three-step halt until I started working with Dylan. It gave me a nice, steady rhythm. But in working with Dylan, two things changed. One was that he had great natural focus; the second was that I had to speed up my heeling pace considerably. His focus meant that at any time that he saw my body straighten, he began to sit. The quicker pace meant that taking three steps to come to a halt just took too long. So I went to the two-step halt and found that it worked better. Sam was ac-

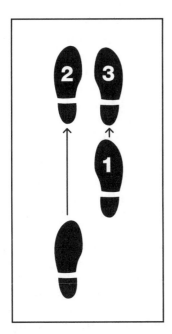

The two-step halt. The dog will be more confident and more precise if your footwork is precise and consistent. This halt pattern encourages quick sits.

customed to the three-step halt, but I reshaped him to the two-step pattern and his sits are now both quicker and straighter. The two-step halt is now my preference.

As you are walking forward at a brisk pace your body should have a slight forward lean to it. I am not suggesting that you make a point of leaning forward as though you were heading into a stiff wind; you should naturally have a slight forward lean, that is all.

I have been to many seminars and heard a lot of opinion back and forth about whether you stop on your left foot or your right foot. There is about an even split of opinion, and plenty of good reasoning to go around. I train my dogs for both, simply because I want to be able to halt quickly without worrying whether my footwork is "correct." However, I do have a preference.

I like to stop using my right foot to "brake" forward momentum, stopping on my left foot and "catching up" with my right. The simple reason is that my dogs are working off my left foot, and if I bring it all the way forward and halt, there is virtually no chance that they will be lagged. On the other hand, I sometimes find a slight lag if I stop on my right foot and catch up with my left. That's because my body shifts ever so slightly with the first stopping step, so the dog is already starting to sit when my left foot catches up. The other reason is practical, for the competitor who shows outside: You often encounter uneven ground. By taking your last step with your right foot, your weight shifts slightly to your right when you stop; if you are on uneven ground and have any imbalance, this will take you away from the dog, thus avoiding such things as stepping on his foot or falling on top of him.

Your dog already knows how to sit and how to do so with proper posture and alignment. You have stimulus control over the sit; that is, you have added the cue ("Sit") and the dog will sit on cue. If you have been really diligent, you have shaped a quick response to the "sit" cue by putting the behavior on limited hold. Now you can incorporate the sit into actual heeling.

Simultaneously as your body starts to straighten on your stop step, say "Barfy, sit." As you are saying "sit," bring your "catch-up" foot up even with your "stop" foot, bringing you to a full halt. At first, Barfy will sit slowly. This is the result of uncertainty (remember, you are adding something new). C/T the sit response even if slow. Remember too that you can only train one thing at a time. You want Barfy to learn that when you stop moving, he sits.

That's the only lesson you're going to teach at first. You're not even going to worry about posture, straight in line, or alignment. Your only concern is that Barfy sits when you stop moving forward.

Once Barfy sits consistently when you stop moving forward, rebuild latency so that he is sitting immediately as your brake foot hits the ground. Then, shape posture, direction, and alignment. At each stage, reintroduce latency once the new criterion is in place. In other words, make the immediate sit a constant throughout.

The sit posture

If you are walking at a brisk pace and using the two-step halt, you will probably not find much of a problem with the dog's posture. He won't have time to rock back. And his readiness to move when you do will tend to keep his body weight forward.

Maintaining alignment with handler's left hip

This will only be a problem if the dog is not properly aligned while walking at heel. If Barfy's ears are in line with your left hip and he sits with good posture, he will remain in line. But when Barfy sits, the distance between his nose and shoulders narrows. So if Barfy is heeling with his shoulder at your hip, you will produce a noticeably forged sit. Similarly, if he is heeling with his nose at your hip, you will produce a noticeably lagged sit. In other words, the antidote to forged or lagged sits is to establish a solid "middle ground' heel position while in motion.

Facing same direction as handler

Together with "close to left side," this is one of the areas where "focal-point" training can jump up and bite you. When the dog trained to a focal point sits, the dog will work to keep the focal point in sight. He will do this by "wrapping" (bringing his head and shoulders ahead of and around the handler's left leg). If the focal point is the handler's hand at waist, the dog will have to "wrap" even slightly further than he does while in motion to keep the hand in sight. One fairly common focal point is the handler's left upper arm. A small dog trained to that focal point may move his front feet slightly to the left as he sits in order to be able to see it.

If Barfy is not crabbing while you are moving, it is unlikely that he will crab as he sits. Use a spotter. If you become aware of any crabbing, reemploy the target stick for a couple of sessions, keeping his nose on the stick while sitting.

Close to left side

Here is another area where "focal-point" heeling can cause problems. The requirement that the dog be "close to the handler's left side" has two aspects to watch for: (a) "as close as practicable," and (b) "without interfering with handler's freedom of motion." The dog that is "wrapped" will interfere with the handler's freedom of motion. On the other hand, the dog that has to move slightly away from the handler to keep a "focal point" in sight will not be "as close as practicable." This is most often noticeable with toy breeds, who may have to lean outward to their left to keep the focal point in sight.

"Scoot sits"

If after the dog has put it together the sit is still slower than you want, pay special attention to the limited hold. Do a series of short forward movements, just enough to get the dog up and moving before sitting again (these are sometimes called "scoot sits"; you will also use them in shaping "front" position). One or two steps is enough (your concern here is the sit, nothing else). The timing you are looking for is that the dog is sitting *at the instant* your "catch-up" foot is moving up to your "stop" foot.

You can use a silent count to gauge the dog's quickness. Let's say that after your left foot catches up with your right, you can count "one banana, two banana" before the dog sits. At first, you will not reinforce anything slower than "two banana." If the dog is not sitting within that count, tell the dog "wrong" and try again. After some reps the dog will consistently sit at "two banana," and will at some point offer a sit at "two ba*na*." When you get this faster sit, jackpot and quit for the day on this exercise.

When you start the next day, your standard is "two ba*na*." If he gives it to you the first time, give a small jackpot. Continue with the session. You will find the same sequence repeating, with the dog at some point sitting at "two ba." Jackpot and quit as before.

Now at some point in all this the dog is likely to "get it," and sit immediately as you halt. Major jackpot. Remember though, you can now only reinforce the immediate sit. Anytime you have to count at all after your left foot has caught up to your right is "wrong." I strongly recommend against using the word "wrong" or anything similar at this phase. Simply, do not reinforce the slower sit. It is enough that Barfy realizes that his effort was not sufficient to earn reinforcement; he will do better quickly enough.

A

B

C

Mace's "tuck sit" keeps him in correct heel position when he sits. The front legs come to a stop (a) and the back legs come forward and under (b) so the dog neither leans forward in a forge or rocks back in a lagged position. The handler clicks as the tuck is occurring, and then treats in the sit position (c).

Fine-tuning

Now that you have achieved a sit that is quick enough to suit you, you may find that some of the other criteria have declined a bit. To some extent this is natural during the time you are introducing and refining new criteria, and often the old criteria return once the new criterion is in place. But if the decline in performance seems a bit more chronic than that, you are now faced only with some polishing work. Again, and as always, begin with the assumption that doggy errors are handler errors in disguise. At any time that you become aware of a problem with the sits, first reexamine your pace and footwork. Ninety-nine times out of a hundred that is where the cure will lie.

The biggest obstacle in this phase is simply being willing to admit that you are probably making mistakes that are causing the dog's errors. If you can own up to that, the rest is easy. If possible, have a training partner you are willing to listen to watch you with a gimlet eye. If no such person is to be found, try to have someone videotape you. If that is not possible, go out in the early morning to a sidewalk in front of buildings with glass windows and watch yourself carefully.

If the dog is straight in line while moving forward, quick sits are straight almost by definition. You may be causing the dog to "crab" by moving too slowly. If so, review that section. Or, you may be causing the dog to veer in-and-out by not maintaining a straight line yourself. This is usually the result of watching your dog too much. Set "targets" for yourself. In the ring, the ring posts do quite nicely. Outdoors you can use trees, telephone poles, light standards, whatever. Indoors you can use doors, chairs, windows, or corners. But if you watch the dog you'll follow the dog, and that will lead you anywhere but in a straight line.

Another common fault in the sit at halt is a "rockback" sit. Typically the handler causes this by coming to the halt too slowly, or in an erratic rhythm. A related fault is a forged sit, which typically results from the handler halting on a dime. The dog then does a nice impression of a crash-test dummy.

When do I introduce turns and changes of pace?

Don't be in such a hurry. My rule of thumb is that you should be able to go thirty strides (about sixty feet) with the dog maintaining heel position on a VR schedule before you introduce turns and changes of pace. Yes, that is a good deal farther than you will ever have to go in the ring (the longest side of any Obedience ring is fifty feet, and with turns at either end you usually heel at most about forty of those fifty feet). But the dog that will stay with you for thirty strides on a VR schedule is a well-disciplined heeling dog. And you will need every bit of that discipline when you go into maneuvering and changing pace.

The heeling maneuvers

There are nine maneuvers that you must perform while heeling: normal pace, fast, slow, about turn, right turn, left turn, half-circle left, half-circle right, and halt. Guess what? The key to each is consistent footwork on your part. No matter how much attention the dog is paying to you, if your footwork is not consistent, you are going to throw the dog off and lose points.

I've already discussed the footwork for the halt, so I won't go into that again. One question I raised in that section was how to distinguish the halt from the slow pace and the about turn. Novice dogs not uncommonly sit (or start to sit) when the handler goes to a slow pace. But a really attentive dog can surprise you on the about turn as well. After all, in that maneuver you are pivoting in place with some very short steps, and it is not hard for the dog to misread the foot cues.

The slow

The Regulations (C3, S6) do not say anything about the "slow" other than that the dog and handler must "noticeably decelerate." And of course, the handler's deceleration must be "smooth and natural."

What is "noticeable deceleration?" Referring back to the metronome, if you maintain a "normal" pace of 120 steps per minute, then a slow pace would be about eighty. The deceleration must be noticeable to the judge. Almost as important, the acceleration back to normal must also be noticeable. In teaching yourself the transition, I recommend that you over-decelerate going into the slow pace, and over-accelerate coming out of it. Once you are comfortable with the feeling of the transition you can adjust it so that it is more "natural."

The most common problem for most new Novice handlers is that their normal pace is too slow. As a result, there is not much deceleration when the judge calls "slow" and even less acceleration when the judge calls "normal." This is exacerbated when the handler watches the dog too closely. Many dogs lose focus on the slow pace. The handler sees this, starts to worry, and then does not resume her original normal pace.

Transitioning to the slow

There are two keys: (1) Take a two-step transition into the "slow," going from 120 to 100 to 80 steps per minute. (2) *Lengthen your stride slightly.* If you keep your stride the same as your normal stride or worse, shorten it, you will induce your dog to sit. Add about one-fourth of the distance of your normal stride, and make your steps long and fluid.

Which foot should you transition with? I don't really think it makes any difference. And as with the sit-at-halt, it is important that you and the dog be comfortable transitioning, regardless of which foot the judge catches you on. The important thing is that the first step into the slow pace be longer and slower than your last step at the normal speed.

Returning to normal pace

Again, this is a two-step transition, quickening from 80 to 100 to 120 steps per minute. Here, it does help if your first quickstep is with your *left* foot, since that will be most visible to the dog. Make your transition steps *slightly shorter than your normal stride* so as to "spark" the dog to move forward quickly.

Shaping the slow

The transition steps

Shape the transition steps *one at a time*. Spot must not forge as you take that first slow-down step. *Remember!* Even if your dog is paying attention, if your deceleration is not smooth and you do not lengthen your stride by about one-fourth, the dog will inevitably forge simply because your change of pace is too sudden and rough.

So . . . *practice your footwork without the dog* until your transition sequence is smooth. Then add the dog. Shape one step at a time. Take four to five steps at your normal pace before beginning the "slow." *As you slow down, C/T at the first step* if Spot holds heel position. If he is forged, simply break it off and repeat. (Again, let me caution against giving any verbal "correction" cues such as "anh-anh" or "wrong"; use simple reinforcement to keep Spot thinking about what you are doing and what you

want from him in return. Every verbal cue becomes a crutch you have to wean yourselves off later.) You want to get three smooth first steps in a row. When Spot has the first step right, go to the second. At each step, you treat and release *up and back* toward you, not forward. While I say generally that "click ends the behavior" and it doesn't really matter what Fido does after you click, in this maneuver you do not ever want to give the dog any sense of charging forward.

Extending the slow over a distance

Once you have a smooth transition, you must build Bowser's ability to hold heel position while going slow over a long distance. The Regulations require that a Novice ring be not less than thirty by forty feet (indoors), and forty by fifty feet outdoors. Usually, you will get the "slow" along the shorter side of the ring. There is tremendous disparity in the way judges call the exercise, and often you will be asked to take only five or six steps. However, the AKC is encouraging judges to extend the distance for the slow, and I have seen more judges call the slow along virtually the entire forty-foot length (this is not too common in Novice A, but is not uncommon in Novice B and is now fairly common in Open B and Utility B). So you should be prepared to go a long distance at this slow pace. This means you have to maintain control over your footwork (stride and pace) and keep the dog focused and in heel position. This is not easy.

Shape distance for the slow the same way you shape distance for normal heeling. In other words, build it through a VR schedule. If you were working in a forty by fifty foot ring and the judge made you do the slow along as much of the forty-foot side of the ring as possible, you would do about thirty feet (fifteen strides). So build up to twenty strides. The greater discipline will be of immeasurable value.

Watch for attention

Buster's actual attention is critical in this maneuver. Many dogs lose focus (and therefore position) on the slow because the slow pace tells them that they have time to look around, sniff, scratch, etc. *You cannot expect the dog to stay in heel position on the slow if his focus is wandering.* The unfocused dog will wander out of heel position or start to sniff the ground while you are going slow, and fail to regain heel position as you speed up again to "normal."

Therefore, in shaping the slow, C/T only as long as Fido's head is at least parallel to the ground. Put another way, his head position will give you a built-in guide as to his tolerance for distance. At any time that his head drops, you have found your outer limit. Build distance through VR.

Shaping the return to normal pace

This doesn't take long. The renewed speed helps recapture the dog's interest. However, you have to train it. As in the transition to the slow, C/T the transition step by step. Give each step two to three sessions. I have sometimes found it helpful to overexaggerate the first step in the first practice session, making it almost a sprint step. This gets the dog springing forward.

As in every maneuver, the first step is critical. *C/T the initial step if the dog speeds up immediately!* Do not go to two steps until the dog is speeding up reliably on the first step. You do not want the dog to get used to catching up to you from a lag. I like to visualize the dog as a "coiled spring" on the slow.

In training the transition back to a normal pace, make your play releases forward and away from you. I favor tossing a small toy forward a few feet after the click, telling Buster "get it," then treating when he brings it back. Deliver the treats in front. Once the dog knows how to stay with you through the two-step transition, the normal pace presents no new challenges as such.

The fast

Unlike the slow, the Regulations are pretty specific about what is required for the fast pace. They state (C3, S5): " 'Fast' signifies that *the handler must run,* handler and dog moving forward at *noticeably accelerated speed.*"

A substantial deduction (three to five points) is mandated "for failure of dog or handler to noticeably accelerate speed forward for the Fast" (C2, S6).

Unfortunately, the Regulations do not define the word "run." The conventional wisdom is that "run" carries its ordinary meaning: a pace in which both feet are off the ground at the same time at some point in the stride.

The dog does not have to run. All the dog must do is "noticeably accelerate speed forward." So if the dog merely lengthens its stride in order to maintain heel position while the handler is "running," that should be sufficient to avoid any deductions. Handlers with large dogs may even find it impossible to run fast enough to cause the dog to do more than lengthen his trotting stride.

In 1990 I participated in a Gaines Western Regional competition, and had the fun of watching a handler named Beth Myer and her Harlequin Great Dane "Ducky." Ducky just about came up to Beth's shoulder. Beth's normal pace was what most of us would consider a fast, and her fast was a world-record sprint. Beth did what she had to do to get—and keep—her dog moving. Caught more than one judge by surprise, as I recall.

The most common handler error on the fast is not accelerating noticeably. Some handlers (even experienced handlers) try to disguise this by making an exaggerated up-and-down motion with their feet *as if they were* running. Justice may be blind, but the judges are not. The Regulations say "run," so *run* (or at least do something very much like it). If you are overweight, at least show an accelerated pace; most judges will be considerate.

Another common problem arises on transitioning out of the fast. Not uncommonly the fast is followed by an about turn and halt. And not uncommonly the judge will call the about turn when you are uncomfortably close to the ring ropes. So the handler must be able to decelerate quickly and do the about turn on a dime.

The fast is in some ways more difficult than the slow because what you do and how you do it will vary significantly depending primarily on the size and athleticism of your dog, as well as your physical characteristics as a handler. Beth Myer with her Great Dane could do a much faster fast than could Gerianne Darnell with her Papillon. Similarly, for example, a person with a long stride is going to have different concerns from a person with a short stride. Since there are so many ways in which this exercise can vary from team to team, I'm just going to lay out what I—an average-sized person with medium-sized dogs—do in shaping the exercise.

Transition to the fast

The first point, as always, is to establish your own footwork. You can't just take off at a dead run. You need a transition sequence that tells the dog that you are changing to the fast.

Again, it is a two-step transition, beginning with the *left* foot (because that is the foot most visible to the dog). Bring the foot up slightly higher than normal, and quickly to the ground with a stride about one-half your normal stride. The second step with your right foot should be the same except that the stride is about half again as long. This will be the length of stride you maintain during the fast. Your stride on the fast should be *slightly shorter than normal.* By making these slightly "choppy" transition steps you'll get the dog moving more quickly.

Be very conscious of your dog's response to your first (left foot) step. There are two principal dangers.

- First, in starting into the fast, you can go too fast too quickly, causing a lag worth (at least) a minor deduction. Part of the answer to this lies in consistent transitional footwork. Part of it lies in maintaining the dog's focus during the normal pace, as discussed earlier.
- Second, if your pace *during the fast* is too fast, and you have a very energetic dog, you may find the dog bolting away from you. When I was first putting Dylan in matches he was a "bolter." At an ASCA trial he ran ahead of me and when the judge called "normal . . . about turn" Dylan went out of the ring and whipped a very neat about turn around the ring post (I thought it was rather spiffy, myself; the judge was not quite so amused). I went through a period of moderating my fast so as to give him time to mature. Now, even with a speedy fast, when we get that sequence of "normal, about turn" he will work tightly with me, staying inside the ring even if we are running right up against the ropes or center post.

Transition to the fast pace

As always, get that first step down before going any further. You should see the dog accelerating immediately as you do. C/T the first step. As with transitioning to normal from slow, you may also toss a toy or ball forward as a "play release" in between click and treat.

Practice the fast until you can sustain it, in position, for twenty to twenty-five steps. You won't usually have the problem with focus on the fast that you might have on the slow. A faster pace always gets the dog more engaged. But what you will encounter is the dog "fading" on you, decelerating to a more moderate (if not completely "normal") pace. This is a special problem if you do not regularly practice long-distance "fasts." The dog gets used to going fast for only a few strides and starts to slow down in anticipation of the transition to normal. For that reason, I never practice short fasts (unless I am "doodling"—see pages 139–140) once I have good distance. In practice I always go fifteen to twenty

steps on the fast. So you have to shape the fast just like you have to shape everything else.

Once that first step is in place, use VR (Appendix A) to develop distance as with the other heeling elements.

Transition back to normal pace

To transition back to a normal pace I like to take a couple of "deceleration" steps, slowing down slightly but not reducing the length of my stride, and then a slightly longer than normal step so the dog doesn't sit (reading the slower steps as a "halt" cue). After that, the stride is normal length.

You may notice that here I do not put any emphasis on which foot to "brake" with. In practicing and shaping the transition out of the fast, you have to "mix it up" thoroughly. Stride and rhythm become the dog's cues, not which foot does what first. Practice going from the fast into the about turn in three steps, two steps, and up to ten steps. Occasionally I will even throw in a halt just after resuming normal pace. To be reliable on and coming out of the fast the dog must be aware that anything can (and probably will) happen. (Early on at a Novice Top Dog competition the judge gave this pattern to start: forward, fast, normal, right turn, halt.) Once the dog understands the need to be ready for anything, his focus will be there.

The critical thing is to make sure that the dog is not forging as you complete the *second* transition step. A slight forge on the first step won't hurt you. But because you will often be making a turning maneuver soon after coming out of the fast, the dog *must* be in heel position at the second transition step.

As you return to normal, lengthen your stride slightly and keep your pace quick (if anything, slightly quicker than your ordinary normal pace). If you have some distance (ten to fifteen feet) before the about turn, resume your normal pace in that distance. Otherwise, use the about turn to bring yourself back to a completely normal pace.

Turns—Shaping and footwork

You should not start shaping turns until you have the dog going at least twenty steps in a straight line, maintaining perfect heel position, on a VR schedule. My progression for teaching turns is as follows: circle right, right about turn; right turn; circle left, left about turn; left turn. The only one of these that you can't fit into the obedience exercises is the left about. However, because it is so useful in teaching the dog to work its rear end around for the left turn, it is an important transitional training step. The circle left and right come into play when you are doing the figure-eight. I start with turns to the right because they are easier for dog and handler.

Circle right

In this exercise you begin by doing circles with about a twenty-foot diameter. *You* maintain a normal (brisk) pace. *The dog* must pick up his pace to stay in heel position. It is very important in shaping this behavior that you avoid the temptation to do any of the dog's work for him. In other words, don't slow down and don't cheerlead. Reinforce step by step.

The first step into the circle right will be with your *right* foot. Take a few steps forward with dog in heel position, then a half-step with your right foot, angling it to the right. Imagining that you are standing at the center of a clock facing 12:00, your first step will be to 1:00. Then bring your left foot forward just enough so that your left heel is slightly past your right big toe. Your left foot will be pointing to about 2:00. This introduces the dog to the footwork you will use in the about and right turns. From there, continue in a circle, with each step moving you one hour further around the clock.

Do not try to do the full circle at first. Start with an arc the distance of about a quarter circle. If the dog can't keep up, cut that in half. It the dog still can't keep up, you aren't ready to start practicing circles yet.

Using the target stick

The target stick is very useful here to give the dog a target slightly ahead of you. This will help him maintain proper position. If anything, you want to feel as if the dog is slightly forged as you go through the circle. Use the "touch" command to cue the dog to chase the stick. Let him touch it after a couple of steps at first and C/T. Gradually extend distance.

Do not ask for sits at all during any of your circle work. There are a few reasons for this. I have yet to see a judge call a halt while a handler is in the middle of one of the figure-eight arcs (though I have heard of it happening), so it isn't something you need to practice for. It is almost impossible for a dog to give you a straight sit when you are on a curve, and there is nothing to gain and much to lose by getting the dog accustomed to giving you crooked

sits. And the circling is partly in preparation for the about turn, in which you want the dog almost forging as he comes around and out. So, no sits while doing circles. If you want to end a circle exercise on a sit, break the circle and walk straight forward at least a couple of steps before having the dog sit.

When you finish each heeling segment, release the dog with an upward/forward release. The reason for this is the same as on normal heeling; you want the dog's momentum always going forward and away. Tossing a ball or toy is good here.

When going in a circle in either direction, you want to be sure to "step" your way through the curve, describing a distinct portion of the arc with each step. Most of us have the tendency to "swing" our outside leg (in this case, the left leg) around. This is a mistake. It causes you to take too much of the arc at once. It does not give the dog a chance to keep up, because the left leg is moving ahead faster than the dog can. So you are creating a lagged position where none is necessary.

Proper footwork on a curve requires that you almost "single-track." Your steps become shorter, only slightly longer than "heel-toe." If you were to draw a curved line on the ground for the circle right, your right foot would be just inside and barely touching the line, and your left foot would be just outside and barely touching the line. Your *pace* doesn't change, only your stride. You will apply the same principle on the circle left, only in reverse.

Do not go to teaching the right about turn until you can complete a full circle three times in a row with the dog maintaining proper heel position. If the dog doesn't understand the principle of being aggressive while maneuvering to his right, you cannot teach the right about and right turns.

After you can describe the full circle, begin doing spirals, closing the circle tighter and tighter toward the center. This will require the dog to continue to accelerate, and will lay the foundation for the outside turn on the figure-eight.

Right about turn

This maneuver is tricky. The Regulations are not much help in defining it. They state (C3, S5), "In executing the About Turn, the handler will always do a Right About Turn."

Do you have this feeling that they aren't telling you everything you need to know? You're right. There are a couple of essential elements. First, the handler cannot "back into" the turn by, essentially, pivoting on her left heel and bringing the right foot back to meet the left. Why not? The Regulations do not say so, nor is there anything in the AKC Guideline for judges. I have been given a couple of reasons (no doubt there are others). One is that it is implicit in the Regulations that while in motion the handler is always moving *forward*. The handler must always be going forward or, at most, be temporarily moving "in place." The "back-up" maneuver is also seen as "unnatural." As a rule, the only handlers I've ever seen use it are people who also show in the breed ring.

Second, you should execute the turn so that you are coming back along exactly the same line as you went out on. Many judges will stand on a line directly behind you (some even immediately behind you). If they are not looking you in the face when you come out of the maneuver, you'll get nicked.

Third, while you are executing a pivot, you cannot "stop" your forward momentum. You must keep your feet moving, and at the same pace as you maintain while walking at a normal forward pace. A typical fault is for the handler either to stop completely for a second or to slow way down to give the dog a chance to "catch up." Both are scoreable faults. If you were really extreme you could be seen as "adapting pace to that of the dog"; this is grounds for an outright failure.

The final thing about the about turn is something that you won't find even hinted at in the Regulations, and that is, when is it called? It is quite often called after the fast pace. A typical sequence is "fast, normal, about turn, halt," with the halt coming within about five steps of the about turn maneuver. This puts a lot of stress on the team. You have to go from fast to normal, almost immediately negotiate an about turn, then come to a halt. The perils are many. If you do a real fast (that is, "run"), you may even find yourself running into the ring ropes.

Bowser can forge coming out of the fast, leading to an out-of-position, wide, *lagged* about turn (one and a half points). Now as you come out of the turn the dog may still be wide, slightly angled, and lagged (one to one and a half points). The almost immediate halt does not give a dog in that position a chance to get straightened out first. So you usually end up with a lagged, crooked, perhaps wide sit (one and a half points). At a half point per fault, this sequence can add up to three to five points in the space of less than twelve steps. And that is to say nothing of what happens when you start up again and the dog is still lagged, wide, and crooked. There are trolls under that bridge, so beware.

All this presents yet another reason for you to make sure that you come out of the about turn on exactly the same line you went in on. If you are likely to make any mistake, it will be to over-turn; this will only add to the problems your dog will have maintaining proper heel position and alignment.

Handler footwork

The circle right has accustomed the dog to "charging" while maneuvering toward the right. Now you are going to formalize that into an about turn. There are a lot of ways to do the about turn. There are good reasons for almost all of them, and I have tried every one I have heard of. Some handlers do a pure "pivot." Having stepped forward with their left foot they just pivot in place and set off again. This makes it almost impossible for the dog to keep up with the handler. I recommend this only for people with insurmountable problems in keeping their balance.

The two most popular footwork patterns are the "T" and what I call the "toe-in" maneuver. They both work, but I find both somewhat difficult to execute.

- The *"T" turn* not only requires good balance, it has a tendency to misdirect the dog. Remember that the dog is following your left leg. When the left foot steps across in front of the right, the left leg is leading the dog past the center line of your body. Moreover, as the dog is moving that way, your upper body is facing only to about 2:00 (taking 12:00 as your original line of travel). The result is a tendency for the dog to swing wide as he comes around, creating all the problems I described above.

- The *"toe-in"* maneuver avoids that problem and the dog will usually come around quite nicely, but is a rather athletic move. I used it for a couple of years, but found it difficult to maintain my balance, and I am not particularly uncoordinated. It's a good maneuver if you show indoors a lot, but if you are outdoors (as we Westerners tend to be) you will often encounter uneven ground, and that can make this maneuver tricky.

I believe it was Helen Phillips who broadcast (on the Internet Obedience line) yet another footwork pattern for the about turn that I think works beautifully. The thing that I really like about it (aside from the fact that I can stay upright while doing it) is that the footwork segues very nicely into the right turn, producing very nice results on both.

- *The first step* in this turn is with the right foot on an angle toward 1:00, the right heel barely past the toe of the left foot.
- *The second step* is a "catch-up" step, bringing your left foot to a spot parallel with the right foot (facing toward 1:00). Note that while the toes are aligned, the feet are angled so that the left foot is actually slightly behind the right. As the dog follows the left foot he will not go past your center line, nor is there anything in your footwork to draw him past that point. It isn't real important how close your feet are in doing this, as long as you feel balanced.
- *The third step* is with the right foot, pivoting around so that the right foot is pointing directly back down the original line of travel (toward 6:00), the heel of the right foot right next to the heel of the left foot. Note that the right foot is now slightly to the right of the line of travel, so you are going to be coming back right along that line.
- *The fourth step* is with the left foot, directly forward along the return line (continuing toward 6:00 based on your original line of travel). It's a half-step only. The next step with the right foot will be a full stride.

Yes, this footwork is "unnatural." But as a practical matter, all about-turn footwork is "unnatural." It simply isn't a maneuver you do in the course of your day-to-day meanderings. The real issue on this maneuver is "smoothness," especially given the typical sequence described earlier. It all comes down to footwork. So? Practice the footwork *without the dog* for at least five minutes at a time, three times a day. Get it consistent, get it automatic. Don't even think about getting the dog involved until you can do this maneuver in your sleep.

Shaping the right about-turn

You have mastered the footwork. Now you are going to shape the turn. Shaping any turn requires that you identify what I will now call "click points," that is, specific points in the turn that the dog should know require him to be in a specific position. I have identified three "click points" in the course of the about turn at steps 2, 3, and 4.

Click point 1 is where you have brought your left foot to catch up with your right. At that point the dog should be in heel position or, if anything, slightly forged. The dog's rear end may be "out," but this will not be scored as the judge does not expect the dog to stay "straight in line" while performing a tight circle.

You do not want a lag, but you certainly don't want much of a forge either because you want a tight "wrap" as you come around. Aim for left hip alignment.

C/T the dog for holding that position at that point, releasing *back and to your right* to build the sense in the dog of continuing to move right sharply. Practice this step until the dog will give it to you three times in a row without either a click or a treat. It takes about a week to be sure of it. Jackpot at the end of the session.

Click point 2 is where you have pivoted on your right foot and are facing back along your original line of travel. The dog should be about in line with your right heel. C/T when he is in that position, giving the treat forward and straight ahead. As else-

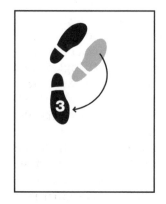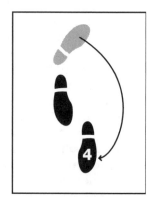

The about-turn. Footwork for the about-turn is always a little artificial—we don't make the maneuver much in normal life. This pattern produces very nice results. Practice without the dog until your footwork is consistent and automatic.

where, using a toy or ball for a "chase/play" release is very useful here. It helps reinforce the "charging forward" mentality in the dog.

Click point 3 is where the left foot has come forward in a half-step past the right. Bowser should be aligned at your left hip, but you should have the feeling that you have to "brisk it up" a tad to catch up to the dog. C/T for left hip alignment, and here very definitely release forward with a toy or ball.

Once you have consistent left-hip alignment, consider the *criterion* of "straight in line." You are going around a curve here, so nobody expects Fido to be "straight." However, if he is not working on a curve that tracks your turn-in-place, he will go wide; the judge will be aware of that. Use the target stick to shape Fido to wrap tightly around you as you step through the turn. This will keep him working closely to your own track rather than wide.

Now you want to add *variable reinforcement* into the training. As you progress through the three points, do not go forward until you are getting each one three times in succession without reinforcement. If you are practicing every day, this should take about a week per step. And as always, no more than three to four repetitions per session.

Once you are all the way through the turn, you can click at one or more of the click points as you progress through, to reinforce "that's right" in the dog's mind. Do this randomly. Be sure to stop right at that point and treat. Then repeat, the next time going all the way through the click point and clicking for the completed maneuver. In this way you can work several repetitions into practicing one turn without simply doing the same thing over and over.

Handler: Give yourself a target when you turn

Something to be aware of on footwork: In doing any maneuver to the right, you always run the risk of *over-turning* somewhat. In other words, instead of heading toward 6:00 (on the about turn) or 3:00 (on the right turn), you find yourself heading toward 8:00 or 4:00, respectively. This will not only throw you off-line. If you correct your line you may well bump the dog. If you don't correct the line, the judge is going to see you as out of heel position.

The way to avoid turning too far and going into your dog is to set yourself a "target" as you come through the turn. *Don't look at the dog!* Find a point at a distance and orient to that. In an outdoor ring (or an indoor ring with ring posts) this is easy: You can use the ring post farthest from your turning

point. Even on a pattern where the judge has you go down the center of the ring, there is usually a center post at the far end of the ring. If there isn't, pick some target outside the ring to orient to before you go in the ring. In an indoor ring with baby gates you can use the corners or the center stanchion.

I have heard it said that turning your head in this manner helps cue the dog. I don't know if that's true or not. I suppose it might if your dog is looking up at your face, but I don't know. Perhaps turning your head helps your body go through the turn smoothly, and that may help the dog; again, I don't know. None of this is the purpose of targeting, and none of these concerns constitutes a reason not to target. By lifting your eyes and sighting onto a target you will pick a straight line for yourself, and this will inevitably assist the dog in coming through the turn cleanly. That is all.

The right turn

Once you have a consistent about turn, you are ready for the right turn. This is now easy. It is, essentially, an about turn cut short. As with the about turn, there are three "click points" to work with.

Click point 1 is on step 2 into the turn. This step is exactly the same as the about turn: right foot taking a half step, pointing to 1:00. The dog now knows what this means: "We're going around." C/T if the dog is tight on your left leg. If you use any toy toss as a play release, toss it forward, and to the right toward 2:00.

Click point 2 is on step 3 with the left foot. Instead of bringing your left foot parallel to the right foot as in the about turn, you will step slightly past your right foot, angling it directly to 2:00. C/T if Fido is still tight on your left leg, and perhaps with his shoulder at your left hip (a tad forged). The "look" to him will now be more like the circle right (the old prepares us for the new).

Click point 3 is on the next right-foot step. This is only slightly longer than heel-toe, right foot pointing directly to 3:00. This is now your new line of travel. You have executed a 90 degree turn by traversing a 90 degree arc. C/T for the dog being at left-hip position; ideally his shoulder will be aligned. This is *slightly* forged, but you want the dog charging through the turn.

To summarize the sequence, in the right turn you start out heading toward 12:00, and end up heading toward 3:00. To traverse that arc, you take three steps: right (1:00), left (2:00), and right (3:00), and forward from there. This sequence demonstrates

The right turn is essentially an about turn-cut short. As with the about-turn there are three "click points." As you refine the dog's responses you will click, stop, and treat when the dog hits your chosen click point in correct position. It's advisable to start with the last click point, and then work on the earlier segments.

why it was so important in the early arc and circle work to discipline yourself to step through the turn. You won't be precise in making these steps if you don't accustom yourself to it early on.

Though the Regulations do not specify how the right turn is to be done, this "arc" through the right angle is completely in keeping with both the letter and spirit of the Regulations. Referring back to C2, S2, "military precision . . . by the handler" *must* be penalized. So if you were to do a ninety degree pivot at the corner, that would (or should) qualify as "military precision" and would earn you a deduction. On the other hand, if you were to describe more of an arc going through the turn the judge could decide either that you were "aiding the dog," or not making a real right turn at all.

Turns to the left

The progression is the same as in turns to the right: circle left, left about turn, left turn.

Circle left

This is the first stage in teaching the dog to move his rear legs to his right ("get it in"). In your foot-

work you will "single-track" as described for the circle right, except that now your left foot will be inside and just touching that imaginary line and your right foot will be outside and just touching it. The dog has to *decelerate* in order to hold proper left-hip alignment. It is not necessary that the dog be "straight in line" while moving to the left, but it is *essential* that the dog not be forged.

Your footwork into the circle left begins with your *right* foot. Take a few steps forward in a straight line, then bring your right foot *across* your line of travel, the heel of your right foot just slightly ahead of the little toe of your left foot, pointed to about 11:00. Now take a half-step with your right foot so that the heel of your right foot is just past the big toe of your left foot, right foot pointed to about 10:00. As with the training sequence on right turns, this will introduce the dog to the footwork he is going to encounter on all maneuvers to the left.

To shape the circle left I prefer to use the target stick, held just at the midline of my left leg. The goal here is to teach the dog to "get-back"; the resulting movement will also serve to bring the dog's rear end in toward my line of travel.

"Get-back"

This applies the fluency explained in Chapter 3 (page 69). Hold the target stick folded in half in your right hand, directly at the dog's nose level. As you start the circle to the left, move the target stick back slightly as you say "get-back." The aim is to induce the dog to take small steps ("tread water") momentarily.

It is good to have a spotter, though you will be watching the dog pretty carefully yourself. This is because you may not be able to see the dog's feet clearly. You will be aware of the dog "treading water" because of the dog's head and body position relative to your leg, but by the time you see that you will be clicking the result, not the motor action that produced it. So have your spotter click at any shortening of the dog's stride, however imperceptible or uncertain.

When I am getting that footwork from the dog consistently I add the cue "get-back." When you are getting a consistent "treading water" response, start to fade the target stick. Note, however, that if you later start to encounter problems with the dog forging, your tools are in place for a "fix." Simply reintroduce the stick and the cue.

As always, C/T that first correct step, and build distance slowly. Don't be in a rush, although you will probably find it easier for the dog to hold heel position on the leftward arc than on the rightward. As the dog's performance of the circle left improves, add spiraling in as you did on the circle right.

Left-about turn ("U" turn)

This is not something you will ever do in the Obedience ring. However, just as the right about lays the foundation for the right turn, the left about lays the foundation for the left turn. Do not begin this exercise until the dog will hold left-hip alignment and keep his rear end in on circles of about eight feet in diameter. As with the right about turn, there are several "click points."

Click point 1 comes on the first step (right foot) as it comes across the left, heel near the left little toe, pointing to about 11:00. Left-hip alignment should be anywhere between Bowser's nose and ears. Rear end should be moving in. This is now familiar territory to the dog. We're moving to the left.

Click point 2 is on the second step (left foot), heel-toe as before, but this time you will point your foot at 9:00. This too is not entirely unfamiliar to the dog, because as you tightened your circles while "spiralling," your left foot tracked more and more toward 3:00. So this looks very much like a tight spiral left to the dog. Left-hip alignment should be around the muzzle area; you really want the dog working back and in here.

Click point 3 is on your third step (right foot), heel-toe as before, but coming around to point at 7:00. Here is where you may first expect to see a breakdown on the "forging" part. Be very attentive that the dog's ears are behind the center line of your left hip. Be prepared to stop right here and reinforce both "get-back" and "get it in." Do not go further until the dog is holding position properly.

Click point 4 is on your fourth step (left foot), heel-toe as before, pointing to 6:00. This is your new line of travel. C/T for correct left-hip alignment (ears at hip). Just as the slow pace felt like a coiled spring, so should the left. The dog should start to move forward again at the instant you are coming out of the maneuver.

Click point 5 comes after the fifth (right) and sixth (left) steps. The right step is about a half stride and the left a full stride. The dog should be straight in line when you take the right step. Your pace and stride are normal, and Bowser is in completely correct position. When you treat, give the treat forward of the dog so that he must forge to get it. If you toss a toy, toss it straight ahead.

The left turn. Each step is a potential click point, informing the dog that he is correct when he slows or gets back as the turn starts, stays close in as the turn continues, and continues out of the turn in heel position and traveling straight.

Left turn

This is a relatively easy adaptation out of the left about. Your footwork will start the same way: right foot across left, heel-toe, pointing to 11:00. Your second step (left foot) will be heel-toe as before, at a lesser angle than on the left about, pointing to 10:00. Your third step (right foot) will be heel-toe, also at a lesser angle, pointing to 9:00, which is now your new line of travel. As with the right turn, you are executing a ninety degree turn by describing a ninety degree arc, only this time it is to your left.

If you have done the circles and left abouts, the left turn really will not present any difficulties. Use each step as a click point, again watching for the two criteria of "get-back" and "get it in." And as before, while in the turn itself you will treat release up and back toward you. As you are coming out of the turn you will treat and release forward.

Handler: Remember to give yourself a target

Remember that on the right turn the concern was that you might over-turn, walking into the dog's line of travel. On the left turn the concern is that you will *under-turn* because the dog is "pushing" into your line of travel. In other words, instead of coming out on a line toward 9:00, you end up heading to somewhere between 10:00 and 11:00. Part of the "fix" for this lies in the training itself. If you have properly shaped "get-back" it won't happen too often. Even so, if you are watching your dog too closely as you go through the turn you will find yourself tending to "under-turn."

As with the right turn, it is good practice to lift your head and sight in on a target point *as you enter the turn.* Keep your eyes on that point until you are completely through the turn. Among other things, this will teach the dog that you are not going to move out of his way. He *must* "get-back" or else he just may get stepped on. This is one of the few exceptions to the general rule that if you want your dog to pay attention to you, you must pay attention to the dog.

Figure-eight

This one is a complete puzzler. The manner of performing it hardly ever varies. Oh, some judges throw in a trick like having you stop halfway through the first circuit, and I have heard of some that have you stop on the arcs, but that is rare. Generally it is a straightforward, standardized, and predictable exercise. Handler and dog make two circuits around two stewards acting as "posts," standing about eight feet apart. There are no changes of pace, no about turn, and usually only two halts.

It is so routinized that I once saw a dog at a match take off on the judge's command "forward" and do the loops all by itself while the handler just stood there dumbstruck. And more than once I have seen dogs stop to sniff a "post" while the handler continued on and then go around that one "post" and trace the handler's route in a loop around the second "post" in order to catch up.

Yet certainly, at least in Novice, it causes more points to be lost than the entire heeling pattern that precedes it. One of my early instructors told me that the reason Novice handlers commonly think they do better off lead than on is that you don't do a figure-eight off lead in Novice. She's probably right.

Some mechanical problems to consider

The most important thing to understand about the figure-eight is that you are not required to execute an "8" as figure skaters used to do. The Regulations (C3, S5) simply state:

> The Figure Eight signifies that on specific orders from the Judge to Forward and Halt, the handler and dog, from a starting position about equidistant from the two Stewards and facing the Judge, shall walk briskly twice completely *around and between* the two Stewards, who shall stand eight feet apart.

How can such a simple little exercise cause so much trouble?

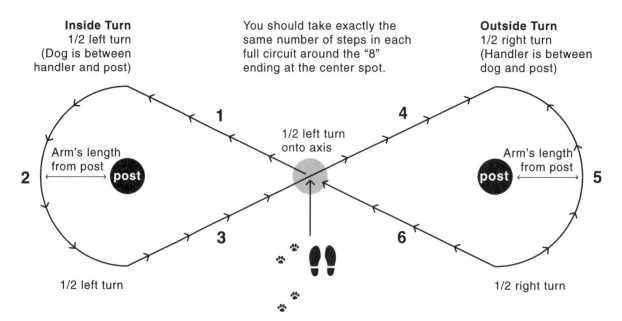

The figure-eight exercise is best taken as a straight line followed by an arc, first in one direction, then in the other.

First, some "geography" (see diagram). The "center line" is the imaginary line running between the two posts. The "center point" is the imaginary midpoint of that imaginary line (sort of like magnetic north). The "left axis" is a straight, diagonal line running from the lower end of the arc on the handler's right through the center point to the upper end of the arc on the handler's left. The "right axis" is a straight, diagonal line running from the lower end of the arc on the handler's left to the upper end of the arc on the handler's right. The arc to the left is the "inside arc" (the dog being "inside" the handler, between handler and "post"), and the arc to the right is the "outside arc" (the dog being "outside" the handler, handler between dog and post).

Starting to the right

OK, call me an old wife telling tales. There are very competitive handlers who start to the right on the theory that this motivates the dog immediately. I will never forget the judge at a sanctioned match who introduced the exercise thusly: "This is the Figure 8. You may go in either direction. If you go to the right, you deserve what you get." If you start to the right the dog has to speed up immediately from a sit at heel. By me, this is unrealistic. It is far easier and, I think, more conducive to consistency to let the dog first take it easy through the inside turn and then build up speed for the outside turn.

That said, however, I do start to the right with Dylan about half the time. At one point during Dylan's Novice career he was getting blasé about the exercise and started taking the opportunity to investigate the left-hand post on our first circuit. I corrected this simply by starting off to the right once or twice. Subsequently, he lost a little pace on his heeling. While this sometimes crops up in unexpected ways (such as, at first, on the fast pace), I noticed it most on the outside loop of the figure-eight. Starting to the right helped correct the problem. So what does it all mean? Read your dog, and do what you have to do.

Maintain a consistent pace

Not uncommonly, Novice handlers—and even some experienced handlers—adapt their pace to that of the dog. They go a little bit slowly into the inside arc, trying to avoid a forged dog and a bump. They then speed up just a bit going to the outside. Most judges will watch to see that you maintain the same pace on the figure-eight as you did in the heel-

ing pattern. If you do not, you can expect to get scored for it.

Improper footwork

Often, handlers do not shorten their stride enough so as to "step through" the pattern while describing the arcs. If you have established your circles footwork as described earlier, you are not going to have any problem with that here.

On the inside turn, with the dog between you and the post, this causes the right foot not to come over far enough. The step is straighter than it should be. This does not give the dog a clear cue as to what is happening, and the dog then does not circle left properly, but instead goes "half-straight" as he follows the right foot. This causes the dog to intrude in the handler's line of travel, causing bumping and forcing the handler to walk wider to avoid the dog.

On the outside turn, with you between the dog and the post, a failure to shorten stride causes the left foot to swing in, away from the dog. This causes the dog to lag and go wide. In so doing the leash will typically tighten. The left-foot "swing" causes the handler to describe too narrow an arc to the right, aggravating any lagging. Though all these faults on the inside and outside arcs are scored against the dog, they are pure handler error.

It is virtually impossible to execute the figure-eight properly if you try to walk it as an actual 8. You will have a difficult time giving accurate footwork cues, and your orbit will be very erratic.

So what's the best way to do the figure-eight?

If you could go straight into Utility the problem would be solved because you don't do figure-eights in Utility. But unfortunately, you have to go through Novice and Open first, and you have to do figure-eights in both those classes. The figure-eight is simply a series of half-turns to the left and right connected by two half-circles left and right. Look at the diagram again. You stand slightly to the right of the center point. The dog is lined up directly on the center point. You will keep your head up and "targeting" at all times during the exercise.

Starting to the left

Take one step forward with your left foot, just as though you are moving forward at heel. Your next step is a crossover, heel-toe, with your right pointing to about 11:00. Sound familiar? It's the start of the left turn. Target that imaginary spot ahead of you. Now, instead of continuing around to the left, you step straight forward with your left foot, continuing toward 11:00 until you reach a point directly in line with the left shoulder of the "post." You should be about an arm's length away from the post's shoulder.

For the inside turn, you are going to do a small half circle left. This is old news by now. You are going to single-track, heel and toe, maintaining a distance of about an arm's length from the post, until you complete the half-circle and are at a point directly in line with the post's right shoulder. Target that spot *as you enter the inside turn* and keep it in sight until you reach it.

For the *right axis,* you are going to enter on the straight diagonal connecting this point with the upper end of the outside arc. You are facing straight ahead. Crossover, heel-toe, with your right foot. It's another half turn to the left. Continue in a straight line. Target a spot about an arm's length away from that post's right shoulder.

For the *outside turn,* as you reach the beginning of the arc, your first step into the arc will be with your *right* foot, angling toward 1:00. This should also sound familiar: It's the first step in all maneuvers to the right. Now you will execute a half circle to the right, single-tracking heel and toe as when doing an ordinary circle right, until you have completed the one-half circle (maintaining a distance of about an arm's length away from the post) and are in line with that post's left shoulder. You are now prepared to enter into the left axis.

For the *left axis,* you are facing straight ahead. Your first step into the axis will be with your *right* foot, and you will continue straight ahead with your left, and so on. Target the spot you used at the beginning of the exercise at the start of the inside arc.

Halts

The Regulations (C3, S5) require the Judge to call two halts, one during and one at the end of the pattern. I cannot remember ever seeing a judge call more than two halts, though it would be permissible under the Regulations. Although I am not generally in favor of memorizing the heeling patterns, I do think it is a good idea to watch the figure-eight once just to see if the judge does anything out of the ordinary with the halts. There are judges who will call a halt after you have completed the inside arc and are proceeding along the right axis. The key is not to anticipate the halt, but to not be surprised by it.

Once in a while you may encounter a judge who calls a halt while you are on the arc. If you run into this, simply break the arc slightly so that you go into your halt on a straight line. Otherwise, you are guaranteeing a crooked sit. When you start forward again, handle it like another half turn to the left or right, as the case may be.

An easy test to determine whether your footwork is consistent

There is an easy way to tell whether your footwork is consistent. Starting with your first step with your left foot onto the left axis, count your steps around a full circuit until you stop at the center point. Then make the circuit again. The number of steps should be the same. If they are, you are maintaining a consistent pace and orbits. Once you can do this without the dog, do it with the dog. Make the exercise as routine as possible.

Why stay an arm's length from the posts?

On the inside arc, if you are closer, you are risking your dog sniffing the post. On the outside arc, if you are closer you will probably cause your dog to lag. Neither result is desirable. Finally, by staying an arm's length away you give yourself a consistent, standard line of travel that you can hold throughout the exercise.

Shaping issues

There really is nothing new. Simply remember to C/T the first step on every maneuver. Since the dog has to go from a "get-back" to a "hurry up," you may wish to use the target stick as you are heading along the right axis to move him forward. Treating forward or tossing a ball ahead for a play "release" is also appropriate here.

If you don't have training partners, you can use a ring post and a large hula hoop to replicate the approximate distance around the post that you should be travelling. Don't simply train with the ring post (bitter experience talking here) because it will cause you to make your circles too close.

Because the exercise can become routine in a hurry, I find it helpful to mix it up during training and at practice matches. For example, I'll do an about turn while going along one of the axes. Or I'll do a complete circle around one of the posts and then come out on the axis. This is not so much as to teach the dog that this is how the exercise is done, but just enough to keep him on his toes.

If you generally practice alone, make sure that you get some sessions in with live people standing as posts. If Bowser is unfamiliar with people standing there he may decide that it's a nice time to go visit.

Transitioning to on-lead heeling

What a strange concept. But all our heeling work is done off lead. Now that you are thinking about showing, you have to get the dog used to wearing the lead in the ring. The good news is that the dog won't have developed any aversive connections with the leash, so you won't be "fighting" the dog. The bad news is that the leash will seem to be in the dog's way, and, depending on the size of dog and length of leash, can take some getting used to.

Once you are up to about fifteen steps in a straight line, I suggest that you put the lead on the dog briefly at the end of the session and do a few short bursts with it on. From then on, in all your training include a brief on-lead component at the end of each practice session. As you get closer to trials, have the leash on for increasingly long periods of time.

However! Never make a leash "correction!" The leash is just a decoration, not a training tool. Hold the leash handle around your left palm, left hand against your waist. Your left hand never moves. At the slightest sensation of any tightening on the leash, stop and do some restructuring as though you were practicing off lead.

Hand position

The Regulations allow you to hold the leash in either hand, or both hands, as long as the hand position is "natural." Off lead, your right hand must always swing free at your side. Your left hand may be in either of two positions: swinging freely at your left side, or "against, and centered in the front of the body, in the area of the waist. The forearm shall be carried, as much as possible, against the body" (C2, S19).

I am an advocate of *always* keeping your left hand in the position described here. While on lead, it ensures that your left hand will be quiet and still, so you won't do anything that might be construed as "correcting" or "aiding" the dog. While off lead, it is completely consistent with your hand position while on lead. With your hand at your waist you avoid problems with touching the dog inadver-

tently. And as with all your mechanics, it becomes a position that you simply do not have to think about.

Now, having articulated that "rule," let me tell you how I have broken it with Sam. As I have said, he is a "crossover" dog. Early on, all our heeling was with my left hand at my side. When I got into "binding" and other fancy leash work, I brought my left hand up to my waist. Sam hated that kind of training. At least, his heeling went into the toilet along with his attitude; I call that "hating." When I got into shaping, I decided to see if it made life easier for him if I brought my left hand back down; it seemed to. So, I have my left hand at my side with Sam, and at my waist with Dylan. All I can say is that it's a good thing they are different colors.

Doodling

Once you have shaped all the maneuvers, some of the best heeling practice consists of "doodling." Doodling is pretty much what it sounds like: random movements within a relatively small area. I "doodle" before going into the ring as a way to bring me and my dog into sync.

A typical doodling session will consist of forwards, turns, halts, circle lefts, circle rights. I like to do all this in a space about twenty feet square. There is no preset pattern. You make it up as you go along. Because the changes are quick, the dog must be focused to respond.

The major thing about doodling is that it should be playful. If the dog "misses," break it off for a moment but do not do or say anything recriminating, nor use any tone of voice that suggests displeasure. Doodling is a game; keep it that way.

Doodling variations

Use turns in place. You can also do rights, abouts, lefts, and 180 degree left abouts without you going outside of an eighteen-inch square (even smaller if you are dextrous). This is not only good heeling practice, it lays the foundation for Utility, where you have to execute several turns in place (articles and gloves).

Another neat little game is to throw in a "get-back" as you are moving forward, and backpedal as you keep the dog at heel. Start with one step back, then two, and build up to five. When you come out of the "get-back" and start forward again, throw in a quick turn or change of pace. Click and treat for especially quick or accurate responses.

You can also do crossovers to the right and left, making the dog cross-step as well to hold position.

Again, this is not something you are going to do as such in the obedience ring, but it heightens the dog's alertness to what might happen.

I will doodle while in the ring at practice matches. Part of this is to keep the dog from learning to respond to the judge's order. So, for example, when the judge calls a left turn I may do a circle right or an about turn followed immediately by a right. Or I may throw an about turn in on the figure-eight. The purpose here is simply to carry the element of surprise into the practice ring. As a matter of courtesy to other handlers, don't make this really time-consuming. Even a couple of tricks of this sort will take you a long way. Remember that you cannot do this at a sanctioned match, where the same rules apply as at an AKC trial.

When at a trial, I don't like to drill heeling before going into the ring (I won't be doing it under the new Regulations allowing "training" on the grounds any more than I did before). You can't do yourself much good practicing a lot before you go into the ring, but you can do yourself some harm. I'll do a couple of forwards, halts, turns, but only within a short distance. As the dog immediately before me is setting up for the last exercise I will do some close-order doodling including quick turns in motion, turns in place, get-backs, crossovers, etc. I will talk constantly to the dog during this activity, using it to establish clear contact between us.

One last thought

Heeling is something you will work on throughout your obedience career. It is akin to a concert pianist doing scales. It is essential practice, but there is no reason to make it boring. Endless repetition without variation will do that. Practice heeling in short spurts of not more than ten minutes at a time. I think carefully about what I want to work on, and keep the sessions crisp and short. The only exception to this is when doing VR work on straight-line heeling, but the VR itself keeps the practice sufficiently randomized that the boredom factor is minimal. Even when you are working on a particular maneuver, always throw in a little doodling "just for fun." It will help keep Fido's mind sharp.

I like to follow a heeling session with an exercise that the dog particularly likes to do. This way, another element of "work" reinforces the heeling. Also, it avoids having the dog become "pattern" trained. Because I train in all classes with my dogs, I may follow heeling with go-outs, or retrieves, or anything else that seems right at the time.

If your dog seems to be getting "stale" on heeling, stop it altogether for a few days. When you go back to it, start with short doodling sessions lasting no more than three to five minutes. Gradually work your way back to a longer schedule. When all is said and done, the single greatest challenge in this exercise is to maintain the dog's enthusiasm. Lose that, and it's a long road back.

The "group" exercises (long sit and long down)

Aside from refining the mechanics of the sit and down, the only real issue that confronts the Novice exhibitor is the "group exercises" (C3, S12), or the long sit and long down. The group exercises in the "Novice class" at any given trial include all the dogs entered that day. If there are more than twelve dogs entered in the class, the Regulations direct that the long sit and long down "shall be judged in groups of not less than six nor more than twelve dogs." If there were thirteen dogs entered, the judge would probably judge them in a single group and nobody would be likely to complain too much.

It is common to hear exhibitors complain of having "group problems," and then explain by saying something like, "Fido has been going down on the sit." In other words, for whatever reason, we tend to think of the long sit and long down in a clump, even though the problem we are having may be very specific. This is, I suspect, one reason why "group problems" can be so difficult to solve.

And while trainers are always only too happy to impart their latest technique for getting a faster sit or a straighter front, most trainers will also tell you that if there is one problem area they hate to have to work on, it's "groups." Though I no longer share that same sense of dread (note, I say "no longer"), I will agree that "group" problems tend to be difficult to solve. This is not because the exercises are complex; after all, the dog is only doing one thing: sitting or lying down. Rather, it is because when you are showing, you often have only a week or two between shows. This does not usually give you the time you need to restructure your dog's performance in this area.

With shaping, the long sit and long down are not difficult to teach; it merely takes time. I have found that with shaping it is not as difficult to solve problems as it was with "traditional" methods. I'll talk about my approach to problem solving at the end of this section.

The group exercises are always done in the same sequence: first the long sit (one minute in Novice, three minutes in Open), and then the long down (three minutes in Novice, five minutes in Open). If you think about the group exercise as a sort of *behavior chain* (which, from the dog's point of view, it really is), this means that all too often the only behavior you reinforce is the down, because that is what comes at the end. So, although the long sit and long down are each *long-duration behaviors* (that is, a behavior that the dog simply continues doing indefinitely until told to stop), there is a "chaining" element from the dog's perspective. This means that before you can expect your dog to perform reliably in the groups you must have solid *stimulus control* over both the sit and the down.

The other thing to be aware of is that we complicate matters by using the word "stay" as a cue associated with both the long sit and the long down. So, to the dog, if "sit" means "stay," and "down" means "stay," why is it wrong to lie down on the sit?

The long sit

This exercise is simplicity itself: You tell Fido "sit," leave his side, walk to the other end of the ring, and wait for one minute while you find out how your heart tastes. Then you return to your dog, collapse in a heap of jangled nerves, and get ready for the long down. Man, this stuff is fun.

Actually, the long sit is not difficult to train. You simply have to be conscious of building the long sit as a distinct, long-duration behavior. Put another way, do not "chain" it with the long down in training.

Formal requirements of the long sit

There is no requirement that the dog sit in any particular fashion during this exercise. The only requirements are: (1) that the dog sit, (2) that the dog not leave the *position* in which he was left (i.e., neither lie down nor stand up), and (3) that the dog not move from the *place* in which he was left.

The more competitive the class or event, the more rigorously the judges will enforce the third of these. For example in Novice A it is highly unlikely that a judge would deduct for a dog that shifted position slightly while holding the sit. But in Open B or at a national tournament, that could cost you a point. For this exercise, you want to train a statue.

Sloppy "sit" posture may contribute to any of these faults. A dog with a "puppy sit" will often reshift his weight, causing him to move from the

place in which he was left. And if the dog does not move in that way, the rolled position may cause the dog to lie down. A well-postured sit is a stable sit that the dog can comfortably hold for considerably longer than three minutes.

So proper posture is essential for a reliable long sit. Fido's forepaws must not be so far forward as to cause him to slouch between his front and back feet, nor should he roll back on his haunches (the infamous "puppy sit"). With proper posture, your dog can hold his position like a statue indefinitely. Once you have proper posture, a straight alignment from head to tail for purposes of heel position and "front" is relatively easy to accomplish.

If your dog has a posture problem, refer back to that section in Chapter 3 on fluencies (pages 57–60), review that section, and solve the problem now. Do not work on extending the time that the dog holds the sit until you have proper posture. If you do, all you will do at best is confirm the incorrect posture. And you will always be struggling against the tendency of the dog to lie down because of the bad posture.

Leaving the dog

You started developing the concept of "hold that position" ("stay") in your *fluency* training, but we did not deal with leaving the dog at that point. If you did the fluency work you have the necessary foundation to build on as you add this element now.

The first problem most dogs have with the long sit or down is that the handler is leaving. Here is the one place where you might think that the word "stay" could be helpful, since you want the dog to distinguish between this exercise, where he must continue to sit while you move away, and heeling, where he moves when you do. The "stay" cue is not necessary for this purpose. Simply say "sit" as you leave.

When I am getting my dog lined up, I use the "get around" cue to bring the dog into heel position. As a matter of *repertoire cuing*, "get around" not only cues Rover to move to my left side, but also to sit. So, I don't have to say "sit" when the dog gets into position. At least, I'm not ready to show the dog as long as I still have to do so.

I used a hand signal with the "sit" cue, bringing my hand down, palm open and parallel to the ground, in front of the dog's nose. I am no longer certain this is necessary, but Sam and Dylan both are very used to it by now, so I have not completely eliminated it from my own ring repertoire, though I tend to think of it as one more handler's crutch.

But I digress, if only slightly. You have to be able to leave your dog before you can start asking for an extended sit. You have to overcome the fact that (a) you have conditioned the dog to move when you do, and (b) Fido is not going to be real wild about you walking away and leaving him there. So give this part of the process a little time.

The journey starts with a single step

Say "sit," take one (and only one!) step forward, and turn and face the dog. Now, you can employ a little footwork here. If on heeling you always step off with your left foot, here step off *with your right foot.* This will be a *foot cue* to remind Fido that this is not heeling. No harm in giving him a *little* help, anyway.

When you face the dog, count one second ("one banana"), then walk back to heel position by going around the dog's left side and coming up on his right. Click and treat, and release him from the sit. Have him sit again, and repeat. And repeat, until he is completely comfortable with the "coming-and-going" process at one step.

Problem: Fido moves

What do you do if Fido gets up when you take a step? Do nothing. Terminate the exercise, return him to position, give him the "sit" cue again, and step with your right foot again. Now, if he stays in the sit when you step with your right foot, click and treat. This lets him know what you are looking for. Release him from the position, and have him sit again.

Now, take a step with your right foot. If he stays still, move your left foot up. If he is still on the sit, click and treat. Release him from the sit, and have him sit again. Now take your step, turn, and if he is still sitting, click and treat. Now, return to heel position, release him from the sit, and have him sit again. Take your step and turn. If he is still sitting, return to heel position and click and treat.

Do not repeat the word "sit!" We humans talk too much. When Fido is having a problem such as moving on the sit, we are tempted to "remind" him to sit by repeating the word "sit" as we move, saying things like "sit, good sit, sit, good boy." Don't do it. The *cue* is "sit." He knows what that word means. If he doesn't (i.e., if he is not sitting 100% of the time on cue, with *zero latency*), you are not ready to be doing this yet. Don't let him off the hook. Use reinforcement, not "cheerleading," to keep him mindful of the task at hand.

Adding time and distance

Now, at one step away, build time, adding a second or two every session until you are up to fifteen seconds. As in your fluency work, this is straight addition, not a variable schedule. When he is comfortable at fifteen seconds, take two steps when you leave him and reduce the time to three seconds. Build back up to fifteen seconds. Now go three steps away, reduce your time again, and build back up again. Repeat, adding a step at a time and reducing and rebuilding time at each step until you are forty feet away (about twenty steps). Note that Fido continues to sit while you are walking away and coming back, so he is actually holding the sit for more than fifteen seconds. In essence, you are getting extra time as a "freebie," given the structure of the exercise.

Don't get dismayed or put off by the fact that this takes time and involves a lot of repetition. There is no substitute for care and patience in building Fido's tolerance for this behavior. I am convinced that (along with the unnecessary confusion caused by use of the word "stay" when leaving the dog) the single most predominant cause for long-term problems in the group exercises is the trainer's lack of patience in the early stages.

Putting the long sit on a variable schedule

Now you are ready for a *variable schedule.* The training goal is for the dog to hold the sit like a statue for ten minutes. This is possible even for a Novice dog if you work patiently. I discuss the concept of a variable schedule in Chapter 2 (see pages 24–27).

Remember always that you are working with two elements: time and distance. At each stage, first add time, then distance. As you add each step of distance, you will reduce the time and rebuild at that distance. Notice, I said *"add each step."* This takes time. If you want a reliable sit, there is no alternative.

You got out to forty feet and Fido held the sit for fifteen seconds. So, fifteen seconds is your "mean." On your next repetition, go just six feet (three steps) away. You will now work on extending time, only with a variable schedule between seven seconds and twenty-five seconds. Work at that level for three days—longer if Fido has trouble with the longer time.

Now, twenty-five seconds becomes your "mean." Work between eleven and thirty-five seconds for three sessions.

Now, thirty-five seconds becomes your "mean." Work between twenty and forty-five seconds for three sessions.

Now you are at a forty-five-second "mean." Work between thirty and sixty seconds for three sessions.

Always remember in these sessions to "yo-yo" up and down from high to low. You can plan out a very specific schedule; don't worry, the dog will never really figure out the pattern. Refer to Appendix A for sample variable reinforcement schedules for training this exercise.

Also, while your "low" is as indicated at each stage, you should always throw in some segments that are even shorter, as low as one or two seconds. It is especially important as you build distance to throw in an easy "surprise!" now and then. For example, you can do occasional "out-and-backs" where you walk out, turn, pause for just a second, and return, click, and treat. Don't make it always just get harder for the dog.

When you are successful at the forty-five-second time, add one step and go back to fifteen seconds, and rebuild your time as before. When you are up to forty-five seconds again, add another step, go back to fifteen seconds and rebuild the time again. Et cetera, et cetera, and so forth.

At the risk of overstating the matter, do not allow yourself to be put off by the sheer quantity of repetitions required to make this work. Any impatience on your part means potential failure in the ring. The good news is that you will find that the dog starts to generalize as you progress, and it will not take as long to go through the variable schedule as you progress. However, even if you spend only one session at each level, put in the time.

Now, when you get back out to forty feet, you can start extending the variable schedule even more. At sixty seconds, your reinforcement range is between thirty and seventy-five seconds. At seventy-five seconds, between forty-five and ninety seconds. At ninety seconds, between sixty and a hundred and twenty seconds. As you can see, with even a few repetitions you are getting in a great deal of time. Your ultimate goal is a ten-minute sit. You get there by building your mean from 120 seconds to 150 seconds, then to 180 seconds, and upward from there in increments of thirty seconds to seven minutes (420 seconds). When you are at seven minutes you can jump the upward time to nine-and-one-half and then ten minutes. The dog should certainly have the patience for the longer schedules by then.

If at any point Fido starts to "break" the sit, either lying down or standing up, you can either reduce your schedule temporarily or add more low-end reinforcers for a session or two.

The "out-of-sight" sit

In Novice competition, the handlers stay in the ring, standing across from the dog for a period of one minute. The "out-of-sight" sit occurs in Open; it simply means that you leave Rover and go to a place where he cannot see you, for a period of three minutes. In Open competition the handlers go behind a blind or some other obstruction. Your goal in training is that Rover will tolerate you being "out of sight" for up to ten minutes. You should train Rover to this degree before entering him in Novice competition. With that degree of discipline, the likelihood that he will ever break a Novice sit is infinitesimal.

Never train "out-of-sight" sits without a spotter or training partner watching your dog while you are out of sight. You must be sure of your dog's safety at all times. When you are ready to start going "out of sight," progress into it gradually. Walk away, go behind a tree or car, and immediately return. If Fido is still sitting when you return, click and treat. Once you are sure that he can tolerate your momentary disappearance, start extending the time that you are "out of sight" to fifteen seconds on a straight schedule, then build the time from there on a variable schedule, just as you did for the sit itself.

Once the dog tolerates you being out of sight for about three minutes, then if you are able to do so, set it up so that you can leave in one direction and return from another. For example, if you train indoors you can leave by one door, go around outside, and return through another.

Introducing distractions ("generalization")

I discussed *generalization* ("proofing") in Chapter 2. Remember, the point of "proofing" is to teach the dog that he can succeed at increasingly higher levels of difficulty, not to "set him up to fail" so that you can "get in a good correction." Put another way, "proofing" in the traditional manner is intended to convince the dog that you always have the power to compel a behavior; generalization in clicker training is intended to convince the dog that he can always succeed.

And remember, though you are training extended sits, there is a rule of reason. Discipline is not mindless robotics. In *Eminent Dogs, Dangerous Men*, Donald McCaig tells the story of a rancher who trained the down-stay so well that one day when his cows broke out of the barn, his dog stayed where he was and was trampled to death. If my dog is faced with a genuine threat to his physical well-being and tries to get away, I'm not going to resent it. I want him to avoid the danger! I take it as a given that he is not going to "break" without really good cause; and if it's good enough for him, it's good enough for me.

Staying in place is for competition, for control, and for safety on the street. I don't want the dog wandering into traffic as we are waiting for the light to change, or onto the highway when we walk from the house to the road to get our daily mail. On the other hand, if a coyote is threatening him, I want him to feel free to save his own life. Keep these purposes in mind in your training. Do not train the dog to hold a stay mindlessly in a situation where no sentient being of sound mind (you, for example) would do so.

I regularly train and practice in public areas, so I always have a certain level of distraction built into my sessions. There may be a ball game going on behind us, or a tennis match to our right, or riders on horseback, or kids kicking a soccer ball around over yonder, or some guys playing dominoes to rap music over at the benches, or a child coming over wanting to pet the "little Lassies." To quote that famous French philosopher Inspector Clouseau, "It's all part of life's rich pageant."

It is best to practice stays in public places as much as possible, as early as possible. Go to a grocery store, stand on the sidewalk, and practice stays with the dog at your side. If your dog is young and a bit skittish, start by having him sit between your feet as you sit on a bench. Make him face outward. Stroke his ears for calmness.

Go to parks where kids are playing, ice-cream trucks are dinging, and weekend athletes are celebrating their prowess. As your dog becomes more comfortable and reliable, expose him to increasingly boisterous situations. Find places where there are birthday parties, perhaps with small rides. Work near merry-go-rounds. Work in increasingly crowded places. Use your imagination. Do this early and often. The more the dog gets accustomed to a general level of hubbub, the less of an effect the events of a dog show will have on him.

As with all other exercises, you will train off lead when in a safe area. However, when you are training in well-trafficked areas like this, use a long line.

Do not use the line to make "corrections" of any type. Hook the line to your belt. That will minimize any temptation to "pop" it, and if your dog "breaks" it will be more secure than if held in your hand. If your dog breaks position, "walk" your hands down the line until you get the dog and regain control with still hands and verbal cues. You may even click as you near the dog, and treat when you get there. The "click" can have a calming effect in this sort of situation.

Next, introduce your dog to the situation where another dog comes over and sniffs him while he is on a stay. Unfortunately, this is a fairly common occurrence even in the Open rings where you would think the dogs (and trainers!) would know better. If your dog "breaks" in the presence of a simple social sniff the judge will likely *not* consider the visit sufficient interference to warrant rejudging you on the exercise (C2, S8). Do this with other trained dogs, first with dogs your dog knows and then with dogs with whom yours is unfamiliar. As with other new criteria, start this working close to your dog and rebuild distance.

After a while, generalization is limited only by your imagination and consistency with the basic rules: Raise the levels of distraction or interference gradually, always give your dog a reasonable chance to win, build on success. I cannot emphasize too strongly that if you want your dog to be able to hold an extended sit under "duress," you cannot wrap the exercise in fear. Reinforcement, not reprisal, will make it work.

Practicing with other dogs

It is important to get in group practice with other dogs. Your dog will probably never do the group exercise alone, unless you are at a Bavarian Lunchenhund Specialty, so you have to accustom Fido to being patient and calm while doing the long sit and down in the presence of other dogs.

Use the presence of the other dogs to establish basic protocol—for example, no visiting before or after the exercise. This is not a social hour. If dogs "visit" while waiting to go into the ring, there is a good chance they will decide to continue the conversation once they are in. Also, what seems a friendly visit can quickly turn into a confrontation. Not a real desirable event when you are about to ask your dogs to sit quietly next to each other for a while.

If your dog has problems with dogs either considerably larger or considerably smaller than he, practice with smaller or larger dogs next to him. Stand close at first, and C/T continuously. Build time and distance as he becomes reliable.

When I am working with other trainers practicing groups, I do several things to "mix it up." First of all, of course, I let the other trainers know what I am doing. They usually regard my antics as a good distraction for their dog. But, I let them know ahead of time. If I am practicing the sit, I usually do not return when the other handlers do. If I am on a variable schedule, I work that schedule. This keeps my dog focused on us and what we are doing, not what everyone else is doing. If I am doing a straight-time practice—for example, we are practicing a straight one-minute sit—I will typically return and release my dog after the other handlers have returned and released theirs. Again, the message is: Wait for me. When I am doing a long variable schedule, I will keep my dog working on the sit while the rest of the dogs do their long downs. If I am doing a short variable schedule and I am finished before the other dogs are done with their down, my dog and I will simply leave the group.

The long down

Dogs that can do the long sit successfully usually have no problem with the long down. The down is the most comfortable and natural resting posture for the dog. It is a considerably easier position for the dog to sustain for an indefinite period of time than is the sit, which is probably why the long down is always the longer of the two exercises.

I find it best to develop time and distance on the sit before doing so with the down. This is because the sit is less "natural" for the dog as a long-duration behavior, so it helps to make that the first subject of discipline. Also, when you have the sit on a variable schedule it will be relatively easy to incorporate time and distance into the down. If you train the down first, however, you will not find the discipline carrying over to the sit quite so readily.

Reminder: Do the down from a stand

Fido already knows how to go down at your side. Here is one area where having him go into the down from a stand rather than a sit is important. It is not hard to see how the two exercises can "blend" in Fido's mind if you have him go into the one from the other, even if you have a momentary "break" in between. You must keep the two exercises distinct.

Reminder: No chaining in practice

I no longer practice long sits and long downs in the same session. For one thing, it would become impossibly dull (but that's mostly my problem). For the dog, I don't put them together because I do not want the dog "chaining" them at all. As a rule, therefore, I train the long sit in one session and the long down in another. I can do them on the same day, as long as the sessions are separated. The long down is a good exercise to practice at home while you are eating dinner or watching television. Rover will be happy to lie down near you. You can work on duration this way, even though it is informal.

Develop the variable schedule as with the sit

Build the exercise through a variable schedule, developing time and distance as you do with the sit. You should get up to about one minute on a variable schedule at forty feet before you start extending time very much on the down. As I mentioned earlier, the sit discipline will carry over to the down fairly readily.

Problem solving

There is bad news, and there is good news. The bad news is that I cannot guarantee that your dog will never break a group sit or down. The good news is that, if you shape the sit and down as outlined (and this may be about a six- to nine-month process), problem solving is not all that difficult.

As a rule, group problems usually first surface on the sit. So the program I outline is geared to that exercise. As I said before, problems on the long down for a dog that has no problems on the long sit are rare.

Remember my "Rule of Three?" Every rule has its exception, and the exception to this rule is on the groups. Here, I use a Rule of One. If my dog breaks a group in a trial, we work on it immediately.

Not all failures mean you have a problem

Some failures are situational. I have, for example, seen lanky, noncoated breeds such as borzois or weimaraners do a fine long sit and break on the down because they are on a particularly hard surface, and their "elbows" hurt. But that is too situational to qualify as a "problem." Stuff happens.

Sometimes, something happens outside the ring to cause a break. One judge told me about a long down with three beagles in the group. The show photographer had set up his photo area just behind the group line, so there was always some level of distraction with squeakies and so forth. But on this occasion he was photographing a poodle, and for reasons known only to himself he decided to use a dog whistle. Well, he blew the whistle and the beagles all popped up, into a perfect "point." They held the "point" until their handlers returned. As it happened, the judge was not only alert to what was going on but gracious, and allowed the three to be judged again.

"Why" the dog broke the group is immaterial; just solve the problem

If you are in Novice you can see what is going on, and may spot something—a noise, or the approach of another dog—that "caused" your dog to break. If you are in Open, because you cannot see what your dog is doing, you probably won't know. If something happened in the ring, the judge will be able to tell you. More often than not, the most she will be able to tell you is something like "he went down after two minutes" or, "he scratched and then sat up." If Fido was responding to something happening outside the ring the judge probably did not see it. So, more often than not, all you are going to know for sure is that your dog "broke the group."

But even in Novice, you often will not really know what happened to cause the break. As a result, a great deal of folklore arises among trainers about the whys and wherefores. "He broke because a little white dog walked past." "He broke because the awning over the stewards' table flapped." "He broke because the German shepherd broke and his best friend is a German shepherd and he thought it was playtime." And so on and so forth. Disregard all of that. It might (barely) make for interesting conversation, but as an aid to training it is pointless.

All you really need to know is that Fido failed to perform the exercise. The other thing you need to know is that once a dog has (say) gone down on a sit at a trial, there is a real risk it will happen again, and soon. "Once is an accident, twice is a lifestyle. . . ." So, do your best not to let it happen twice.

First question: Have you maintained a *variable schedule?* First answer: probably not. This is not meant as a criticism. You did a lot of work getting the dog ready to show, you are showing, you have limited time to train. You have to work on other things like retrieves. It's only natural that you do shorter practices—especially because Rover *never* breaks a group in practice.

"Come to Mama"—Not

Here's the scene. It is the Open class at the Kennel Club of Beverly Hills. They are about to do the second group of the day. Two friends of mine from Pasanita have volunteered to steward the ring. In groups, this means that they stand about halfway across the ring, one at each end of the line of dogs, watching for any misbehavior. It is very late morning on a summer's day, and already hot.

The owners leave, and after about a minute a cocker spaniel gets up and starts to walk slowly across the ring. One of my friends, a jovial lady, takes the dog by the collar and gently leads her over to the steward's position. As it happens, the way the sun is positioned my friend's body casts a shadow over the cocker.

The owners return. The cocker's owner is not pleased, but is on her best behavior as she repositions the dog for the long down. The owners leave again, and as the cocker's owner is leaving the ring the cocker gets up, walks purposefully over to my friend, and plops down right next to her again. To say my friend was embarrassed would be a considerable understatement. I was able to console her by letting her know that with her coloring, red is definitely her color.

This is an object lesson in something. Of what, I have never been entirely sure.

So, when Rover breaks that group in competition, *immediately* go back to your variable schedule. Work at about a one-minute to a one-and-one-half minute mean in the intervening week. Do not practice any long downs. If you really worked through the variable schedule the first time through, this will quickly resolve the problem. It works as a simple reminder to Rover of what you expect.

If Rover breaks a group the next time you show, you have a real problem. Don't just keep showing, hoping the problem will resolve itself. Typically, it will not. You may find that you have to make a hard decision—probably to stop showing for a few weeks at least. You have to break the dynamic. You have to reestablish the behavior on a variable schedule, and you now know that it is going to take some time.

This is also a time to remember the problem of the *behavior chain.* Especially if you are showing a lot, and do not maintain variable and differential reinforcement in practice, the group exercise may become (from the dog's point of view) a behavior chain in which reinforcement only occurs after the down. And what happens to an "intermediate behavior" in a behavior chain when that "intermediate behavior" is not reinforced? It tends to become extinct. This can easily happen to the long sit when paired with the long down.

After Sam had his CDX and had never broken a group in three years, he suddenly started going down on his sits. After several frustrating failures I bought a little sand-cast figure of a sleeping sheltie; I call it "Sam's long sit." Finally, at one trial he went down before I was even halfway across the ring. I finally got the message: It was time to retrain. I had to pull Sam's entries from three shows, but money was no longer the issue. As things were going the money was wasted anyway.

The first thing I did (after I was done banging my head against the nearest tree) was reestablish the variable schedule. I worked him back up to ten minutes. That took about a month. Next, I started reintroducing him to group practices. I put him on the sit and did variable reinforcement. Finally, I let him do a three-minute sit. When he finished we left the group and he got his *jackpot.* We did that a few times, and then I reintroduced variable reinforcement in the group, having him hold the sit while the other handlers went through the sit and down. I reinforced on my own schedule.

I was training Dylan's groups at the same time. That gave me a really diabolical idea. With them side by side, I would have Sam hold the sit while I put Dylan on the down. That has, in fact, become kind of a standard technique for me. If I have both of them waiting for something, I will put one on a sit and the other on a down. I figure, if they can ignore each other and keep their minds on what I have told each of them to do, they will do just fine in the ring.

My training practices gave me another ploy. I work my dogs at the same time, so one is always waiting for the other. So, I would have Sam sit whenever he was waiting for his turn to practice. I would reinforce *randomly,* and I mean randomly; I

would go over to him and C/T whenever I hit a little break point with Dylan. That could be after a minute, or after five minutes. I didn't know when I was going to deliver the reinforcer, and neither did Sam.

All this went on for a period of about two months. Then I went to some Show-and-Gos and practice matches for exhibition only (FEO). All I did was groups. And all I did on the groups was the sit. At first I pulled Sam from the group after the sit and we went for our jackpot; later, I had him sit while the other dogs went through the whole routine, just as we had in practice.

This was also when I figured out about not using the word "stay." I found that if I said "sit" when I left, he had no problem; if I said "stay," there was some degree of likelihood that he would go down. So I just stopped saying "stay." At the time, I didn't give the matter any more thought than this: Sam does better if I don't use the word, so I won't use it *with him.* Then I decided to take the same approach with Dylan; it worked very well. I have since used it with all my students, and it has worked well with them also.

I didn't enter Sam in a trial again for about six months. That was partly to give the program time to work, and partly due to my own schedule. Six months might seem like a long time. I have no theoretical position on the issue except to say that when confronted with a group problem (or any problem, for that matter), you have to be willing to give the solution the time that it takes. It will not serve you well, ever, to get "halfway home" and jump back into the fray. Take the time you need, do it right, and don't put yourself in the position of having to do it again.

The stand for examination

In Novice competition the stand is the "bridge" between on- and off-lead work. You have completed the on-lead heeling pattern and the figure-eight, and you are about to go to the off-lead heeling pattern and recall. It is not at all uncommon to see "the wheels start to come off" in this exercise because the dog, while not necessarily "actively resisting" the handler's command to stand, does not respond readily and briskly to it. Sometimes the exercise becomes something of a wrestling match. I can't help but think that this makes the judge a bit leery about what is to come. It also creates an unhelpful tension between dog and handler, right at the moment when "teamwork" is at a premium.

In Utility competition, the stand is integral to two exercises: the signals, and the moving stand (for examination). In each, the dog must halt standing in heel position and not move forward except on command. In the signals exercise the dog has the benefit of the handler stopping when the dog does before proceeding on the direction of the judge to a spot about thirty feet away. In the moving stand the dog must come to a "freeze" while the handler continues forward without hesitation.

Now, it is possible to complete your CD—even with high scores—and never teach your dog to stand on command. You are permitted to handle the dog physically in order to get him to stand, and I know several handlers who do just that: They lift the dog into the stand and stack the dog. One of my competition students did this with her boxer, believing that she would never go as far as Utility. Sure enough, she got as far as Utility, and now she was faced with teaching her dog the stand so she could get her UD before the dog was too old. P.S. She succeeded.

So I strongly suggest you resist the temptation to take the easy way out in Novice. Teach your dog to stand from a sitting position and teach the stand as an immobile exercise. It is another "fluency" that will make your life immeasurably easier on down the road.

What the Novice stand requires

Structurally, the stand is the easiest of the Novice exercises. The Regulations say that "The principal features of this exercise are that the dog *stand in position* before and during the examination, and that the dog display *neither shyness nor resentment*" (C3, S8).

So there are *three principal physical components* to the finished exercise: (1) The dog must stand, and (2) the dog must remain immobile in a stand while the judge "goes over" the dog, until (3) the handler has returned to heel position and the judge calls "exercise finished." And there are *two "social" components:* The dog must not show shyness or resentment. I'll talk about them in that order.

The physical requirements:
The dog must stand

The stand is unique in obedience competition. It is the only time in any class that the handler is per-

mitted to handle the dog physically. The Regulations provide that "The handler will stand and/or pose his dog off leash by the method of his choice, taking any reasonable time if he chooses to pose the dog as in the show ring" (C3, S8, ¶1).

Presumably, if your judge knows terriers, you could lift your Westie into a stand using its tail, because that is how the dog is posed "in the show ring." I wouldn't recommend it, though. The reason you are permitted to handle your dog to your heart's content is that scoring on the stand does not begin with the judge's initial command ("stand your dog and leave when ready"), but when "the handler has given the command and/or Signal to Stay, except for such things as rough treatment of the dog by its handler or active resistance by the dog to its handler's attempts to make it stand. Either of these shall be penalized substantially" (C3, S8).

Fortunately for most Novice handlers, dogs that "resist [the] handler's attempts to make it stand" usually take a passive-resistance approach, requiring the handler to execute something resembling a Sumo move to get the dog off the ground. It isn't "active resistance" so usually doesn't get scored, but it tells you that the dog doesn't understand the exercise, it often forebodes disaster on the off-lead heeling, and it sure ain't pretty.

How the stand should look

There is no need to execute a "show stack." There are no "style points" in this exercise. All you need is a posture that Fido can hold comfortably and reliably while a stranger approaches and touches him. The easiest way to figure out what is comfortable for your dog is simply to watch him from the side when he stands on his own. As a rule, you will see that the *front feet* are (a) directly under the elbow joint and (b) parallel to each other, and the *rear legs* positioned so that the hock is directly below or just slightly behind the point where the tail crosses the pelvis (what I call the "tailset"), with the feet directly below or perhaps slightly back of the hock joint. The dog standing in this manner is balanced and comfortable and less likely to move than a dog standing with his feet askew.

Don't "overstack" the stand

As a rule, I don't do any "stacking" at all. Woody never liked the stand, and any handling at all made

The stand: A show "stack" is not required in obedience. Harpo has a nice, natural, balanced stand. His front feet are parallel and directly under the elbow joint. His hind feet are under the hocks with the hocks under or just back of the tailset. This stance is comfortable so the dog is less likely to move.

him nervous. So I just left him alone regardless of how he looked. His front feet could be crossed, and he wouldn't move. Sam swings his rear legs all the way back and his front legs are in perfect position every time, so I don't touch him either. Dylan swings his back legs about ninety percent of the way back about seventy-five percent of the time, so with him, while I was still figuring out how this shaping stuff really works, I sometimes lifted his rear to get the legs properly positioned. But that's it.

Point of interest

The Regulations do *not* require that the stand be done from a sit. The judge will tell you to "stand your dog and leave when ready." Remember, the stand comes after the figure-eight. You have released the dog and removed the leash. The dog is probably standing throughout this activity. If the dog is standing on his own, odds are that he is standing naturally and comfortably. If so, simply check his posture and, if satisfied, make sure you are in heel position (nothing more embarrassing than to lose one point on the stand due to handler error! I should know, I've done it and it cost me a Dog World) and leave. However, you should teach your dog to stand from a sit, because this gives you more control over the exercise. If you have not already done this, then review the discussion in Chapter 3 at pages 72–75.

The dog must not move when you leave

We've come all this way, and we haven't discussed the "stay." If you read the sections on the long sit and long down, you know why not: I have dropped the word from my vocabulary. I don't use it with the stand any more than I do with the sit or down. I don't even use it in the Utility signals stand or moving stand. In the first, I am leaving the dog on a stand after we come to a halt; when I leave, I simply repeat the hand signal for the stand. In the second, I am leaving the dog on a stand without breaking stride. So when the judge says "Stand your dog" I say "stand" and give the hand signal for the stand. In Novice, when leaving the dog I do exactly the same thing. It works just fine.

In training the long sit and long down you have already conditioned the dog to accept you leaving his side. It will be easier now because the dog is already conditioned to the process, and you are leaving him on a stand instead of a sit. Even so, go through the initial step-by-step procedures, as you did with the sit, until you are able to take five steps away. In Novice, you are only going to go three steps away, but as in everything else, I advocate "overtraining." If you regularly go five steps away and only take three steps in the ring, your dog will be completely comfortable.

"Setting" the stand

If you did not work on "setting" the stand while doing fluency work, you must do it now. Review the description in Chapter 2, the fluency section (pages 72–75). The critical element is that as you press on the withers and rear end you should feel an answering pressure up from the ground. It is not enough that the dog is not moving; you want to feel a responding "push." That tells you that the dog is well planted.

The TTouch Palliative

It may be helpful if I expand slightly on the TTouch methods here. This is not "clicker training" as such. However, as I have discussed, TTouch associates quite nicely with clicker methods. This is holistic training. We are working with mind, spirit, and body. Especially because the stand can be a source of stress—it is not a natural resting posture for the dog and the dog has to tolerate the approach of a stranger—it is beneficial to do what you can to make the dog as relaxed as possible.

A   B

The stand will be more secure if you can feel an answering pressure when you push down on the dog's withers. Here Morgan uses Ttouch™techniques—the "Python Lift" (a) and "the Butterfly" (b) to encourage Harpo to set his front legs and "plant" himself immovably on the ground. Harpo seems mystified and a bit worried by this new experience, but a click for the right muscular response will reassure him and show him what he's supposed to do. With both hands occupied, Morgan might use a verbal click.

As indicated, I use the TTouch "python lift" to set the front legs. Kneel slightly in front of and slightly to the side of the dog. Encircle the dog's left leg with your hands. Work in the space between the carpals (ankle) and elbow (knee). Start about half way up and "lift" with a light stroking pressure upward.

At first the dog will probably lift his foot. Quietly say "anh-anh" and gently return the foot to the ground. If necessary, release the leg (keeping your hands close but off the leg) and allow the dog to replace his foot himself. This is very much a matter of "feel." Repeat. After one or two reps the dog will leave his foot on the ground and you will feel muscular action downward. I don't recommend clicking here because the sound can disrupt the process. Soft sounds are best.

As the dog's leg feels more "rooted," confirm it with a verbal C/T ("good"/treat). Repeat on the right leg, from the right side. When you have done the "lift" on both front legs, stand up and from the dog's right front press down on the shoulders once more, C/T. You can also use soft verbal reinforcers. The dog should now feel very solidly in place.

You can also use the python lift or the butterfly on the rear legs. The butterfly is less invasive than the python lift and introduces Fido to that touch. Put your hands around the leg and massage in an up-and-out motion with your thumbs. Start with a gentle pressure (just enough to move the skin of your eyelid without bothering your eye) and increase it as the dog learns to resist the upward pressure.

The dog must remain in place

As with the sit, when the stand is under stimulus control the "stand" cue means "Stand right there until I tell you to do something different." However, unlike the sit, here you are working somewhat against instinct. A dog is naturally inclined to lie down or sit while remaining still, particularly if confronted by anything stressful (such as a stranger's approach). In the normal order of things, standing is something the dog does when "on the alert"; it is a precursor to an act: either going forward to confront an enemy or prey, or running away ("fight or flight"). Remember this as you develop the stand and encounter some uncertainty in the dog. It is a triumph of will (and conditioning!) for the dog to stand still and accept the approach of and physical handling by a stranger without moving away from or greeting that stranger.

At the risk of repetition, there are two elements to the Novice stand: the "remain in place" and the examination. You must spend time getting Rover generally socialized to being petted and touched all over, by yourself and others. This is a matter of general socialization. Don't put it together with the stand until the long stand is solid.

As with the sit, shaping the long stand involves the dog standing still for longer and longer periods of time between reinforcements. In other words, like the sit and down, the stand is a "long duration" exercise. Build up to a period of one minute. There is no time limitation in Novice; it typically takes at least half a minute from the time you leave Fido until the time you return. Looking ahead to Utility, it is well to establish real patience now so as to preempt problems with anticipating the down signal.

If you read the preceding section, this is going to sound very familiar. Start by standing at the dog's side. Beginning with one second, build up to fifteen seconds on a "straight-line" schedule. Remember that "click ends the behavior." If Fido moves *after* you click but before you treat, that's okay. On the other hand, if Fido does not move after you C/T, be sure to release him and have him stand again for the next repetition. Be careful not to try to go too far, too fast, in this phase, because Rover is strongly conditioned to sit when at your left side. If you see him starting to sit it is a good sign that you are asking for too much time, too quickly.

When you reach fifteen seconds, go to a *variable schedule* and build up to one minute (your progressions are twenty seconds, thirty seconds, forty seconds, fifty seconds, sixty seconds). Remember to "yo-yo" up and down.

Now add distance. Take one step, turn, and face Rover. Go back to about seven seconds, rebuild to fifteen, then repeat your variable schedule up to one minute. Repeat to two steps, then three, four, and five.

Introducing the examination

From the very earliest days you should have been socializing your dog to human contact. It should therefore be no great shock to the dog's nervous system for a human besides you and your significant other to touch him. And the Novice exam is not exactly a massage session. The Regulations direct the judge simply to touch the dog three times: once on the head, once on the back, and once on the rump (C3, S7).

Return to the position one step away from your dog. Have him stand for seven seconds and then have someone he knows come up and do the Novice "exam." Begin with one touch, at the with-

ers. C/T. When he is comfortable with that, go to two touches (shoulders and back—C/T after the second touch) and then three touches (shoulders, back, and rump—C/T after the third touch). Rebuild your distance up to five feet, repeating this sequence at each step.

Now, increase the level of difficulty by asking Fido to accept a Utility examination. I do this with the Novice dog in order to be certain that my dog is completely comfortable with the exercise; also, especially if you are showing in Novice B, you will encounter judges who "overexamine" the dogs. This is not out of any desire to trick you. Judges who are certified for Utility may go a long time without judging Novice, and habits can be hard to break.

In the Utility examination, "the Judge approaches the dog from the front and examines the dog by going over it with his hands as in dog show judging, except that in no circumstances shall the examination include the dog's mouth or testicles" (C5, S11). Note that while in Novice the judge is using one hand only, in Utility she will use both hands. The examination will start at the shoulders and work back to the rear legs.

Return to your position one step away. Have your training partner approach the dog and put both her hands on Fido's shoulders. C/T. When Fido is comfortable with that, the examiner puts both hands on his shoulders and then runs both hands down his forelegs. C/T. Then add the sides to the progression, then the back, then the tailset (not the tail!), then the rear legs. At each stage, C/T when the progression is complete.

When Fido is comfortable with the full examination at one step, go to a distance of two steps, and repeat. Then three steps, four, and five. You will find it all increasingly easy, but work through the progression even if each step takes only one session.

No "shyness" or "resentment"

If you have socialized your dog well and you go through the process I have just described, you will have no problems with "shyness or resentment." If anything, because you have been patient and made the "approach and examine" process so consistently and completely reinforcing, you may encounter the opposite problem.

At Sam's very first match in pre-Novice, when the Judge came up to examine him Sam reared up on his hind legs, put his paws on the Judge's hand, and grinned up at him. The Judge looked rueful and said, "I sure hate to fail a Sheltie for being too friendly."

If your dog is at all skittish, the time to work him through that is not while you are perfecting the long stand, but outside the context of any particular exercise. Put him in places where he can receive pats and attention from lots of people, and do it regularly. Soon, it will no longer be a big deal for him.

One of my pet-class students has a Portuguese water dog that is leery of people. For several weeks we did a class exercise where every student in the class walked up to him, one by one, and gave him first a pet, then a touch with a brush. The handler C/Ts with every contact.

Another little ploy for working through leeriness is to develop the cue "go say hi." I worked this out with Sam and Dylan. Being Shelties, they are naturally reticent with strangers and other dogs. "Go say hi" tells them that it is okay for them to approach. The easiest way to develop this cue is to have a stranger kneel in front of the dog with a piece of bait. When the dog indicates to the stranger, C/T. In short order Fido will move, if only with one foot, toward the stranger. C/T. When the dog is willing to step to the stranger to get the bait, say "go say hi" just before the dog moves and you C/T.

At first the Portuguese water dog would shy back from the approaching stranger. When we introduced "go say hi," he would immediately walk forward for the greeting. After three weeks the cue became extraneous.

A practice ("generalization") note

Sometimes you would never know that Obedience judges are experienced dog people. Handlers with large dogs may encounter judges who are leery of their dogs. Handlers with small dogs may encounter judges who think the best way to approach a small dog (who might be nervous) is to creep up on him, not unlike Dracula sneaking up bloodthirstily on an unsuspecting victim.

Woody hated the stand. For about three months, he would stay still but almost literally melt into a puddle. I still don't know how solid bone could be so malleable. Then he got "comfortable" with standing upright, but became the master of the forty-five-degree lean. He could lean away from the judge until you wondered if he was somehow exempt from the law of gravity, but never take a foot off the ground. All in all, it took about eight months to get him to stand steadily for the exam.

After all that, I took him to a sanctioned match. The judge thought he looked a little shy (observant judge), and did the Dracula creep. Woody's eyes went wide. He leaned, and leaned . . . and just as he was about to break a young boy outside the ring dropped his bicycle with a tremendous clatter. Woody was in the treetops. The judge turned to me and said, "Obviously that noise spooked him, so I'm not going to fail him for moving." It took me another month to get his stand back.

It was all worth it, though. At one of his Novice trials Woody was under a judge who was a tall, hearty fellow with a large Stetson hat. The judge walked right up to him, touched him one-two-three, backed away, and Woody didn't bat an eye. Our photograph from that day is still one of my favorites.

The point of all this is that you can expect that your dog will encounter judges who will spook him on the exam portion of the exercise, for whatever reason. So make sure, once the stay is *firmly* in place, that you have people go over your dog in all sorts of ways, wearing all sorts of clothes and hats, approaching in all sorts of ways. Let him see it all, and earn lots of clicks and treats for putting up with it all. Use your imagination to mix the process up as much as possible.

A note on the release

After the handler returns to heel position and the judge says "exercise finished," some handlers take a couple of steps forward and have their dog sit, and then release the dog. I never liked that little taradiddle, and I don't see too many still doing it. The problem with it is that, rather than a long-duration behavior, the stand now becomes a behavior chain, with the sit being the ultimate behavior. Guess what? The dog now associates the sit with the stand, and the stand itself is not reinforced. So guess what lurks. . . .

I am adamant about separating the sit and the down, and equally so about separating the sit and the stand. Under no circumstances should you ever give the dog the idea that the sit has any appropriate place in the exercise once the dog is on the "stand" cue.

Release from the stand with an upward motion of the arms, inviting the dog to bounce upward out of the stand. In the ring, I like to play for just a moment after releasing from the stand, and then go back to the place where the heeling pattern will start, using

A moment of play can be useful between exercises. Judges don't mind a playful moment ("Shows good attitude") but be careful to use a brief play release frequently in practice, so things don't get out of control in the ring.

either "let's go" or "heel" to bring the dog back under control.

I like to let my dogs play for a moment between exercises, and generally recommend it. However, if you are going to indulge in this, do a lot of this in practice so that Fido doesn't "lose it" in the ring. Judges don't mind a playful moment ("shows good attitude"), but you are in an area where it is very easy to lose points, even though you are between exercises.

The Regulations provide that "praise and petting are allowed between and after exercises, but points must be deducted from the total score for a dog that is not under reasonable control while being praised" (C2, S22). In Novice, you can use the collar only to "gently" guide the dog between exercises (C2, S23); it is a substantial deduction (typically scored a zero in the B classes) if you physically guide the dog at all in Open and Utility (C2, S23).

Finally, there is "misbehavior" (C2, S25). "Misbehavior" includes "any uncontrolled behavior of the dog such as snapping, barking, or running away from its handler, whether it occurs during an exercise, between exercises, or before or after judging." Conduct that the judge can construe as misbehavior "must be penalized according to the seriousness of the misbehavior, and the Judge may expel or excuse the dog from further competition in the class." Heavy stuff. There are handlers who do not play with their dogs at all while in the ring for the simple reason that once the dog starts to play it is impossible for them to bring the dog under control with a verbal cue only.

Rather than eliminate play from your ring repertoire, condition the dog to play reasonably and return to control. The Canine Good Citizenship test used to have a segment that was perfect for this: The handler would let the dog play for about ten seconds, then put the dog on a sit or down. You should condition your dog to stopping play "on a dime," and returning immediately to heel position.

When I release Dylan he bounces up and down once or twice, I give him a quick tousling of his ruff, and he is back at heel. Sam's favorite play is a brief wrestling match: I grab his ruff and shake it, he puts his forepaws on my arms. Again, it lasts for a couple of seconds and it's back to business. It's a positive and legal form of interaction. Just keep it under control.

If your dog does "lose it," remember some real basics such as the fact that you originally shaped Fido's name as a "recall" cue. Call his name with sufficient clarity to catch his attention and get him back at heel. Do not let your hands be active at all, since any hand motion is likely to get him going again. Move quickly to the starting place for the next exercise.

Handling note: Handler's posture

The Regulations do not impose any requirements on how you stand after you have left your dog. You are only required to stand with your hands at your side when the dog is coming toward you to a "front" position. The Regulations are entirely silent as to hand position in any of the stationary exercises, except insofar as you might do something that really strikes the judge as an additional cue.

Some postures other than "hands at side" have a cue-like quality, but are not scored as such. I like to adopt a relaxed posture: hands folded at my chest or behind my back, weight slightly shifted to one side. The first person I saw do this was Pat Cook at the Sacramento Cycle Classic; since her dog placed in the top ten, I decided it was something you could get away with. This posture tells the dog that I am not going to ask him to do anything, because it is visibly different from the posture I take when I am going to call him or give a signal. This is the same posture I adopt in the group exercises, and it serves the same purpose.

Finish, front, recall

I'm titling this section in this way to make a point. The recall is a *behavior chain* that ends with the front-and-finish. Actually, the recall is probably the most fundamental behavior chain in competitive obedience and, as a behavior chain, an essential fluency. With the exception of the "return-to-heel" element of the Utility moving stand exercise, every exercise in Novice, Open, and Utility that involves the dog working away from the handler ends in a recall-to-front.

The Open drop on recall and the Utility signals recall are "true" recalls in that they are specifically cued. In all the other "performance" exercises—retrieves, broad jump, scent discrimination, directed retrieve, and directed jumping—the recall-to-front element is an "uncued" part of the overall chain. The "cue" is a *repertoire cue.* The dog simply has learned that whenever he is coming toward you, having completed some task "out there," he is to come to front and sit. For this reason—assuming, of course, that you have properly trained the recall in the first place—you do not have to reteach the recall with every exercise.

The recall is a behavior chain. As a rule, we shape behavior chains from back to front. In putting the recall together, then, think of it as a "finish, front, and recall." Because you have done fluency work, you can modify this "rule" somewhat, in that you do not necessarily have to reshape every element of the chain from back to front. However, when putting the fluencies together, it is still best always to do so from back to front. This is always the most reliable way to educate the dog as to any chain. So, let's begin at the ending.

Shaping the finish and front: Some general considerations

It's a simple, if rather astounding, fact of life: Once you get your scores into the mid-190s, prog-

ress into the rarefied atmosphere of 198 and up depends almost entirely on two things: straight sits at heel, and straight fronts. The reason is that if you are scoring in the mid-190s you are not getting more than one to two points off in heeling; your dog is performing the principal portions of each other exercise correctly; you are not contributing any significant handler errors to the scoring; and your team is not receiving any substantial deductions. So what is left to score? Fronts and finishes.

You can easily do the math. A front where the dog's head is aligned but the rear is crooked is worth half point. Get four of those in Open, and you have lost two points (that's a 198 if everything else is perfect, 197 if you lose one point heeling, 196.5 if Fido bobbled or mouthed the dumbbell). Get six of those in Utility, and you have lost three points (that's a 197 if everything else is perfect, 196 if you lose one point on heeling, 195.5 if Bowser scooted up a tad sitting up on signals, 195 if he sits a wee bit crooked when you turn for the articles, and so forth, there being seemingly no limit to the things you can get nicked for in Utility). Now, add to each crooked front a crooked sit at heel on the finish—and your deductions double. Now add to that slightly crooked sit at heel a slightly lagged or forged sit . . . 'nuff said.

A word of comfort to the new Novice competitor. You are not going to fail the recall if Fido comes when called, even if he neither sits in front nor does a finish. Why? Because neither the front nor the finish is a "principal feature" of the exercise (C2, S10)!

I once knew of a fellow who primarily trained field dogs. He wanted a CD on his dogs, but did not want to teach them things that would interfere with their field work, so he never taught them a finish. (I'll leave for another day the question of why a finish should not interfere with field work.) What did it cost him? Three points. And he typically scored in the mid-190s in Novice. You couldn't get away with that in Open and Utility, of course, but he wasn't interested in those titles. He knew what he wanted, and he lived with what it cost him.

You not only won't fail if your dog does not do a finish, you won't even fail if your dog doesn't do a front, but goes directly to the sit at heel. What will that cost you? It depends. It's a substantial deduction (three points; C3, S11) for the failure to sit at front. Having failed to sit at front, it doesn't really matter what your dog does at that point. Now, you will be given the order to "finish." Your dog must move into the heel position; a slight shift of the butt won't suffice. So let's suppose that Fido came all the way around to heel rather than sit in front, and you give the cue "heel." Fido may look at you and say, "Hey, dad, I'm already there." So he is. Three points more (C3, S11). Now, let's say that Fido is sitting at heel and you say "get around," and he goes around you in a circle and sits back at heel. He's done a finish. Now he will only be scored for sitting crooked, etc.

The point is not that some cues are better than others, but that *neither the front nor the finish is a principal part of the recall exercise.* Therefore, even the failure to perform both will not cost you more than six points.

That said, the quirk in the Regulations is that although it is not explicitly stated as a principal feature of the recall exercise, you can nonetheless fail if the dog does not end up close enough to you that you can touch the dog without stretching forward or moving a foot (C2, S11). So if Fido does not come to front but wanders away from you to one side or another, you would receive a zero—not because he did not sit in front but because he ended the recall portion of the exercise at a place too far away from you.

So what's the moral? Train your finishes and fronts and make sure they are under stimulus control. For the finish, this means that Fido does not move from front except on cue. For the front, this means that Fido learns that the cue for "sit in front" is the action of coming toward you from a distance, whatever else he may also be doing (retrieving, jumping, etc.).

The finish

Every recall or recall-related exercise ends with a finish in which the dog moves from the front position to the heel position. One exercise—the Utility moving stand—ends with a finish but no front.

We have already covered "heel position" as a fluency. In beginning training you should teach Bowser to *find heel position* from wherever he is in relation to you. With this in place, it is not difficult to move to the formal "finish."

If you have trained Bowser to find heel from only one side (typically, this will be the right side), it is *essential* to teach him to find heel from both sides. In other words, he should be able to do both the "go-behind" (to your right) and "swing" (to your left) finishes.

This is a handy training tool. By having both a swing and go-behind in place, I can use the finish as a kind of reinforcer. By sending the dog to the right

(and not delivering a reinforcer) I am saying, "That wasn't quite right, I want you to do it again." By sending him to the left (and delivering a reinforcer) I am telling him, "success!" Thus, the swing becomes a kind of jackpot. Obviously, this is something I get to only after each finish is thoroughly trained. So, except when I am training the finish as such, the direction that I send the dog tells him whether we are going to move on to something else, or if there is still work to be done. Once this is in place, it gives me a very useful communication tool in the ring.

Having both finishes in your repertoire helps in the ring in a lot of ways. The simplest is that you can never tell when you might need to cue Bowser into heel position, or from where. Novice dogs, especially Novice A dogs, are often highly distractible. If your dog loses heel position or worse, starts to run away, in addition to wanting him readily responsive to being called, you want him to be able to find heel and get back under control easily. So wherever he gets to and whatever he is doing there, you want him comfortable and confident about coming back to fully correct position.

Also, if Bowser always finishes in one direction, he may well start to anticipate you sending him in that direction. So even if he never "anticipates" the finish by eliminating the front, this can cause him to tend to come to front slightly hitched in the direction of the finish. If he doesn't know which way you are going to send him, he will be more inclined to find a neutral "front" position.

Even in Novice (with only one front-and-finish), having both ways of doing the finish in place gives you an option if you need it. Let's say Bowser has come to front but he is off-line to your left. If your only finish is to the right, he may not make it all the way around—or line up straight if he does. By having the swing finish in your repertoire, you stand a better chance of getting a straight finish even if the front is crooked. No sense in piling up those half points.

When you get to Open and Utility with their multiple fronts, having both in hand is valuable. In Open I will typically alternate swing/go-behind/ swing/go-behind. This serves several purposes. The first swing is a +R for doing a successful drop on recall. (Dylan sometimes does a "push-up" instead of a full drop; if he does, I give him a go-behind. He has been doing this long enough to recognize that as a "Thpbbbpppt.")

In Open there are two retrieves: the retrieve on flat (ROF) and the retrieve over high jump (ROH).

A

B

C

The "Pop" swing finish gives Sam a chance to celebrate. The dog leaps up and switches from front to heel position in mid-air. The slightly crooked sit may cost us a half point but Sam enjoys this behavior, so I use it as a "Work's all done!" signal and a jackpot reinforcer.

Because of our training history, the go-behind on the ROF reminds him that there is another task to do and operates as a sort of VR. This is helpful on the ROH because he has more things to think about, and the "boost" I get from that little bit of VR improves his focus. Now when I give him the swing after the ROH it is a jackpot +R for completing both retrieves successfully.

Last there is the broad jump. I always send him to the right for that finish. There just isn't enough room for my dogs to do the swing the way they like to do it (with a "pop" up and to the left) without seriously rearranging the boards. A smaller dog can do the swing, perhaps even with a pop; mine cannot.

In Utility, I extend the use of the go-behind and the swing as communication. On the articles (two retrieves) and directed jumping (two go-out and jumps) exercises, I send the dog to my right after the first, and to my left after the second. And I always have the option of sending the dog to the right if he has flubbed an exercise. Remember, if he *expects* a swing as a "congratulations" movement and gets a go-behind instead, he has heard me tell him that he didn't get the job done properly. As a rule, this gets me a heightened performance on the next exercise. For that reason, I may even use it if he did the exercise "correctly" but desultorily.

Training the finishes (applied targeting)

In developing the targeting fluency, you taught Rover to move in a full circle to your right and to your left. To train the finishes you are simply going to refine these motions so that the dog ends up at heel position after moving in either direction. You are then going to fade the target stick so that the cue for the finish becomes a simple left- or right-hand signal.

The "go-behind" finish

In Chapter 3, Fluencies, I said that I prefer the swing finish. But I teach both. In one respect the go-behind is preferable as the first finish to teach because it is the simplest. The dog goes to his left, circles behind you and ends up sitting at your left side. Nothing to it. The only real "trick" to this finish is keeping the dog moving briskly as he goes behind you. The space between the point where he disappears on your right and where he resurfaces on your left I call "Death Valley." You can't see him, you don't know what distractions he is encounter-

ing, and (of course) there isn't a thing you can do about it.

I saw one dog go behind his handler, spot a kid with an ice cream cone outside the ring, and go for the cone. One of my first instructors sent her dog to her right, and stood there waiting for him to complete the finish. After a few seconds she noticed the judge was laughing. So were the ring stewards. So was the crowd. She finally broke down and looked behind her and there was her dog, chasing his tail.

You have already taught Buster to move in a full circle to your right. Now tighten the circle so that he is moving close around you. Start with Buster in front of you—whether he is sitting or standing is not immediately important. The target stick is in your right hand. C/T him for a couple of touches to get him going.

Now move the target stick to your right, but instead of turning with him, stay stationary, swing the target stick behind your back, and then quickly bring it around in front of you and over to your left side to give Buster a target to orient to as he comes around you. As he arrives at your left side and touches the stick, C/T.

Has Buster sat at heel? That depends on how consistent you were in your fluency work. He should have learned that when he is at heel, if he is not moving, he is on a sit. So, "heel position" should be a repertoire cue for the sit. If he sits when he gets around to heel, count your blessings and go on. If he does not, do yourself—and your dog—a favor and worry about one thing at a time. The first thing to worry about is that you are giving him proper hand and target stick movement, especially that you are getting the stick behind your back and around to your left in time. Work on it until your timing is perfect. You can't ask your dog to be any sharper than you are. Once you are sure about your own handling, become demanding about what Fido is doing. If you are cuing him around properly with the stick and he is not sitting, give him the "sit" cue *immediately before* he touches the stick, and before you C/T.

The "go-behind" cue

Unlike other exercises where we get the behavior "off-cue" and add the cue when the behavior is in place, you are always cuing the finish (whether the go-behind or the swing). This is simply because you *induce* the finishing movement with the movement of the target stick.

Because you begin training with the hand movement with the target stick, the easiest cue to estab-

Use the target stick to shape the go-behind finish.

lish for the go-behind is the motion of your hand to your right. I like to use the hand signal rather than the verbal command, even in Novice, because it conditions the dog to keep his attention on me at all times. Also, it avoids fumblemouth. When completing my CD with Woody I was very nervous. It was

my first! He was at front, the judge said "finish," and I—with great enthusiasm and verve—said to him "finish!" He looked up at me as though I had "eaten of the insane root that takes reason prisoner," and then moved around to heel just to let me know that he knew what was going on even if I did not. I can still see him sort of shaking his head and seeming to sigh as he moved.

Fading the target stick

Martin and Pear (*Behavior Modification, What It Is and How To Do It*, 5th ed., 1978) define *fading* as "the gradual change, on successive trials, of a stimulus that controls a response, so that the response eventually occurs to a partially changed or completely new stimulus." At this point, what is the stimulus for the dog to move around to the right and to heel position? It is the target stick in your right hand, moving to the right. You have to fade the target stick from the picture.

If you have been using a wooden dowel you will have to shorten it. If you have been using one of the commercial models, fold it in half. If you have the kind that folds in quarters, fold it in half for now.

Folding the target stick and then holding it further toward the end allows you to "fade" the target until the go-behind finish can be cued by the hand movement alone.

The target end of the stick is now closer to your hand. Have your palm open and fingers extended. Hold the stick between your thumb and your palm. Your hand is now in the "signal" position; you will keep this "look" constant from now on. The signal is with your hand open, palm facing the ground.

Over successive repetitions, bring the target end closer and closer to your fingertips, until there is little or nothing of the target end showing. If you are using a wooden dowel, you will want to make several of successively shorter lengths, ending with one that is about the length of your hand from the heel of your palm to your fingertips. If you are using a commercial model that only folds in half, just slide the folded stick further and further up along your palm so that less and less of the end shows. If you have a quarter-fold model, fold it first into half and then into quarters, and the end can virtually disappear.

There is no recipe for how many repetitions you will require. Let the dog direct you. As long as you are getting repeated responses to the motion with the target stick visible to some degree, you can continue to lessen its visibility. If at any time the dog seems confused or uncertain, slow down, back up a step, and rework.

When you have reduced the visible end of the stick to a nubbin and the dog is moving around to heel in response to your motion, hold the target stick so that it is in your hand, but no part is visible past your fingertips. Make your hand motion to the right. With all the repetitions you have done fading the stick, the probability is that he will move with your hand motion. C/T on his arrival at heel position. If he doesn't move, you have gone a bit too fast.

The final step is to reduce your hand motion so that it becomes a snappy movement to your right, covering a total distance of about twelve inches. You can reduce it even further; my signals for the finish now barely cover three inches in either direction.

The swing finish

The advantage of the swing over the go-behind is that in the swing the dog is never out of your sight. The movement is inherently quicker, so this finish tends to be brisker than the go-behind. Finally, you can easily get the dog to "pop up" as he starts the swing, which makes for a nice, jazzy move. That's especially impressive with a large dog.

It is usually easier for large or long-bodied dogs to do the go-behind accurately because they can wrap their body around yours. In the swing the dog

A

B

C

D

Shaping a swing finish with the target stick, you start with the dog in front of you and stick in your left hand, and lead him past your leg and around toward the front again into heel position. Make the loop smaller and smaller until the dog comes into a straight sit; then fade the target stick and use the hand movement alone as the cue.

has to reverse directions, and this can be hard for the larger or longer-bodied dog to do accurately. If you are working the swing with such a dog, you are almost compelled to teach the "pop up" move at the start.

The swing motion

In the swing finish the dog goes to his right, and after he is past you on your left pivots 180 degrees to his left, coming around to sit at heel.

To shape the swing you use the target stick in your left hand instead of in your right as you did for the go-behind. With Fido sitting at front you bring the target stick to your left, giving Fido plenty of room at first to make the pivot. When his tail is about even with your leg, bring the target stick around toward your body and forward so he will follow the stick into heel position. Think of it as "stirring the soup." It's harder to read about than to do.

Gradually tighten the loop on the swing until Rover is making the swing in a tight space. The wider the loop on his swing, the greater the chance that he will sit crooked. Fade the target stick over time in the same manner described earlier.

The "pop" motion

Some dogs, when figuring out how to make the swing, will naturally decide to pop up as they do it, simply because it is easier for them to make the turn if they do so. Now, when I say "pop up" I am not talking about the kind of spectacular "flip" that Patricia Burnham did with her greyhounds, where the dog gets virtually as high as the handler's head. Go for it if you want, but it's a bit beyond me. All I want is for the dog to hop up into the air getting his front feet off the ground and doing the pivot while in the air, settling back into heel position when he lands.

Shape the pop after you have shaped the basic swing. This way Bowser will know where he is going. In your initial fluency work on targeting you had Bowser rear up on his hind legs to touch the stick. Now you use that motion to *shape* the pop. It works best if you start with Bowser in motion a bit, or at least standing, rather than sitting still, simply because his momentum will help you get the desired response. Once he understands what you are asking for, it is not difficult to transfer that to the front position.

Start with Bowser in front of you, but don't worry about front position as such. Hold the target stick above but near Bowser's head. "Bounce" it a bit to induce him to jump up to touch it. C/T the jump. Your hand motion will look like this: Raise your left hand (holding the target stick), palm open, up and out to your left, so that at the completion of the hand motion your palm is facing the dog. Next have Bowser jump to the stick from a sit. Next put Bowser on a front. Have the target stick in your left hand. Give your pop signal, up and to the left. C/T the jump.

Now you want to add the swing into heel position. After he is consistently jumping to follow the stick, simply bring the stick down and past you so that he follows it past you to touch it. Next, bring it past you and around so that he follows it into heel position. Give each progression the time that it takes. Usually, if you teach the swing first and then add the pop, Bowser gets the idea quickly.

The front

In the words of one of my first tutors, "Fronts are everything." In Novice you have one front-and-finish; in Open, four. In Utility, you have six fronts and seven finishes. There are two primary difficulties: getting the dog to hit the front position accurately, repeatedly; and teaching the dog to hit front from almost any angle.

Angle fronts may not seem important to the Novice competitor. The recall is on a straight line, so why should angling be a problem? But even for the Novice competitor, things are not so simple. For someone who primarily competes indoors, it may be true that your Novice dog will never have to come to front from an angle. For the outdoor competitor, it is rarely if ever true. For one thing, it is difficult to walk across the ring in a straight line outdoors, especially if the center poles are offset. Also, when outdoors you are often on uneven ground with bare patches, places where something yucky has been, and so on.

Dogs respond to these things unpredictably. The dog coming "straight" in may arc for any number of reasons; once he arcs he has to be able to come back to front. I once saw a Weimaraner on a recall charge toward a bare patch of ground, jump to his left to avoid it, and then regain his straight line toward his handler, seemingly without breaking stride. At one Open trial the judge was starting the recall in a corner of the ring that about half of the dogs wanted nothing to do with. We humans could not see anything wrong, but those dogs certainly could sense it, and for most the recall was disrupted in one way or another (coming in slowly, leaving the sit before being called, etc.). One Rottweiler in Novice got his nose to the ground as he arose from the sit and kept it there all the way across the ring, never so much as looking up once to see where his handler was—and still ended up more or less in front position.

In Open and Utility you encounter fronts combined with retrieves. The greatest difficulty in this regard is in Open. Fronts following the Open retrieves will almost invariably be at an angle because the dumbbell will usually bounce to one side or the other. In the ROH the dog not only has to come back to you at an angle, but take a jump in the process—which may add its own elements of slewing the dog off line. Open also requires Bowser to hit front after the broad jump, which demands that the dog turn 180 degrees from his line of flight on the jump. In Utility, although the dog goes out and returns on an angle in the directed retrieve (gloves) exercise, and returns on an angle in directed jumping, you are at least facing him head-on as he returns to you. Nonetheless, especially on directed jumping, Bowser often has to adjust his line of travel to find front. So Bowser has to be able to find front from almost any position to your right or left, from any distance.

In 1990 I participated in the Cycle Western Regional in San Bernardino, California, and took the opportunity to watch some of the legends work. I wanted to get a start on forming my own "mental picture of perfection." To that end, I watched Andrea Vaughn and her golden retriever "Rocky" in Open. Rocky's fronts were astounding. Regardless of how the dumbbell bounced, when he got about eight feet away from Andrea, he lined up dead on target and came in like a spaceship on a tractor beam. I watched from a position behind her, and on each front you could see exactly the same amount of haunch on either side of her. That image of the "perfect front" has stayed with me to this day.

Repeating fronts

Bowser also has to learn to find front again, and again, and again. Once you have taught him what exactly "front" is, do a ton of repetitions to get him accustomed to hitting the position without being reinforced with a C/T every time. After all, he isn't going to get that reinforcer in the ring. Use a high number of repetitions to create a high level of probability that on any given occasion, it will be right.

I have stated that, when in doubt, when it comes to repetitions "less is more." You want to quit on a success and quit while you are ahead, and all too often a trainer can ruin a good session by doing repetitions for no particular purpose other than to do repetitions.

However, a behavior is not learned until the subject can perform it with a high degree of reliability. And one way to measure reliability is quantitatively. To put it crudely, if Fido does the behavior one hundred times, how many times out of a hundred does he do it properly? That's your "reliability ratio." Professional trainers, working with assistants, will train their animals for hours at a time, ultimately putting them through thousands of repetitions in a short period. So they may be looking at a "reliability ratio" of 9,990 (or higher) out of 10,000. The chances that the animal will perform the behavior correctly on any one given occasion become quite high.

Now, you and I are not likely to do 10,000 repetitions of a single behavior with a single dog in a lifetime, much less in a few weeks or hours. But let's say that you do ten repetitions and get eight successes. Your "reliability ratio" is 8:10. Put another way, the odds are two in ten that on any given occasion you will get a "miss." If you build up to a hundred repetitions and get ninety successes, you have used the higher repetitions to build a greater frequency of success and, therefore, a greater degree of reliability. If you do 1,000 repetitions with 990 successes, you have raised the odds in your favor even more.

So at some point in training every behavior, and especially any behavior that must be repeated often with a high degree of precision and without specific reinforcement for each performance, you *must* use high numbers of repetitions to build that "reliability ratio" in your favor.

This always raises mind-boggling discussions about how "some dogs tolerate high repetitions better than others," and so forth. There is some validity to what can only be termed these "myths," but only some. For example, Jack Russells are hyperactive, and so "busy" that it is difficult to keep them focused on multiple repetitions. Or, shelties and other "smart" dogs tend to resist high numbers of repetitions because they "get bored and start thinking up variations." True enough in each case (feel free to add your own), but with one proviso: *only unless, and only to the extent that, you fail to condition them to tolerate high numbers of repetitions* in the expectation of reinforcement. To some degree this is a question of the proper use of *variable reinforcement.* And, to some degree, this is a matter of your imagination.

I have discussed using VR elsewhere. Whenever you extend your VR schedule, you accustom (condition) Fido to working longer, or harder, *or repeating the same behavior multiple times* to get his reinforcer. So you can use "scoot fronts" and other means of getting rapid multiple repetitions as a method of VR. You want Fido to work a little harder, a little longer, a little more precisely, but you don't want to push it so far that he quits.

Perhaps an analogy will help. Imagine yourself blowing a bubble with bubble gum. If you get your wad ready and blow as hard as you can, it will just splatter. Blow carefully, extending the bubble a breath at a time and making sure you always have enough material available, you can get a large bubble. With repetitions, you are blowing that large bubble. You are constantly extending Fido's capacity to do more work, but gradually so that the bubble does not burst. It's up to you to know your dog well enough to know where that balance lies.

So be inventive with variable reinforcement. Fido must be able give you two, three, five, seven fronts in a row, all correct, without reinforcement (that is, without clicking or treating). When you do deliver the reinforcement, because you have asked for several performances per reinforcer, make the reinforcer something of a jackpot. Extra effort merits extra rewards.

Imagination also plays a role; you want to increase repetitions without benumbing your dog or overwhelming him with the challenge of having to be right again and again and again. First, build the basics carefully with reasonably high repetitions so that you get a high ratio of success from the very beginning. Second, as you add new criteria (or refine existing criteria), reduce the number of repetitions so that you are getting correct responses every time. Third, change the puzzle: Use different angles, distances, or distractions to vary the "look" or "feel" slightly so that you are not simply asking the dog to repeat exactly the same movement indefinitely. Get enough repetitions with each variation that you can be confident of what the dog will do, but keep the variations coming.

This is a nice early training stage in which to introduce Fido to repertoire reinforcement. At the start, in training the front as such you will C/T for correct fronts. Ultimately, you have to get away from this because you will never have an opportunity to reinforce the front as such in the ring. Let's go back for a moment to the concept of using the swing finish as a reinforcer. At some point in the training process you will have put the front and finish together as a behavior chain, so that Fido only gets the C/T after the finish. How do you then reinforce fronts without "breaking" the chain? Once the chain is in place, you only *allow* the dog to finish after a straight front (or several straight fronts). This way, the finish reinforces a correct front. An alternative is to put the swing finish into your repertoire as a "jackpot." Send Fido to the right, the front was so-so; send him to the left, it was perfect.

The "front" cue

As is so often the case, there is no "right" or "wrong" as to the cue you choose to use, only good reasoning. In the immortal words of Tom Lehrer when describing the New Math, "It doesn't matter what answer you get, so long as you do the problem right."

I have two recall cues: "come" or "here," which means "Get over here but don't worry about coming to front," and "front," which means "Assume the proper position in front of me." In the Novice recall I use "front" as my recall command. In the Open drop on recall, I use "here" for the first call, and "front" for the recall after the drop.

The two cues are useful in training and in daily life. I am often calling my dogs to me without needing (or particularly caring about) a formal front. "Come" and "here" serve that purpose. If I used "come" to mean both "get over here in close proximity" and "give me a formal front," it would not be a clear cue. The formal front would inevitably suffer. Reserving the cue "front" for that specific application solves the problem.

Another way to look at it is that, for competition purposes, I train the recall as a long-distance front. Fido is doing exactly what he always does—finding front from some odd position—only at a distance of forty feet. So by using the cue "front," I am being completely clear as to what I'm expecting at that time.

I add the cue when first defining the *topography* of the front position. Fido learns that "front" is a *position that he comes to* at the end of a behavior (coming to me). I have Fido sitting directly in front of me, properly aligned (even if I have had to move to get proper position). Say "front" immediately before you C/T. Repeat a few times. Then, introduce "scoot fronts." Take a step back, induce Bowser to move with you if you have to, and say "front" *simultaneously as* he scoots forward to a point directly in front of you, click as he starts to settle into position, treat when he is fully sat.

Make the step short—just enough to get him moving, but not far enough that he has any real chance to lose alignment. You want to see his rump coming up off the ground, but he should not come up into a full standing position. A half step back is usually sufficient. What if the dog "skews" out of position? Simple: Don't click, don't treat. Wait a beat (break the connection between the two events), back up again, and deliver the "front" cue again. If he is in correct position, C/T. Almost invariably you will see Fido put some extra effort into the second front. The overall effect is very similar to what you get with variable reinforcement. By rewarding the front achieved through that extra effort, you make it more likely that you will get that extra effort again.

Teaching the dog to work his rear end (redux)

In Chapter 3, Fluencies, I discussed basic approaches to teaching the dog to work its rear end. Now you need to refine the dog's consciousness of the skill. Very often, when coming to front, Fido will line his head up properly but his rump will end up wherever it happens to land. Fido has to learn to think about adjusting his rear end into alignment with his head as he lines himself up with the center line of your body.

"Chuting"

Is this the place to say "Don't chute the dog?" I didn't think so. Sorry.

"Chuting" involves a process of having the dog work through a progression of chutes in a V shape, the smaller end flattening at your feet. You set up the chutes in front of you. Just in front of your feet the chute is just wide enough to give your dog room to sit comfortably but not swing his rump to one side or the other. At the other end the chute is wide enough to allow Fido to enter comfortably. The sides serve as an obstacle, compelling him to arrive at a straight front.

You typically start with two broad-jump boards on their sides, giving you a chute with six-inch sides. From there you work down to 2×4 boards painted white, first on edge and then flat, 2×2 boards, then 1×1 boards; you then shorten the length of the board so that you end up with a chute about eighteen inches long or less, you then go to uncolored boards, etc.

It's a lot of work and, generally speaking, I think it is more work than is necessary. I went through a chuting program with both Woody and Sam, and I cannot say that their fronts were any better than Dylan's, with whom I have not done any chuting work (with one small exception, described later). I do not use chutes with any of my students, and their dogs' fronts are consistent.

Put another way, the chutes serve as *negative reinforcers.* This does not make their use sinful, but it helps clarify how they work. The aversive element is that if the dog sits on the chute, he will not enjoy the experience. He "removes" the aversive by sitting properly between the boards. This can make him conscious that something unpleasant (not direly unpleasant, but unpleasant nonetheless) happens if he doesn't line up properly, and that can trigger the thought processes. So this is a behavior in which judicious application of negative reinforcement can assist you.

But, as with all negative reinforcers, there are problems. First and foremost, negative reinforcers primarily teach Fido how to avoid the unpleasant consequence. So as you reduce the size of the chutes and their aversive quality diminishes to the point of being nonexistent, Fido may find that he is not experiencing unpleasant consequences *even if* his front position is incorrect. It didn't bother Sam to sit on a half-inch PVC pipe in the grass. And so? You end up reinforcing incorrect fronts. All that elaborate chute work can easily end up vaporizing the behavior.

If you have been consistent with delivering *positive reinforcement* as the dog moves his rear end to avoid the chutes, you may be able to fade the negative reinforcers successfully. But as with any combining of positive and negative reinforcers, this requires exquisite timing and finesse. Also, you will inevitably go through a period of working the dog through the absence of the negative reinforcer altogether, *and that is where the real training will take place.*

So as a rule, I prefer not to complicate the training process. Teach the position, introduce motion a step at a time, reinforce continuously until the position is established, and put each level of the front on a variable schedule before going further. The standard recipe works. The only real issue is your patience and persistence.

The Plexiglas rod

The Plexiglas rod is a tool I sometimes find helpful in two situations: working with crossover dogs, and when angle fronts (described later) become acute. This is sort of a low-key chute method, easy to bring into play and easy to fade. It doesn't work well unless you have laid the groundwork by teaching the dog how to work his rear end.

Keep your hands at your sides and hold the rod so that it will reach the ground when held at a forty-five-degree angle to the ground. Don't make it shorter or it will not serve the very specific purpose for which this is intended, that is, to cause Fido to shift his rear end as he comes to front. The rod is stationary at all times; never use it to tap the dog's rump. Holding a rod in each hand, have the clicker in one hand, held between thumb and rod. From the front, the "look" of your posture is exactly as it is if you are awaiting the recall in the ring.

The critical thing here is that the clicker is acting as an *event marker*. That is, you are identifying a specific muscular action as "correct." Timing is essential: Your click must immediately respond to Fido *adjusting his rear end* to maneuver it around the rod and into a centered position. You must click the movement of the rear end, and not simply the finished result of a centered front. The reason for using two rods is that once Fido gets used to adjusting his rear in one direction, he will start to overadjust. The second rod provides a passive restraint to prevent him from overadjusting very far.

Once Fido is adjusting consistently, you can fade the rods by first holding them down at your side, and bringing one or the other out only if you see the dog lining up to one side or the other. Again, click when the dog makes his adjustment, not when he comes to the final position. From here, it is a simple matter to eliminate the rods entirely.

Angle fronts

A very good way to do multiple fronts while making the dog work his rear is to do angle fronts. Introduce these after you are able to get multiple straight "scoot fronts" taking six steps straight back. Now you can increase the level of difficulty.

Start with the dog sitting directly in front of you. Facing straight ahead, take one step back to the right to a position between 5:00 and 6:00. Deliver the "front" cue as you are stepping backward. To get to front, Fido must not only move forward, he must also adjust his rear end slightly to his left.

When introducing angle fronts, you must be very conscious about working with *increments of behavior. Click as* Fido is moving his rear, not after he plants it on the ground. Remember, you are reinforcing muscle memory, not just results. Fido may adjust his rear end, but not quite all the way. *C/T the movement* and increase the range of motion with differential

reinforcement. This way, you will get more movement and, ultimately, the amount of movement necessary to achieve that straight front.

Once you are getting the amount of movement necessary to achieve that straight front, C/T the result. Put another way, you can get too much movement. There is a point at which he is straight. C/T that result to define how much movement you want.

Once Fido gets the idea of moving and shifting to his left, repeat the same process but to a position between 6:00 and 7:00. Now he is moving and shifting to both sides. Now you can do multiple repetitions, three or four to the right, three or four to the left, then mixing them up (one left, two right, two left, etc.). You want to get repeated straight fronts in each direction. Now put the fronts on a variable schedule, C/Ting after two, three or four.

Next you are ready to increase the angle slightly. Your next step will be to 5:00 in one direction and 7:00 in the other. Go through the same progression as before. Continue to increase the angle. Ultimately, you should be able to step directly to your right and left and Fido should find front.

So far you have been working with Fido directly in front of you. Now you have to add distance. When you are getting consistent fronts while stepping back to 8:00 (this is enough of an angle for you to be fully confident that he understands how to work his rear in both directions), sit the dog about two feet from you in front, offset to either the left or right (between 5:00 and 6:00, or between 6:00 and 7:00). To get to front the dog has to find a line from the offset position, and then work his rear end into line as he comes to the sit.

Go through the same progression as you did in the first sequence. When you have worked up to an 8:00 angle, increase the distance by one step, and start again. At the same time, continue to work fronts from the "direct-in-front" position, sharpening the angle all the way out to 3:00 and 9:00. Be aware that as you make the angle increasingly acute, your progressions must get smaller because it is harder and harder for Fido to locate the position. Be certain always that you give him a reasonable chance to succeed.

Although fronts involve a lot of repetition, I never find the work boring. It is a constant puzzle for the dog, and demands a lot of attention from you as the handler. I get a lot of pleasure out of watching my dogs work through the mechanical problems involved in adjusting and centering as the level of difficulty increases.

Sometimes, as you increase the distance, the dog's awareness of "front" will break down unpredictably. He may hit it nicely from ten feet, and lose it altogether from fifteen. When that happens, reduce your distance slightly or decrease the angle slightly, and retrace the learning process. Build both distance and angles carefully.

Ultimately you are going to build distance up to forty feet. The cue is always "front." Even as you are working longer distances, always include some sessions where you work at distances between six and ten feet. By and large, Fido will naturally tend to orient himself to front somewhere within that range, so keep him conscious of it and keep his competency at making the necessary movements at that distance sharp.

A variation on angle fronts is to *circle backward* to the left or right, having the dog "chase" you into the front position. This is especially helpful if Fido is having trouble "getting" the idea of moving his rear very far. He can't help but move when you circle, and you can C/T the motion.

Once you have established various angles and distances, then in a given session you may work them all, mixing up angles and distance. Again, you will be doing a lot of repetitions per session, perhaps twenty or more. So you have to mix it up to keep it interesting.

The last step is to have Fido find front while carrying the dumbbell, leather and metal article, and glove. Leave him on a sit holding the article, and call him to front. You are, in essence, training the next-to-last step in each of these retrieves ("bring the thing to front"). Go through the same progression with each. You won't have to spend days or weeks at each level, because Fido already knows what to do. But run through the angle progressions anyway. This simply teaches him that he can find front while carrying something—anything.

Fido must remain in place until you call him

The recall involves a brief "sit/remain in place." You have developed (or are developing) the sit as a long-duration behavior independently. In your front training, as you leave the dog, remember never to use the word "stay." Instead, simply remind him to "sit" and step off with your right foot as you leave.

It is best that you train the long-duration sit up to about one minute before you introduce it into your front work. This will let you be pretty certain that you have the long sit under

stimulus control before you introduce motion from a distance.

Remember too, in Novice your group sit will be across the ring, and ultimately you will be calling Fido to front from across the ring. There are various tricks for dealing with Fido anticipating a recall on the group exercises, but one that you should employ in your front training is to vary the time that you wait before calling him to front from a distance, gradually extending that time up to as much as a minute. And sometimes, mix it up even more by leaving him, walking to your established distance, returning to heel, and releasing with a C/T. This will keep him reminded that he must always wait to see what you are going to ask him to do.

Latency

Latency is a fancy word for "response time," or the gap between cue and performance. Ideally, latency in any given exercise is zero. On fronts, Fido must respond immediately to your "front" cue and move into position without hesitation. So, latency is another criterion you must shape for. At each progression, latency will decline slightly as Fido absorbs the new level of difficulty. Don't worry about it at first. If you have made zero latency a habit in all your training (and of course you have!), quickness will return as understanding emerges. If latency is something you struggle with, then once you are getting the correct position you can reintroduce latency criteria by reinforcing only the fastest responses.

The recall

The description of the recall exercise in the AKC Regulations combines the recall itself, the front, and the finish. But for training purposes—and accurate understanding of the criteria of the exercises—the recall as such is the action of the dog coming to you from a distance. That is a completely separate aspect from the front and the finish. You want a speedy recall. The Regulations require that the dog come to the handler "at a brisk trot or gallop." You want as close to a full-tilt run as you can get.

"Enthusiasm" in this context is easy to understand: The dog must be enthusiastic about getting to you. This means that the recall must *always* be reinforcing, and you must not do things in the course of training to "spoil" that enthusiasm. At a presentation I gave to an obedience club, someone asked me how I trained to get a speedy recall. I answered, "First, tell me how you trained to get a slow one." The fact is, the recall should be naturally brisk to fast, simply because there should be nothing more reinforcing to the dog than getting to you immediately.

Woody had great recalls in both Novice and Open. He did not barrel across the ring—he came in at a steady, brisk, and unhesitating pace. There were dogs that came faster, but Woody never got scored for not coming fast enough. I didn't worry about his speed because he worked at the speed that enabled him to get the job done. And he did get it done: On the drop on recall at one Open trial the judge got fascinated with how straight Woody was coming to me—and forgot to give me the drop signal.

There is no point to "cheerleading" to get a fast recall. As long as your dog works at a brisk, steady, unhesitating pace you will be fine. And, if Turid Rugaas is right, it may well be that "cheerleading" seems like agitation to the dog, and may trigger stressed responses (such as arcing or slowing down). If your dog knows what to do and wants to come to you, his speed will be just fine.

The recall is a long-distance front

You did the necessary groundwork for the formal Recall in your fluency training. If you did not follow that program, refer to it now. I am not going to reiterate those basics; here, I am simply going to note some points that are essential to polishing the exercise for competition purposes.

You will train front to a distance of forty feet. Fido will learn through that process how to come to you from a distance, orient to front while he is moving toward you, and end up in correct front position all from the front training. As you complete that program your recall cue will be . . . "front."

With that in mind, the finished product does not really present any new issues. The only thing you need to worry about is that you do nothing to spoil the latency you have achieved through your front training.

The recall must always be reinforcing

The easiest way to "spoil" the recall is to associate it with any sort of negative consequence. Remember, the dog is out there, off lead, free to come or not. Give him any good reason not to come, and he will stay away from you. In this regard (and this is something all trainers "understand"), perhaps the most important rule is that you never call the dog to you for any sort of punishment. Remember the

"hippie" mother and her apparently recalcitrant child? That is an instance of undermining the recall by punishing the subject for coming to you. Whatever happens out there, you must *always* deliver positive reinforcement for the dog's act in coming to you. Deal with other problems separately.

If, for example, you call Rover and he sniffs at the local doggy e-mail post for a moment, you have a choice to make. You can walk over and get him; if you do, you are free to deliver a negative message if it suits your purposes. Or, you can wait for him to respond to your cue; if you do, you *must reinforce* him for coming to you, however long it took for him to make up his mind.

If the recall ever starts to break down, go back to your "name-as-recall" training and remind the dog about immediate responses and coming to you at the slightest hint.

Do not associate the recall with stress

One of the main things that communicates stress to the dog is bending over toward the dog as he approaches. We tend to misconstrue this behavior because to us this is a means of delivering affection. But our reality is not the dog's reality. When one dog wants to assert dominance over another, a typical first move will be to put his head over the other dog's shoulders or back. This typically triggers one of two responses: pugnacity or fear. When you bend over your dog, you are mirroring this dominance movement. If you bend toward Bowser as he is coming to you, you are asking him to place himself in a dominated position. That is completely against nature. The most comfortable thing for the dog is to approach another being straight-up, with no posturing on either side.

When training the recall, at all times stand straight, but relaxed. With this posture you are allowing the dog to approach without giving him any confrontational signals. You are in a calm, welcoming posture. There is no reason for the dog not to come all the way to you, and every reason for him to do so; you are not only the person he wants to come to most, but there are no stress signals attached to the event.

Remember that whatever stress you introduce into the exercise in practice will be magnified in the ring. You will be excited, and Fido will pick up on that. So if he is at all tense about approaching you on the recall under normal conditions, he will be doubly or triply so when competing. This is not to say that you cannot be excited in the ring (a fella's gotta have some fun!), but that you must be careful to keep your excitement from negatively affecting your dog's performance. Excitement can be a positive or negative stressor. If you have not introduced negative stress into the exercise in practice, the chances are all the better that the excitement will produce "positive" stress in competition.

Another reason not to bend over is that it will be helpful to you if Fido learns that he must always come all the way to you to get his treats. If you bend over, then you can deliver the treat at arm's length. If Fido gets used to stopping about an arm's length away in practice, it will only be worse in the ring. Regardless of where in the recall you are clicking or why, always make Fido come all the way in to get his treat and always deliver it to him from an erect standing position. Even though it can cost a half point or so, I would much rather have Fido sitting with his front paws on my toes than backing off even an inch.

The legacy of negative reinforcement

With the *crossover dog*, there are some typical problems you may confront from previous mistraining. In "command-based" training, the trainer uses a leash pop to "motivate" the recall. As a reinforcement issue, this is negative reinforcement. "Fido, come" is followed by a leash "pop" (presentation of the aversive in anticipation of a less-than-immediate response), and the leash pressure is "taken away" when the dog comes. In effect, Fido is coming to you "for fear of something worse" happening if he does not. The same principle extends to use of the electronic collar. This device is simply negative reinforcement* carried to an extreme degree, and is very susceptible to misuse—and abuse—in training the recall. Stay away from it.

Another negative reinforcement tactic for training the recall is to use something behind the dog as a "motivator." I have seen this done various ways. Some trainers have a partner standing behind the dog throw a can filled with rocks or coins at the dog's rear as he is going toward his handler. Some

---

*There are a lot of opinions about E-collars, and I don't really want to get into that debate. Most people (even "traditional" trainers) who "reject" them do so on essentially humanitarian grounds. On that point, all negative reinforcement involves application of some sort of "punisher," and therefore all negative reinforcement is subject to abuse. As a scientific proposition, the E-collar differs from the slip and prong collars only in degree, not in kind—they are all methods of applying negative reinforcement in training.

trainers have a board attached to a long line, which they pull toward them behind the dog as the dog comes forward. In my view, all this is unnecessary, counterproductive (possibly harmful), and wasteful. When the dog is waiting to be called, I want the dog completely calm. When the dog is coming to me, I only want the dog thinking about where he is going, not what is (or may be) creeping up behind him. Very often the judge is walking toward you behind the dog as the dog comes to you. Do you really want your dog worrying about what the judge might do from back there? I think not.

"Cheerleading"

Another major, but perhaps more subtle mistake is to "cheerlead." Of all the things we do, this may be the most anthropomorphic. We think that because we are cheering, the dog is pleased and encouraged. In fact, the opposite is most likely true: The dog is perceiving stress. We have a hard time perceiving "happy noise" and arm-waving as stressors. But the issue is not how we humans perceive this sort of behavior, but how the dog perceives it (as far as we can tell). Noise is generally a stressor for a dog, or a sign of stress in a dog, as is excited physical movement. When a dog is approaching and perceives a stressful situation, there are three typical reactions (these fall into what Turid Rugaas calls "calming signals"): The dog will slow down, or continue moving but in an arc toward the other dog, or stop and back away. It does not take much analysis to realize that these are not qualities you want in the recall. If you are seeing these behaviors on the recall, recognize that the origin is probably not "disobedience," but uncertainty caused by cheerleading.

Trainers cheerlead to speed up the recall, but this begs the real question: Why has the recall slowed down? Assuming you have not injected stress into the picture, recalls slow down for the same reason any behavior slows down: Rover is uncertain as to what you expect. In other words, somewhere along the line you have raised or shifted your criteria too far, too fast. By cheerleading, all you are doing is layering stress upon confusion. This is no solution. Eliminate cheerleading from your repertoire.

So what's left?

If you take away all your negative reinforcers and "motivators," your crossover dog's recall will probably slow way down. In that case, relax all your recall criteria but one: Fido comes to me. Retrain the behavior from scratch with simple clicks and treats, reinforcing Fido for coming to you, wherever and whenever. Let him off leash in a safe place, and any time he orients to you C/T. Do not respond negatively to "slow to orient to me," but respond positively to "he looked my way." Do not respond negatively to "not fast enough," but respond positively to "coming at his chosen speed." If you have an established recall cue (such as "come"), eliminate it for the time being. Establish the cue "here" to confirm for Fido that something new is happening.

When Fido is willingly orienting to you and readily moving in your direction, work on his chosen speed. Use differential reinforcement to identify for Fido the faster movements as the ones that merit reinforcement. You can start by jackpotting faster movements, then making the faster movements the new norm. If you are feeling especially thrilled and want to give other happy messages, do so *after* you have C/T'd the behavior. Praise is a primary rather than a secondary reinforcer.

Another good way I have found to speed up the recall is to cue it while playing chase-and-retrieve games with the dog. Get the dog running at good speeds, and say "here" while he is heading in your direction. Click when he gets to you. You may often find that he is not really interested in a treat. The real reinforcer in the play situation is the opportunity to play some more. So, play. It will loosen you both up.

When you are getting something closely approximating the speed you want, start to reintroduce the formalities (sit and remain, sit in front, etc.). But don't be in too much hurry. Somewhere in here lurk the criteria that you introduced too quickly the first time around. Most likely, the problem arose with the front. All too often the spunky recall gets squelched in the quest for the perfect front. You will often see Fido come in with really good speed, get about six or so feet from the handler, and then slow down in order to orient himself.

So for a while, until you have eliminated all the problems with the simple "come to me" aspect of the recall, train the front as described earlier, *but train it separately from the recall* until it is as precise as possible. As Fido becomes comfortable with "front" you will find latency improving in that behavior. The recall gradually stops being "come" and starts to become "front." It does sometimes happen that changing the name you give the exercise, along with the topography, helps eliminate problems in the "old" way of doing things.

Open:
Step Two to the UD

At the risk of repetition, let me restate the recurring theme of this book: Train as much as you can, as early as you can. The more your dog learns, the more your dog will know. The more your dog knows, the easier he will be to train. Learning—whatever the subject or activity—involves certain sequences of receiving, processing and applying information. Dogs "learn to learn," just as people do. Every new lesson, if done precisely and consistently with what you have done before, aids the dog along this path. And as you travel that path with your dog, you "learn to teach."

If you have followed the progression to this point, you have given your dog a good dose of necessary basic Open training when you were doing *fluency* work, and I hope that you continued that training while you were emphasizing the Novice exercises.

When I started my first dog, the notion that you would do anything other than Novice training until you had your CD was heresy. Open and Utility—to say nothing of doing something completely different, such as Agility or Tracking—were forbidden, not invited (fortunately, this is changing as more and more trainers are becoming interested in doing more and more things). A trainer I very much admire, Robin by name, had a sheltie named Jazz who was an elegant working dog. Watching Robin work that dog, in the days when I was going through my first pet obedience class at Brookside Park with Woody, was what really inspired me to get into Obedience. I saw Jazz jumping over a high jump, picking up a dumbbell, and coming back over the jump

and thought, "If I could ever get a dog to do that, I'd die a happy man." Early on she told me, "Novice is what you do so you can get to Open, and Open is what you do so you can get to Utility, and that's when you have fun."

The fundamental disadvantage of training the classes sequentially, however, is that you make it unnecessarily difficult for yourself to progress. The practical disadvantage to teaching Novice, getting your CD, then training Open is that you are setting yourself up for a period of at least twelve months, perhaps as long as eighteen months, before you will be trialing in Open. That's a lot of "down time." Except for the first sixty days after you get your CD,* you can't show in any regular classes during that period, and there are few opportunities to show in nonregular classes. I sometimes suspect that this is part of the reason there is such a drop-off from Novice to Open—that, and the fact that there is often so much "reconstructive surgery" to be done that you burn out before you ever get into an Open ring.

Another disadvantage in waiting to finish your CD before doing any Open or Utility work is that it will be just that much harder to make the essential transition. In Novice the emphasis is on the dog *staying with* the handler. In Open and Utility the dog

---

*As I am writing this the AKC is floating a proposal to allow exhibitors to continue to show in Novice B indefinitely after obtaining their CD. It didn't happen with the February 1998 rules changes, but it is still in the wind, and word around the campfire is that an advisory committee will be formed to consider this as well as other new proposals.

has to work *away from* the handler. If you don't introduce the dog to this concept early in your training, it can be difficult to get the dog to be comfortable with it later on. My first dog was very soft, and it took almost six months to get his retrieve in place. Looking back, and giving due weight to my having been a hamhanded newbie clunk, I think a major part of his problem on the retrieve was that, having spent over a year becoming convinced to stay with me at all times, he just didn't understand that he now had permission to leave my side.

Don't forget about heeling

Maintain the foundation

You have done considerable work shaping heeling in your Novice training. The foundation is there. However, as many handlers move into Open they focus heavily on what I call the "performance" exercises (drop on recall, retrieves, and broad jump) and very little on heeling. It is therefore no particular surprise that heeling "falls apart." After all, behavior that is not reinforced tends to extinguish. The good news is that behaviors shaped through operant conditioning tend to be resistant to extinction if the only "non-reinforcement" involved is simply a failure to practice them routinely. It is relatively easy to reestablish the behavior when you start reinforcing it again.

You don't need to do long-duration heeling constantly. In fact, I find that as we get into the advanced work our practice sessions are better if we focus on short, crisp sessions of doodling and straight-line VR up to fifteen or twenty steps. It is also a good idea to practice your changes of pace for long distances, as you are more likely to encounter demands such as ring-length slows in Open and Utility than in Novice.

Practice session structure

When training in Open (and Utility) I typically devote the bulk of my time in any given training session to the performance exercises. But I am always sure to do some heeling at the start *and end* of every session. Ending with heeling intensifies the reinforcing nature of the exercise because it is the last thing we do before "quit and jackpot."

In a typical session, I will start with some seven- to ten-step straight-line, normal-paced heeling. I do an abbreviated VR schedule, cutting my usual

schedule about in half. In the middle I will break it up and do some doodling: quick turns, circles, turns in place, chassé right and left. Then I'll do fasts (three or four in succession, seven to fifteen steps) and slows (same) and finish up with straight-line heeling, VR to 10 steps, three to five repetitions (reps), normal pace. This session may take ten minutes.

Sometimes I give the dog the luxury of doing very little heeling, and on those occasions we will do two reps straight line (short, long), doodle, one rep each fast and slow, two reps circles right and left. I mix up the sequence. This session may take five minutes.

I watch for problems and reshape if necessary, but my primary concern is that the practice be zippy and varied. If I have had a problem in the first session I will typically close with a brief (two to three minutes) session in which I focus on the problem we worked on at the beginning. That way, the very last thing in the dog's mind is being reinforced for correct performance of a behavior he was struggling with.

Of course, each dog brings his own problems to the table. Dylan, for example, tends to try to cut short the inside turn on the figure-eight. So when I'm doing circles left I am sure to reinforce frequently at various points during the inside turn so that I make him conscious of maintaining heel position throughout.

Do you work on a problem behavior first, last, or somewhere in between? It depends on the severity of the problem. If it is something serious I may work on that only, to the exclusion of other things. If it is not very serious but I know I'm going to do a lot of repetitions, I will do it early so that I am not working a tiring dog. If it is something minor (and I consider "drifting in" on the figure-eight to be minor), then I'll work on it toward the end, and let "problem solving" be the behavior that triggers the jackpot reinforcement. These are my precepts. As with so many other things in training, though, this is an issue that is encompassed within the trainer's "art." You have to know your dog.

Even if I plan to emphasize heeling in a training session, and do a lot of work before going to the performance exercises, I will often do a quick "doodling" session with some short straight-line work after the performance exercises. This keeps the dog from getting too used to the ring "pattern." You are going to show in Open more than in any other class, and the Open exercises tend to become stale (Utility, on the other hand, is a never-ending adventure). So it will serve you well to mix up the exercise sequence during your practice sessions—even interspersing the Open exercises with some Utility exercises. My typical practice setup is a "versatility" ring with all jumps set up. This not only lets me do whatever I want, it keeps the dog alert to responding to the cues I give him, and not just what he expects when he sees the ring "look" a certain way.

How often should I jump the dog? And how high?

My show year follows the seasons. I show from mid spring to early summer, and again from mid fall to early winter. I give myself three months or so between cycles to train new things and reshape the old. During my training cycles, I jump the dog as often as I must for training purposes. Generally speaking, the jump heights are low. My dogs jump twenty inches in shows (I have taken advantage of the now-lowered jump heights to reduce the height by two inches, though I still overtrain), so my practice jumps are usually set at fourteen to sixteen inches (roughly the height of the shoulder—see pp. 96–104).

During show season, I don't do a lot of jumping practice. If there is just a week between shows, I may do some cavalettis just to let the boys have some fun. If I do jumps, it is to address a specific issue that has arisen in the ring. For example, Dylan tends to cut the right-hand side of the broad jump. We'll do broad jumps in our practice sessions to work on that. Sometimes Sam has trouble hitting front coming off the jump. We'll do high jumps (either several at a low height or one or two at full height) to work on that. If they aren't having any problems, I may not do any jumping at all, especially if there is only one week between shows. This, again, is a matter of the "trainer's art" and you must base your judgments on what you know about your dog. But I find, as a rule, that when I am in a show "run," less is often more at practice time.

The performance exercises

I use the term "performance exercises" to refer to all the exercises other than heeling and group sits and downs. In Open there are four performance ex-

ercises: drop on recall (DOR), retrieve on flat (ROF), retrieve over high (ROH), and broad jump (BJ). In Utility there are seven (signals, which is combined with heeling, articles or scent discriminations, directed retrieve, moving stand, and directed jumps.

Constructing behavior chains

These exercises are all *behavior chains.* They consist of a series of discrete, identifiable behaviors that must be performed in a given sequence, typically on more than one cue, in order to comprise a single exercise. Within the overall chain there will sometimes be a "mini-chain" of several behaviors that must be performed on a single cue.

For example, in the ROF, the dog must (a) sit at heel until directed to retrieve the dumbbell, then (b) go away from the handler, retrieve the dumbbell, return to front, and continue to hold the dumbbell, (c) deliver it to the handler's hand on cue while remaining in the front position, and (d) return to heel on cue. When the chain is fully trained, there are four cues: "sit," "fetch" ("get it," "grok," whatever), "give" (or "thank you"—my personal favorite), and "heel."

The "sit" and "heel" cues direct the dog to do one thing only. The "give" cue actually incorporates *two* behaviors: (1) remain in place and (2) deliver the dumbbell to me. The "fetch" cue tells the dog to do *five* things: (a) go out to the dumbbell, (b) pick it up, (c) bring it back, (d) sit in front, and (e) hold the dumbbell in his mouth until you give him the cue to deliver it to your hand. So in both the "fetch" and "give" cues we have mini-chains within the larger overall chain.

A chain is any sequence of behaviors in which only one behavior—the end behavior—is specifically reinforced, regardless of whether you deliver more than one cue. (If you only skimmed the discussion on repertoire reinforcement and repertoire cuing—see pages 35–38—this is a good time to review those concepts.)

In every recall or recall-based exercise, the reinforcer is delivered after the finish. For that reason, not only is the "front-and-finish" a chain, but the finish is the culmination of every recall or recall-based behavior chain. I think that understanding the "front-and-finish" in this way also helps to emphasize the importance of having these behaviors fully under stimulus control, as well as in adding them as fluencies at the end of various chains.

Backchaining

There are two key principles in shaping a chain. One is *backchaining.* The other is making use of fluencies. In backchaining, we teach the last behavior first, then add the second-to-last behavior, then add the third-to-last behavior, and so forth. In this way, the dog is always going from something new to something known. This gives the dog confidence in approaching the new task, because he always knows where he's going in order to earn reinforcement.

If you don't quite see the point, try a little experiment. First, memorize the previous paragraph this way: Memorize the last sentence first and say it. Now memorize the second to last sentence and after you say it, repeat the last sentence. Finally, memorize the first sentence and after you say it, repeat the next two sentences. You should find yourself increasingly comfortable with the last and second-to-last sentences. Now add the title of the subsection, and you'll have it down cold.

Now go to this next paragraph. Memorize the first sentence first, then the second, then the third. Even though the paragraph is simpler, you will probably find the memorization more difficult.

So generally, it is best to build a chain from back to front. With the exception of the Utility moving stand, the last piece of every recall-based exercise is the finish. The second to last piece is the front. The third to last piece is the recall (dog comes to front from a distance).

Using fluencies

Fluencies are the "wild card" (if you will) in this construct. Remember, a fluency is a basic, learned behavior (or skill) that can be combined with other behaviors or skills to produce a larger behavior. As a rule, once a fluency is established (trained and under stimulus control) you can "tack it in" anywhere in a chain, without regard to backchaining principles. Jumping is a fluency; you don't have to reteach Fido how to jump every time you need it in a new exercise, you simply tell him when he is supposed to do this thing that he already understands.

The same holds, for example, in teaching scent discrimination. You don't have to teach the dog to pick up an article because he already understands that part; you do have to teach him how to know *which* article to pick up. But the retrieve, *as a fluency,* is already there. Put another way, if the retrieve

is not already present as a fluency you are not ready to teach scent discrimination as an Obedience exercise.

When working with fluencies you may still backchain, but you are not locked in to that approach. You can put chains together in a way that is simply logical. For example, returning briefly to the recall, once Fido has learned that "every time I come to Big Guy I sit in front and only go to heel when he tells me to," that chain itself becomes a fluency. So whenever you are teaching a new recall-based exercise, you do not have to reteach "front-and-finish" as the "first step" in backchaining the exercise. When Fido picks up the dumbbell you simply give your recall cue, and he should know what to do from there.

Drop on recall (DOR)

The drop on recall is the "terror" exercise in Open A; it is the exercise where all good Open A dogs "go to die." I have no hard statistics to back this up, but based on watching a lot of Open A rings I would venture to say it is the performance exercise that Open A competitors most commonly fail. It does not have to be that way.

In the DOR you leave your dog as if for an ordinary recall. The dog must come on cue, drop on cue (which you give after receiving a signal or verbal order from the judge), come to a sit in front on cue (also after you get a signal or order from the judge), and finish on cue. It is a simple behavior chain, but one that causes most new Open dogs (and handlers!) immense difficulty.

If you have done fluency training you can construct this chain out of existing fluencies. The dog knows how to come, drop in motion, come to front, and finish. Viewed in this way, the only thing "new" in the drop on recall is the specific chaining of the fluencies.

Formalize the drop in motion

In the fluency stage of training, you taught Rover to drop in motion. This simply meant that whenever Rover was in motion, whether walking at your side, running around aimlessly, or coming toward you, if you told him "down," he went down. The drop on recall simply puts this fluency into a specific context. It is really no more difficult than that. The only issue is getting the drop under stimulus control, but if you really trained the fluency this will not be difficult.

Stimulus control over the drop

In your early training you taught Rover that you may ask him to drop at any time. So he is already conditioned to respond to the cue. He must, however, be able to recognize the cue for the drop readily, as well as understand that unless and until he sees that signal or cue he continues as before.

So the burden is on you, the trainer, to make the *discriminative stimulus* (that is, the cue to drop), completely clear. I prefer to use a hand signal, for several reasons. Using a hand signal forces my dog to keep his eyes on me at all times. Also, voice can get lost in the hurly-burly of the ring. I have a video of Woody in Open A; just as I said "down" the PA came on right above our ring. You can see him hesitate and then, because he was (apparently) not sure he had heard the command, continue to come in to front. I did not consider that a failure (though we NQ'd the exercise), because he did what he had been trained to do: keep coming unless he was sure he had heard the verbal cue. From that time on, though, we went to a hand signal.

Voice can also be erratic. As I have noted before, *tone of voice* is very significant to the dog. In the excitement of competition you are unlikely to maintain a consistent vocal quality. One friend of mine, who is a very experienced competitor, gave a very squeaky "down" to her dog one day. Her dog missed it entirely and she repeated it, this time quite definitively. (The judge did not realize that she had "squeaked" the first time; she told him she had given a double command and took her NQ. Sportsmanship uber alles.) I find it far easier to maintain a consistent hand signal (though it does take work!) than to maintain a consistent vocal quality.

Another point is that all too often handlers who rely on voice for the "down" command deliver the command in a loud and peremptory tone. I hear no other command bellowed in the ring the way that one is. And often, the tone is not only loud but almost abusive. The handler seems to believe that the only reason the dog will drop when commanded is if the handler delivers the command like a Marine Corps drill instructor addressing a moderately deaf recruit on his first day. The Regulations frown on "excessively loud" commands and say they should be "substantially penalized" but they rarely if ever

are; more's the pity. And for the spectators, the handler's tone in this exercise conveys a completely wrong impression of what Obedience is—and should be—about. You can avoid this problem altogether by using the hand signal exclusively.

Finally, the more you work with hand signals, the more the dog will have to learn to pay close attention to you. And the sooner the dog gets used to working from hand signals, the easier it will be to train the Utility exercises, in almost all of which the signal and not the verbal cue is the most significant element. The Regulations require that the signal be "a single gesture with one arm and hand only, and the arm must immediately be returned to a natural position." As with most rules, this leaves some room for interpretation and if you watch enough rings you will see considerable variation in the way handlers give their signals. My mantra for signals is that they be "smooth and continuous," with the "exception" that on the drop signal a slight hesitation at the extended position—just enough to be sure that you have fully extended the hand forward and up—is acceptable.

Conditioning the signal

If you have not already conditioned your dog to the hand signal to drop, go back to the Chapter 3 fluencies section and review that portion (see pages 66–72). When giving the signal the palm should be open, fingers together, facing the dog with your arm fully extended. I favor extending the arm more or less from the shoulder to about head height when fully extended. Others raise their arm straight up. This is purely a matter of personal preference. Whatever signal you use, make sure that it always looks the same and that you always deliver it with the same rhythm. Missed signals are usually the handler's fault.

Rover must be able to go down from a stand at a distance of thirty feet before you fully incorporate the signal into the drop on recall. In this way you will be sure that he understands the signal, and that you have distance control. And guess what? You will have one-third of the Utility signals exercise in place already.

Start the signal training at as close a distance as you must to get an immediate response from the dog. Extend your distance one or two steps at a time all the way to the thirty-foot distance. Stay at each increment for two or three days, doing three to five

A good, clear "down" signal. Your Utility signals should always look the same and be delivered with the same rhythm. Have a friend video tape you so you can check for unconscious "extra" signals such as leaning forward. The dog should drop as the arm starts to go up, with zero latency or lag time.

Rover looks at you as if he has never seen the signal before. So you may find yourself taking a smaller increment at times, perhaps even "yo-yo-ing" forward and back a step or two if required. You have to be sensitive to these sticking points, and work through them carefully. Remember too, this "sticking point" may crop up at more than one place along the continuum. So be watchful.

Remember latency

Latency is "response time," that is, the gap between cue and behavior. As always, you are working for *zero latency* (i.e., no gap between signal and behavior). Start your count *as you start to raise your hand into the signal.* Rover should be on the ground by the time your hand gets to the top of the signal. If he is not dropping until your hand is fully extended—or, worse, after your hand starts to drop—the latency period is too long and the response is unreliable.

Get zero latency when you are up close, and do not extend distance at any point in the progression until you have zero latency at whatever distance you are presently. Otherwise you will only build a slow response into the exercise, and when you get to full distance you will not have any reliable response time.

Aside from the general desirability of maintaining zero latency, it is critical in the drop on recall because the dog must respond immediately to your signal. The Regulations mandate a "substantial deduction (three to five points) . . . even to the point of zero" for a "delayed or slow response to the handler's command or signal to Drop [or] for delay or slowness to Down." You can be into some serious points if your dog (a) is slow to halt his forward motion and (b) drops slowly. Be sure to make quick response time a constant feature of your training regimen, and don't be afraid to "go back to kindergarten" at any time that latency starts to increase.

The "Sphinx" or "accordion" down

This is another important training element. The "Sphinx" or "accordion" down is a one-piece motion. It is, therefore the fastest way for Bowser to drop. Train this down using "get-back" so that Bowser learns it as a "backward-moving" rather than "forward-moving" exercise. This will prevent

reps a day. Be careful about extending distance. You will find that the dog does quite well within a certain distance, but suddenly his responsiveness declines. Maybe dogs do have some working concept of distance control. For example, you might do just fine up to about ten feet away, but at twelve feet unwanted forward movement. And because it integrates the two elements you are most likely to be scored on—stopping in response to the signal and dropping—it gives you the most reliable way for the dog to perform the exercise.

The other virtue to the Sphinx down is that the dog is in a ready position to get up and come to you. If he has dropped from a sit into a down, he is likely also to be rolled slightly. This will slow his response to the signal to come.

Stimulus control over the down

The next danger area is that the dog will anticipate the second recall command. It is common in Open B for the judge to wait a few seconds after the dog has dropped before giving you the second recall command. It is a score of zero if the dog does not remain down until called or signaled.

This brings us back to what by now should be familiar areas: *selective reinforcement* and *variable duration schedules* (VDuS). With selective reinforcement you regularly, periodically, reinforce only the down. Drop the dog and C/T. You may walk in to deliver the treat and then call him to front, or release him from the down to come to you for the treat. Or you may use the opportunity for a play release such as tossing a ball between your legs. Let your imagination be your guide. While doing selective reinforcement pay particular attention to latency and form.

With the variable duration schedule you will build your dog's tolerance for holding the down. Your goal in training should be that Rover will hold the down for fifteen seconds before being called. This is overtraining the time that you will require in the ring. Build the time to about five seconds on a straight-line progression, then use VDuS to get to fifteen seconds. Once you are at fifteen seconds, vary the release both as to time and type. Sometimes call to front, sometimes release.

Another way to mix things up is to drop the dog more than once during the recall. This reminds the dog that this is basically a "drop in motion" exercise, and that the cue may come at any time. As always, as you mix these tactics up, remember that your fundamental goal is for Rover to keep his mind engaged on the task at hand and not go on automatic pilot. He will have ample opportunity to experience predictable patterns in the ring, so avoid them as much as possible in training.

Maintaining speed on the "recall" portion

Very often, in traditional training, making the dog responsive to the "down" command slows the recall. A common theory is that the dog slows down because he is unsure of the exercise, and will speed up again once the exercise is learned. This has some validity, and proves to be the case just often enough to sustain life. But it does not always hold true.

Let me return for a moment to Turid Rugaas and her theory of "canine calming signals." Two of the most common such signals that she identifies in a dog approaching another dog are arcing and slowing down. Perhaps not coincidentally, these are two of the behaviors that we commonly see in the recall. We owe it to ourselves to ask whether we are doing things that are triggering these "calming signals" in our dogs. For example, I noted earlier that many trainers get very "military" in giving their "down" command on the DOR. I think it probable that the dog perceives this as stress. One also wonders if things some trainers do in the cheerleading vein are also perceived by the dog as a lot of noise that indicates that the handler is stressed just as a dog that is barking wildly would be. I have no definite answers, but these are things that a handler encountering "slow-down" problems on the recall owes it to herself to consider.

Conditioning the speedier response
First, determine whether you have a problem

Before you start working on Fido's mechanics, you might find it helpful to examine what, if anything, you as the trainer might be doing to cause or contribute to the problem. If you are able legitimately to eliminate any issues you may be causing by your own behaviors, either in training or in the ring, you may turn your attention to the dog. If you think you have a problem with your dog slowing down, you must not rely on your own subjective impression of the dog's speed. You will need some objective baseline data to work from. This requires some record keeping on your part. You will probably find it helpful to have a training partner to do the logging for you. All trials are done on a *continuous reinforcement* (i.e., 1 : 1) schedule.

Start with a straight recall. Log the dog's performance time, that is, the time it takes him to get from the starting point to you. The dog is not going to cover the distance at the same speed every time, so over successive trials (at least ten, more if you are able) you will find a mean (average) time that it takes him to cover those thirty-five feet. Just to frame the discussion, let's say that his fastest time is three seconds and his slowest time is four and a half seconds, so his mean is 3.75 seconds. It's important to take actual time trials so that you are not relying on your own perception of how fast he is moving.

Now, take it one more step and set markers (small orange flags such as are used in tracking are fine) at one-fourth, one-half, and three-fourths of the way across the ring and time the dog's speed to each marker. Take at least ten trials at each marker. You will now have some baseline times for the full-length recall and for the segments. Your question now is, does the addition of the down signal slow down the dog's time?

Now, do a second series of time trials to each of the three markers, this time giving the dog the down signal when he gets to the marker. As before, do at least ten trials at each stage. Let me emphasize here that all you are doing so far is gathering information. So, do not respond at all to the behaviors your dog gives you other than to reinforce at the end of each trial. *This is not training!* This is simply determining what retraining, if any, you must do.

Once you have all this data in place, sit down and compare the times on the trials where you added the down signal to the trials where you did not. Are the times within the same parameters? If so, has the average changed? In other words (and these numbers are purely imaginary), the parameters for getting halfway across the ring may be from 1.5 to 2.25 seconds with no down signal, creating an average of 1.875 seconds. But with the down signal added the majority of times may be closer to 2.25 seconds, creating an average of 2.1 seconds. You want to bring the average back down, and at least now you know what you are working with and for.

You may discover other things. For example, you may find that with several repetitions the trial time improves. This may tell you that the dog is becoming more comfortable with the exercise. There may be several reasons for this: You may have put the cue in place too early, and Rover is gradually figuring out what the word means; or, you may have asked for "too much behavior" too soon, and Rover is gradually figuring out what the exercise itself is; or, with successive repetitions you may have (inadvertently or otherwise) gradually reinforced the faster responses at the expense of the slower. If you

can figure out why Rover's performance improved in this particular case, it will give you insight into improving his performance on other exercises.

If you do have a problem . . .

Your data will tell you (a) what the problem is, if any, and (b) what the scope of the problem is. You are now more than halfway down the road to curing it. The next step is to plan your remedial program. There are several possible problem areas you must consider. Slowing down may indicate a lack of stimulus control over the recall itself or over the down. This may be caused by not having fully established the down, or not having done sufficient repetitions at each stage (see pp. 162–163), or having been inconsistent with reinforcement, or not having correctly transferred "food reinforcement" to *repertoire reinforcement.* The analysis is yours to make. If any of these things are involved, you will have to "go back to kindergarten" and reshape or restructure the exercise as may be required.

Another possibility is that you are inconsistent with your delivery of the signal. If you are uncertain about this, then have someone critique your motions to be sure that you are delivering the signal the same way every time. Remember that dogs are very visual animals and respond most strongly to body language. Variations in the way you deliver the signal or extraneous motions (of which you are probably entirely unaware) may significantly alter the "look" of the signal to the dog, and hence affect the dog's responses to it.

As one example, I see handlers in training who give their signal and do not get a sufficiently quick response. The handler may then take a step toward the dog, lean the upper body forward, etc. If the dog then responds, those additional motions have become part of the signal to the dog. You aren't going to do those things in the ring, so you must eliminate them from your "repertoire" in practice. A very innocuous motion may become part of the cue as Rover perceives it. At the very start of teaching Dylan scent articles I first tossed the article a few feet for him to retrieve. My hand motion forward became part of the cue for "find it," and I had to reshape to eliminate the association.

If your signal is consistent but Rover still drops slowly, you may address the decline in speed with *differential reinforcement.* Starting with the *average* speed, reinforce only that speed. Anything slower you simply do not reinforce. Reinforcement will tend to produce an increasingly high number of performances at your former average; not reinforcing slower recalls will decrease their frequency, or tend to extinguish the response, in favor of the faster ones. Now you can "crank it down" a notch by identifying the slightly faster recalls and reinforcing those, going through the same process of reinforcement/extinction as before. Do this at first with straight recalls, then with recalls that include the drop signal.

The retrieve*

An essential, complex behavior chain

The retrieve is part of two exercises in Open (ROF and ROH) and two in Utility (scent discrimination [articles] and the directed retrieve). Properly taught, the retrieve is more than just "get that dumbbell." It means (a) "Get whatever I tell you to get and bring it to me" and (b) "If at first you don't see it, keep going until you do." That *attitude*, that whatever Fido is going for is "out there" and his job is to find it, is essential to a reliable retrieve. That same willingness to "go and keep going" will also contribute to reliable Utility go-outs.

The retrieve exercise is a classic, complex *behavior chain.* The dog must (1) sit until (2) directed to get the dumbbell; (3) go out to the dumbbell; (4) pick up the dumbbell; (5) hold the dumbbell firmly without mouthing; (6) return to the handler with the dumbbell; (7) sit in front; (8) remain in front and continue to hold the dumbbell until cued to deliver it to the handler; and (9) finish on cue. There are three handler cues: "stay," "get it" ("fetch," "take," or whatever), and "heel." But because it is a chain, there are cues and reinforcers built into every step.

To get a clearer picture of what I'm talking about, let's briefly review *repertoire cuing* and *repertoire reinforcement.*

Repertoire cuing means that, in a chain, completion of one behavior is the cue for performance of another. This arises in any situation where the dog must perform more than one behavior on a single cue. Repertoire reinforcement means that proper performance of one behavior is reinforced by performance of a successive behavior. The two concepts are related. Completion of behavior A cues

performance of behavior B. And performance of behavior B reinforces completion of behavior A. Let's look at the ROF to see how this works in practice.

In the ROF, on the single cue "get it," Fido must (a) go away from you, (b) pick up the dumbbell, (c) come back to you with the dumbbell, and (d) sit in front until you (e) take the dumbbell and (f) cue him to finish.

The delivery of the dumbbell and the finish are cued separately. If you look at the sequence of behaviors to be performed on a single cue, you can see them as a series of related cues and reinforcements.

"Take it" is, obviously, a cue to find the dumbbell. In training, you can use "take it"—and therefore the action of retrieving—as a reinforcer for a proper stay while you throw the dumbbell (if you like, you can even treat the throw as a cue to "remain in place" rather than as a "chase" cue). Allowing Fido to go get the dumbbell reinforces the stay (if Rover anticipated the "take it" cue, you would not allow him to complete the retrieve). Picking up the dumbbell cues the return, and the return reinforces the pickup (if Rover did not find the dumbbell, or pick it up, you would not allow him to return). The recall cues the front-and-hold, and the front-and-hold reinforces a proper return.

This is not just an exercise in abstract theoretical symmetry. Keeping these concepts in mind can smooth the training road. By thinking of one behavior as a cue for another, you can work more consistently toward making a certain series of behaviors habitual. And by understanding how one behavior reinforces a preceding behavior, you can introduce increasingly high levels of differential reinforcement for that preceding exercise.

This is related to, but slightly different from, the *Premack Principle.* The Premack Principle states that the opportunity to perform a behavior with a high probability of occurrence (that is, one that has been strongly reinforced) can be used to reinforce performance of a behavior with a lower probability of occurrence. While repertoire reinforcement allows you to use one behavior to reinforce another, there need not be any significant difference in the probabilities of occurrence of either. The real significance of repertoire relationships (cueing and reinforcement) is to allow you to use successive elements of a chain to reinforce and cue each other.

You may also use repertoire reinforcement to reinforce smaller elements of behavior. For example, if your dog really wants to barrel out there for

---

*See Appendix E for a discussion on fitting the dumbbell to the dog.

that dumbbell, keeping him on the sit for *variable* periods of time will reinforce not only the sit, but also the explosion out of the sit toward the dumbbell. Be careful with this: If you were to extend the waiting period too long you would undermine that enthusiasm. But it is something you can play with.

Repertoire reinforcement also helps clarify why you should train the retrieve as a "give it to me" rather than a "get it" exercise. In other words, the essential skill is the dog returning and delivering the object to the handler. That is the ultimate reinforcing act. To the dog, then, getting the object is a desirable thing to do not because it is rewarding in and of itself, but because it enables the dog to earn reinforcement by delivering it. Put in terms of the earlier discussions on repertoire cuing and repertoire reinforcement, the act of picking up the dumbbell cues the delivery, and the delivery reinforces the pickup.

Delivery to hand from formal front

I am assuming for purposes of this discussion that you have gone through the retrieve fluency training described in Chapter 3. If not, now is the time. You must have the basic elements in place before putting the finishing touches in place.

The first thing to work on, once the retrieving fluency (go on cue to get the dumbbell, pick it up, and bring it back) is in place, is to incorporate the front into the recall-and-delivery. Just as with the drop on recall, where you created a chain by connecting the existing fluencies of come and drop in motion, with the retrieve you are also creating a chain by welding fluencies together rather than "backchaining" in the strict sense of the term.

Front is already a fluency; that is, Fido understands that when he comes to you he sits in front. In all probability, when you were having Fido bring the dumbbell to you from a stationary position you found him sitting in front more often than not, even though you were not asking for it.

Retrieve is also already a fluency. Fido knows what it means to go out, pick something up, and return it to you. Maintaining the sit is also already a fluency. And so, in terms of the behaviors in and of themselves, you are not really teaching anything new. You are instead deepening and extending existing behaviors, and relating those behaviors one to another in a behavior chain or sequence.

Front-with-dumbbell is different from front-without-dumbbell

As a position, front is front is front. But as a behavior, front when Bowser is carrying the dumbbell is different from when he is unencumbered. Now Bowser not only has to think about hitting the correct position, he has to remember to hold the dumbbell. So front with dumbbell is, if not an entirely new behavior, certainly a new criterion that you have to structure in consciously.

Shaping the front-with-dumbbell

You are ready to add the front-with-dumbbell when the dog is coming reliably at a distance, and bringing the dumbbell to your hand without mouthing (rolling the dumbbell around in his jaws). Start by going back to "scoot fronts" as you worked them in the basic front, only now with Bowser holding the dumbbell. Remember, you only train for one thing at a time. At first, don't worry about "straight" or even "quick"; the important thing is that the dog get to front and sit.

Though Fido has been bringing the dumbbell to you without mouthing it, you may see mouthing when you add the front. This may be due to the additional criterion, or it may be due to nothing more than Bowser lifting his head to look at you as he sits in front. *The reason for the mouthing is not important.* You cannot eliminate the requirement that the dog come to front and sit, nor do you want to eliminate his focus upon you. So, you have to teach him to sit in front and watch you while holding the dumbbell without mouthing it.

You cannot train two things at once. But remember, here you are not shaping the front. That already exists. You are shaping the front-with-dumbbell. And, your fluency training should have established a solid basis for Fido to hold the dumbbell without mouthing. So, as we have seen elsewhere, you are not so much shaping something new as you are putting two existing fluencies together in a single (albeit complex) behavior.

To eliminate mouthing, retrace the front training (beginning with Fido in front, adding distance, scoot and angle fronts, etc.) but with the dumbbell in *his mouth at all times!* Do not move to a new step in the progression unless and until Fido is performing the existing level while keeping the dumbbell still in his mouth.

What do you do if Fido mouths the dumbbell? Simple: Do not reinforce. Remember, behavior that is not reinforced tends to extinguish. You may have to wait him out at first. In that case, be ready to reinforce any stillness of the jaws. Often, after a dog has mouthed the dumbbell a few times he will close his mouth on it, if only for a second. That is where you C/T. You have to be alert not to miss those moments, because if you do not catch them you will deny yourself the opportunity to deliver reinforcement at all.

Refrain from any physical actions such as rapping the dog's underjaw. This is aversive and unproductive, and can cause physical harm to the dog. There is one physical inducement you can use, which is to tap the ends of the dumbbell lightly; this will cause Fido to tighten his jaws reflexively. Fido's jaw-tightening will happen at the instant you tap the dumbbell, so you must C/T *immediately as you tap the ends.*

Stimulus control over front-with-dumbbell

Stimulus control over the front means that the dog understands that releasing the dumbbell is not "automatic" once he gets to front. This adds another repertoire cue/reinforcer link in the sequence. Returning to you with the dumbbell *cues the front.* The front will, at first, reinforce the return (recall with dumbbell). That means, for now, you do not add the finish in. You want to reinforce when the dog has brought the dumbbell to front.

There are two ways to do this, and you will usually employ both. First, extend the time that elapses between the moment Rover comes to front and the time you cue the release. Then put it on a variable schedule, and work up to about twenty seconds. This is important not only to be sure you have control over the behavior, but also because judges work at different speeds. A helpful variation on this tactic is occasionally to send your dog to heel while he is still holding the dumbbell. Even though you are unlikely ever to do that in the ring, it will confirm to the dog that he is to hold the dumbbell—and continue to hold it—until you ask for the release.

Second, have the dog give you two and three—up to as many as seven or eight—repetitions on the fronts before taking the dumbbell from him. The front is one exercise that plainly benefits from drill. Also, fronts are a behavior for which you must establish a high number of repetitions per reinforcer, given the number of times Fido will have to perform that behavior in the ring without direct reinforcement.

The finish

In both Open and Utility you have many opportunities to use the finish as a reinforcer for the front. Of course you can do this in Novice as well, but it becomes important in Open and Utility because the front is repeated so often in the ring, and there is never a time when you can reinforce it specifically.

Sam and Dylan love to do the "pop" swing finish. With either dog, if he is in front and I simply say "heel," nine times out of ten he'll pop to the left. It's a celebration move. Most dogs who learn to "pop" the swing enjoy it as a physical release.

In Open, I use the "go-behind" finish in the ring for two purposes. On the DOR, I use the "pop" swing as reinforcement for a good drop. I use the "get-around" on the ROF to remind the dog that there's another retrieve to be done yet, and the "pop" swing after the ROH to tell him "done retrieving, well done." Of course, this is subject to amendment as we go (there is training, and there is handling and although the two intersect they are distinct). Dylan's "go-behind" finish is more accurate than his "swing"; if he misses the "swing" on the DOR, I won't use it again after the ROH. When I do this, it tends to make him drive even harder on the finish from the broad jump (I see this as an example of "extinction burst" behavior).

In Utility, you do two "send-away" exercises twice: scent discrimination and directed jumping. In each, as a rule, I use the "get-around" after the first and the "pop" swing after the second. Sam sometimes gets very pleased with himself, particularly after jumping; when he does, even if I send him right, he goes left. Oh, well. (This has never cost me points, because he is going to heel on command.)

The completed exercise

The last step in the progression is to reincorporate distance as the "new" criterion, once all the other criteria—taking the dumbbell on cue, holding it, and delivering it to you on cue—are in place. Your original fluency training established Fido's ability to take the dumbbell when thrown to a distance. So again, this is not "new" except in context.

As I noted when discussing fluencies, because the emphasis is on Fido returning to me with the dumbbell, I have not encountered the problem of the dog going to the dumbbell, picking it up, and not coming back. However, now that you have added the front and finish, you want to reintroduce distance carefully so as not to lose the other criteria. Extend the distance about three feet at a time, and do not toss the dumbbell further if there is any "play" or "mouthing" of the dumbbell during the return. If you have done all the front shaping carefully this should not be a problem, but be watchful for it.

The high jump

Before getting into jumping specifics, let me reemphasize a couple of points. First, your dog's physical structure is critical. Whether choosing a puppy or an older dog, be careful that your dog of choice has good front-end layback and proper rear-end angulation. Know the breed standard, and make sure that your dog conforms to it. This is not for looks. The structural physical requirements in the breed standards are meant to assure that a given dog is capable of doing the work the breed is intended to do. A poorly structured dog will have a limited jumping career and will always be more susceptible to injury than the well-structured dog. If you have an adult dog who is not well structured, don't shoot him. Simply be careful in your jump work not to expose him to unnecessary risks. Do a lot of low cavaletti work to allow your dog to develop a smooth, low-arcing jumping style.

Second, do not put the specific formal exercises together too fast. All the jumping exercises—the Open retrieve over high (ROH), the broad jump (BJ), and the Utility directed jumping—are entirely constructed of fluencies. Jumping, the recall, and front/finish are present in each. The ROH requires an established retrieve. Both the BJ and the precursor to the Utility jumps—the go-out—rely as well on targeting (though you can train the go-outs as a retrieve if you prefer). You will not find it hard to put the fluencies together as required, if you have developed them properly in the first place.

One of the major causes of uncertain jumping is that new trainers all too often start jumping the dog when the dog has nothing in his mouth, then suddenly add the retrieve to it. This might not seem like a big deal, but jumping while carrying the dumbbell is a considerable step up from jumping "empty-mouthed." So once Fido is a confident jumper, create a collateral fluency: jumping with object in mouth. Have him do cavaletti sequences carrying the dumbbell and articles. This will make him as fluent jumping when retrieving as when not.

Some mechanics questions

Stutter-stepping and "popping"

The Regulations state that "minor to substantial deductions, depending on the specific circumstances in each case shall be made for the dog that . . . displays any hesitation or reluctance to jump." There are two signature characteristics of the hesitant jumper: stutter-stepping and "popping." Neither is likely to be scored so long as the dog maintains continuous momentum toward the jump, but if either starts to appear in your dog you should recognize that you have a problem and start retraining.

Don't confuse stutter-stepping with "gathering." A confident jumper will approach the jump at a trot (some, faster). As the dog approaches, depending on the distance from his starting point to the jump, he will adjust his stride and lead foot so that he takes the jump comfortably. In this "gathering" process, though, the dog will not show any noticeable loss of momentum. There will be no loss of pace. When the dog stutter-steps, he will lose pace and will approach the jump hesitatingly.

"Popping" represents a downward progression from stutter-stepping. It is as far as an unconfident jumper can go to avoid a jump without actually refusing to take it. The dog will come to virtually a complete halt before taking the jump, and will take the jump almost vertically. The dog has no rhythm, and no sense of how to gauge the jump. The "pop" is also unhealthful for the dog; it puts great strain on the rear legs in pushing off (it takes greater effort to jump from a standstill, without momentum, and straight up than it does to jump from a run on an arc), and great stress on the front end in landing (due to coming down vertically on the front legs).

If you have not gone through a jump conditioning program with your dog, you will probably see one or the other of these problems, at least in embryo. Do not go forward into regular Open and Utility jumping work until you have put your dog through a proper conditioning program. From a scoring or performance point of view you will only be asking for trouble. From a health point of view you will be putting your dog at risk.

General physical conditioning

Notwithstanding the recent rule changes lowering the jump heights, it is essential that your dog be in good physical condition if he is to jump regularly, or he will be at risk of injury. After all, jump heights have been lowered in the past, yet the incidence of injuries continues at a noticeable rate. Canine injuries are pernicious. Dogs are very good at not revealing injury. Don't confuse this with "nobility." More likely, it is an atavism: An injured dog is a hindrance to the pack, and is at risk of being attacked and killed by healthy members of the pack. Dogs can suffer a slight muscular injury and disguise it until it shows up as a serious problem. Usually by the time you notice it, mild therapy is insufficient. This is yet another reason to massage your dog regularly; your touch will stimulate responses, making you aware of problems you might not otherwise notice until the injury is serious.

Proper physical conditioning of your dog is your paramount responsibility. It is as important to proper jumping as training proper jumping mechanics. The canine athlete should be lean, slightly underweight if anything. Look at the breed ring: Observe all the hefty canines. Now look at photos of dogs in the wild: Observe all the lean and hungry types. Which do you consider the more likely athlete? You cannot feed your dog full rations, get him out for something resembling exercise a couple of times a week, and expect him to perform well in jumping exercises on show day. This is true whether the dog is jumping one and a half times his height at the withers, the same as his height at the withers, or stepping across a chalked line drawn in the grass.

Building the retrieve over high jump (ROH)

The retrieve over high (ROH) is a complex *behavior chain*. The dog must sit, stay, go-out, jump, pick up, return, jump, come to front, deliver, and finish. These are all fluencies. Before you can even think about training the ROH, you must have each of these basic skills in place. If you don't have the fluencies in place, you will find yourself in a huge muddle trying to teach the basic skills as well as the completed exercise. The training approach that follows here presumes that you have already trained

the fluencies. If you have not, do so before going forward.

Adding the jump to the carry

Fido learned to carry the dumbbell confidently both in fluency training and in working on the ROH. Now, you can add the jump to the carry. This is done in two parts.

First, go back to your basic cavaletti work, and have Fido carry the dumbbell through the ground poles and low jumps. You do not have to retrace the whole jump-training program; you are not conditioning jumping, but shaping jumping while carrying. The more you do, the more comfortable Fido will become with jumping-and-carrying, and the more confident he will be with carrying the dumbbell while jumping over the high jump.

"Mouthing" is usually not a problem while jumping. Even a dog that carries the dumbbell loosely while moving on the flat will hold it more tightly while jumping. However, you should not introduce carry-and-jump until you have solved any mouthing problems you may have had while training the ROF.

Developing jump height

When Fido is comfortable jumping while carrying the dumbbell, the only matter left is to build to the full jump height. Again, I recommend reading the programs in books like *Jumping From A to Z*, where the progression is fully and carefully laid out. Whatever your preferences for a program, follow it sincerely. Here are a few things I am adamant about:

- Build height carefully and slowly.
- Train the bar jump and high jump simultaneously.
- "Overtrain" to a height two to four inches higher than your dog will normally have to jump, but do not jump the dog at that height often.
- Do not practice at full height regularly. Repetitive jumping should be at a maximum of about shoulder height.

Build jump height in gradual increments

The reason for the first is obvious, and the principle is well known to trainers. In part, it is a matter of plain physical conditioning. Each new height takes some getting used to. But there is what one might call a "psychological" (I hate it when I do that) element as well.

As long as Fido can see over the jump, he will typically demonstrate little or no hesitancy in taking the jump. However, at a certain point the jump will get just high enough that he cannot see over it until he is in the air. When you get to that point, Fido must take the jump on faith, that is, with no hesitancy in believing that there is a safe place to land on the other side. This does not come about by "show-and-tell" (I have seen trainers walk their dog around the jump to "explain" that everything is OK). This comes about through carefully developed progressions.

Train the bar jump and high jump simultaneously

I train the bar jump and high jump simultaneously as a carryover from the initial jump conditioning, and also to avoid any problem with the dog becoming resistant to or confused about the bar jump after lots and lots of high-jump training. I even go so far as to have my dogs perform the retrieve over both the bar and the high jumps. The fluency is: When I say "jump," you jump, whatever is in front of you. Doing this also helps avoid uncertainty as the heights go up.

Overtrain the jump height

Overtraining the height does a couple of things for you. First, it gives you a dog that will be completely confident at his normal height. Second, it will avoid problems if the dog encounters a jump that is (or seems to be) higher than he is used to. Even if you have reduced your dog's jump height under the new Regulations, uneven or sloped ground can create a situation where the normal-sized jump appears higher than usual. Overtraining height gives your dog the confidence to handle this calmly.

Do not practice regularly at full height

Do not practice at full height regularly; there is simply no need to do so and you risk injury to the dog. I have seen more than one nice working dog brought down by physical injuries caused or exacerbated by repeated jumping at full height. The excuse for repeatedly jumping the dog at full height is that he has a "jumping problem" that can only be addressed at full height. This is simply untrue. The vehicle for resolving any problem with your dog's jumping mechanics is cavaletti work, not innumerable repetitions at full jump height.

Avoid "quick fixes"

Too many handlers rush their dogs into jumping without laying a proper foundation, then get frustrated when the dog does not jump properly. And all too often, these same handlers resort to "quick fixes" to "cure" the jumping problem.

One such "quick fix" is to "trick" the dog into taking the jump with some room to spare by running a trip wire across the jump, about one inch above the top board. I think this borders on the sadistic. If your dog truly cannot elevate to the necessary height, then you should not be jumping the dog. On the other hand, if the problem lies in the dog's jumping mechanics—which is more often than not the case—then the trip wire will not do you any good.

A variation on this is to have a training partner with a "jump stick" standing beside the jump, ready to thrust the jump stick out slightly above the top board of the jump, "compelling" the dog to clear the jump better. This has all the vices of the trip wire, with the additional problem of timing. Any misstep in inserting the jump stick can throw the dog off his rhythm and possibly disrupt the jump altogether.

I can not repeat this too often: You can best solve mechanical problems in jumping through cavaletti work at low heights. There is no substitute for patient work in the initial conditioning. And remember, the dog has to work through his jumping mechanics for himself. You cannot really help him, simply because it is a behavior employing muscles, joints, and movements. You have no real choice but to give the dog the time and means to sort his jumping problems out, and to provide reinforcement as you see the mechanics improve.

If your dog has been jumping well but suddenly develops a jumping problem, first check for possible physical causes. As I noted before, dogs often hide injury, and by the time you become aware that there is a problem, the injury may be rather severe. Include an eye examination. If you exclude physical problems, then return to cavaletti work and build back up to regular jumping.

Adding the front to the jump-and-carry

Once your dog is comfortable jumping, add the front as he comes over the jump to you. Again, you are now simply working with established fluencies and putting them together in a specific sequence.

You have worked with front on the recall, the drop on recall, and the retrieve on flat. So, you may not find that you have much of a problem with the front when Fido is coming back over the high jump. Or . . . you may see a problem arise. As with the front-with-carry, the problem will arise simply because you are adding a new criterion. In the ROF, that new criterion was the presence of the dumbbell; you have taken care of that. Now your new criterion is the presence of the jump.

Your jump-and-front training will start with Fido sitting across the jump from you, at the distance that he takes his cavalettis, and with the jump at about one-half his normal jump height. If you want to start as low as eight inches you may do so, but you will probably not find it necessary. You will be directly across from him. Think of this as long-distance front work, with a jump in the middle.

Call Bowser to front over the jump. Don't worry about his jumping mechanics as you introduce front. Set the jump at a height sufficiently low to minimize problems, but don't make a big deal out of them. You have done a lot of work getting the mechanics in place, and they will return once Bowser absorbs this new element.

Get Bowser coming to a straight front on a straight line, then introduce long-distance angles. Again, this is familiar ground to him except that the jump is between you and him. The reason you have to introduce angles is that you never know where the dumbbell is going to land when you throw it. Make sure you are always facing straight ahead, no matter how sharp an angle you require him to come to you on. You will most likely find that Bowser straightens out the angle before taking the jump; that is what you want him to be doing.

Because the "click" will not end the behavior (that is, Bowser is not going to stop in mid-air), you can click when Bowser adjusts to a straight line before taking the jump. This will reinforce his preparatory behavior. If you are going to do so, treat when he gets to you even if he does not sit in front. Once you are confident that he will make the proper adjustment as required, you can eliminate that click and reinforce for the front as such.

Putting it all together—Adding the retrieve

Fido will jump on cue. He will carry the dumbbell on the flat and over the jump. He knows how to

come to front with the dumbbell. Now there is only one element left to fold in—the actual retrieve.

Over, touch, and return

The first step is to introduce the peculiar discipline of the ROH: going out and coming back over the jump. The rule for Bowser in this exercise is, "If you *go out* over a jump, you *come back* over a jump." "Over and back" simply has to become a *habit*. The corollary, of course, is, "If you went out on the flat, you come back on the flat." This will avoid problems in rings where the judge sets the ROF close to the ROH.

Begin the retrieve training by having Bowser go over the jump to a target stick. Put the target stick out about fifteen feet from the jump. On the cue "over," Bowser should go over the jump without any problem. As he lands on the other side, tell him "touch." He should go to the stick without any problem. If he seems to have trouble with the fifteen-foot distance, reduce it at first to about ten feet, then extend it to fifteen and even up to twenty feet.

Click as he touches the stick. Immediately after you click, tell him "over" again. Because of the click, he should be orienting back to you for his treat. If he shows any confusion, say "come" as well. Treat when he returns to you.

Progressively fade the cues. The first cue you will fade will be "touch." This will not be much of a problem, since you have been reinforcing the touch with the click. He will quickly put "touch the stick" into the sequence. Also, it will remind him of the "go-out" training you did in the fluency training stage.

Now, when he is going readily to the stick, do not click but wait until he is turning back to you. This "return" element should also come together as the "touch the stick" element does. Now eliminate the "come" cue and simply say "over." Click as he clears the jump, and treat as he gets to you. You are now reinforcing the whole package—dog goes out, touches stick, and returns. The returning jump now reinforces the action of touching the stick.

The next step is to make the "jump-and-touch" completely fluent, which means that you move the target stick around from side to side and back and forth. The idea here is to remind Fido that the target is out there and he is to go to it. The practical implication of this is that when you throw the dumbbell you can never be entirely sure where or how it will land. Introduce Fido early to the idea that he may have to jump and go anywhere to complete his task. And, of course, he always returns to you over the jump. Do this until, on the single command, "over," Fido will take the jump, go to the target stick no matter where it is, and return to you over the jump. Now you can add the retrieve.

Over, fetch, and return

Step one is to have your dog pick up the dumbbell at rest on the other side of the jump. You have established the reinforcement pattern by using the touchstick, so now you simply transfer it to the dumbbell. Place the dumbbell (do not throw it) about ten feet to the other side of the jump.

At the start, set the jumps low, about the height of the dog at the elbows. Taking his full height is not an issue at this point. You want the jump sufficiently low that Rover can concentrate on the task at hand—getting the dumbbell and bringing it back—without worrying about other things. Rebuild height once the over–fetch–over sequence is soundly in place.

The cue sequence is "over," "take it," and "over" (you should no longer need the "come" cue). Rover knows what to do when he sees the dumbbell on the ground, and he knows what to do when he is on the other side of the jump from you. You should be able quickly to fade the "take it" and "over" cues just as you did with the touch stick.

Move the dumbbell around as Rover becomes more fluent with jumping and retrieving. Place it close to and far from the jumps, and move it from side to side. Practice this retrieve aspect as thoroughly as you can, including "burying" the dumbbell in high grass (if you show outside at all).

At first, do not worry about the front when Rover returns. Some trainers allow sloppy fronts during this stage, but I would rather have no front at all than a sloppy front. To avoid any confusion here I use my "jump-up" cue (hands out and up as Fido comes to me) to have the dog put his paws up on me to deliver the dumbbell. Once all the pieces are in place it is a simple matter to reinstate the front. Click the pickup and treat when he returns; once the pickup is reliable, C/T the jump. When you are getting a good out, over, fetch, and return you can add the front. All this is before you introduce the throw.

Be sure in all this practice that you are giving Rover ample room to approach the jump from your side. Give him room to find his stride. It will also help him find front if he does not have to pull up too short after taking the jump coming back. Know what your dog's working stride is, and be sure to place yourself at least that far from the jump or, if anything, a little farther. You can never predict what Rover will have to contend with on the far side of the jump while coming back, but you can make your side of the setup predictable. Use a measuring stick of some sort until you can gauge the distance to the jump accurately by eye.

Adding the throw

The most important aspect here is that Rover must not anticipate the initial "over" command. Handlers with dogs who are enthusiastic jumpers and retrievers often encounter this problem, and once in place it can be very difficult to eliminate. These dogs become adrenalized in the ring and, no matter how consistent the handler is in countering the anticipation in training, it can pop up at any time.

Put in strict behavioral terms, before you can ask the dog to retrieve the thrown dumbbell you must first have "remain in place while I throw it" under *stimulus control.* Far better to have "remain in place" under stimulus control from the start than to try to reassert stimulus control over the stay once it has gotten out of hand.

Reinforce "remain in place"

Back to *repertoire cuing* and *repertoire reinforcement* for a moment. It may help you to think of the throw as a cue for Rover to remain in place. Put another way, when Rover sees the dumbbell thrown, he should take that as a cue to remain where he is until released, rather than as a cue to "chase." On the other end, releasing him to jump and retrieve reinforces "remain in place."

The most straightforward approach is first to reinforce "remain in place" in the context of throwing the dumbbell. Go back to the flat for a couple of repetitions; throw the dumbbell, do not give the retrieve command, hold Rover in the sit-at-heel position for three to five seconds, and C/T. After a couple of repetitions, let Rover get the dumbbell. In this way, the retrieve becomes a reinforcer for remaining at your side (put another way, being allowed to get the dumbbell is Rover's reward for waiting until you tell him to do so, an example of the Premack principle in action).

Now move to the obstacle and repeat. Watch Rover very carefully while he is at heel position. You don't mind a show of eagerness, but there should be absolutely no movement forward at all until you send him to the jump. If you notice any tendency to "hitch" forward, simply keep him in heel position slightly longer, up to five or seven seconds. Make sure he is solid at remaining at heel position before you allow him to go for the dumbbell.

Some dogs anticipate by taking the jump when the dumbbell is thrown. (I knew one dog that was so eager that when his handler threw the dumbbell he took off, cleared the jump, and the dumbbell came down and hit him on the head. Now *that's* anticipation.) Some dogs anticipate by going on the judge's order to "send your dog." So, it will also be helpful in generalizing this exercise to have a training partner give you the judge's orders. The point is to teach the dog to listen only to you. Vary your response to the "judge's" directions. If you send your dog, vary the time that you wait after hearing the order "send your dog" before saying "Rover, over." Sometimes, do not send Rover at all. In other words, mix it up until you are certain that he understands that the only thing that matters is what you tell him to do.

The broad jump

Not everything makes sense in life

One explanation for the Open and Utility Obedience exercises is that they reflect actual working tasks that a dog might have to perform were he actually doing some work for you instead of competing for ribbons. Much of Utility, for example, relates to hunting activities. Some correlation to working tasks can also be drawn for the Open performance exercises. The drop on recall resembles the drop that a herding dog has to do while moving sheep. The retrieves have some relationship to bringing back game.

For the life of me, though, I cannot visualize what the broad jump is supposed to reflect. I have heard from several folks that the broad jump is supposed to be like the dog jumping over a stream. Okay, I can see that—but only to a point. The exercise not only requires that Bowser "jump the stream," but that he come around 180 degrees to sit in front of the han-

dler. There is no way in the world I'd expect to be standing in a stream (walking, yes) while my dog jumps it, and even if I were I cannot imagine why I would want my dog, having jumped over the stream, to circle back into the water and sit in front of me. All of which is a way of saying that, structurally, the broad jump has to be just about the silliest of all obedience exercises.

The exercise is made worse by the way it is mistrained. Most handlers focus on the problem of getting the dog to come to front, rather than on the dog properly clearing and extending past the jump. As a result, the dogs learn to turn either in the air or immediately upon landing. Given the dog's structure, both of these are recipes for injury. Let me emphasize, though, that the risk of injury is not inherent in the exercise, but rather in the way it is taught.

Distance is not a big concern

The distance for the broad jump is twice the height of the high jump. This is not a problem. If your dog is jumping the high jump properly, he will be in the air about twice as far as he is jumping high, and perhaps farther if he jumps on more or less of a flat arc. Sam jumps twenty-two inches on the high jump, and forty-four inches on the broad jump. The forty-four inch jump is so short for him that he can practically stretch across without leaving the ground. When I trained his broad jump I had him jump sixty inches; that at least required him to exert himself. Dylan has to put a little more effort into it to clear forty-four inches, but not much. So the real problem with this jump is not the distance is too great, but that dogs get lazy with it. Clearing the broad jump just isn't that much of a challenge.

To keep the dog from getting lazy, you have to make sure that you build some degree of arc into the jump. It is also a good idea to "overtrain" the distance so that the dog gets used to putting some real effort into the jump.

Building the arc

I don't think it's particularly healthy for the dog to take a really high arc over the broad jump. I've seen some dogs going over the broad jump as though it were the high jump, but given the problem with turning and coming back to front, I think too much height only accentuates the risk of injury. I like to see the dog describing an arc over the broad jump at about elbow height. That's enough to insure elevation, but not so much as to create any unnecessary shocks to the joints on landing and turning.

While you won't have set the jumps at competition distance, Rover will be familiar with the look of the broad jump from your cavaletti work. He already knows that there is more than one obstacle, and that he has to clear all of them.

If Rover has become a confident jumper through the cavaletti work, you may not find it a tremendous problem to get proper arc on the broad jump. He has already learned how to approach a jump and clear it, and having found his normal jumping stride he will pretty much take every jump the same way, compensating only for height. The problem with the broad jump is that he will perceive the jump as being at a very low height, so you want to help him get it in his mind's eye that the jump is a little higher than it looks.

Shape the arc at first by a combination of setting the middle board on edge, and putting a jumpstick right over it, at a height of about twelve inches (this would vary depending on the height your dog jumps). The jumpstick should be about half the width of the broad-jump boards, and set on the left half of the jumps. This will help accustom the dog always to jump on the left half and not to cut toward the right-hand corner of the boards as he is jumping. You stand across the jumps from the dog, facing him, on what would be the right-hand side of the jump as you look at it. Stand about ten feet from the end of the jump. Do not worry about Fido coming to front. You are only interested in his arc as he clears the jump. Click as he clears the middle board, and treat when he gets to you.

You may find this to be a good place for a training partner if you cannot get a good look at how Fido is taking the jump. Have your partner watch from the side of the jump and do the clicking as Fido clears it. When Fido is taking the arc consistently, fade out the jumpstick. First replace it with a white round stick, then a brown dowel, then a clear plastic dowel. Spend about a week with each one, still leaving the middle board on end.

When you are down to the clear plastic dowel, lower the middle board to its proper position and go back to the plain white dowel. Then over the next three to five sessions, fade back to the clear plastic dowel. Always remember, *click as the dog is clearing the middle of the jump!*

As you are going through the process of fading the visual stimuli (jumpstick, broad jump board on edge), apply *differential reinforcement* (DR). With differential reinforcement, you reinforce only the best performances. You will have done dozens of repetitions asking Fido to clear the boards at a height of about twelve inches, and even if you were using a training partner you should have developed something of an eye for what that twelve-inch-high arc looks like. Click *only* when you get the desired arc. If Fido gives you something less, simply walk him back to the starting point and have him do it again.

This is an example of differential reinforcement. You withhold reinforcement of a given behavior in order to allow it to extinguish while at the same time reinforcing a "better" behavior. With VR, the behavior you are not reinforcing is acceptable, but you are going for "more"—a faster recall, a straighter sit, a longer stay. With DR, the behavior you are not reinforcing is not really acceptable. A jump over the boards in which the dog clears them by an inch is not at all what you want. With DR you establish a floor of acceptable performance below which you will not allow the dog to go. Your consistent refusal to reinforce subpar performances serves to extinguish anything less than what you really want.

Extending the line of travel past the jump

The second essential element in the broad jump is that the dog not turn to you immediately, but continue forward for two or three steps before turning. Now, this is not written into the description of the exercise. But this is essential if you are to avoid having the exercise deteriorate when you add the front. In a sense, the description of the exercise you want to convey to the dog is "jump, go out, then come to me."

The first tool for teaching this is the target stick. Place it in the ground about ten to twelve feet past the end of the jump, on the left side of the jump. After Rover clears the boards, tell him "touch" and have him continue out to the target stick. Click as he touches the stick, and treat.

Overtrain distance

As I discussed in the high-jump section, *overtraining* does not mean training past the dog's endurance or capacity, but rather training beyond what the dog will normally encounter in the ring. You "overtrain" the sit/"stay," for example, when you have the dog hold the stay for five minutes.

A

B

Set-up for a targeted broad jump. (a) Side view. (b) Front view. The location of the target stick encourages jumping over the left side of the boards. The dog then goes out to the stick before returning to the front position. This shaping procedure reduces the chance of corner-cutting, twisted and possibly injurious landings, and lost points.

Overtraining is a common technique among champion athletes. Sprinters, for example, will run dashes on an upslope. It is the same principle: By demanding more than is required in practice, you increase the likelihood that you will get what is required in actual performance.

On the ROH, I usually overtrain by two inches. In the broad jump, I overtrain by about six inches to a foot. The reason for this is that even enthusiastic jumpers can get lazy once they know for sure how high or how far they have to go. As with most things, behavior tends to recur at the minimum level necessary to sustain reinforcement. As I noted earlier, the distance the dog has to jump on the broad jump is not much of a problem for most dogs, which is why lazy jumping is a particular problem

Click! Laurel Hahn is shaping Baron to clear the broad jump with adequate height. If the jump is good enough, Baron gets a click at the peak of the jump. If there's no click, he has to try again. At this point the front is not required; if Laurel clicked, she'll go to Baron after the jump is completed to give him his treat.

on the broad jump. Overtraining will help you avoid this.

Unlike the high jump, there is no particular problem maintaining the extra distance for the broad jump. The dog's arc is long and flat, so there is little or no risk of injury so long as the dog is not turning in the air or immediately upon landing. Once I have the extra distance in place, I keep it there in practice.

Adding the front

You can add the front once Fido is consistently jumping at the left one-third of the boards, and consistently extending two to three steps past the last board before turning. At first, you will not be standing beside the boards. After Fido clears the boards and touches the stick, call him to front. Do this from various positions past and to the left and right of the boards. The idea here is to make the dog completely *fluent* at going well past the boards and then coming to front.

Do not let him get sloppy about touching the stick. If he starts to just "nod" at it as he goes by, or to cut short before going to the stick, go back to reinforcing touches and do not let him come to front unless he has touched the stick. This is another example of repertoire cuing and repertoire reinforcement. Jumping the boards cues touching the stick; touch-

A

B

C

Adding the front: The front is already a well-learned behavior, as is going out to touch the target stick. Laurel uses them as a chain, with verbal cues, to shape a safe and correct return to front. The jump is reinforced by the cue, "Touch!" to which Baron responds with enthusiasm (a); the touch is reinforced by the cue "Front," to which Baron also responds briskly. Baron's front is a bit far from the handler, [c] but she now will click and treat for the whole chain, and then work on the front position separately if it continues to be less than perfect.

ing the stick is a cue to come to front (and because it cues the front it has a reinforcing quality), and coming to front reinforces the touch.

You then fade and eliminate the target stick. One way to do so is to put the stick farther out (about twice the normal distance), and click for the number of steps that Rover takes before he gets to the area where the stick had been. If it took him three steps to get there after landing, click after he takes five steps; then cue the front. In this way you use the stick to keep him oriented forward, but transfer the criterion from touching the stick to taking *x* number of steps.

Rover is most likely to cut the corner of the jumps when you establish your position to the right of the boards (from the dog's starting position). You can neither prevent nor solve this problem if you have

not been careful in the various stages developing toward this point. Do not be in a hurry to get into position. As you move in that direction, keep several points in mind:

- Is Rover maintaining a consistent arc over the boards?
- Does Rover consistently jump over the left half of the boards?
- Does Rover consistently go to the touchstick before coming to front, wherever you are?

How many repetitions?

This is the perennial question. The number of repetitions depends on the complexity of what I am asking Rover to do at any given time. When I have all the elements of the broad jump in place, I may do eight or ten reps in a given session, changing each one slightly from the one before, but always demanding the same level of performance. This is one reason I move around the boards in various directions when doing fronts. Each change, however slight, gives the dog a new puzzle to solve and keeps his mind engaged.

As a rule, there is nothing wrong with a high number of repetitions as long as there is a purpose to each one. Nor is there anything wrong with "drill," as long as you are insistent that each repetition be correct. If you get an incorrect behavior, do not simply repeat it. Do what you must to get a correct behavior the next time, reinforce it, and continue.

I will also tend to do fewer repetitions of the complete exercise when we are trialing frequently. I find it more helpful to drill on details between trials than to work the whole exercise over and over.

Problem: Rover walks the boards

This is a hard problem to diagnose. Usually it arises for one of two reasons: Either the dog is injured, or the trainer has not been precise with articulating the *criteria*. Injury is always a primary consideration if your dog has had the habit of cutting to the right too quickly upon landing. The greatest risk is of a shoulder injury on the right side, making it painful to extend, as well as to land and turn.

Assuming that your dog is free of injury, do a little rethinking of the exercise and your training approach. Seeing the broad-jump exercise as a *behavior chain*, the single cue "jump" triggers three behaviors: clear the boards, turn, come to front. As often happens in training chains, once the middle pieces are in place, reinforcement tends to come only when the dog comes to front, so both dog and handler tend to reduce the exercise to a somewhat bizarre front and finish.

One preventative is simply to be consistent in the early stages about clicking the jump. That is, continuously reinforce a correct jump over the boards. After you have the entire exercise in place, selectively reinforce the jump—that is, *click as* the dog is clearing the jump and treat without asking the dog for a front. In this context, the "treat" may consist of tossing a ball or a toy out ahead of the dog's jumping path and letting him chase it. (Play is a primary reinforcer, the same as food, physical contact, etc. We don't normally use it in training because it is disruptive of the session, but this is an instance where you can easily integrate play into training as a reinforcer.) In this way you simply remind the dog from time to time that the object is to take the jump and extend past the last board before coming to you.

Utility: Are You Having Fun Yet?

Utility is the most rewarding and enjoyable of all competition Obedience classes. It asks the most of the dog and handler, separately and as a team. This is not so much a matter of the physical difficulty of the exercises as it is of the mental stamina required of the team to work its way successfully through the various pitfalls that the class presents.

The complex and subtle demands of Utility scare a lot of folks off. The good news is, if you have shaped your dog's Obedience behaviors as described in this book, neither you nor your dog will find the heightened demands of Utility insurmountable. You have built concentration and focus into your training from the earliest days. You have learned to be precise about what you ask of your dog, and your dog has learned to work to a high standard at all phases of his training.

Moreover, you have done the fluency work, so all the physical skills required for your dog to perform the Utility exercises are in place. From here on it is primarily a matter of formalizing and refining what the dog already knows. So relax and have a good time.

The signals exercise

Some general considerations

In the signals exercise the handler must cue the dog with hand signals only; verbal cues are not allowed. The signals exercise is a complex sequence, but it is not really a single behavior chain. It consists of a long-duration exercise (heeling on signal) followed by a chain of four discrete behaviors, also performed on signals (stand, down, sit, and recall), ending with the front and finish. If the dog fails to perform any one of the signaled behaviors he fails the entire exercise.

The core problem in the signals exercise is that the dog *must not anticipate* the next signal in any way. The dog that sits on the "down" signal, or after lying down but before you give the "sit" signal, for example, may be said to be anticipating the recall. So all four features of stimulus control come into play here. Before going into the specifics of the various signals exercises, it is worthwhile to review what stimulus control involves, this time in the specific context of this exercise.

Stimulus control redux

1. The dog does behavior X on cue X. The dog stands when you give the stand signal. This is complicated because you have by now spent untold hours training Rover to sit while heeling at the first hint that you are halting. Expect to put some time into this one, and when you get it expect to get stands at halt when you need a sit until Rover works it all out.
2. The dog does not do behavior X on cue Y. The dog does not sit when you give the stand signal. Also, Rover does not sit when you give the down signal. If you have not trained the "fold-back" or

"accordion" down, you may encounter some problems here.

3. The dog does not do behavior Y on cue X. The most common place you will encounter this is the dog sitting on the stand cue. Another place it may arise is the dog not doing a full down but doing a "push-up" (going halfway down) in anticipation of the sit and recall.

4. The dog does not do behavior X except on cue. Watch for Rover to anticipate every signal at some time or another during the training process. The most common anticipation event will be to pop back up into a sit after the down, but it is not the only one. Use all the techniques I have described elsewhere in this book to work past these tendencies.

Distance makes the task grow harder

All the Utility signals exercises after you leave Rover on the stand are done at a distance of about thirty feet. This can be a problem. Not to get unduly obscure, but the tricky part of distance is distance. Dogs have some sort of "zone of control" concept. I don't know that it is exactly the same, but it may be related to the "fight or flight" zone often discussed in terms of aggressive responses to other dogs. Dogs will be quite responsive when you are close, and increasingly less responsive as you put distance between you. I don't think this is necessarily a function of you having force-trained your dog, though it is possible that the fact you are close makes the dog think that force is always possible. Another consideration is that as you add distance, the dog may become aware of distractions at a distance as well, whereas when you were close, his "close-up focus" tuned them out. Whatever. As I have said, I have no idea what really goes on in those little doggy brains.

You have to work through the "zone of control" issue, one step at a time. Yes, it takes time. So it goes. There are no shortcuts. If the down from a stand is not *completely* reliable in training, it will "fall apart" (simply because it was never really there in the first place) in the ring. And if you go into the ring before this exercise is fully under stimulus control both nearby and at a distance, and Rover does not perform it, you will find your training going in reverse in a hurry.

Every step away from the dog is a new criterion, so make sure each existing step is completely solid before you go forward. This involves two things: (1) that the dog is performing the exact behavior, and (2) that the latency period at each step is zero. If you increase distance while the behavior is sloppy or slow, you will only be building those problems into the next step.

You have a simple way to tell if "latency = zero" in signals work: Rover should complete the signaled behavior before you complete the signal. At first, Rover will perform the behavior *after* you give the signal, just as he performs a behavior on verbal cue *after* he hears the full cue. In signals work, the start of your hand motion is the cue for Rover to start the behavior; he has to watch just long enough to be sure what it is you are asking of him, but no longer than that.

Rather than using variable reinforcement here, I prefer drilling with large numbers of repetitions, as many as twenty or thirty in a single session if necessary. You can usually expect to spend three to four days at each new level, which means that you can do as many as 120 repetitions at each level. Don't let that daunt you. You and your dog need them. However, before going to a new level, I will put the existing level on a variable schedule. I do not go above a 3 : 1 ratio, though; I simply find no need to do so.

Do not be surprised if you spend more time at some stages than others along the way. Each dog's "zone of control" is going to be different, and you will likely find the phenomenon reasserting itself at various points. That is, you may hit a sticking point at about six feet, and then everything goes well until you hit about fifteen feet. Just be watchful for and responsive to the issue.

The signals heeling exercise

Heeling—Nothing new here

From a training point of view the signals heeling will not create anything new for you if you have trained "automatic" heeling as described in this book. In fact, it will prove to be the easiest part of the exercise for you. Rover already moves when you move unless you tell him to stay, so you really don't need to add anything to what you do already. Be mindful that the Regulations do not *require* you to give any signal; they simply do not permit you to give any verbal commands. You "shall use signals only" in this exercise, but "moving forward at the heel without any command or signal other than the natural forward movement of the handler's body shall not be considered as anticipation."

As a practical matter, I think it is a good idea to do your heeling from Novice through Utility silently, using a movement of the left hand as the cue. Don't show in Novice until your dog works on that basis. This way, signals heeling holds no terrors whatsoever because it is what you have always done.

If you have not trained "automatic heeling" (see pages 110–140), now is the time to do so. Bowser should be so attuned to you that your leg movement alone is sufficient to get him up and moving with you. If you as a Utility A handler are relying on Bowser paying enough attention to you that he will catch a signal at the start of this exercise, you may well find yourself in trouble. Yes, you *want* that kind of focus, but don't start your Utility A career assuming that you have it. Bowser will, however, easily become attuned to your movement, so he will stay with you even if he is not catching your signal.

Keep the signal modest

Very often Utility A handlers get into the habit of giving really dramatic signals. I have seen people who, in heeling, bend their knees and swing their left arm in almost a windmill fashion. The signal is so exaggerated and complex that I am always surprised that they are not NQ'd; I write it off to the generosity of most Utility A judges.

It is not hard to get your dog to respond to even slight signals if you have conditioned your dog to do so throughout your training. The simple formula is to start with as much of a signal as you need to induce the behavior, then fade it down bit by bit until it is only as much as necessary in the ring. Not only does this look better while you are working, it keeps the dog focused because you are always asking him to perform at the same level.

The signals stand exercise

To the extent that the signals stand poses a problem, it does so as a component of heeling. From the time Bowser was small and insignificant, a mere warm little puppy with his eyes barely open, you have trained him to sit when you come to a halt while heeling. "Sit straight, sit fast" has been your mantra. Competitors, judges, and bystanders alike have stood in awe as Bowser's rump hits the ground within nanoseconds of you stopping your forward progress. You have done demonstrations at seminars on the topic, been written up in *Front & Finish*, and speculation about how you accomplished it has been the subject of untold rumor and slander on the Internet. Your dog's excellence on this matter has made you a legend in your own time.

And now, look at the dirty trick you are about to play on your poor, unsuspecting pooch. When you come to the end of the heeling pattern, instead of him slamming his rump into the ground he has to stand. This is an unconscionable, egregious change in the "rules of the game." And no doubt, your puppy will make you pay for your treachery. So let's consider the matter carefully.

The stand, even the stand on signal, is not new as such. It may, however, be rusty if you have not worked on it since Novice—which you probably have not. After all, it does not come up in Open, and why aggravate yourself training things you don't need? Well, this is why. You still need it.

Before trying to incorporate the signal stand into heeling for the signals exercise, go back to kindergarten and make sure that you have the stand on signal under **stimulus control**. There are several things to be conscious of in this process. First, reinforce the stand as an *offered behavior*. In other words, go back to free shaping for a bit. Second, add the cue as a hand signal only; *do not* use the verbal "stand" cue. When Bowser stands, simply lower your right hand over Bowser's head, and C/T. It is immaterial for these purposes whether you are getting the stand from a sit, or if Bowser stands after moving. The point is simply to reinforce the stand as an offered behavior and put it on a hand-signal cue.

Don't concern yourself with your body language at this phase of training. Ultimately you must eliminate any extraneous body language (particularly, turning at all toward Bowser as you give the signal), but this is not a concern now. Your only concerns are the offered stand, and associating the hand signal as a cue. Do about ten repetitions a day for about a week.

The next step is to associate the stand informally with motion. Don't insist on a stand at halt in heeling as yet. Simply have Bowser moving near you, give the signal, click immediately (so that he does not have a chance to sit), and treat. Make the signal very obvious; ultimately you will fade it as you refine the presentation, but for now the critical considerations are that he recognize the signal and remain standing after you present it. Continue with a high number of repetitions (ten or more per session) for about a week.

Now you can add the stand to "left-side walking." Start by making this a "moving stand" exercise (not to be confused with the moving stand exercise that I discuss later. When is a moving stand not a moving stand? When it's a moving stand. Get it?). In other words, the point of the exercise is that

Using the Video Camera

The video camera may be one of the most important training tools you have. This is especially true if, like me, you do most of your training on your own. But it is also true if you have a training partner, if only because most people find it hard to be as critical of you as you are. The video camera gives you an unvarnished record of what you are doing at any given time.

You should use the video camera at all stages of training, but it becomes very valuable in Utility training because of the emphasis on body language (signals). You want to watch for extraneous motions of your hands and body as you are giving the signals. Not only can such motions be considered "extra commands" causing you to fail the exercise, but they become part of the stimuli for the dog and, as you try to get rid of them, you will find the dog becoming confused because you are no longer giving him all the "signals" that you have accustomed him to.

So, videotape your training sessions and review them.

The other thing to do is videotape your ring performances, and compare the "look" you give the dog in the ring with the look you give the dog in training. More often than not, these "looks" will be different, and this in turn will help explain why your dog's performance in the ring is not as accurate or consistent as his work in training.

Bowser stand at the end of your forward motion. Take one step forward and deliver the stand signal. Do not allow Rover to walk forward at all after you deliver the signal (here is where the "kick-back" stand, which trained the stand as an immobile exercise, earns its keep).

How do you "not allow" Rover to move forward? Simple: Be faster than immediate with your C/T. Your click should *anticipate* the stand, so that you *click at the instant all four feet are still,* and not one instant later. Deliver the treat quickly after the click, and do not let Rover leave the stand in any way to get it.

Gradually build the distance you move before giving the stand signal. Be aware that the more distance you cover, the more this will look like regular heeling, and the more inclined Bowser will be to sit when you come to a halt. This is why I don't consider it necessary to go to variable reinforcement in training this exercise. One stand, one C/T. You are working against a long- and well-reinforced tendency for Rover to sit when you stop. For that reason, putting this exercise on a variable schedule could cause considerable confusion.

Leaving Bowser in place on the stand

The last portion of the stand exercise is that you leave Bowser on the stand and go across the ring for the remainder of the signals. In line with the principle I discussed on the long sit and long down, I use the same signal for "stay in place" as I did for the stand, that is, right hand coming down directly over the dog's head. This confirms to Rover that he is on a stand; the "stay" is simply an extension of the stand.

The signals down

If you trained the down on a signal for the drop on recall, this is pretty familiar territory. If you did not do so, go back to Chapter 3 (Fluencies—see pages 66–72) and the Open drop on recall section (pages 174–179).

The only unfamiliar element now is distance, as I discussed earlier. If you trained the down from a stand as described earlier (see pages 174–179), even that is not new because you built up to thirty feet in that training before incorporating the signaled down into the drop on recall. But if you did not do that training then, do it now.

The accordion down

If you trained the down from a sit (or simply allowed Bowser to go into the down that way because you didn't think it mattered), you are going to have some major reworking to do. *You do not want Rover going into the signals down by progressing through a sit!* There are primarily two reasons for this. First, the down will be unreliable and you will find Rover stopping halfway through the down. This is not good. You will have enough of a problem with Rover sitting on the down signal (or popping up into a sit after going down but before you signal the sit) without giving him the added incentive of going through the sit on his way to the down. Second, the physical action of Rover going through the sit will cause him to inch forward, costing you points.

You want Rover to drop directly in place into the down, folding back into the accordion (or "Sphinx") down. I detailed how to train this in the earlier discussions (see pages 66–72). If you haven't trained this already, there is no time like the present.

Old habits die hard—if they really die at all

As you are building the accordion down, work at a very close distance until the form is consistent, and build distance slowly. The problem with retraining is always that old habits not only die hard—they in fact never truly die. I think of them as words written in chalk on a blackboard. You can erase and erase, but there is always some "dust" left over, keeping the earlier writing visible through the new.

"The moving finger writes; and having writ moves on: nor all thy piety or wit shall lure it back to cancel half a line, nor all thy tears wipe out a word of it." Old Omar Khayyám is perhaps a bit cosmic for present purposes, but there is a truth here. Train for the behavior you want from the beginning, and do not reinforce behaviors you don't want. That way, when problems arise (as they invariably will), you can "go back to kindergarten" and retrace an established learning curve rather than "reinventing the wheel."

Sometimes you read about a prizefighter whose trainers are trying to change from a slugger to a boxer. All goes well in the gym, but the first time someone bangs him in the snoot, he's back to slugging. In the same vein, a major-league pitcher was quoted once as saying that all pitchers basically throw the way they did when they were seven years old. The trick for them as adults is to keep their mechanics that clean.

Behaviors that are learned early have a long history of being reinforced, and so are remarkably resistant to extinction. The good news is that if you trained the behavior properly the first time around, when it "falls apart" for any reason it will be relatively easy to reestablish it. But if you did not train it properly at first, then when under stress, even if you have retrained the exercise correctly, early patterns will always tend to reassert themselves. I suppose this is the source of the old saw that "you can't teach an old dog new tricks." More accurately, I guess the saying should go, "It's tough to teach an old dog to do an old trick in a new way." But it can be done.

For this reason, if you are retraining the down for Utility signals to get an accordion down rather than a down-from-sit, you will want to do large numbers of repetitions; I mean hundreds, even, at every stage. You have to establish a very strong reinforcement history for the new behavior in order to have confidence that it will prevail over the "old habits." Your reinforcement schedule will be continuous until you have built to a high level of reliable responses (forty-nine out of fifty or better) at each level of distance. As always, though, before going to the next level put the existing performance on a variable schedule (3 : 1 is sufficient).

Also, because you are establishing a new behavior, do not reinforce any "almost good" drops. Know exactly what you are looking for, and reinforce that behavior and only that behavior. It is either a clean Sphinx down, or it is not. There are no gray areas, no "good enough for government work." Be clear about what you want, insist that Fido give it to you, *click only for that*—and in the fullness of time you will get it. Be vague about your expectations and inconsistent with your reinforcement contingencies, and you will get inconsistent results—and it won't be the dog's fault.

Remember latency

Latency is another major issue here. As you demand only a certain type of drop, you will find Rover's response time slowing somewhat. That's OK. If he has to slow down a bit to get it right, let him do so (*relax existing criteria when introducing a new criterion*). But don't add or shift any criteria, and especially do not increase distance until you have latency at zero at your present distance.

The signals sit

There is nothing new to teach concerning the sit as such, *except that* you do not want Rover "hitching" his front feet forward at all as he comes up out of the down. The ideal motion is that he push up on his forelegs and tuck his rear end forward to come into proper position. You will tend to get this if you taught him to sit that way from the stand or while in motion. Rover may be inconsistent. If so, then be alert to those times when he comes up into the sit with the proper motion, and selectively reinforce it.

The sit signal

Unless you introduced your dog to signals during fluency training or as a matter of principle, this is completely new. Everyone has their own preferences on how to do the sit signal, so I'll just stick with mine.

Mechanics

I like to alternate hands from signal to signal. I do the down signal with my right, the sit signal with my left, then the recall signal with my right again. The initial motion for both the sit and recall signals is rather similar, and this avoids any risk of confusion between them. The risk is real because, in Open, I use a recall signal to call my dog from the drop on recall. Also, the recall is the reinforcer for the sit, so if I create any confusion the dog is likely to resolve it by performing the reinforcing exercise.

The sit signal is a circular motion with my left hand, palm open toward the dog. Tuck your left elbow against your side and keep it there at all times; this dictates the diameter of the circular motion you will make and also the distance your hand will be from your side. Starting with my hand at the thigh I bring it up to about waist level, hand away from my body the length of my forearm, then in a circle back away from the dog, ending up with my hand at about stomach height. My open palm faces the dog at all times.

Remember that the signal must be smooth and continuous, so don't make a huge deal out of the circular motion and do not "hitch" before describing the circle.

Training the response

You will always be asking Rover to sit from a down. Ultimately you can use the hand signal to have him sit from a stand if you like (when Rover will sit from a stand on signal you know his response is fluent), but in this exercise he starts from the down position.

Before you introduce Rover to the signal, be sure that your own mechanics are consistent. It is impossible to emphasize this too strongly: Next to their sense of smell, the strongest skill dogs have is their ability to read body language. Dogs communicate through body language more than anything else. Our dogs are always reading and responding to our body language, though we don't always seem to realize it.

With signals, we are explicitly asking the dog to respond to body language. For body language to be a communicator, it must be specific, clear, and consistent. So whether you do the sit signal as I have described or in some other way, make sure that you

are performing the motion consistently before introducing it to your dog.

Training for zero latency

The sit in response to your signal must be immediate—that is, there must be zero latency. It is not hard to teach an immediate response to the signal *if* Bowser already has an immediate response to the "sit" cue. Standing close to the dog, begin the sit signal and say "sit" *as you bring your hand up and into the backward circle.* Do not draw the word "sit" out (for some reason people have a tendency to do this with a sibilant "s" so that they are completing the word as they are completing the signal); keep the word crisp. In this way, the verbal cue will be complete before the hand signal is complete. This way, Bowser is responding to the first part of the hand signal, not the last.

Now you may well get a somewhat confused response, manifesting itself in a slow sit in response to the verbal cue. He'll be watching your hand at the same time as he is responding to the verbal cue. The hand signal at this point is a distraction. On the one hand, Bowser knows what a signal is (he has seen signals for the down and recall). On the other, a signal to sit is completely new. Just as you gave yourself time to perfect the signal before introducing it to Bowser, now you must give him time to learn what it means.

Fading the verbal cue

Before you do anything else—either add distance or incorporate the sit into the signals sequence—you must eliminate the verbal cue. You have to know that Rover will sit reliably in response to the hand signal only. The first step is to *watch the dog*. You will know if he is picking up on the meaning of the hand signal if he is sitting up from the down at the start of your hand motion, almost before—or at least simultaneously as—you vocalize the "s" in "sit."

The second step is to start fading the verbal cue simply by lowering volume. Assuming you start with your voice at conversational level, gradually reduce it to a whisper. At the same time, eliminate any movement of your lips (remember, lip movement is body language!). You can do this easily by "smiling" throughout.

Work at a distance of about three feet (close, but just far enough away that he can see your signal clearly), using both verbal and hand signal, for about three to five days. Give it time. After the third day, give him both the hand signal and whatever is left of your verbal cue for one repetition; on the second repetition, give him the hand signal only. Rover should sit in response to the signal. If he does, *jackpot*.

Don't delude yourself into thinking that he now knows the signal. It's still too soon for that. But he has the idea. For the next couple of days, your ratio of hand signals only to signals + verbal cue should be about 4 : 1. I find it most effective to continue starting with the combination and then eliminating the verbal cue on successive repetitions. This virtually eliminates the possibility of initial failure. I can then build on success.

You can be confident that Rover knows the hand signal when he responds to it at the first repetition. This should take about five sessions. If it takes a little longer, do not despair. Double-check that your signal and general body language are consistent, and be patient.

Adding distance

The issues here are familiar by now. Add distance a step at a time until you are at forty feet. Remember that you will encounter "zone of control" issues throughout, so don't take any leaps. If your dog readily responds at each step, maintain that distance for a couple of days and then take another step. You may also want to move from side to side, a few feet in either direction, so that Fido is responding to the signal even when you are not directly on a straight line in front of him. This is because you may well not walk away from him on a straight line, and you want to be sure that you being "off line" will not disrupt his performance.

Putting the down and sit together

You can do this before you add in the recall. Do not do it, however, until both the down and the sit on signal are reliable at forty feet.

In putting the down and sit together you will encounter anticipation issues. If your dog has the "accordion down," you won't have to worry overly much about the dog sitting on his way down, but be alert for it. It will happen. If it does, do not "correct." Simply withhold reinforcement, release him, and do it again. If it happens twice in any set of ten repetitions, isolate the down and selectively reinforce the accordion drop.

Vary the time that you hold Rover on the down between three and fifteen seconds before giving the sit signal. This will underwrite the patience he will require in the ring, and will help avoid Rover learning to regard the down as a repertoire cue for the sit. You can (and should) selectively reinforce the down from time to time by C/Ting the down without having Rover sit first. You can do this in a couple of ways. Click, walk in, and treat. Or, click and release Rover from the distance to come to you.

While the down should never become a repertoire cue for the sit, the sit will become a *repertoire reinforcer* for the down. You can, and should, use it this way. Teach Rover that he only gets to sit when he does the down properly—and holds it until you "release" him into the sit. Why is the sit so reinforcing? Because it is the precursor to the recall.

The signals recall

If you trained the recall on signal for Novice and Open, there is nothing new here. The signal for the signals recall is exactly the same as in those classes. You probably won't even have much of a problem with anticipation here, because you have done considerable training already with Rover waiting on a sit for the recall cue. Nor are there any new issues on the front and finish. Put another way, recall, front, and finish are a strong, established, and completed *fluency*. This part of the exercise is all old business, and once Rover knows that this is how the exercise ends, it will "come together" for him nicely.

Training with a high number of repetitions

Overall, the central problem in all the signals exercises is consistency of response. Many times handlers try to cut corners. In any set of (say) five repetitions, the dog may miss two. So the handler says "he knows it pretty well," and it's on to the next step. You can "get away" with this in Novice and Open; it is impossible in Utility, where Bowser's focus and mental stamina are at least as important as (if not more than) his ability to perform the exercises as such. For the dog to know an exercise "pretty well" is, in fact, not to know it at all. A woman is either pregnant, or she is not. A dog either knows the exercise, or he does not. There are no gray areas here. As long as the response rate is inconsistent, the learning phase is still in progress. You cannot build on that which is not itself established.

You will only get a high response rate with high numbers of repetitions. This does not mean that you go through the pattern (down, sit, come) mindlessly ten times a day. It means that while training each, and in putting them together, you do at least twenty repetitions a session, and more if necessary, such that your response rate is eighty percent or better at each step before progressing. Chart the responses so that you can do the calculation. Do not take another step until Fido's response rate is into that high range.

This you will do "in the laboratory," that is, in a training place that is familiar and comfortable to your dog, before you introduce distractions of any significance. It will take a while, but the exercises must be perfect "in the laboratory" before you take them "on the road." And, when you take them "on the road," you will go all the way back down to the beginning of the learning curve and rebuild. It is a retraining process.

Yes, Fido will have considerable ability to **generalize** by now. So why do I reemphasize all this when discussing signals? Simply because *proper performance of the signals exercise requires absolute focus on you*. Rover must learn how to tune out distractions completely. No other training of any other exercise accomplishes this as thoroughly as does signals work, simply because if Rover misses the signal he doesn't get to perform the behavior, which means he doesn't get to earn a reinforcer. Rover must be comfortable, attentive, and completely responsive, regardless of conditions.

It will also help you to watch Rover's body language for stress signs. When you leave him on the stand, he should stand as though he were awaiting the stand for examination—that is, naturally. If you see him hunched (back "up" or head somewhat down), or the ears back, or he is panting, understand such signs as stress indicators. A very strong signal is if the dog's head is turned at all (other than in immediate response to a loud noise) while he "watches" you. This is a primary *calming signal* and tells you that Rover perceives considerable stress in the situation. Most likely, this arises because you are not really comfortable with his work and you are asking too much of him at the time (for example, you are putting him in a trial before the exercise is perfect in practice).

Whenever you see these (or similar) indicators, you will also see slow response, or no response. Here is a situation where "corrections" are your worst enemy. The dog perceives your stress, and is to some extent stressed himself. How, then, will it help anything for you to charge in and, for example, "pop" the dog into a down? An aggressive physical response can only make matters worse.

The issue is not that the dog did not respond to your signal. The issue is that the dog perceives the situation in a way that interferes with his ability to respond to your signal. The question becomes not "why is this dog stressed?" but rather "what am I doing to stress the dog?" This approach at least has the benefit of turning one's attention to the handler, which is where all problem analysis must begin.

There is something of a "mantra" that has gained currency in the last couple of years. It goes something like this: "Train with positive reinforcement, use 'corrections' only after your dog really understands the exercise but does not perform it." What this statement overlooks is that (a) if your dog really understands the exercise—specifically, understands what behavior will trigger reinforcement, and (b) understands the cue for the exercise, then (c) he is not likely to fail (much less refuse) to perform the exercise unless something specific is interfering with his performance. If you accept this truth, and are able to trust your dog, then you will understand that things always happen for a reason; therefore, a particular "failure to perform" must be analyzed, not "corrected." Most of the time, a dog's failure to perform is caused by the handler asking for too much behavior, or escalating criteria too rapidly, or being imprecise in delivering the cue, or communicating the handler's own stress to the dog. Sometimes, the "failure to perform" is not a failure at all but simply a reflection of good stimulus control (for example, the dog that does not respond to a cue that he may not have clearly heard or seen). In none of these situation is it "fair" (much less an appropriate teaching tool) to subject the dog to an aversive.

Scent discrimination (articles)

There are many methods used to teach scent discrimination. With Woody I used the "tie-down" method (lashing the articles to a board or to a bolt in the ground), and it seemed to be working fine until I realized that when he had his nose down it wasn't to sniff the articles but to nudge them to see which one moved. That was the one he picked up.

So when training Sam I went to Janice DeMello's "Around the Clock" method, which worked quite well on the whole. I found myself reducing the amount of cheese a little more quickly than she suggests, mostly because Sam seemed to spend a lot of time licking the cheese, after which he seemed to forget what he had gone out to do.

I've now gone to a straightforward *shaping* approach. Scent discrimination is actually an easy fluency for Fido to learn (see pages 104–108). The problem is not that the dog cannot easily learn that you want him to find the article that smells like you, but that we cannot, as humans, readily understand what the dog is really doing. The dog's sense of smell is so extraordinary that we humans have no sensory organ that even remotely compares to it.

What we don't know, we don't trust. As Glen Johnson put it, "in scent work the dogs are asked to perform something which the trainer cannot see, hear or feel and whether the dog is actually performing correctly or not cannot be accurately deduced since the vagaries of scent are, as yet, a mystery. One correction applied when the dog is actually performing correctly could have a lasting detrimental effect" (*Tracking Dog,* 1977, p. 7).

Not knowing what the dog is really doing, we trick up our scent discrimination training not because the dog needs it, *but because we do.* If, however, we can take the leap and decide simply to *trust the dog* to do what he knows how to do best, scent discrimination "training" need not be difficult at all.

In training scent discrimination you are not teaching the dog "how to scent." Johnson writes, "What a dog smells, or how scent behaves, or just what scent is should not even enter the novice's mind when attempting to train a dog in tracking. The only important thing is the *type of behavior desired* in the finished product of a handler-dog team." What is true in tracking training is equally true in scent discrimination training. You want a certain **behavior.** You really have no reason (or right!) to interfere in the dog's sensory processes that get you to the point at which that behavior appears.

Training scent discrimination simply means educating the dog as to *which article* out of several you want him to retrieve. But let's clarify something. Although throughout this discussion I'll refer to scented and unscented articles, Bowser is not really choosing between scented and unscented articles. None of the articles are truly "unscented"; you will impart scent to the articles as they are in your car, and even as you carry them to the ring. Not to worry. The dog can easily tell the difference between a fresh and stale scent, as well as distinguish between intensity of scent. You can even pick up an "unscented" article lightly by the bell and place it on the ground, and Bowser will be able to distinguish that

from the one you have scented directly on the bit. So scent discrimination training is simply a matter of communication: I want the one that smells *the most like me*, not the ones that smell like anything else.

At the beginning of the training you are concerned only that the dog retrieve the correct article and return it to hand. You need not be particularly concerned about the sit in front or the finish. This is partly because you want to focus on the one essential skill: locating and retrieving the correct article. Also, as in other complex exercises, the sit in front and the finish are, by now, a well-established fluency. You will tend to get the sit in front without asking for it.

"Scenting" the article

"Scenting" the article simply means imparting your scent to the bit. You cannot avoid imparting some of your scent to the bell ends, but this is incidental. The concentration of scent will be on the bit, and that is what you are going to teach the dog to orient to. How much do you "scent" the article? Most of us have a tendency to overscent. This can be a problem, particularly outdoors on a hot day. The scent may be sufficiently strong to make the article distasteful to the dog. If it is windy, the scent may also "travel" to a neighboring article. I have also been told by some tracking trainers (who I believe "should know, if anybody knows at all") that rubbing the article too much actually changes your own scent. Scent is really carried by microscopic skin cells, so rubbing creates friction, causing the molecules in the cells to move around faster, so it is possible that the scent they communicate changes depending on how "hot" you make it. I do know that when I scent the article heavily my dogs seem to have a little more trouble with it than when I scent it lightly. That's good enough for me.

Find out how much scent your dog needs. Practice articles at different times of the day to see if the necessary amount of scent changes from the cool of the morning to the heat of the afternoon. It may not make that much difference, but it is handy to know. Also, practice in breezy and even windy conditions to see how these conditions affect your dog's ability to get to the correct article readily.

Using articles to play

In the initial scent discrimination work I find it helpful to start with a few (no more than five) play retrieves. This may be partly due to working with shelties, who are indifferent retrievers. As you progress it becomes less and less necessary to do play sessions, and by the time you progress to having four or more articles on the ground, it is probably unnecessary entirely. Gradually reduce the number play retrieves you do before the scent work; do not just eliminate them altogether in one fell swoop.

The metal article

It is best to start scent discrimination work with the metal article because Rover will more readily recognize that it is your scent that you are asking him to identify than he will with leather, which carries its own desirable scent. Not uncommonly, dogs with a reliable retrieve with the wooden dumbbell will easily carry that over to the leather articles. Leather is not unpleasant to the dog, so it's an easy transition. It's not always so with metal.

The best way to prepare early for scent discrimination work is to introduce your dog to having metal in his mouth at a very early age, and keep metal in your dog's toybox forever. Otherwise, you may well face an extended period of getting the dog accustomed to the taste and feel of metal in his mouth.

I made the mistake with Dylan of not introducing him to metal until he was already accustomed to wood and leather. It didn't occur to me that this would be a mistake, because neither Woody nor Sam had any problem with metal. Dylan, however, quickly decided that metal was an alien plot to eliminate shelties from the face of the earth, and he was not going to fall for that trick. It took many sessions to get him to take the metal article consistently.

This isn't a "retrieve" problem so much as simply a comfort problem. Leather and wood are chewable; metal is not. Metal has a funny taste. I am told that scent is different on metal than on leather (also affecting taste). Get your dog used to the taste and feel of metal in his mouth from his earliest days as a puppy, and make playing with a metal retrieve toy as much a part of your repertoire of games as anything else. It will save you a lot of grief and aggravation further down the road.

The cue ("find it")

The most common cue is "find it" or "find mine." I use "find it." Every time Rover indicates the scented article, say "find it" immediately before you C/T. Start this before you put the articles on the ground.

Developing the retrieve

The scent discrimination exercise is an "identify and retrieve" exercise. It requires that the dog (a) "find the one that smells the most like you" and (b) bring it back to you. I deal with the *fluency* for this work in Chapter 3 (see pages 104–108). There you developed Rover's ability to indicate and then locate the scented article. Now you are going to add the retrieve element and teach Rover to work an increasingly large pile of articles. As always, the approach is to give the dog the opportunity to succeed at first, then increase the degree of difficulty gradually so that the dog can still succeed while having to work progressively harder to do so.

You want Rover to *offer* the scent retrieve. Do three to five play retrieves with a scented metal article to "get Rover in the spirit." Do not do any fronts or finishes; keep him always working in front of you. Still using only two metal articles, place them on the ground about two feet away from you, and about twelve inches apart. Wait for Rover to go to the articles on his own. If he shows no disposition to go to the articles, pick up the scented one and toss it lightly near the unscented one. Because of the play toss, he should go out and get it. After a couple of those, toss the article as he is getting his treat from you and give him the opportunity to decide to go for it on his own. From there you can go to placing it on the ground as he watches.

Repeat the cue "find it" every time he indicates to the correct article, and click *immediately* when he indicates it. You will use **continuous reinforcement** throughout this training. Together with sharp timing on your clicks, this will give the dog a constant flow of information from you as to what you want and whether he is giving it to you. This will help you immensely in the ring, because you will be establishing good latency. Fido will know immediately when he has the correct article, which means that he will be less likely to fall into the habit of searching the pile even after he has identified which article is the correct one. Your goal is that he go directly to the pile and retrieve the scented article immediately when he locates it.

At first, you are only concerned that he *indicate* the correct article. However, you will probably soon find Rover picking up the article after he indicates to it. All well and good. After all, you have trained him to retrieve, so this is a fluency at work. Indeed, he is putting the two behaviors (scent discrimination and retrieve) together on his own, and you want to encourage that sort of inventiveness.

If Rover does not start picking up the scented article on his own, the time to start asking for the pickup is after you have had one full session in which he has indicated the correct article every time as you have moved it around the unscented article. Now as he indicates the correct article you can remind him to "take it," and click when he lifts it from the ground. Here you are clicking the pickup, so if he drops it and returns to you for his treat, that is okay. When Rover is consistently picking up the correct article, click for the delivery to you.

Although it is not necessary to train this exercise fully as a blind retrieve (see pages 210–211), it will not hurt to incorporate blind retrieve concepts into the training. If you show outdoors, and especially if you have a small dog, you will have times when the articles are difficult for Rover to see. Make sure that you do some sessions with the articles hidden in tall grass, or even in a small depression so that Rover cannot see them until he is close to them.

What if he picks up the wrong article?

Remember Johnson's warning: even a small "correction" in scent work may produce undesirable results that you will struggle with thereafter, forever. If Rover gets the wrong article, you are going to rely exclusively on *extinction*. Simply, do not reinforce Rover for indicating or getting the wrong article.

I said just before that continuous reinforcement and timing were key to problem solving. Here is an example. You should have been clicking *every time* Rover indicated the correct article, and *before* he picked it up. Now, when he indicates the wrong article and you do not click, that gives him a piece of information; the absence of reinforcement (remember, this is a 1 : 1 schedule!) in and of itself sends the message "wrong." If Rover does not realize almost before he has the article off the ground that he has the wrong one, you are probably being too slow with your clicks.

If he gets back to you with the wrong article in his mouth, *say nothing*. You cannot use the word "wrong" or some similar extinction cue here, because you would not be addressing what is in fact

the "wrong" behavior. The error lies in identifying the unscented rather than the scented article, not in bringing what he has "found" back to you. The time to say something like "wrong" would be when Rover was indicating the incorrect article (but if your timing with "wrong" was that good you would be at least equally adept with the timing of your clicks, and the absence of the click would communicate the necessary information anyway).

So, say nothing. Simply take the article from the dog silently—and wait. At this stage I do not even look at him, but off in the distance. Now you have withheld reinforcement three times: once when he indicated the wrong article, once when he picked it up, and once when he returned it to you. Rover will definitely know that something is amiss. Give him time to figure it out. I have waited as long as two minutes for the dog to return to the scented article.

You may find the dog looking around, a bit confused. If he looks at the scented article, C/T. Again, you are giving him information: "That's the one." Now, wait again. It will only take a couple of trials before he goes back and gets the correct one.

Once he gets the correct article, replace the one he picked up with a completely clean one. Put the new unscented article back where the first unscented article was and the scented article back in the position that caused Rover the problem. Send him again. You may have two or three failures before he "gets it." Once he goes directly to the correct article, C/T and you are done for that session.

Try, however, to do another session that same day. Start with the articles in the positions you last left them. Rover should go directly to the correct article. You can then do two or three repetitions, moving the article around each time. If you get two or three correct pickups, it's time to stop.

A generalization note on scents and such

Lassie *must* get used to retrieving your scent out of a pile of articles with other, unfamiliar human scents on them rather than just "cold" but familiar scents. After she is comfortable with basic scents, mix it up a bit. Put articles with stronger scents (even food scents) out there and condition her to bypassing them in favor of the one that has your scent. You simply do not know what the dog may encounter on the ground, and you should be prepared for everything—or at least, as much of everything as you can whip up in your imagination.

The silly season: Food smells on your hands

Perhaps the most curious practice I have heard of is that of some handlers who like to get the smell of their bait (liver, Rollover, whatever) on their hands when they go into the ring. Some judges have been known to tell handlers to go wash their hands, which if anything is even more curious. It's a toss-up.

You don't need anything but your own scent. Handlers who feel the need to "juice up" the smell are simply falling victim to what I discussed at first: the inability to trust their dog's olfactory powers. Such a practice is not necessary, and may even be counterproductive. Practice the exercise consistently and learn to trust your dog.

On the other hand, avoid chemicals such as perfume, cologne, sunscreen or insect repellent. These not only interfere with your scent, they are positively obnoxious to the dog. If you must apply such things, do so before you leave the house. Preferably, wear latex gloves while putting the stuff on, so your hands don't get the smell on them. If you don't have such gloves, wash your hands thoroughly before you leave and make sure not to get any of the stuff on them again before you go in the ring.

Topography of the exercise

Point 1. Involvement of other people

There are three elements to the exercise as actually done in the ring that are noticeably different *to the dog* from how you have practiced the exercise until now. When in the ring, you will always start the exercise with your back to the articles pile, and "turn-and-send" Spot to find it; there will be someone else placing the articles in the pile (and imparting some scent to them); and there will be someone else taking the scented article out and placing it in the pile.

The scent of a stranger on the "unscented" articles

The scent of a stranger is a critical issue, because while the "unscented" articles actually have scents—the "cold" but familiar scents of your car, your other dogs, and so forth—the scents are all familiar. The scent of a stranger adds something new, and Spot may be completely thrown off. Some stewards impart no more scent than is inevitable when handling the articles to put them on the ground and spread them around, and some stewards put real effort into scenting up each article, particularly in Utility A

where they seem to think this will be especially helpful to your dog.

I don't have someone else start placing the articles for me until my dog is retrieving both leather and metal articles, at a distance of about twelve feet. At that point I know that my dog is certain as to the physical maneuvers involved and is as close to 100% reliable with both metal and leather articles as I can expect.

A stranger places the scented article

There seem to be two aspects to the problems created by the judge placing the article in the pile. One is that because you have always gone out and placed the articles, the dog is certain that there is an article in the pile for him to find and bring back. Now the dog has to become similarly confident even though someone else has placed the article, and Spot was facing away from that person as he did so. The other is that by going back and forth to the pile you established a scent that the dog can track into the pile. The dog no longer has that scent to orient to. So the dog has to develop a new awareness of how to get to the pile. It helps that you and Spot are facing the activity while the steward is setting out the whole pile, but not much. Most dogs I've worked with do not really process the fact that the article is out where they have seen the other articles being spilled. They have to learn that is where the article is.

When you first have your training partner place the scented article in the pile, start by facing the pile with your dog as your partner takes the article from you, goes to the pile, and puts it down. This will not help Fido pick out the right article but it will inform him that this person is putting the article out there for him to find. It is an easy step from that to turning your back while your partner places the article.

Point 2. The "turn-and-send"

As a fluency, you have practiced the maneuver for the "turn-and-send" since your "Beginning Utility" work, in the form of doing turns in place while "doodling." The "turn-and-send" is nothing more than a right about turn-in-place.

Until 1996 you were required to have the dog sit at heel before sending him to the articles. Now, you have a choice. You may turn, have the dog sit at heel and then send him, or you may turn and send him without first having him sit. It's up to you, but it's a choice you must make in practice and stick with.

If you turn and send Spot without a sit-at-heel, the Regulations only allow you to give the "command or signal to retrieve," which you must give simultaneously as you turn. Properly executed, the dog "slingshots" out toward the articles as you execute the turn; there should be no hesitation in the dog's movement around and forward as you turn. This maneuver is nice for the dog because it avoids the problem of the dog forging around in his eagerness to go for the article. The maneuver is nice for you because you don't risk points off for a crooked sit at heel after the pivot (remember, the exercise starts when the judge gives his first order, which in this exercise is "turn and send your dog"). There is also little risk of points off for anticipation and the like. As far as I have observed, it seems that handlers with the more manic retrieving dogs are using the single movement (turn-and-send with no sit at heel), while handlers with more deliberate working dogs are sticking with the two-part sequence. Your dog, your call.

When sending the dog out, you may use *either* a verbal cue or signal, but not both. Since almost everyone settles on a verbal cue ("find it" or "find mine"), this becomes another new wrinkle for Spot to work through. In Open, both retrieves are preceded by you throwing the dumbbell. You not only don't throw the article in this exercise, you don't even place the articles in the pile. Also, in the other "send-away" exercises (directed retrieve and directed jumping) you are permitted to use *both* a cue and a signal. You will do a lot of **stimulus control** training in those exercises, giving the dog a hand signal but requiring that he wait for the verbal cue; here you will require that he go on one cue only.

This also creates some problems for the handler, because you will get very used to giving both a verbal cue and a signal and may find yourself lapsing into doing both on this exercise. Again, this is a very important place to have either a gimlet-eyed training partner or a video camera. Keep very mindful of *anything* you do physically that is in any way suggestive of physical cuing.

Developing the puzzle

Fido has to (a) identify the correct article from among more and more "unscented" articles and (b) look in different places to find the scented article. The progression throughout is to add one scented article at a time, then vary positioning of the scented article among and around the unscented articles.

Varying the number, location, and arrangement of scent articles keeps the puzzle interesting and develops fluency in the dog: skills that are well beyond what is required in competition.

A couple of preliminary notes. First, use the same scented article throughout every session. Rescent every couple of repetitions, but don't overdo it. By the time you're done, it will be quite ripe. Second, I refer to "80% reliability" throughout this discussion. By this, I mean that Spot finds and returns the correct articles at least ten consecutive times out of ten trials in any given session. This may mean that you do thirty trials in a session, but so be it. If he seems to be getting stale, quit and do something else for a bit, then come back to it. But do not add distance or articles so long as Spot is less than 80% reliable at whatever level you are working.

Last, the progression outlined here involves four principal variants: (1) the article material (metal or leather), (2) the number of articles on the ground, (3) the distance Bowser has to travel to get to the pile, and (4) the position of the scented article in relation to all the unscented articles. I explain the first three elements as I go. As to (4), with every successful repetition you must place the scented article in a different place relative to the unscented article(s). You should "box the compass," that is, move it from side to side, front to back, and corner to corner. Generally, place the scented article within six to nine inches of the nearest unscented article(s).

Stage 1: Metal only, two to six articles

Start with one unscented metal article on the ground. When you have 80% reliability with two articles, go to three (one scented, two unscented), and so on. Work with metal articles only until you have six articles on the ground (one scented, five unscented). Next build distance, adding about three feet every session until you are up to about twenty-four feet away from the six articles. Ultimately you want to work at a distance of thirty feet, but twenty-four feet is enough for early training purposes. You will reduce and rebuild distance throughout; every time you do so it will take less time to go through the progression than previously, but go through it nonetheless. Once the dog is at the pile, his extraordinary scenting ability will get him through; it is your responsibility to make sure that the mechanics of getting him to the pile are impeccable. At any time that performance breaks down, take one step back and get it back on track before going further.

Stage 2: The turn-and-send

When Spot is working with at least 80% reliability at twenty-four feet, introduce the "turn-and-send." Reduce distance to six feet with the six articles on the ground. Stand with your back to the articles, Spot sitting at heel (also facing away from the articles). Place the article in the pile, return to your dog, turn and send (don't worry if Spot tries to turn a bit to watch you; he won't know where the article is by sight anyway). Spot should not be having any problems with the scenting aspect of the exercise by now, so you are both free to concentrate on this maneuver. Rebuild distance about three feet at a time to twenty-four feet, working for over 80% reliability at each stage.

Stage 3: Have someone else place the articles

Once the dog is comfortable with going about twenty-four feet to the pile from a "turn-and-send" with you placing the scented article, have a training partner place the articles. Start at a distance of about six feet, facing the pile with your dog as your partner places the scented article. Repeat several times until Spot is going readily from your side when you send him. Then you can introduce the turn-and-send. Work at six feet with the full sequence, including the turning maneuver, until you have 80% reliability, then rebuild distance. Your partner should do the whole routine just as it will be done in the ring, including touching the "unscented" articles as she

puts them on the ground. Have your training partner scent the articles in various ways, sometimes touching lightly and sometimes heavily.

Your training partner should place the article you have scented the way the judge will, using a pair of tongs and a clipboard if possible. This will give the dog optimum exposure to the "look" of the exercise in the ring. Have different people do this for you from time to time so that the dog doesn't get used to just one other person's scent on the articles. From this point on, as you add each variation first do it placing the article(s) yourself, and then have your training partner place the article(s). If possible, have your partner place the article for you at each stage before increasing distance or adding unscented articles. If you primarily train alone, you may have to do several progressions alone between sessions with a partner. In that case, when working together have your training partner place the scented article in two or more of the variations you have worked through in the interim.

Stage 4: Add unscented leather articles

When you have 80% reliability with the turn-and-send at twenty-four feet, reduce the distance back to about six feet, and remove one of the unscented metal articles and replace it with an unscented leather article. Rebuild distance to twenty-four feet. In the same manner, replace the metal articles one by one with leather until you have one scented metal and five unscented leather articles on the ground, at a distance of twenty-four feet.

Stage 5: The scented leather article

Now introduce a scented leather article. Place it on the ground with an unscented metal article, about six feet away. When you have 80% reliability as before, replace the unscented metal article with an unscented leather article. When you have 80% reliability with the two leather articles, add an unscented metal article. Then, replace that with an unscented leather article, and so on. When you have six leather articles on the ground (one scented, five unscented) with at least 80% reliability at six feet, rebuild distance as before.

Stage 6: The "double retrieve"

Until now, though you have done many repetitions in each session, you have been working with either a leather or metal article only. However, scent discrimination is a "two-retrieve" exercise: Spot must retrieve one leather and one metal article. The sequence is up to you; I use metal first and then leather, for the same reason I start the process with metal. If there is anything out there that might confuse the scent, it is more likely that my dog will readily locate the scented metal article than the scented leather article the first time out. With that one successful retrieve under his belt, the leather article is simple.

Introduce the double retrieve when you are back to a distance of twenty-four feet with the six leather articles. Reduce the distance to about twelve feet. Start with the scented metal article. If Spot retrieves it, repeat with the scented leather article. Some dogs handle the double retrieve with no difficulty (after all, they are already conditioned to retrieving both types of article; the only difference is that they are now retrieving each instead of just one or the other). If this switch causes Spot some confusion, give it a little time. If necessary, reduce distance to six feet. If he is really confused, take yet another step back and do a little bit of play, tossing first the metal and then the leather article. I have not yet encountered a dog that did not absorb this transition in at most two sessions. Rebuild distance to twelve feet as before.

Stage 7: Building the pile

When you are working at twelve feet with Spot retrieving both articles with 80% reliability, start building the pile by adding unscented metal articles one at a time until you have twelve articles (one scented, eleven unscented) for him to work through. When you have 80% reliability at twelve feet, rebuild distance but now go to thirty feet. There is no limit to how many articles you can put on the ground in practice (I have used as many as twenty, and I have heard of trainers who use up to 100 at a time), though there will never be more than ten on the ground in the ring.

Some trainers will move the scented article away from the pile to make sure their dog knows to look for it wherever it might be, but I am not a fan of this practice. The article is never thrown in the ring, and it will always be near the others (usually in the midst of the pile—if anything, you may find the articles are too close together, not too far apart). Therefore, there is no real reason to move it away from the pile, and this can be detrimental. If Fido gets used to working away from the pile in practice, you may find him not going directly to the pile in the ring or, if he does so, you may find him first working the pile and then looking away from the pile to see if there is anything he has missed.

It is helpful to vary the distance between articles, placing them anywhere from twelve inches apart to having the scented article right next to, or on top of, an unscented article. Another good variation is to scent all the articles but one and leave them out for forty-five minutes to an hour. Then, scent the article to be retrieved and do the work. This will teach Fido to locate and retrieve the "hottest" article in the batch. This is especially helpful if you intend to campaign your dog, or if you are showing on a "circuit" of three or four shows in a weekend. In such cases you may not be able to fully "de-scent" the articles, and Fido has to know that it is truly the one that smells *the most* like you that you want him to get.

How long does all this take?

It takes as long as it takes. Most dogs can learn the essentials of the scent discrimination within a couple of weeks. The real time involved is in *generalization* and gradually expanding the dog's puzzle-solving abilities. For this reason, practice articles every day until your dog is working the full pile at a distance of thirty feet, even if you do not have the time to do anything else on that day. Once you've reached that level it is no longer necessary to drill constantly, but it is helpful to play with the puzzle to keep him interested.

The critical element to maintain as time goes on is *latency*. Keep your practices brisk: "Fido, go to the pile, locate the right one and bring it right back." Do not let your dog get into air-scenting (circling around the pile several times, then diving in and retrieving the article) or pausing while at the pile.

Place the articles in different places in the practice ring

The most common place for the judges to lay out the articles is next to one of the jumps, with you by the other jump. However, there is nothing in the Regulations that directs where the articles are to be placed, and judges can and will lay the articles out anywhere in the ring. The layout that seems to cause the dogs the most trouble is on the center line between the jumps, so that the dog has to go past the jumps to find the articles. That placement invites the dog to do any number of things other than find a scented article. The most common effect is for the dog to confuse scent discrimination with the directed retrieve and head all the way to one of the ring posts.

Make sure in your practice that you randomize where you place the articles. Place them by, between, and under the jumps. Put them by fences and gates, and right at someone's feet. Have Fido pick them up off of cement, grass, sand, and mud. Utility is meant to be a demanding class, and you cannot rely on the ring always being the way you want it, or the articles being laid out in the one way you have always practiced.

When in the ring . . .

The preliminaries

The judge will designate two articles for you to remove from the bag, and those articles will be placed on a chair or stool inside the ring before you start the signals exercise. At the start of the scent discrimination a steward will take the rest of the articles, in your articles case, and lay them out at a spot about twenty feet from where you are standing. You and the dog will stand facing the steward while he does so. This is to allow the dog to see that there are in fact articles out there. Some dogs are so good at attention that they don't notice, but that's another story. You will not have an article in your hand at this point.

The steward is to touch the articles as he places them. Some stewards make quite a production out of it. Particularly in Utility A, some judges seem to think this will be helpful to the dog. I don't think it is, particularly, because the dog can easily get caught up in investigating this new phenomenon, but there you are.

The "turn-and-send"

When you have scented the article the judge will take it from you, usually by having you place it on her clipboard, and will take it out to the pile. You and the dog must turn and face away from the judge as she does so. The judge will not touch your article with her hands; if she needs to move it once it's on the ground she will either use the corner of the clipboard or a pair of tongs. When the article is in place she will instruct you to "turn and send your dog."

Searching the pile

In describing the performance of this exercise, the Regulations state that the dog "may take *any reasonable time* to select the right article, but only provided it *works continuously*." In discussing how this exercise is to be scored, the Regulations provide that "there shall be no penalty for a dog that takes a reasonably long time examining the articles provided the dog works *smartly and continuously*."

Your first few times in the ring, you may find that Rover is slower at the pile than he is in practice. Don't let that throw you; the critical thing is that he not stop working the pile. With the method I outline here, dogs tend to become very quick in identifying and retrieving the scented article. This is because the communication is precise, and they are not reinforced for "hunting" but only "finding and returning." When you are practicing, don't even think about "correcting" if Rover takes a while to get to the right article, nor even if he indicates the right article but goes on to sniff the others before picking the right article up. One of the purposes of all this practice time is to allow him to get as comfortable as possible figuring the puzzle out for himself. Your interference will only be destructive to the goal. I cannot emphasize it too strongly: *Scenting is the dog's specialty.* Let him do the job as he knows best; that includes giving him the time he needs to figure it out for himself.

The judge is mandated not to deduct for the amount of time it takes the dog to find the correct article, as long as the dog works the pile "smartly and continuously" and does not pick up an incorrect article first. If he picks up an incorrect article, drops it, and then picks up the correct article, this will be a substantial deduction. It doesn't matter if the dog steps on articles, as long as he doesn't play with them. It doesn't matter if the dog nudges an article with his nose, as long as he doesn't pick up an incorrect one. Keep your breathing calm and controlled.

Some dogs are air-scenters. The air-scenter will circle the pile with his nose in the air, sometimes making three or four circuits around the pile before diving in and grabbing the correct article. This habit can be a major concern. There are some judges (a minority, but they are out there) who do not regard air-scenting as "continuously working" or "examining" the articles. The greater problem is that the air-scenting dog is more readily distractible than the dog who is working with his nose to the pile; as long as the dog does not completely stop working the pile you should get only a substantial deduction for a momentary stoppage, but it is not something you want to struggle with. If you go through the training sequence properly you should be able to avoid air-scenting.

The delivery, front, and finish

Once the dog has the article, the exercise becomes a normal retrieve, and all deductions applicable to the Novice recall and the retrieve on flat apply. Fido must come to you briskly and promptly, bring the article to front, hold it without mouthing until told to release it, and then return to heel on command. Here is one place where having both finishes in place can be helpful. I use the go-behind for the first finish; this tells my dogs that they have more work to do. I use the swing for the second finish. They enjoy the swing, so it is a positive reinforcer. It also tells them, "exercise finished."

When day is done: What to do with the used articles

If you have back-to-back trials or are on a circuit, you may be concerned about the articles you used on day one being "contaminated" for day two. I tend to think that this is not a problem. I practice every day with the same articles, using different scented articles each day, and the dogs never show any confusion by picking up the articles I used the day before. Your scent may still be on it, but it is "cold" compared to the "hot" scent you have just imparted. Together with the variation described earlier of working with "cold" and "hot" scented articles, this helps keep your dog strong in looking for the article with the "strongest" (as opposed to the "only") scent.

If you are entered in a tournament in which you may do two rounds in one day, or are on a multiday circuit, it is advisable to carry a complete set of extra articles in a separate bag or box, and replace the articles you just used with the extras. Even though Bowser is reliable, there is no point in risking unnecessary incidental scent contamination.

The directed retrieve ("gloves" exercise)

In the directed retrieve the dog is presented with three gloves laid out at one end of the ring. One glove is at each corner (gloves 1 and 3) and one in the middle (glove 2). The dog and handler face away from that end of the ring as the steward lays the gloves down. On direction from the judge the team turns to glove 1, 2, or 3; the handler then sends the dog to retrieve the glove.

Retrieving the glove is usually not a problem for a fluent retriever. Most dogs will transition from a solid retrieving object to a cloth object with little or no difficulty, and if you have played tug-of-war and chase games with furry squeakies you will have even less trouble.

Some dogs seem to enjoy "killing" the glove—shaking it vigorously, tossing it in the air, worrying it on the ground, and so forth. Many dogs that "kill" the glove have played a lot of tug-of-war games. The cloth item in their mouth puts them into that play mode. This you have to *extinguish* by reinforcing a steady "take-and-hold" just as you did with the dumbbell. Also, reinforce zero latency on the recall portion of the exercise to keep the dog conscious at all times of the real purpose of the exercise, which is to return to you with the glove. This same *shaping* process applies particularly to dogs such as terriers, who apparently respond to the glove as "game" and "kill" it for that reason.

Marking

No, we're not talking about the dog identifying its territory. "Marking" refers to the process of showing the dog the direction in which you want him to go in order to perform the exercise. Before the handler sends the dog, the handler brings his left hand down next to the dog's head and "marks" to the glove, which is about sixteen to twenty feet away. If you show indoors the gloves will be readily visible. If you show outdoors, they are sometimes slightly hidden by uneven ground or tall grass. I even once had a steward step on the gloves after he put them on the ground. Seemed a bit excessive to me.

Mechanics of marking

The "mark" is described in the Regulations as follows: "The handler will then give his dog the direction to the designated glove with a single motion of his left hand and arm along the right side of the dog." The handler also "may bend his body and knees to the extent necessary in giving the direction to the dog."

You introduced Bowser to the fundamentals of "marking" in your fluency targeting work. Technically, the "mark" is a *discriminative stimulus*, delivered as a two-part signal. In the first part, you bring your left hand and arm down next to Fido's head, the palm of your left hand open and facing you, fingers together to form an "arrow." In the second part, you thrust your hand toward the target glove. The Regulations require that the two parts combine into a single motion, but in training your dog (and yourself) it helps to break the signal into two separate parts, then fade the separation so that they become one.

When I was first taught marking, my instructor told me to give the command "mark" to get the dog to look at my hand. I don't do that any more. If I am getting any "look-away" behavior when I bring my hand down next to the dog's head, I simply wait the dog out and C/T the dog for looking at my hand. I stay at that point until the dog is looking at my hand every time I bring it down. In this work I always maintain a *continuous reinforcement schedule.*

When the dog is looking at my hand every time, then the "get it" cue and thrust of the hand become the reinforcer for the dog looking at my hand. But there is no point in introducing the cue and signal to retrieve the glove if the dog is not looking at your hand. This is a major reason to make the two parts of the signal separate at first.

Common error: Dog goes to middle rather than corner glove

Assuming that the dog actually understands enough to go out to retrieve something, somewhere, the most common error that I see is that when the handler turns to the corner, the dog nonetheless goes for the middle glove. There are probably a lot of reasons for this. The dog does go-outs and recalls down the middle of the ring. Also, whichever way you turn, the middle glove always comes into his field of vision. And, often, the handler does not deliver the signal definitively enough in the ring, thus not presenting his dog with the same *discriminative stimulus* as in practice.

There are four aspects to working on this problem. First, train a blind retrieve. Second, once the blind retrieve is established, always work with distractors on the ground. Third, develop distance slowly. Fourth, practice your "mark" signal so that you are delivering it the same way, every time.

Train a blind retrieve

I lay no claim to having invented the blind retrieve. I first read about it in Bill Koehler's book on Utility Dog training. Field dog trainers do it all the time, up to distances of 100 yards or more. The Border collie who runs out 200 yards to pick up the flock is doing a sort of "blind retrieve"—the dog cannot see the sheep but he knows they are there if he only goes out far enough to find them. The blind

retrieve is a critical skill for any advanced retrieving work.

Simply, the blind retrieve teaches the dog to go in the direction of your "mark" until he gets to the target, even if he cannot see the target to which you are directing him when he starts out. More than that, the dog has to go with your "mark" even if he can see another target—but not the one to which you are directing him. Full *stimulus control* over this element means that Bowser goes in the direction you send him, and nowhere else, until he finds what you have sent him to find. You cannot work on the blind retrieve until you have established the concept of marking and the dog is fluent at following your mark.

To set up the blind retrieve, first set up three posts as they will appear in the typical ring: three across. As you face the poles, the #1 pole is at the left-hand corner, the #2 pole is in the center, and the #3 pole is at the right-hand corner. As you do each of the progressions you will be moving the glove toward the appropriate pole. When you turn to either the #1 or #3 poles, you are facing the short end of the ring, and you will be on about a thirty-degree angle. I discuss footwork later; if you have worked on "doodling" you will not have any problem with the turn-in-place. This is the only time in any of the classes that you are sending the dog toward a corner of the ring. Because this demands some "counter-conditioning," train the corner gloves first, and the center glove last.

Use continuous reinforcement in training the blind retrieve. Add distance when you are getting very high ratios of success (90%—forty-five out of fifty retrieves—or higher). Also, because the directed retrieve becomes a rather elaborate puzzle-solving exercise, there is no substitute for repetition. Practice the blind retrieve every day, or at least at every training session. Work it at least four times a week.

Blind retrieve for glove #1

The essential element in training the blind retrieve is that you are always sending Fido to a "hidden" target to which he must go even though other visible targets are out there. You cannot be certain that the blind retrieve is reliable until you have successfully trained the blind retrieve in all directions with other gloves visible on the ground. On the other hand, once you have a reliable blind retrieve you should encounter no problems with the exercise.

Facing the #1 ring post, dig a small hole about four feet from you on a line toward the #1 post, and put the glove in it so that it is not visible at dog's-eye level from more than a foot or so away. Send Fido to the glove. Since he does not have far to travel, he will find it immediately. At first, C/T when he locates the "buried" glove, then shift the reinforcement to him retrieving the glove to you.

Build distance to thirty feet, which is considerably farther than he will have to go in the ring. Add a couple of feet every two to three sessions. When you get to thirty feet, add a distractor, that is, a visible glove on the ground in the #2 position (i.e., toward the center pole). Return to a short distance, place the second glove in sight, and send Fido to the buried glove. As you rebuild distance with the buried glove, add the same distance with the visible glove, gradually moving it all the way out to the center pole. Ultimately Rover is going all the way to the #1 pole with the center glove visible at the #2 pole.

Blind retrieve for glove #3

Repeat the same process, now sending Rover to the #3 pole. Start with no other gloves on the ground, then add the #2 glove as before.

Blind retrieve for glove #2

You will repeat the same process as you did for the corner gloves, except that when you add the visible gloves you will put both the #1 and #3 gloves down. The reason for this change is that when Fido is going to the #1 or #3 gloves, the only other glove he will see is the #2 glove. But, when he is going to the #2 glove he will always see both the #1 and #3 gloves. So, get him accustomed to the "look" from the beginning.

All gloves visible

The final step is to have all gloves visible when you send the dog. However, do not do this until you are certain that he will go all the way to the indicated glove when it is buried.

A "one-glove" retrieve

Once you have worked all three gloves out to the pole, when you practice any of the directed retrieves you will only do one retrieve at a time. This is because he must get the right glove of the three the first time, and there are no "do-overs." As they say in basketball, it's "one and done." If you want to do several directed retrieves in a given session, separate the retrieves with one or two other exercises. If

Rover gets the wrong glove, do not have him repeat to "get it right," but do something else for a bit and try again. At any point that you find him going twice to the wrong glove, go back to the blind retrieve, shorten distance, and rebuild.

Work with additional distractors present

To be truly reliable, Fido must go to the marked glove regardless of what else is on the ground. For people who show indoors, this may not often be much of a problem. But people who show outdoors regularly encounter things blowing into the ring, such as bits of paper. We also encounter distractors such as people eating hot dogs close to the ring ropes. So to fully generalize this exercise, put distractors on the ground that the dog must pass to get to the mark. Work the distractors with a blind retrieve at first, then go to a visible retrieve when you have reliability.

Mechanics of the turn-in-place

It is entirely up to the handler which way to turn when preparing to send the dog. I turn to the right for the #1 and #2 gloves, and to the left for the #3 glove. Some handlers turn to the right for all three, simply extending the range of the pivot as necessary. I don't know of any particular compelling reason to do it one way or the other.

The turn-in-place is simply a pivot such as you would do in "doodling." There are a couple of points to be aware of for scoring purposes. You can use only a verbal cue to move the dog, not a signal. Fido must be in heel position after the pivot, and you cannot reposition the dog in any manner after he has sat after the pivot. Be very mindful of excessive motions while turning, as these can earn you substantial deductions. The significance of this is that, while you are not allowed to give a signal, a slight movement of the hands will cost you a few points but will not cause you to fail the exercise. Nonetheless, you want "quiet hands" throughout. Use a video camera in practice to see whether you are unconsciously incorporating extraneous hand motions into the movement.

The moving stand and examination

In the moving stand and examination ("moving stand"), dog and handler proceed forward on the judge's instruction for about ten feet (five steps).

The Judge then tells the handler to "Stand your dog." The handler then "will, without pausing, command and/or signal the dog to stand, continue forward ten to twelve feet and turn around, either to the right or left, and stand facing the dog. The dog must stand and stay in position." The Judge then examines the dog and, upon "command and/or signal" the dog shall *return to Heel position*" (that is, there is no front in this exercise).

Typically, this is the easiest Utility exercise to train, *assuming that the stand is completely fluent.* If the dog accepts the examination appropriately, there is little or no risk of failure. Even if the handler breaks stride slightly when giving the "stand" cue and signal, this will result only in a two- to three-point deduction at most.

Conditioning the stand itself

The critical feature in this exercise is that the dog must become immobile in the stand position while you proceed forward with no interruption in your forward motion. This sets the moving stand apart from the signals stand, because in the signals exercise you and the dog both stop at the last halt with Fido standing, and you proceed forward only on the judge's direction.

The moving stand exercise demands a completely fluent stand, which means "have all four feet on the ground and stay there until I tell you to move." You will have this in place through your fluency and Beginning Utility training.

From the handler's point of view, there is a training issue and a handling (competition) issue. The training issue is that, to make the stand effective, you must be very sharp in timing your click. The handling issue is that you must give the stand cue/signal while moving without pause. Since it is virtually reflexive to hesitate for a second to make sure that Fido has actually stood, you have to get the stand in place before adding your continuing movement. You will develop this comfort in training. It is another case where use of a video camera is invaluable; it will give you a set of eyes to see what you are really doing when you give your dog the stand cue. Be scrupulous about eliminating any hesitancy forward when you give the cue, as well as any extraneous motions toward the dog.

The examination

The Utility examination differs from the Novice examination in that it is more thorough. "The Judge approaches the dog from the front and examines the dog by going over it with his hands *as in dog show judging* except that in no circumstances shall the examination include the dog's mouth or testicles." The Judge will also not make any particular point of inspecting the dog's ears or feet. What the Judge typically will do is stroke the dog very thoroughly along his back, sides, and hindquarters.

Accepting the Utility examination is purely and simply a matter of socialization. It will hold no terrors for you if you socialized Bowser well as a puppy and conditioned him for a Utility-type examination while showing in Novice. As usual, I again suggest *overtraining* the exercise by having people go over Fido very thoroughly, including touching his head around the mouth; if you know people who are comfortable with dogs, even have them touch your dog's gums and teeth lightly (once you are certain that your dog will readily accept that sort of handling). If Fido becomes **conditioned** to a pretty intrusive examination in practice, he will have no problem with accepting the examination he will get in the ring.

If your dog has any trouble with the examination, build his tolerance through early and continuous reinforcement, having him first accept the approach from the front *and the side.* (Judges are not particularly scrupulous about approaching "from the front"; many seem to regard "front" as any position that is not "behind" the dog. They are not going to change, so it's up to you to have your dog prepared for all contingencies.)

Next, have him accept the examination along the body. This is "out of sequence," because the judge will touch the head first. However, in conditioning, it is easier for a dog to accept contact with his body than with his head. So, treating this as a sort of **behavior chain,** shape it by **backchaining,** working first on the body, then the head.

Once the dog is accepting an examination along the body, follow it immediately with examination of the head. Typically, this will involve patting the head and then stroking the head with both hands along the side and to the rear of the skull. When Rover accepts an examination on both body and head, reverse them and have your partner do the head first. You are now over the hardest part of reconditioning the examination.

The recall to heel position

In your fluency work, you trained heel position as a fluency by calling Fido to heel from various positions away from you to the front, back and side. This portion of the exercise simply employs that fluency.

There are no real problems with stimulus control, if only because there is no other exercise that replicates the topography of this exercise. It doesn't "look" like anything else the dog will ever do. Simply make sure that in your training you are, at first, completely clear in your cue and signal to heel.

You can approach this aspect of the exercise with complete relaxation because, as always, the finish is not a principal portion of the exercise. "Return to handler" is a principal feature of the exercise, but this does not mean "return to heel" for purposes of determining whether you have a qualifying performance. Even if Fido does not go to heel (and this means, even if he does a front instead) *it is not a failure.* It is a failure if the dog fails to return at all, or is so far from the handler that the handler could readily touch the dog's head "without moving either foot or having to stretch, but not to the heel position," but it is only a substantial deduction if the dog returns to a place where you could touch him without having to stretch, even if not in heel position.

You also must work on latency, which in this exercise primarily arises in the dog's return to you after the examination. Except that there is no front, this involves precisely the same issues that arise in training the recall, and you will reduce the dog's response time (here, the time it takes him to traverse the ten- to twelve-foot distance between you) the same way you reduced his response time in recall training.

General considerations

The moving stand gives most handlers a minute to relax and catch their breath, and get ready for the directed jumping exercise. It is probably consciously interspersed between the directed retrieve and the directed jumping. If these two exercises were in sequence it is probable that the dog would go out to the same place where he had just gone to get the glove. The moving stand gives your dog a moment to "forget" the gloves exercise before doing the go-outs.

Because the moving stand quite literally involves nothing really new except your not stopping after giving the stand cue, most handlers find it fairly easy to train and maintain. In the ring, it should also be an opportunity for you to catch your breath and get ready for the last big event. Since it is the one chance you have to relax in Utility, take advantage of it and do so.

Directed jumping, part 1: The go-out

The directed jumping exercise is a complex behavior sequence involving two go-outs, two sits at a distance, two jumps, and two fronts and finishes. I cannot quite decide whether this is one *behavior chain,* or two linked behavior chains. Without having fully resolved that issue, I have found that it helps in training it to work toward making the exercise one long, if rather complex, behavior chain.

I don't show indoors very often, so I haven't shaped a go-out for indoor situations. If you show regularly in rings with baby gates it is a relatively simple matter to teach your dog to *target* the center stanchion. I have attended seminars given by well-known instructors from back East who say they cannot imagine how they would train a dog to do go-outs without the benefit of the reasonably predictable indoor setup. Essentially, you have to train your dog to go-out to nothing, that is, to maintain a straight line in the direction of a "mark" (see pages 209–210), ignoring all distractors (jumps and ring posts). If you have a strong go-out-to-nothing, you should have no trouble switching from an outdoor to an indoor venue.

There are two principal aspects to the directed jumping exercise: (a) the go-out and (b) the jumping. Though together they form a behavior chain, the sequences are really discrete. I train them—and so discuss them—separately.

Requirements of the go-out

The go-out is defined in fair detail in the Regulations, but you have to read the Regulations together with the Guidelines for Judges to understand how it is really scored. The principal feature of the go-out is that the dog go away from the handler on command to a distance at least ten feet past the jumps and stop on command. The dog that does not go at least ten feet past the jumps must be scored zero. Rover will not fail the exercise if he stops but does not sit, the sit not being a principal feature of the exercise. However, if you give a *second command to sit,* this will cause you to fail the exercise. This is the only exercise in all Obedience where a second command given on a nonprincipal portion of the exercise will cause you to fail the exercise. With any luck at all, the AKC will someday eliminate this anomaly.

If the dog goes more than ten feet past the jumps, the dog will not fail the exercise if he stops on cue, as long as he does not stop until told. However, the dog that goes more than ten feet past the jumps but less than "about twenty" feet will usually be a dog that stops on its own. The only situation where this is not the case is when the dog is heading toward one of the corners, and the handler stops the dog before he gets all the way there.

The requirement that the dog go "about twenty feet" past the jumps is interpreted in the Guidelines for Judges to mean that the dog go to a spot between anywhere from eighteen and a half feet to twenty-one feet past the jumps. Working in a fifty-foot ring, as a practical matter your dog should end up about five feet from the other end of the ring. The Guidelines prohibit judges from marking the twenty-foot distance in any way. "About" means "about." The dog should stop in the "approximate center" of the ring. Taking the nineteen- to twenty-one-foot distance as the diameter of a circle, "approximate center" is anywhere within eighteen inches of the center line of the ring.

The handler is completely on her own in deciding when to give the cue to the dog to stop; there are no directions from the judge. This means that you must have sufficient depth perception to know when your dog has gone at least ten feet past the jumps. If you have trouble with this, set out flags or other markers at ten feet and fifteen feet past the jumps so that you can learn to recognize the distances readily.

Go-outs are unusual also because this is the only exercise in any of the classes in which the handler can control the dog's actions when the dog is working away from the handler. It is therefore the one exercise in which the greatest overall amount of teamwork is involved, especially if the dog is going away "off course," toward one of the corners instead of toward the center of the ring. This is why it is so important to understand "the grid" and be able to correlate what is happening with the scoring as your dog goes off course with the next phase of the exercise, that is, the jumping.

As long as the dog goes more than ten feet past the jumps and does not stop moving forward until

The Go-Out Grid

X = Point Deduction for Off-Center

	3	2.5	2	1.5	1	.5	0	0	.5	1	1.5	2	2.5	3	
	3	2.5	2	1.5	1	.5	0	0	.5	1	1.5	2	2.5	3	0
20 feet	3	2.5	2	1.5	1	.5	0	0	.5	1	1.5	2	2.5	3	0
	3.5	3	2.5	2	1.5	1	.5	.5	1	1.5	2	2.5	3	3.5	.5
	4	3.5	3	2.5	2	1.5	1	1	1.5	2	2.5	3	3.5	4	1
	4.5	4	3.5	3	2.5	2	1.5	1.5	2	2.5	3	3.5	4	4.5	1.5
	5	4.5	4	3.5	3	2.5	2	2	2.5	3	3.5	4	4.5	5	2
	5.5	5	4.5	4	3.5	3	2.5	2.5	3	3.5	4	4.5	5	5.5	2.5
	6	5.5	5	4.5	4	3.5	3	3	3.5	4	4.5	5	5.5	6	3
10 feet															

Y = Point Deduction for Short Distance

Point loss in the go-out and directed jumping exercise. *The dark line at the bottom of the grid here represents the ten-foot distance. The dark center line represents the center line of the ring. The dark 3-sided box at the top represents "about twenty feet." As long as the dog is in that "box" you will receive no deductions. The dark lines at the top and center are the X (horizontal) and Y (vertical) axes. The X and Y grids give you the points off for being off-center (X axis) and short of the "about twenty feet" distance (Y axis).*

cued to sit, the dog will not fail the go-out portion of the directed jumping exercise. The Guidelines indicate that the judge is to visualize a grid between the ten-foot and twenty-foot mark, and out to each side of the ring. Each square in the grid is worth half a point. There are six sections between the ten- and eighteen-and-a-half-foot distance, and six sections to each side. So, for example, if the dog went fifteen feet out and all the way to one side, there would be one and a half points for distance and three points for center, for a total deduction of four and a half points on that go-out alone.

To calculate your deductions, simply add the points for each. For example, if the dog goes all the way to twenty feet out and all the way to the corner, it will be a three-point deduction (3X + 0Y). If the dog goes fifteen feet out and half-way to the side, it will also be a three-point deduction (1.5X + 1.5Y). If the dog goes just past the ten foot line but stays in the center, it will be a three-point deduction (0X + 3Y). If the dog goes just past ten feet and all the way to the corner, it will be a six-point deduction (3X + 3Y).

Aside from showing myself to be real clever, there are a couple of reasons I am addressing this in such detail. In training, you are of course concerned with maximum accuracy. That is, Fido should always go straight out and sit on cue at about twenty feet past the jumps. But, as with everything else, you are going to struggle with inconsistency. Even after you have more or less resolved the distance problem, you will still have times when Fido wanders off course. It will help if you make a chart of this grid in your training book, and use it as a reference point for gauging Fido's accuracy in practice. Then, through differential reinforcement you can gradually shape the dog closer to the center line and the twenty-foot distance.

A training note: Do not practice go-outs immediately before or after practicing the directed retrieve. My preference is not to practice them in the same session at all. The reason is simply that in training with a blind retrieve, the two exercises "look" almost identical to Fido, and if you do several repetitions of go-outs and then go to the directed retrieve, you are making it highly likely that Fido will go to the center pole regardless of your mark. So make it easy on yourself. Do not work the exercises in the same session until both are completely reliable.

As I commented earlier, this is a true teamwork exercise. It is very important when showing that

you know what is happening as the dog goes off course so that you can make an informed decision as to when to stop him. Part of the decision will be based on which jump he is going to take. For example, if he is going to take the right-hand jump and he is heading for the right-hand corner, you can stop him halfway across that scoring quadrant. You will take only a two and a half- to three-point deduction. But if he is going to take that same jump and is heading for the left-hand side of the ring, you may want to let him go all the way to the corner so he has a better angle to take the jump from. Note that this also would be a three-point deduction. The good handler recognizes that there will be points deducted, and works with both the points and jump issues.

The go-out as such is a mini-behavior chain consisting of the sit at heel, the go-out ("away"), and the turn-and-sit. Both the "away" and the turn-and-sit rely on fluencies that are already developed, but they are unique in context. So we're going to more or less build this chain backward. Actually, we will develop the four necessary fluencies (go-out, turn-and-sit, directed high jump, directed bar jump) independent of each other, along essentially parallel tracks. The really tricky parts come when we start putting them together.

The "turn-and-sit"

When the dog sits, he need not be facing the handler directly. The problem, of course, is that if the dog is facing one jump or another, he will tend to go in that direction. So in shaping the turn-and-sit you want the dog to turn 180 degrees with regularity. The turn-and-sit is a *mini-behavior chain.* The sit fluency is already in place, so all you need to do is put it together with a full turn.

In some ways this isn't as hard as it sounds. When you call the dog's name and say "sit," Bowser's natural inclination will be to turn to face you. However, the dog will be in his "comfort zone" once he can see you clearly. Given the dog's superior peripheral vision, this means that the dog can easily get accustomed to turning only to a point roughly halfway between ninety and 180 degrees. If you rely solely on the dog's natural inclination to turn toward you when he hears his name and a command, this is what you will end up with. The fluency you are going to rely on to shape a proper turn-and-sit is *targeting.*

Step 1: The stationary turn

Shaping a full turn is easy to do using the target stick. Put Rover on a stand and step behind him, about eighteen inches away from his rear end (the correct distance will depend to some extent on the size of the dog). Hold the target stick directly in front of you, straight up-and-down. Say "Rover, touch." The dog will turn toward you, and as he does he will see the stick and touch it. Be sure you are holding the stick just far away enough that he can make a complete turn without bonking into the stick, but close enough that when he turns he will not have to take a step forward to touch the stick and can touch the stick immediately as he completes the turn. Click as Rover completes the full turn and touches.

When the dog will turn and sit reliably with you close behind him, move a step away at a time until you are about six feet away, still holding the target stick. When you give the "touch" command, step forward so that, as before, the dog does not have to move forward to touch the stick.

You will now introduce a new cue: "Turn." Say this *as the dog is turning* and immediately before you C/T. You are going to fade this cue in a little bit, but it is a necessary bridge in fading the "turn-and-touch." Return to your original position. You can have the target stick in hand in case you get some confusion, but keep it behind your back or otherwise out of sight. Give Rover the "turn" cue, clicking as he completes the 180-degree circuit. Rebuild to a distance of about six feet.

Adding the sit

Now you can add the sit. Return to your original position, give Rover the "turn" cue and, *as he is turning,* give the "sit" cue. C/T when his rump hits the ground. Do ten to fifteen repetitions a day, and after three to four days give the "sit" cue without the preceding "turn" cue. Rover should turn and sit, facing you directly. As with other behaviors where every performance must be correct, I favor staying on a *continuous reinforcement* schedule. I cannot think of any particular reason ever to put this behavior on a variable schedule. Now you are in position to build distance, at first without any motion forward. Your goal is that Rover will turn-and-sit facing you on the sit cue at a distance of fifty feet. Do not add motion until you have achieved this level.

Step 2: The turn-and-sit in motion

When the dog will turn-and-sit without moving forward with you at a distance of six to eight feet, you are ready to introduce the sit in motion. However, you can't do that until you have started to get the dog to go away from you and put some distance on the basic go-away.

The "go-out"

The critical question is, how do you get the dog to go out in approximately a straight line, for a sufficient distance? There are two fairly standard approaches. The first is to train the go-out as a blind retrieve (see pages 210–211). The idea here is to capitalize directly on the "marking" training. There is nothing wrong with that per se, and in fact the two exercises will work together in many ways. The synergy between the exercises can become a source of trouble, however, and I have encountered problems with this approach. For one, dogs I have trained that way tend to go out with their heads down to the ground, looking for the retrieve object. I prefer the dogs to go out "heads-up." For another, I have found a tendency for dogs trained to do go-outs this way to tend to go to the #2 glove on the directed retrieve. Nonetheless, as I say, there is a synergy between the two exercises that you will take advantage of in this training.

The second traditional approach is to shape the dog to go to the center pole. You can easily get into trouble that way as well. For example, dogs shaped to go to the center pole have been known to disregard the "sit" command in order to get all the way to the pole. And, typically, a "pole-trained" dog has learned that the pole is a target and will touch or even lick it in hopes of there being some food on it. Not the best of form. It also happens that a "pole-trained" dog may spot one of the corner poles and go there instead.

There are a couple of other instances where a dog shaped to go the center pole can get in trouble. Not all rings are set up with a center pole; often there are actually four poles along the go-out end of the ring, two at the corners and two offset from the center. The dog who is conditioned to go to the center pole as a target may become lost. This will either cause the dog to go to one of the corners, or one of the offset posts, or to stop short of the thirty-foot distance in confusion.

Straight, full-distance go-outs are critical. Returning for a moment to the "grid" I discussed earlier, deductions can easily pile up in this exercise. Two four-and-a-half-point go-outs will give you nine points off before you even get to think about things like taking the right jump, ticking the jump, straight fronts, etc. The good news is that directed jumping is judged as a single exercise, so you have nineteen and a half points to lose before you fail. The bad news, however, is that poor go-outs are often a prelude to mistakes in the jumping portion, particularly if the dog does the go-out to the wrong side of the ring.

So there are two critical goals in the shaping process: (1) developing the dog's understanding of "straight," and (2) developing the dog's willingness to keep going forward until stopped. Taking all these factors into consideration, the approach that is most likely to establish a reliable go-out is to shape the dog to "go-out to nothing."

The "go-out to nothing"

In a nutshell, the fluency is for the dog to understand that whatever is "out there," even if nothing is seemingly "out there"; he starts out straight and keeps going straight until you tell him to stop. The "go-out to nothing" is, as you can see, a variation on the blind retrieve discussed in the section on the directed retrieve. You are employing exactly the same concept: " 'It' is out there, if you just keep going far enough." In this case, "it" must be out there eighty or more feet away so that Rover has no conditioning to stop short.

Step 1: Go-out to the target stick

The first thing is to condition the dog to "know" that there is something out there to go to. When I started training this exercise I first used a white squeaky toy on the ground, but this quickly developed drawbacks. Primarily, the dogs started heading for anything white that they saw on the ground. Bits of white paper on the ground are not exactly rare in outdoor shows, so it was time to rethink my tactics. The target stick was a natural. I just stuck one end of the stick in the ground. At first, I put a band of white tape around the stick at a spot roughly at the height of the dog's nose. Now he had a target. *Click* as the dog touches the stick, and have him return to you for the treat.

Here is a primary example of how the click serves as what the early dolphin trainers called a **bridging**

stimulus. It marks the correct behavior (touching the stick) and allows delayed delivery of the primary reinforcer without diluting the significance of the conditioned reinforcer.

As you have already consistently reinforced touching the stick, you will very likely find Rover offering the behavior without any stimulus other than the presence of the stick. Welcome the offering. The end product will be a highly energized go-out. Begin by standing about eighteen inches away from the stick. You will fairly readily be able to move to about ten feet away and have the dog go regularly, absent a cue, to the stick and touch it. When I trained Dylan this way he was very quickly running laps, out to the stick, click, back to me, treat, back to the stick.

Now add the cue. By now, the pattern should be very familiar to you (and to Lassie as well). *As the dog is still moving away from you and is about to touch the stick,* say "away!" I like "away" as the cue because it is completely distinctive and lilts nicely off the tongue. Then "back the cue up," saying "away" increasingly closer to the moment that Rover leaves your side, until the cue is acting as the stimulus for the dog to leave your side altogether.

At the same time, build distance. Your goal with only the target stick in place is that the dog go at least seventy-five feet to touch the stick. A very easy way to build distance is simply to take one step backward as Fido is running away from you. Fido won't even notice the added distance, but don't in-

Using the target stick results in a nice "heads-up" go-out. Harpo is also learning to ignore the jumps and other distractions around him, and go straight away from his owner.

crease distance by more than two steps in any given session.

Go-outs past distractions

So far, Fido has been going to the stick without anything to distract him from it. Now, you are going to add distractions. Start with a single ring pole, with the target stick about ten feet past it. Stand next to the pole, and send Fido to the target stick. Take a

The ring posts and rope mark the end of the ring, but the target stick is set up outside the ring, well beyond competition distance (top). Sam ignores the distractions and goes right to his target. He is learning to go straight out from the handler, to any distance, and without relying on the ring perimeter for information. The next step will be to fade the target stick.

step back as he is going toward it. Next repetition you will send him past the ring pole. Do not add another step until you are getting nine trials out of ten in which he goes past the ring pole without giving it so much as a nod.

In your next session, place the target stick two feet further out, and start one step behind the ring pole. As Fido is going to the stick, take another step back. Repeat your trials at this distance until you are getting at least an 80% correct response rate on a continuous reinforcement schedule. Continue building distance in increments of moving the stick two feet and taking one step back until you are completely across the ring, and the stick is forty feet past the ring post. You are now, essentially, doing go-outs to eighty or ninety feet.

Now, you can change the "look." Instead of a single ring post in the center, set two posts up, about ten feet apart. The object is for Fido to go between the posts to the stick. Repeat the same distance progression as you did with the single ring post. The next aspect to the "look" is that you add a ring rope between the two posts. You may also place the posts farther apart; this will not add any new training issues. The final aspect to the "look" is that you put the jumps out, in the position they will occupy in the actual ring, that is, about twenty feet apart. Now, as you back up across the ring, Fido will not only have to pass the ring post or rope, but the jumps as well.

Fading the target stick

In part, this will be a product of added distance. But you also need to eliminate the stick itself. When Fido is doing eighty-foot go-outs past the center pole, replace the target stick with a one-eighth-inch wooden dowel with no white end or other marking on it. This will quickly give you a "blind go-out" because Rover will not be able to see the stick until he is fairly close to it. Return to your original distance, get at least ten go-outs to the new target, and rebuild distance. You will find it fairly easy to return to full distance by now. Next, replace the dowel with a clear plastic wand, such as you can get from a drapery house. This will give you a completely blind go-out. Repeat the entire sequence.

Incorporating the turn-and-sit

When you have eighty-foot go-outs to the clear plastic wand, you can incorporate the turn-and-sit. Return to your original distance position, and send him to the target. Tell him "sit" just before he reaches it. Click the sit and let him return to you for the treat (again, you are utilizing the "bridge"). Build distance as before.

As you are adding the turn-and-sit, it is important that you not fall into any consistent patterns that can create *superstitious* behaviors in Rover. The fluency is that Rover go forward until you tell him to stop, and that he stop (and sit) wherever you happen to tell him to do so. When you are doing go-outs to eighty feet, this can be anywhere inside or outside the ring between you and the target. I will sometimes stop the dog after he has gone twenty, or even just ten feet. On the next repetition I will send him a long way out.

Don't worry that stopping him short of the far end of the ring will cause him to stop there later. You are teaching Rover that the rule is "go until I tell you to stop." In order for him to fully understand this, you have to randomize the distance often until he is showing no uncertainty about this concept. In any given set of twenty repetitions, I will typically have my dog stop outside the ring about twelve to fifteen times, at the ring rope about three to five times, and short of the ring rope two or three times. I will follow each "short" go-out with at least two beyond the ring; often the first of these will be all the way to the target.

Troubleshooting: Avoiding the arc

A very common problem, particularly with herding breeds, is that the dog arcs as he is going away from you to the stick. You will start to notice this as you get over twenty feet away from the stick. This is completely instinctual, and relates to the arc a herding dog would naturally employ when going out to pick up a flock. It is an example of what Marian and Keller Breland described as *instinctive drift* in their 1961 article "The Misbehavior of Organisms." In essence, this theory recognizes that regardless of conditioning, animals with a strong instinctive drive will tend to "drift" toward the instinctive behavior. So if you are working a herding dog, you may expect that regardless of how stringent you are in conditioning, the dog will have a tendency to "drift" toward arcing on the go-outs.

Just as you do not respond aversively to seemingly "wrong" things the dog may do in scent discrimination (see pages 201–203), it is important not to respond aversively to any such "drift." In the words of Little Richard, "the boy can't help it."

What you need to do is be very observant for the emergence of the arc; when you see it, reduce distance and reintroduce the target if necessary to reaffirm "straight." All in all, the best weapon against the arc is a very high number (even hundreds, if you need them) of repetitions to the target at various distances using continuous reinforcement.

Directed jumping, Part 2: the jumps

Directed jumping follows the go-outs. Together with the go-outs they comprise a single *behavior chain*. The Regulations refer to this as the "directed jumping" exercise, but exhibitors almost universally refer to it as "go-outs." I think this is because the go-outs are really the harder part of the exercise; most dogs do the jumping element pretty reliably. You have already introduced Fido to the concept of "directed jumping" in your fluency work (see pages 46–52). He has learned the high jump, the bar jump, the associated cues, and the concept of following your hand toward the jump. Now you can formalize all this into the directed jumping exercise.

Because there are two go-outs and two jumps, Fido has four opportunities to fail to perform a principal feature of the exercise. Well, nobody said Utility was easy. For this reason, it is very important that you do not put the go-outs and jumps together while you are teaching. Be *certain* that Fido has consistently good go-outs and consistently takes direction to the jumps before putting them together. By

Karla gives Harpo an "away!" cue for the go-out, with the ring jumps in place. This strong cue may be gradually faded until Harpo will leap into action on either a hand signal or a verbal cue.

"consistently" here, I mean that you have a success rate of 80% or higher on each before combining them.

Giving the signal

It is important to remember what the Regulations say about signals and extra commands. Your signal must be "a single gesture with one arm and hand only, and the arm must immediately be returned to a natural position." Or, as I say, "smooth and continuous." Every bit of body language other than the movement of your hand toward the jump may be construed as an extra command. Now, this last is never construed entirely rigidly. It is not unnatural to turn your head slightly toward the jump that you are indicating, and as long as you do not make this a gross motion you are unlikely to get nicked for it. As with so many other Utility exercises, using the video camera in training will be immensely valuable.

Different people do the signals differently, and there really is no "right" or "wrong" to it so long as your motion complies with the rules. I like to bring my hand up to about shoulder height, palm facing the dog, my hand the length of my upper arm from my body, then extend it out toward the jump, at shoulder height. This makes for a smooth, clear, definitive motion that I can easily, consistently repeat. Others more or less swing their hand up from their side and out toward the jump. As I say, it really does not matter, as long as your signal gives the dog a clear look at the direction you are indicating, and you are consistent in practice and showing.

One of the reasons I like "two-part" motions for my signals is that it forces me to maintain the same pattern all the time. It's hard to get sloppy. Because signals are body language to the dog, consistency is critical. Everyone who has shown in Utility has blown an exercise because the dog "missed" the signal. More often than not, this is because the handler did not deliver it definitively. Nerves can make you rush or give an "incomplete" signal. This is not the dog's fault, but you fail just the same. The other reason I like the "up and out" signal is that it helps keep my body upright. I find it easy to lean toward the jump when I'm more or less swinging my arm in that direction. I can't think of any good reason to invite handler error of that type.

You can give both a verbal cue and a hand signal. It does not matter what your verbal cue is. At a Cycle Classic in 1994, one handler in Super Dog gave her Border collie the hand signal with the verbal cue

"Easy!" This is entirely proper under the Regulations; she needed the "easy" cue because her dog was an enthusiastic jumper. The only requirement here is that you must deliver the verbal simultaneously with the hand signal. I say the dog's name as I am bringing my hand up, and the cue for "bar" or "high" as my hand hits full extension to right or left.

If you practice consistently and have gotten Fido used to responding to cues delivered in a conversational tone, then you don't need to make a big production out of the verbal cue. Say the word just loudly enough that the dog can hear it. The verbal cue *should* be extraneous because the dog *should* be following your hand.

That said, I also suggest retaining the separate terms for the bar and high jump. If I am giving a verbal, I don't want it to be at all confusing to the dog (though I must confess I am probably more concerned about this than I should be; I once signaled Sam toward the bar jump and said "over," and he took the bar jump anyway—good dog). So, bar is "bar" and high jump is "over." Throughout their jumping career, from the time my dogs are first introduced to cavalettis, those are the words for each jump, so there is nothing new in that regard in this training.

Latency

As with the signals exercise, you want Bowser responding to your hand signal—that is, to be up and moving toward the jump—before you complete the signal. There is a fine line here, because while you need immediate response you also want the dog waiting just long enough to be certain of the direction you are sending him. There is often a fine line between latency and anticipation. In many instances you will get away with slight anticipation because your signals or cues are so close to the behavior that the judge cannot really score it. That is fine. To me, it shows you and Bowser working tightly and well together. In this exercise, though, anticipation can do a lot of damage because it will often mean the dog goes the wrong way.

Perfecting the exercise

Thanks to fluency work, Fido will follow your hand toward the jump. However, so far you have only asked him to follow you from a short distance, and usually in motion. Now you are formalizing the exercise; he must take the direction from about forty feet away, from a sit, with you also motionless. So while the concept of taking direction is not new, the mechanics of this exercise are.

Setting up the practice "look"

Would it surprise you to read that there are different schools of thought on how to set up the practice "look?" Obedience people have differences of opinion on everything except the fact that the sport involves dogs. Given the recurring legend about one well-known midwestern judge and exhibitor training a potbellied pig to do Open work, even that may be a point of dispute.

One approach to setting up the practice "look" is to start with the jumps close together, and gradually move them apart. I tried this with my first dog, and never really liked it. The closeness of the jumps was, I thought, confusing for the dog. And also, you go through a lot of practice before the dog ever sees the setup the way it will appear in the ring.

What I came to prefer was setting up the ring the way it actually looks. (Actually, I train in a "versatility" mode, and will do both Open and Utility exercises in any given session, so I usually have all three jumps set up in the practice area. But that's another discussion.) So the jumps are about twenty feet apart right from the start. The dog and handler move, but the ring always looks the same.

Set the jumps at your low practice height (about the height at the elbows; we are developing the dog's understanding of signals, so don't make height an issue). I start with dog and handler each about ten feet from the jump, facing each other (so you are about twenty feet apart), lined up with the inside post of the jump. It is almost a straight jump for the dog. The dog is at the distance that is pretty comfortable for him to approach and jump, and you are just far enough away that he can come to you comfortably.

Given your positions relative to each other and the jump, there is no chance Fido will be confused about which jump you want him to take. Nonetheless, do it right—this is his time to learn signals and your time to learn to give them. Use videotape on yourself so you can be sure you are giving the same signal the same way every time. Give a clear, slow (at first) signal as you say "over." Click as he clears the jump (you are reinforcing his correct decision—the click here also works as a *bridge*) and treat when he comes to front.

Now you repeat the exercise but going in the opposite direction. So if your first signal for the jump was to your right, it will now be to your left. In this way you introduce Fido immediately to the concept that the jump may be in either direction and it is your signal that counts. Repeat at least five times in each direction. At this distance, you should get

A   B

Karla helps Harpo learn the high jump signal by giving auxiliary cues. The dog has been placed in a sit near the correct jump. The handler also stands near the jump. She uses a verbal command, and she maintains the visual signal while the dog executes the maneuver. She will click as the dog takes the jump. As Harpo's response to the signal becomes fluent, Karla will return her hand to her side immediately.

a ten-for-ten response rate almost immediately. Now go to the other jump, and repeat the entire process. The jumps are low, so there is no stress on the dog. You are giving him a look at each jump from each direction, five times each. Repeat this for two days.

On the third day, take one step toward the middle of the ring and two steps back. Move the dog the same distance. On the fifth day, take another step toward the middle of the ring, and two more steps back. Continue in this manner, extending the distance back from the jumps and toward the center, every two sessions. At the end of about ten sessions, you and the dog will be at the center of the ring, each twenty steps back from the jumps.

Go through this progression on each side, always working back and forth from left to right as described earlier. If at any point the dog seems uncertain, stop where you are and give him an extra day or two. This system is almost guaranteed not to produce any missed signals. The other advantage to it is that the dog is always seeing the ring as it will be in competition, and is adjusting gradually to his ultimate position in it.

As you go through this progression, you should also be practicing your full-length go-outs, between the jumps. However, do not combine them with jumping until Fido is reliably taking both jumps, to the right and to the left, at full distance. It is also a good idea to separate the exercises in time by doing something else between the two.

What about "front and finish?"

At this stage of practice, do you want Fido to give you a front when he comes off the jump? On the one hand, the front should be completely fluent by now. Fido should be sitting in front reflexively when he comes to you. You have practiced this so consistently that any recall-type behavior is a *repertoire cue* for the front. You are not asking for it, so you do not need to click for it when you get it. However, it can confuse the issue. If you start getting sloppy fronts you risk creating a problem over the long haul because you can create a superstitious association between the new exercise and crooked fronts, even though you are not reinforcing the fronts specifically.

To avoid this problem, my preference is to eliminate front when I am working on some new recall-type exercise until the new exercise is fluent; then I add the front back in. To do this I simply give my "release" cue to the dog as he comes to my front so

he pops up toward me in play rather than giving me a formal front. Does this not create a superstitious association as well? Not really, simply because "sit in front" is such a strongly conditioned behavior. At least, this is not anything you cannot get rid of quickly by reinserting the "front" cue once the directed jumping element is in place. In this exercise I do not ask for fronts until the dog is giving me correct responses eight times out of ten at full distance. Now I can reintroduce that element without risking dilution of everything else I am trying to teach.

Since I am not asking for fronts, I do not worry about the finish except insofar as I need Rover to "get around" so that we can repeat the exercise going the other way. However, for this I just use a "get-around" or "doodling" maneuver. I will C/T only occasionally for a correct movement here. When I reintroduce formal fronts I use the two types of finish: The first is to the right to tell Bowser there's still work to be done, and the second is to the left to celebrate work well done. In practice I will occasionally supplement the second finish with a small jackpot.

Putting go-outs and jumps together

When you put the go-outs and jumps together, remember always that jumping is the *repertoire reinforcer* for proper go-outs. In other words, the dog only gets to jump when the go-out is correct. Never allow the dog to take a jump unless he has gone at least forty feet out, more or less to the center of the ring. Whenever you allow the dog to jump from a position away from the center of the ring, you are reinforcing an improper go-out. This will come back to haunt you in the ring. I should note that although this exercise has an element of repertoire reinforcement, you do not want repertoire cuing to come into play. Each behavior is on its own cue, and must be fully under stimulus control. Rover is not to decide for himself when to stop, or which jump to take when.

Because Fido is used to taking the signal from a sit, and because this is somewhat reminiscent of the recall sequence, you will not usually have much of a problem with him moving from the sit. If any problem arises, it will be in him not sitting on cue. As I discussed in the go-out section, this will not fail you in the exercise so long as he comes to a stop. However! In practice, he must always sit, and sit quickly.

When you are putting go-outs and jumps together, when do you click? You don't need to click the go-out, because "permission to jump" works as your reinforcer. If you click when he comes to front, you have missed the principal feature of the exercise, that is, that he take your signal to the correct jump. So, I click when Fido is clearing the jump, just as I did in practice. When I get to the point where we are doing both jumps in one session, I do not click the first jump at all, but use going through the second jump as the reinforcer. If the dog is going for the incorrect jump I cut him off with the word "wrong" and start again.

Multiple repetitions—Enjoy the variety

There are myriad ways to mix up the practice sessions so you can get a large number of repetitions done in any given session. Do not feel that you have to stick with any given pattern. One of the beauties of this exercise is that it allows you to create all sorts of different puzzles and "looks" for the dog. Take advantage of it.

For example, you can switch directions by sending Fido on the go-out, having him take the jump, then leaving him at that end of the ring, going to the other end, and repeating that same jump only to the other side. You can then repeat with the other jump. You can also mix up alternating the jumps so that you do two high and one bar, three and one, or four and one. Or do two high, one bar, and one high. Keep shifting it around so that Fido does not get used to a single pattern. Don't always start with one jump or the other, nor with one direction or the other. Keep careful charts so that you avoid unin-

tentional patterns. Such patterns may stick with him as superstitious associations and carry into the ring.

The overall goal in training is that Fido learn to focus on you, read your signal, and respond to what you are telling him, not what he expects to do. This sounds very much like the goal in all training, but this is one exercise where you really have to have it. Some dogs get into the habit of glancing back and forth from one jump to the other, and taking the jump they last looked at regardless of your signal. Judges are aware of this, and will time their order to you so that the dog is looking the wrong way (sneaky devils). So in your practice, sometimes send Fido to the jump he is looking away from. In other words, don't cut any corners. Fido must be focused and thinking in order to perform this exercise successfully. It is up to you in your training to develop those qualities.

An additional element in the training is to send Fido past the ring ropes while doing long-distance go-outs, and have him sit and jump from a spot ten to twelve feet outside the practice "ring." In this way you stop him from expecting to stop at the ring rope, which in turn will slow the go-out and gradually lead him to shorten his go-outs.

The finished product is a joy to watch. Your dog moves across the ring briskly and unhesitatingly and swings around into a neat sit. Your signal is crisp, smooth, and continuous and the dog jumps unhesitatingly. Then, he does it again. Sigh. A perfect ending to a perfect day. Now, you can take your heart out of your mouth and start breathing again.

Who's In Charge Here?

Some thoughts for the pet owner

This book is written primarily for the Obedience competitor. However, most people who own dogs and need to train them are not Obedience competitors. I was not when I got my first dog. Most people who become involved in Obedience competition start out with pet training, but only a very small percentage of pet owners go into competition training.

Can clicker training work for you as a pet owner? Yes, unequivocally yes. It is easier to use than traditional training methods, you get better results faster, and it is considerably more relaxing for both you and your dog. I have taught many pet owners basic obedience, enabling many to put a Canine Good Citizen title on their dogs. If you were to do no more than do the fluency work described in Chapter 3, you would have a well-trained and socialized dog.

You have to train your own dog

There are many commercial trainers who will "train your dog for you." You can send your dog to their facility, or they will come to your house, but in either case they are doing the work. Then, at a certain point, they "hand the dog off" to you. They tell you the basic commands, give you a couple of sessions with the dog, and away you go. This method of training your dog has a high rate of failure. Don't do it. You have to train your own dog.

Training is a relationship between dog and owner/handler. It is the means by which the dog learns to respect your authority, to understand what you expect, and what to expect in return. The person who trains the dog is the only person who can truly control the dog. Even in our house, with clicker-trained competition obedience dogs, Sam and Dylan respond less immediately to direction from my wife than they do from me. This reflects nothing but the fact that I, and not she, am the trainer.

Dog ownership entails responsibility, and training is the way you fulfill that responsibility. The time demands are not great. With clicker training you can dedicate ten to fifteen minutes a day, three or four days a week, to the task and reap enormous benefits, both as to behaviors you establish, and in the relationship between you and your dog. So please, do not look for shortcuts, nor for someone else to do "the dirty work" for you. Besides, in clicker training, there is no "dirty work." It's fun. And it's your dog, so you train him. A clicker-trained pet is a joy forever, and much of that joy lies in the training process itself. Enjoy the ride.

The "Alpha" issues

Ethologists—people who study the "character" of species and interaction among species—tell us that dogs see the world primarily in "pack" terms. I have no reason to disagree with this. If you watch any set of dogs for any period of time you will see them sorting out which is the leader and which is led. Why is this important from a behavioral point of view? Simply because instinctive behav-

"Can clicker training work for you as a pet owner? Unequivocally, yes. It is easier to learn and use than traditional training methods, you get better results faster, and it is considerably more relaxing for both you and your dog."

ior patterns will tend to assert themselves in even very well-trained dogs.

A good trainer understands "instinctive" behavior and makes use of it. It is not always enough simply to look at behaviors, decide what you want to reinforce and what you do not. Certainly, that is essential. But it is also important to have some sense of what is going on behind the behaviors. Often, this will give you a key on how to apply different reinforcement contingencies in order to change or modify the behaviors. The dog's instinctive tendencies are part of the clay with which we work when sculpting behaviors.

In your family, of course, the humans must be "Alpha." The dog must be made clear as to who gives, and who takes, orders. Put another way, it is a question of discipline. Now, discipline as I use the term is not the same as "punishment." We tend to confuse the two concepts. When we punish a child for some malfeasance, we say we are "disciplining" the child. This causes us to equate the concepts, when in fact they are very different. True discipline—a developed understanding of what behavior is required and when—virtually eliminates the need for punishment.

Clicker training creates discipline because it teaches the dog to produce voluntarily the behaviors you want. Through clicker training you teach your dog what behaviors will be reinforced (i.e., will get the dog what he wants) and which behaviors will not get the dog anywhere. Becoming the leader is, above all, a simple matter of establishing and sticking to those rules. Most pet behavior "problems" are really the product of the owner having ignored good behaviors and reinforced undesired behaviors without being aware of what he was doing at the time.

As a pet owner you must be very clear that dogs are physical, not verbal, beings. We humans talk everything to death. Dogs vocalize very little, and typically only in certain well-defined and recognizable situations. Forget everything you ever saw in a Disney cartoon: A dog's barking is not language in any sense that we use the term. A dog's language is body language, and you owe it to yourself to learn to read and respond to it. Investing in books such as Ian Dunbar's *Dog Behavior* or Turid Rugaas's *On Talking Terms With Dogs* will profit you immensely.

Terry Ryan and others, including the Monks of New Skete, have written on "Alpha behavior" in the home. I'm not going to recapitulate their viewpoints here. Suffice it to say that there are a few points that I believe any wise pet owner will attend to.

Alpha controls the food supply

I often hear of dogs who will not allow their owner to approach while they are eating. Not in my house. I got Woody, Sam, and Dylan as puppies, and from the first day they learned that I put the food down, and I can pick it up whenever I want. I would even brush them while they were eating. Skipper came to our house at three and a half years of age, and he had a reputation for aggressiveness (entirely undeserved, we were to learn). So I felt it was important to introduce him to this rule immediately. The very first time I put his dinner down, I picked it right back up. I did this at random over the next two weeks. To this day, with any of my three boys, I can pick up their bowl while they are chowing down and get nothing more than an anxious look.

Mealtime has also proved to be a delightful opportunity to train tricks. Each of my dogs has a trick he has to perform before his food goes down. Sam rears up on his hind legs ("yee-hah!"). Dylan does a stand (for a hyperactive sheltie, that is asking a lot), and Skipper spins. I've gotten him up to three spins at a time, both to the right and to the left. It's hard to know how this fits into the larger picture. I've been told this reinforces my "Alpha" status because I am making their eating conditional. I don't know about that. To me, it's just fun.

Leader goes first

If you have more than one dog, watch what happens when they gather by a door or gate and you open it up. The most assertive one will push his way through first. Leaders go first. In our house, that's usually Dylan, though Sam can assert himself if he wants. Skipper is always last. These aren't my rules; the boys have sorted this all out for themselves. Recognize the dynamic, and use it. Make it a rule that if you are going through a door or gate with your dogs, you go first. I'll talk later about using behavior modification techniques to help you get this under control.

Leader controls the territory

Who gets the place of choice? Who gets to sit on the sofa? The leader decides. If Fido is on your chair, you try to move him, and he resists, watch out. He is trying to control the territory. This is a very common way in which dogs "take over." In our house we have "dog friendly" furniture, so allowing the dogs up on the sofas and chairs is not a housekeeping question. It is, to put it bluntly, a control question. Sometimes they get up and down as they please. But when I don't want them up, they don't get up. And when I want them off, they get off. I use "off" as the cue, and when they respond by getting off I reinforce them for performing the cued behavior rather than "punish" them for having gotten up in the first place.

Application of clicker training

The most important thing to understand is that "dominance" does not suggest or require physical force. "Dominance" is authority. Authority derives from respect. When your dogs respect your leadership, you have authority. If they do not respect your leadership, you will never have authority regardless of how forcefully you handle them physically. Clicker training is a fast way to win your dog's respect.

Early in my association with the dog I introduce the clicker to him at mealtime. I click, and put the food down. So right from the beginning, I teach him that delivery of the food is connected to something I am doing. If I take the food up, before I put it down I click again. The food is there, I control it.

You can teach basic *cues* such as "off." If your dog is on the sofa, sit nearby with clicker near at hand. Sooner or later, he will get down. When he does, C/T. You are reinforcing the behavior of getting off the sofa. As with any behavior, Fido will soon *offer* it in expectation of a reward. Don't disappoint him. When he is getting off the sofa, say "off" just as or just before he is moving. Then, click. This will establish the cue. And as always when delivering a cue, do so in a calm, conversational tone. Loud noise communicates nothing to the dog except volume.

"Click/treat" establishes pack authority

What is the essential clicker dynamic? Click, and treat. The "treat" is something the dog wants. Typically you use food, but you may use other doggie desirables (petting, play) as well. But consider the dynamic: In order for the dog to get what *he* wants, he has to do what *you* want (**reinforcement** is always *contingent*). He does not get what he wants for free. He has to sing for his supper, by doing something to make you click. By using food treats, you are controlling the food supply with this method. The dog knows you have something good to eat, and you will decide when to give it to him. He learns quickly that the key to you deciding to give the food to him is his behavior.

Dogs will "test" your relationship with them, just as children will. In clicker training you are creating a context for that testing. Instead of testing by growling, the dog tests by offering behaviors. Excuse the anthropomorphism, but: The dog is always asking himself, "What will work? How can I get him to give me the food?" And step by step he learns: by sitting; by lying down; by walking under control at your left side. As you teach each new behavior in this way, two things happen. *You establish your leadership* by setting and enforcing the terms for reinforcement, *and you empower the dog* because he learns what he can do to get you to deliver.

You may think that "empowering the dog" is contrary to the goal of pack authority. It is not. In context, it simply balances the equation. In the wild, for example, the pack members know what they have to do in the hunt. If they do it, everyone benefits and the Alpha treats them well. If the pack members had no way of knowing who was who, there would be anarchy, not authority. "Empowerment" in this sense does not mean that the subordinate takes over, but that he knows what he has to do to please you. He can then freely choose to do it.

Can the dog freely choose not to do what you want? Certainly. Are there no consequences? Yes, there are. In the training context, choosing not to do what you want means that he gets no reinforcement. When you have conditioned the dog to *expect* reinforcement in response to behaviors, withholding reinforcement is a powerful corrective measure.

Are there ever times when physical intervention is needed? Yes. If my dog has his head in something nasty and I call him but he does not come, I will go over and get him by the collar and drag him away. Sometimes obnoxious behavior calls for a scruff shake together with a low growl. In working with a student with a field dog that would break away to chase squirrels or Papillons I once set the dog up on a long line. When he took off east I took off west, and the backflip that the dog experienced stopped his running away for several months.

So sometimes these things are useful. But they are the exception, not the rule. In the five years I have been doing clicker training, physical "corrections" of any sort have comprised less than 1% of what I do. Physical "corrections" are not "training"— they are not the way you establish your relationship with the dog. They are the means for suppressing an undesired behavior in order to gain control in moments of crisis. You have to know how to do it (it is not easy) properly so you can do it once and be done with it. Ineffective physical intervention will always do more harm than good. If you don't have experience in this realm, do not use aversives without instruction, and never overreach. A powerful case in point is the so-called "Alpha roll" illustrated by the Monks of New Skete in their book *How to Be Your Dog's Best Friend*. One pet owner I knew tried this maneuver and almost got a face full of teeth for her trouble. In my view, this retarded the development of her authority because the dog learned the wrong lesson: He learned that if there is a physical confrontation, he will win.

By themselves, punishers are not enough. Punishers, at most, help to suppress undesired behavior. They do not teach desired behavior. So, together with your punisher you must also present an alternative: some way for the dog to win. Otherwise, as a rule, the undesired activity will reemerge. Put another way, having made it clear what I don't want, I must now let the dog know what I do want, and reinforce him for giving it to me.

If I drag the dog away from the garbage, when we are safely away I should release the collar, call him from a short distance, and C/T for him coming to me. If I have given Dylan a scruff shake because he was nipping at Skipper to prevent him from going out the door (yes, sometimes the little brat will do that sort of thing) and wouldn't stop with a "that'll do," when I release his scruff I have to C/T for the result (standing quietly, whatever).

This requires a sea change in our way of looking at things. As a society, we are used to punishment and the expectation of punishment. Seven of the Ten Commandments are written as "thou shalt not." As Murray Sidman in *Coercion and Its Fallout* points out, our own sense of right and wrong is maintained primarily not by being rewarded for "doing the right thing," but by being punished for doing the wrong thing. As Sidman says, "Supposedly our sense of right and wrong, our conscience is really only a sense of wrong." He goes on to point out that "Those to whom we entrust the tasks of monitoring and managing our behavior—our teachers, police, religious leaders, social agencies and government officials—urge us to behave honestly and ethically, in conformity with the legal and moral principles that help ensure society's survival. But only the naive expect us actually to conform to those principles unless we are made to."

As a society, we are not geared to responding to good behavior positively. You get a ticket for running a red light; have you ever received a commendation for stopping at every red light you came to? We are conditioned to negative reinforcement; we know what we are doing is good because it staves off some bad consequence.

So it isn't any surprise that we approach our dogs the same way. A trainer who was adamantly against the use of food treats said, "Why should I reward my dog for sitting? That's what he's supposed to do. I don't get rewarded for doing what I'm supposed to do, why should he?" As a society, we punish crimes but only tolerate lawfulness. Traditional trainers have carried this social dynamic into their training. Behavior that triggers a response is undesirable behavior, and the response is punishment. Proper behavior goes unremarked-upon. So the sim-

"As a pet owner you will get far better results if you train your dog to be a thinking, conscious participant, willing to do what you want because you have established that good things will follow when he does so. Clicker training is how you get there."

ple answer to the trainer's question is: You should get rewarded for doing what you are supposed to do, and so should your dog. Life should not be lived in a state of sullen obedience being grateful only that we have solved all the ways to avoid the wrath of God.

As a pet owner, you will get far better results out of your dog if you train him to be a thinking, conscious participant, willing to do what you want because you have established that good things will follow when he does so. This dog will not sit still when a visitor comes because he is afraid you will smack him, he will sit still because he expects to get the attention he wants. Clicker training is how you get there.

Solving behavior problems

If you are starting to train before problems have arisen, congratulations! Many pet owners decide to train their dog when they realize they have a problem, and at that point are not interested in theory but in simple solutions. Unfortunately, there are no truly simple solutions; even effective "quick fixes" will break down if you do not follow up with consistent training. The behaviors you see in your pet are behaviors that you have helped establish through an entire history of interaction and reinforcement. To solve those behaviors you have to come to terms with that history and understand the basics of what

you have done (reinforcement) to help create the behaviors.

In Chapter 3 (Fluencies) I discuss how to train the basic essential behaviors (sit, down, remain in place, come, left-side walking). I'm not going to repeat any of that here. As I explain here, the basic behaviors not only make for a well-mannered dog, they are a major part of the *positive reinforcement* toolkit for eliminating unwanted behaviors. There are no shortcuts. Basic training is essential.

How to change undesired behaviors

As Karen Pryor points out in *Don't Shoot the Dog,* there are eight ways (and only eight!) to change a behavior. There are four negative and four positive methods. They are:

Negative	Positive
1. Shoot the dog	1. Train an incompatible behavior
2. Punishment	2. Shape the absence
3. Negative reinforcers	3. Put the behavior on cue
4. Extinction	4. Shift the motivation

We've talked about **punishment.** *"Shooting the dog"* may sound frivolous, but that's what you do when you "put the dog down." Sometimes, that is the only humane and responsible solution to a particular problem, especially if the dog has become an unpredictable biter. This is the type of situation that has gotten so far out of control that it is impossible to say that you can establish a normal relationship. I have encountered very few dogs that I thought fell into this category. In each case the client has asked, "What would you do if your dog was like this?" And I have always answered the same way: "My dog wouldn't be like this in the first place." Except for the rare case when a dog's violent behavior is caused by something like a brain tumor, having to put a dog down for aggressive or violent behavior means that you have failed as an owner. Things should never have gotten that far. On the other hand, if they have gotten that far, you owe it to everyone concerned to eliminate the problem. But before you get another dog, think it over.

You know when you put a dog down that you will never have that particular problem with that particular dog again. But you also know—if you are willing to be honest with yourself—that if you do not do things differently with your next dog you may face the same problem again. A woman in one of my classes had a cocker spaniel who was a chronic, unpredictable biter. She told me that this was the third cocker she had that developed this behavior. The cockers were not the problem.

Negative reinforcers or setups in which the dog can avoid discomfort by doing the right thing, may work, but they are difficult to deliver properly. And you can see why I prefer to limit their use. They do not bring us toward "obedience" as a willing activity of the dog. Rather, "obedience" is simply what you get when you have eliminated all other possibilities, assuming you are ever truly successful in doing so. The typical result is an ever-escalating cycle of confrontation or a sluggish, reluctant, minimally compliant dog.

Extinction is "negative" because you are not delivering anything positive in response to a behavior. As negatives go it is relatively nontoxic, but few people have the patience for it. The principle of extinction is that a behavior that is not reinforced will tend to disappear. But before the behavior disappears it typically intensifies (an *extinction burst*). A mother can ignore a child throwing a tantrum for a while, but she usually has a breaking point. And then what happens? The mother gives in. Or, she swats the child and then gives in. In either case, the child has gotten what he wanted. By caving in during the extinction burst you actually reinforce the worst of the undesired behavior. All too often, this is all that we accomplish.

You can best solve most pet behavior problems by training basic desired behaviors early and maintaining them through regular training. Five to ten minutes a day, four days a week will get the job done with most dogs. Then, when you encounter a behavior that you do not like, use the desired behaviors along with extinction to eliminate the undesired behavior. Let's see how this works.

Train an incompatible behavior. Your dog jumps up on someone who comes to the door. If you have trained the sit, you can use it here. The dog cannot jump up on someone if he is sitting. This also works for door-dashing. You are not punishing the undesired behavior but giving the dog a positive alternative to it.

To apply this method, first train the sit and have it *on cue.* Then, go through a process of having people come to the door who will reinforce the dog for sitting when they come in. Start with members of your family. Have them go outside and ring the doorbell when the dog does not expect it. You C/T the dog for sitting when the doorbell rings, and they C/T the dog for remaining sitting when they come in. When the behavior is reliable with family, enlist

A   B

Rubi likes to jump up on people to greet them. Christy extinguishes the behavior by asking friends to pat Rubi only when all four feet are on the ground.

some friends in the project. Fairly quickly, the dog will learn that the path to getting what he wants when someone comes to the door is to sit.

Shape the absence of the undesired behavior. Frequently when I meet a new dog that has no manners and is jumping all over me, I introduce myself by shaping the absence of jumping all over me. I put my hands behind me (hand movement entices the dog to be rambunctious) and sidestep the dog when he jumps up. At any moment when all four of his feet are on the ground, I click and treat. In every case, the dog learns quickly that goodies follow if he isn't jumping on me. Notice that I am not really teaching him anything *positive*. I have taught him *not to do something* by rewarding him for not doing it. If my aim is to teach him to sit when greeting someone, I have made no progress in that direction. Put another way, now the dog knows what I don't want; I still have to teach him what I do want (though, as between jumping up and "four feet on ground," I do want "four feet on ground").

Putting the behavior on cue usually goes with "shaping the absence." If I can put a behavior on cue, I "own" that behavior. Sticking with the example of the dog jumping up on me, once I have reinforced and achieved the absence of that behavior by rewarding the dog for having all four feet on the ground, I can put the undesired behavior (jumping up) on cue by extending my forearm in front of my body and saying the words "paws up." Now the dog can discover that if I say those words and hold out my arm, he has permission to put his paws on my forearm and get some face time.

Shifting the motivation is an essential element in all of this. You have to understand *why* the dog is doing a certain thing. Usually it will be for attention or food. So you find ways to deliver those things in response to desired behaviors, eliminating the need for the dog to engage in undesired behaviors in order to get them. We often encourage undesired behaviors by the dynamic of getting angry, delivering some punisher, and then it's "kiss and make up." The subject of our actions becomes willing to en-

"A clicker-trained pet is a joy for life, and much of that joy lies in the training process itself." Clicker training builds mutual trust and understanding. As Angel and Ethel head for the training grounds, no leash is needed to keep them companionably together.

dure the punisher because of the desirable result that follows. So while we think that we are eliminating the undesired behavior with the punisher, we are actually encouraging it with the consoling that usually follows.

In shifting the motivation you will do best if you have specific behaviors in place—rather than just the absence of an undesired behavior—that you can shift the motivation to. If the dog wants attention, make it *contingent* on a sit, not just on stopping jumping up. If he wants food and gets it by stealing from the kitchen counter when you aren't looking, make getting food contingent on him lying still while you prepare dinner—and then give him some scraps from the cutting board. If you don't like the dog begging while you are eating, put him on a long down and give him a table scrap or two as a reward when you are done. The formula is always the same: Teach the dog that he will get what he wants by giving you what you want.

Dylan gets agitated by the strangest things. Of course, he is a sheltie, but that doesn't explain everything. One of the things that sets him off is when my wife sets up the coffee pot at night. He used to go into a frenzy, barking and jumping and generally being a lunatic. To this day I have no idea what it was about making the coffee that got him going. But . . . my wife started rewarding Dylan for being silent when she made the coffee. At first she was doing well to get a few moments of silence. Bit by bit she was able to extend the period of silence until he got to where he is now. He'll run into the kitchen and stand at attention without making any noise. And every night he gets a Snausage. He knows so well, now, what is expected that she could probably get by without treating him for his silence, but she's established a rule she and Dylan can live with: You be quiet, you get your Snausage. Fair is fair.

Sometimes there are unintended, collateral consequences. Both Sam and Skipper have gotten into the game as well. Neither of them ever gave a hoot about Debra making the coffee. But they very quickly saw that Dylan got treated for standing there quietly, so they started standing there quietly with him. They have absolutely no idea what this is supposed to be about, but they know that if they stand there quietly they will get a treat, so Debra reinforces them anyway. As I say, fair is fair.

Appendices

Variable Reinforcement and Long-Duration Behaviors

Variable reinforcement strengthens a given behavior because it develops the dog's understanding that if he keeps going he will "win." But, like the gambler at the slot machine, he just never knows quite when. You gradually extend the dog's willingness to work for longer periods of time or to give you multiple repetitions in order to earn reinforcement.

The schedules outlined here are representative. They are "recipes." In actual training, as you get used to them and accustomed to reading your dog, you will adapt them to suit your own needs. There are only a couple of "musts."

You *must* "yo-yo" up and down with the occasional "surprise" thrown in. This way the dog does not get the idea that the work only gets harder. The "surprise" element keeps the dog focused, especially as you get into longer times or increasing repetitions. I also believe strongly in ending the session on a short trial. This optimizes the dog's chances to succeed at the end, thus ending the session on a high note.

You *must* be sure that the dog's behavior at each level is established on the variable schedule before going to the next. How do you know? As a rule of thumb, expect each level to take about a week. Sometimes dogs get "stuck," and more time may be required. Sometimes everything is just rolling along, and less time may seem necessary. Be careful about this, though. Remember, in doing VR work you are always playing in the borderlands of extinc-

tion. When a behavior like this "falls apart," that's what you are seeing. More often than not, it is the result of not reinforcing when you get "bursts" but always asking for "more."

I am sometimes accused of being conservative about escalating the criteria. Guilty as charged. As a plea in mitigation, this is only because in my experience most obedience trainers err in trying to go too far, too fast. Doing it right the first time is always easier than having to do major repair work later on.

I am also sometimes accused of being disinclined to put behaviors on a variable schedule. Again, guilty as charged. I tend to be of the view that most competitive obedience behaviors are very specific, and that the risk of confusing the dog as to what I expect outweighs the benefits of putting every behavior on a variable schedule. So I tend to reinforce at a very low ratio, usually 1 : 1 and rarely above 2 : 1. In escalating criteria I do not look so much to having the behavior on a variable schedule as I do to having a very high percentage of success (80% or more) over a large number of trials.

When you C/T, always release the dog from the exercise. If you are heeling, stop and treat (don't ask for a sit in this work). If the dog is on a sit or down, let him up and re-sit him for the next event. Regardless of what you are working on, *don't worry about what the dog does after you click.* Remember, *click ends the behavior!* Once the behavior is done, it's done.

Schedule 1: Heeling

Level 1 ("mean" = 5 steps): 5 steps, 2, 6, 3, 7, 3, 5, 1, 7, 4, 3, 5, 1 (52 steps).

Level 2 (7 steps): 7 steps, 3, 10, 5, 8, 4, 7, 2, 5, 10, 3, 7, 2 (73 steps).

Level 3 (10 steps): 10 steps, 5, 8, 4, 12, 6, 10, 3, 7, 10, 5, 12, 1, 10, 3 (106 steps).

Level 4 (12 steps): 12, 6, 10, 4, 15, 7, 12, 6, 15, 8, 12, 2, 10, 4 (123 steps).

Level 5 (15 steps): 15, 7, 12, 8, 13, 6, 20, 2, 10, 7, 15, 9, 20, 12, 8, 15, 7, 3 (202 steps).

Level 6 (20 steps): 20, 10, 12, 8, 15, 9, 17, 10, 25, 15, 3, 20, 10, 25, 13, 5 (217 steps).

Level 7 (25 steps): 15, 25, 12, 20, 5, 15, 25, 2, 18, 30, 12, 25, 15, 30, 25, 12, 3 (299 steps).

Level 8 (30 steps): 25, 30, 15, 20, 10, 17, 35, 5, 25, 30, 15, 20, 35, 17, 30, 15, 5 (344 steps).

I have totaled the steps at each level to make clear what is happening. You are getting substantial increases in the amount of heeling done from one level to the next, but *to the dog* it does not seem so bad because it is in "doses" measured by the VR schedule.

This schedule varies from 50% below the "mean" to two to five steps above the "mean," depending on the level. In this respect it differs from the textbook VR pattern of (±) 50% around the mean. In my experience it is usually too difficult for a dog to do a VR heeling schedule at that level once you get past ten steps. This progression has been effective with my own dogs and with my students' dogs.

I have interposed intermediate levels of seven steps between five and ten, and twelve steps between ten and fifteen, but after that I go up in increments of five. This is because I have noticed dogs having a hard time making the jump from five to ten and from ten to fifteen steps; but once you are at fifteen the jump to twenty and five-step jumps thereafter, are not so tough. If you notice your dog having a hard time making a leap at some other point, reduce the progression.

You can extend the mean up to forty steps. I recommend this if you are planning to trial in the combined classes (Open and Utility) because it will develop both the mental and physical stamina required. Otherwise, thirty steps (about sixty feet) on this VR schedule is sufficient.

Schedule 2: Sits and downs

There are two elements to the sits and downs: time and distance. This schedule shows a progression from no steps to one step. Apply the same principles laid out in this progression as you increase to infinity (going out of sight).

If your dog fidgets and moves at all out of position, simply return and re-sit him. This nonreinforcing response will tell him that he made a mistake without being punishing. On the next sit, shorten your distance by half and do a shorter interval. I usually go out the half distance, turn, face the dog for a count of "one banana", return, and C/T. Then you can return to your original schedule.

Level 0 (0 steps): This is actually in two parts: first, standing by the dog's side, and second, standing directly in front of the dog. Remember, you have *already* built up to fifteen seconds in both positions.

Level 1 (dog by your side):
(1) 15, 7, 10, 22, 1(!), 7, 15, 5(!), 22, 10, 7, 15, 3(!), 22, 1(!) (2 minutes, 42 seconds)
(2) 22, 11, 15, 3(!), 7, 33, 11, 22, 1(!), 15, 11, 33, 22, 5, 33, 3(!) (4 minutes, 7 seconds)

Level 2 (directly in front of dog):

Step 1: Reinforce the dog for holding the sit while you move your right foot forward. When he is consistent with that, reinforce for holding still while you step with your left foot. When he is consistent with that, reinforce for holding still while you turn and face. Give each of these events about ten trials.

Step 2: Repeat (1) and (2) above for two sessions. (3) 33, 16, 5, 24, 45, 1(!), 16, 8, 33, 45, 3(!), 16, 10, 33, 5(!), 24, 45, 16, 1(!) (6 minutes, 48 seconds). Your next two levels are (4) 45 seconds (22 to 67) and (5) 67 seconds (33 to 100).

Level 3 (1 step away in front of dog): (1) and (2) for one session each; (3) through (5) for two sessions each.

Level 4 (2 steps away from dog): same progression.

Level 5 (3 steps away from dog): same progression.

And so forth. You want to get to a distance of thirty steps away before going out of sight.

Don't be afraid to break the schedule up

I cannot repeat too often or emphasize too strongly: The schedules are recipes. Whether they apply as written to your dog is something you must discover for yourself. One of my students has a German shorthair pointer, very birdy, and particularly interested in chasing little, fluffy white whatnots. She has found it necessary to divide the increments in half throughout. When she first came to me, she was using a tie-out stake for stays. That was gone in two weeks. But to this day she has to work the stays constantly especially around distractions. This is a simple (if aggravating) case of instinctive behavior being strongly at odds with conditioning.

Unofficial Awards, Events, Titles, Scoring Systems

Dog World Award ("DWA" or "Will Judy"): Presented by *Dog World magazine* to any dog qualifying for a title in three straight shows with scores in each show of 195 or better. Will Judy was the founder of *Dog World Magazine,* and veterans of the sport often use his name to refer to the award.

Super Utility: Initiated by *Front & Finish* before the AKC instituted the UDX. Awarded to any dog qualifying in Open B and Utility at the same trial on three occasions.

Delaney System: This is not an official AKC ranking system. It is publicized primarily through *Front & Finish* magazine. It is tabulated quarterly and annually. Until February 1996, dogs received points for class placements—one point for each dog defeated in the class, plus points for High in Trial— one point for each dog in the trial. *Front & Finish* changed the system in February 1996 to eliminate the points for High in Trial.

First and Foremost (formerly the Shuman System): Tabulated on the calendar year, points are awarded to dogs that qualify in Open A and B and Utility (not necessarily combined) according to a schedule based on the score achieved.

Ken-L Ration Dog of the Year: Awarded to the dog that accumulates the most OTCh points during the calendar year. In 1995 the winner was Joanne Johnson with Shetland sheepdog OTCh Jo's Expensif Hobi of Redfield with 1,263 points (an average of a little more than 100 OTCh points per month). *Front & Finish* also keeps running tabulations on lifetime OTCh points. As of the end of 1995 the lifetime leader in OTCh points was Dick and Kay Guetzloff's Border collie OTCh Heelalong Chimney Sweep with 6,909 points (and still showing!).

Pup-a-Roni Tournaments: These were first called "Gaines" and then "Cycle" Tournaments. The Cycle Dog Food Company started these events, sponsoring three Regional tournaments and one Classic tournament every year. Pup-a-Roni took over sponsorship as of 1997.

To qualify for a Regional you must have three qualifying scores (need not be consecutive) producing an average of 193 or better during the year before the close of entries. To qualify for the Classic you must either have three qualifying scores producing an average of 195 or better during the year before the close of entries, or achieve a placement at one of that year's Regionals.

There are now four classes at these tournaments: Novice, Open, Utility, and Super Dog (Open and Utility combined). The events consist of three shows (Red, White, and Blue) over a period of two days, so each team will show once on one day and twice on another. As much as anything the tournaments test the mental and physical stamina of both dog and handler.

If you are a new handler and get qualifying scores I strongly recommend entering. The experience is unlike any other. Both the competition and the judging are top notch. Ordinary trials will never seem so daunting again.

AKC Invitational: First begun in 1995, it is open only to dogs with the OTCh and entry is by invitation only. Twelve dogs from each breed group are invited, with a maximum of four from any given breed. The tournament occurs over two days. On each day the dogs perform a mix of Open and Utility exercises. On the first day all dogs compete, performing each of the exercises twice. The exercises are distributed among six "stations" (rings). The top four dogs receive placements. On the second day those thirty-two dogs compete in an elimination event. The dog that wins on the second day will have to win five times that day.

There are also other national events such as UKC's Top Gun Tournament and the World Series (held annually in Detroit). If you are interested in these events you can get entry information through the sponsoring organization or *Front & Finish.*

Standard Heeling Patterns

In my very first Novice A trial the judge called this pattern: forward (@8 steps), left turn (@8 steps), halt. Forward (@3 steps), right turn (to rope), left turn (to corner), about turn, slow (@10 steps), normal, about turn, halt (@3 steps). Forward, left turn (at center), fast, normal, about turn, halt (@3 steps). Wowie! Pretty scary. Fortunately for me, my first dog didn't have great focus. He was, as my first "tutor" so kindly put it, "very alert." In practice we did a lot of "doodling" to keep him interested. So this pattern was like mother's milk. The only things missing were the turns-in-place and the circles right and left.

Fortunately, that kind of pattern is a rarity (though at a Top Dog competition one year we did get this one in Novice: forward, fast, normal, right turn, halt—that separated the Alphas from the Betas real quick).

There are three common heeling patterns: the "L," the "F," and the "C."

The "L" uses two sides of the ring. It's not uncommon for the judge to start you on the long side, so a typical sequence (starting just inside the steward's gate) might be: forward, halt, forward, left turn, slow, normal, about turn, halt, forward, right turn, fast, about turn, halt.

The "F" uses two sides of the ring and the center line. A typical sequence (again, starting just inside the steward's gate) might be: forward, halt, forward, left turn, slow, normal, about turn. At this point the judge may call another halt. Then, normal to the center line, right turn, fast, normal, about turn, halt. Some judges who use the "F" pattern call the last halt shortly after the about turn during the on-lead portion to have you in position for the figure-eight, but have you go down the whole length of the ring off lead to have you in position for the recall.

The "C" is an extended pattern using two and a half to three sides of the ring. The judge who calls this pattern is looking for consistent heeling over distance. A typical sequence might be: forward, halt, forward, left turn, slow (30 feet), normal, left turn (forward @20 feet), about turn, halt, forward, right turn, fast (30 feet), normal, right turn, forward the length of the ring, then either an about turn, halt, or simply a halt.

Problem Solving

Problems always arise. Dogs are dogs, not robots, and even well-learned behaviors can fall apart. I have seen some of the best dogs in the country blow the drop on recall, forget to sit when heeling, go down on the long sit, you name it. You have to accept it that you are never going to have a finished product. The ideal is that the basic behaviors are so well conditioned that when glitches arise you can repair them quickly.

There is no way, in a book intended to address general training concepts, to give "how-to" solutions on all the various problems that arise. What I want to do here is set out an approach to problem-solving and a few examples of how it can work.

The rule of three

Any time I confront a problem, I apply my "Rule of Three": one is a mistake, two is a trend, three is a lifestyle. In other words, anything can go wrong once, with no significance attached to it other than that something went wrong—once. Usually a minimal reminder of what I expect is enough. If the same thing happens again, either the very next time the dog has the chance to offer the behavior or very close in time, I am looking at a trend. Because "three is a lifestyle," I will regard the mistake as serious the second time it occurs, and not give the dog the chance to make the mistake again. At one time in his Open career Sam started going down on the long sit; after the second (consecutive) time he did it I pulled him from the next three trials he was entered

in and retrained the long sit until I was certain the problem was solved. So sometimes this can cost you time, and money. But applying the rule seems to forestall long-term problems in the exercises, and I recommend it accordingly.

Rule 1: Take responsibility

The dog is never wrong. Whatever the dog does is the product of your training. So if the dog makes a mistake, it is the product of some mistake in your training. You are the trainer, you created the problem, you must figure out how to fix it.

You can develop a solution for solving virtually any behavior problem with the "A, B, C" formula. **A** is for antecedent: What came before? Look at the dog's own history, as well as the history of what you have—and have not—done with the dog. **B** is for behavior: What is the dog doing, what do you want to change? **C** is for consequence: What has reinforced the behavior you now regard as a problem? In analyzing both antecedent and consequence you will have to look closely at what you have—and have not—done to help create and reinforce the situation.

Part of understanding how to fix the problem is to have a way to see how you created it. This means you ought to keep a training log. If possible, videotape your training sessions and keep the tapes as long as possible. This will give you a concrete record of what you did, when, and (one hopes) why. It will also give you a way to see things that were precursors of the problem that you missed (or perhaps simply decided to overlook) at the time. Figuring out what went wrong, and why, will not only help you work through a specific problem, it will help you avoid similar mistakes in the future.

On the other hand, don't beat yourself up. Problem solving is a great opportunity to expand both your understanding of training and your dog's understanding of the exercise involved.

Rule 2: Structure the session so that you can progress by reinforcing something desired rather than extinguishing something undesired

This rule is applicable to all *operant conditioning* work, but it is especially important in problem solving. It is all too easy to get caught up in the mindset of "I'm getting rid of a problem." This causes you to think in terms of squelching unwanted behavior rather than in terms of reinforcing desired behavior. Yes, you are getting rid of a problem, but you are going to do so by establishing something new. That is what you must focus on.

Resist the temptation to get into verbal extinction cues such as "wrong" or "anh-anh." Any time that you face the apparent need to employ such cues you have gone too far, too fast. Particularly in problem solving, you have to break the problem behavior down as far as possible to allow the dog the best opportunity to succeed and give you something positive to build on.

Rule 3: Do not reinforce the mistake

It is a common error to let the dog continue working through an exercise after having made a mistake. By doing so, you reinforce the mistake because you send the dog the message that he can do Step A wrong and still go forward to Step B. When a glitch happens, break the exercise off immediately, fix the glitch, and do not allow Fido to continue past that point until he is doing that behavior correctly (see *repertoire reinforcement*).

Rule 4: Isolate the problem

Don't try to solve the problem by keeping it clumped in with the surrounding behaviors. The dog did not do X. Identify what X is as specifically as possible, isolate it and work on it as a discrete problem.

Rule 5: Don't be afraid to "go back to kindergarten"

It is often helpful to adopt the mindset that "the dog doesn't understand at all what is required here." I sometimes go so far as to say, "We have to retrain this as a completely new behavior." By doing so, you will put yourself in a "training" mode, and approach the training in a positive frame of mind. Retrace the learning curve as far as you must to get the behaviors that you want.

Rule 6: Induce and reinforce the correct behavior

Having identified the problem, do what you must to induce the correct behavior, reinforce it, and then see if the dog will *offer* it on cue. Remember, as a general rule a behavior is not really in place as an operant until the dog will offer it freely in expectation of reinforcement.

Rule 7: Don't be afraid of repetitions

Once a problem has taken root, it is difficult to displace it, and you will probably never displace it completely. You should get a very high percentage of successes (80% or higher) over a large number (100 or more) of repetitions on any newly refined behavior before you can comfortably consider the problem "solved." And even so, be on the alert for the old behavior to raise its ugly head at any time.

Rule 8: Reintegrate the restructured behavior into the chain during the same session if possible, but don't try it unless you are sure you have solved the problem

Successfully solving a particular problem should allow the dog to continue toward another success. Since the behavior following the problem behavior will typically act as a repertoire reinforcer, it should be quite reinforcing to the dog to get to do the following behavior after working on the problem.

If you are going to do this, be careful. Don't invite further error in your enthusiasm to get the exercise back in one piece. Let's say, for example, that I have problems with straight go-outs. If I decide to let Fido jump, *I will do it after I have gotten and reinforced* a good go-out. I will go to where he is, C/T, and then return to my original position and let him take the jump. I will not have him do another go-out in hopes that he will get it right and I can then use the jump as a *repertoire reinforcer.*

People may argue as to whether it is really necessary to finish each session on a success, but I personally have no doubt that this is generally a good rule, and it is an almost mandatory rule when you are working on solving a problem. If I am fighting a problem and making no headway, I will go so far as to reduce the behavior to some level where I am certain to get a success, get the success, and quit for the day. Almost invariably, the next time we return to that behavior I will see progress.

Fitting the Dumbbell

Fitting the dumbbell

There's a lot already written on this subject. Konrad Most probably has the most sophisticated analysis. Milo Pearsall and Patricia Gail Burnham also have excellent discussions, as does Barbara Handler. There are just some basic concepts to point out here.

Fitting to the bite

The dog will carry the dumbbell in the gap directly behind the canines. The dog's mouth should close completely over the dumbbell, but the dumbbell should not be so loose as to "roll" in that space in the jaw. Put the dog on a table so you can see the jaw easily, and test with different thicknesses of dowel to see which fits most easily.

Most obedience equipment suppliers produce dumbbells in standard sizes, though some will turn them to specifications within certain limits. You can get them made in three pieces (two ends and a bit) or in one piece. If you get the dumbbell in one piece you are probably going to be restricted to certain thicknesses unless you are fortunate enough to have access to someone who can make one completely to your order. Fortunately, the standard sizes will fit most dogs comfortably. I have slightly oversize shelties, and they accommodate a half-inch bit easily.

Fitting to the skull

The other aspect of the fit involves fitting to the skull, which has two aspects: the width of the bit, and the height of the ends.

The dumbbell should be just wide enough to leave about a quarter inch on each side of the dog's muzzle. If your dog has significant wattles or dewlaps you may want to allow a half to three-quarters inch, depending. You don't want the dog's lips to be pinched on the pickup. If you leave too much room, however, you will give the dog leeway to pick the dumbbell up loosely, which may invite mouthing or accidental drops, particularly when the dog is jumping. I also have found that giving the dog a narrow target to focus on generally makes the dog more precise in his actions.

The ends should be high enough to be visible when the dumbbell is in grass cut any higher than a putting green, but not so high as to obstruct the dog's vision when he is holding it. I am more concerned about the latter than the former. Why? Because if Bowser cannot see the dumbbell when he goes out to get it, I expect him to keep looking for it until he finds it. With a small dog in particular, if you show outside you will often encounter grass that would be high enough to hide the dumbbell even if the ends were fluorescent. The dog has to know to keep looking. However, if the ends are too high the dog will not see the high jump clearly, and you will also find him tossing his head and rolling the dumbbell trying to get it out of his way. Again, most of the prefabricated, single-piece dumbbells will have a proper width and height.

Wood or plastic?

The Regulations allow either white plastic or wooden dumbbells. The plastic dumbbells are about seven to ten percent heavier than the wooden dumbbells. For dogs that are innate retrievers with a hard mouth, plastic is often better. It takes more abuse, won't break at inopportune times, and the additional weight will contribute to a stronger "hold."

For dogs that are not innate retrievers or are soft-mouthed, the wooden dumbbells are usually preferable. If you use a wooden dumbbell, it may be an all-natural color, or natural on the bit with white ends. As someone who shows outside most of the time, I favor the latter. An all-brown dumbbell can easily be lost against a brownish background, and you can never be certain that you are going to have a nice green surface to work on. Also, if the grass in the ring has not been cut short and the dumbbell "buries" in the grass, it will be easier for the dog to sight in on a dumbbell with white ends. While I expect the dog to keep looking if the dumbbell is "hidden," I have no qualms about giving the dog that much help, at least.

One-piece or three piece?

The Regulations impose no restriction in this regard. The problem with a three-piece dumbbell is that it is more readily subject to breakage than the one-piece. The ends are glued to the bit, and can be knocked loose over time.

Also, most people who use the three-piece have gone to it so they can get a bit that is smaller than would ordinarily be used for the size of ends that they need. This can arise, for example, with sighthounds. The problem here is that the bit is not really strong enough for the stress that it is going to encounter, and the dumbbell may break in the center. In general, it is best to use a single-piece dumbbell unless you really require an odd-sized bit. If you have to go to a three-piece dumbbell, order several and use them interchangeably in training so that you always have replacements on hand. You never know.

Glossary of Terms

American Kennel Club (AKC): The largest and most influential purebred registry in the United States. The AKC sponsors breed championships and working titles in various fields including obedience, hunting, tracking, and lure coursing. Except for the OTCh, which precedes the dog's name, all working titles come after the dog's name (e.g., Pollyanna's Lucky Dog CD).

Anthropomorphism: The attribution of human qualities or characteristics to nonhuman entities.

Articles: The leather and metal items (usually a form of dumbbell) used in the Utility scent discrimination exercise.

Attention: A term in traditional dog training. The dog is focused on the handler to the exclusion of any distracting events, animals, or people. Many people train "attention" as a formal posture. In shaping, the critical element is *focus;* attention is a given.

Aversives: A negative response to a behavior, intended to suppress ("extinguish") the behavior. An aversive may be verbal or physical, but generally a verbal aversive ("No!") has at one time or another been paired with some physical aversive. I often use this term where others might use the term "punishment" or "punisher" because I think those terms have been somewhat loosely defined and employed.

Behavior: Simply, anything a dead dog can't do. Without getting into all the possible permutations of what does and does not constitute behavior, for our purposes a behavior is any muscular activity that is or can be made voluntary through conditioning.

Backchaining: The typical process of training a *behavior chain,* in which you start at the end or last behavior and train "backward" to the first behavior.

Behavior chain: Any exercise consisting of a series of linked behaviors that must be performed in sequence. The chain may be performed either on a single or on multiple cues from the handler. Chains performed on a single cue have "internal" cues built into them. See *repertoire cuing.*

Bridging stimulus ("bridge"): A term developed by early dolphin trainers such as Bob Bailey to refer to use of the CR at a distance. You can click a correct behavior at a distance, and then have a period of time (a few seconds or longer) to deliver the primary reinforcer. The significance of the click is not lost in the interim, as long as there is no behavior more complex than coming back to you in between the click and the treat.

Broad jump: In the Open class, the exercise in which the dog jumps across a set of boards lying flat on the ground and then comes to front position. The distance across the boards is twice the height that the dog jumps on the high jump.

Calming signals: Turid Rugaas, a Norwegian ethologist who works extensively and primarily with dogs, has identified about thirty "calming signals" that dogs give each other to "cool down" a stressful situation. Some of these same behaviors (e.g., turning head away, moving slowly while approaching, and arcing while approaching) crop up in competition. It is my opinion that it is probably helpful to regard these sorts of behaviors as calming signals rather than as some form of disobedience and to analyze what you as the handler may be doing to cause the dog to perceive that you are stressed, and therefore you need to do something to reduce your stress or, at the least, stop communicating your stress to your dog.

Companion Dog (CD): The Novice title, earned by achieving three qualifying scores ("legs") in three different trials under three different judges at an AKC licensed or member trial. There are typically about 7,200 to 7,500 CD titles awarded annually.

Companion Dog Excellent (CDX): The Open title. You are eligible to compete for the CDX after completing your CD. There are typically about 2,400 to 2,500 CDX titles awarded annually.

Conditioning (of behavior): Broadly speaking, the process of bringing a behavior under stimulus control. Generally, conditioning is of two types: respondent or operant.

Conditioned reinforcer (CR): Something you *teach* the dog to like by associating it with a *primary reinforcer.* In some of the literature you will see the CR referred to as a "secondary reinforcer." I avoid this simply because I think the word "secondary" suggests that the CR is somehow less important than the PR. In fact, it becomes more important in the training process.

Conditioned stimulus: Some stimuli are organic; thirst is a stimulus for you to drink water. Other stimuli must be conditioned; that is, the subject must learn that an otherwise neutral event (such as a word) requires some particular behavior in response. *Cues* are a common conditioned stimulus.

Contingencies of reinforcement: Generally, this refers to the three-part analysis of behavior: Antecedent, Behavior, Consequence. That is, the "contingencies of reinforcement" are those things that precede the behavior, the behavior itself, and the result of that behavior, and their interaction.

Continuous reinforcement: Reinforcement at a 1 : 1 ratio, that is, one reinforcer for every behavior. There is an ongoing debate over whether you need to move off of a 1 : 1 ratio before increasing or shifting your *criteria.* As a rule, I do not impose more than a 1 : 1 ratio unless the exercise demands it, nor do I typically go to more than a 2 : 1 or 3 : 1 ratio in training, though there are trainers who can and do go much higher. See also *differential reinforcement, random reinforcement,* and *variable reinforcement.*

Criteria: The specific performance elements that you are training for at any particular point in the training curve. Related to but distinct from *topography.* Shaping is a process of raising criteria incrementally until you get to the finished product. The finished product is defined by its topography.

Crossover dog: A dog that has already been trained by "traditional" methods.

Cue (on cue): A stimulus that tells the dog that a given behavior is required at this time in order for the dog to earn reinforcement. A cue may be verbal, visual, or tactile. Clicker trainers use the word "cue" instead of "command" to denote the fact that with the cue we are communicating information to the dog as to what behavior will earn reinforcement at a given point in time, rather than compelling the dog to do something.

Differential reinforcement: A method for raising your criteria for a behavior by only reinforcing behaviors of a certain type or quality—for example, reinforcing only the quickest sits or the highest jumps.

Directed jumping (go-outs): A four-part exercise in which the dog must leave the handler and jump a bar jump and a solid high jump, as directed by the judge. On signal and command from the handler the dog goes to the far end of the ring ("go-out"), stopping on command. The handler then directs the dog to take either the bar jump or the solid high jump. The team then repeats the go-out and the dog takes the remaining jump on direction from the handler.

Directed retrieve (gloves—Utility): Handler and dog are at the center of the ring with their backs to one end. Three gloves are laid out: #1 at the left corner, #2 at the center, and #3 at the right corner. On direction from the judge the team turns to face the designated glove and the dog must retrieve that glove on direction from the handler.

Discrimination: In clicker training this term refers generally to the process by which the dog learns to identify the cue or stimulus for a given desired behavior from cues or stimuli for other behaviors that are possible under the circumstances. In competitive obedience the Utility class demands a high degree of discriminative ability.

Discriminative stimulus: A prebehavior event that becomes associated with a given behavior earning or not earning reinforcement. In the scientific jargon, S^D is a stimulus that has become associated with positive reinforcement, and S^{Δ} is a stimulus that has become associated with extinction. As Martin and Pear point out (pp. 106–107), a given stimulus may serve both functions: When seated at the dinner table, "please pass the pepper" is an S^D for passing the pepper, and an S^Δ for passing the salt. You have **stimulus control** when the subject has learned the appropriate response to the S^D and all other possible responses have been extinguished.

Disqualification: Not the same as NQ. Disqualification may threaten the dog's eligibility to compete or the handler's good standing with the registry. A dog will be disqualified if it is blind ("without useful vision"), deaf ("without useful hearing"), or changed in appearance for cosmetic reasons (other than ordinary breed grooming). A dog will also be disqualified for attacking or attempting to attack any person in the ring. If you are disqualified you will be ineligible for any award at that trial and may not compete again until reinstated by the AKC. See also *excusal.*

Excusal: A dog will be excused if it attacks another dog or appears dangerous to another dog in the ring. A dog will also be excused for lameness ("any derangement of the function of locomotion") or if it is taped or bandaged in any way or has anything attached to it for medical or corrective purposes. A dog will also be excused if the handler "trains" in the ring or practices an exercise in the ring either before or after he has been judged. Finally, a dog may be excused for "any display of fear or nervousness by the dog," or any uncontrolled behavior of the dog such as snapping, barking, or running away from its handler, or for fouling the ring. The AKC will declare any dog ineligible to compete that is excused three times for attempting to attack another dog in the ring.

Extinction: A consequence that does not strengthen a behavior will weaken it. Over time, behaviors that are not reinforced (strengthened) are subject to extinguishing (weakening and ultimately disappearance).

Fading: The process of gradually changing, diminishing, or eliminating a cue or stimulus for a behavior. You may either change the cue completely (for example, changing from the verbal "heel" to a hand signal) or you may extinguish an extraneous element in the cue (for example, gradually eliminating the target stick in teaching the dog the finish).

Fluency: A learned skill. A basic, fully conditioned skill, which is the foundation for a more refined skill, and can be added into a new behavior chain without having to "backchain" it in.

Generalization: The ability to perform the same behavior in any environment or under any set of conditions. Or, recognition of the meaning of a cue or stimulus regardless of extraneous stimuli. I use "generalization" in this book instead of "proofing" (see *proofing*).

Go-outs: In Utility, that portion of the directed jumping exercise in which the dog leaves the handler's side on cue and goes to the opposite side of the ring, about twenty feet past the two jumps, and stops, turns, and sits on cue from the handler. See *directed jumping.*

Green dog: A dog that has not previously been trained for competition. Competitors also use this term to refer to a dog that is competing but still new at it.

Group exercises: In Novice and Open. There are no group exercises in Utility. In Novice, the sit is for one minute and the down is for three. In Open, the sit is for three minutes and the down is for five, with the handlers out of sight of the dog for each. (See also *long down* and *long sit.*)

Heeling: Used in this book to designate the formal heeling exercise required in competitive obedience. Distinguish this from *left-side walking,* the informal walking used in initial shaping and by the pet owner.

High jump: The solid obstacle jump in the Open class. In the AKC the dog must jump the high jump once in Open and once in Utility. In the UKC the dog must jump it in all classes. AKC jump heights currently are set at the height of the dog at the withers rounded up to the nearest two inches, with exceptions for very small and very large and certain large dogs, as set out in the Regulations. UKC jump heights are uniformly set at the nearest two inches to the height of the dog at the withers, rounded down to the nearest two inches. So, for example, a dog measuring seventeen and a half inches at the withers will jump eighteen inches in AKC, and sixteen inches in UKC.

Instinctive drift: A phenomenon documented and analyzed by Keller and Marian Breland (now Marian Bailey) in their article "The Misbehavior of Organisms," published in *American Psychologist* (November 1961). The Brelands had been engaged in commercial training of animals using operant conditioning for close to twenty years, and in that time had worked with thirty-eight species totaling over 6,000 individual animals including reindeer, cockatoos, raccoons, porpoises, and whales. They noted a recurring pattern of "breakdowns of conditioned operant behavior," using examples in chickens, a raccoon, and pigs. The pigs were to pick up a disk, and drop it in a box. After many weeks and months, the pigs' behavior would degenerate into "rooting." The observed "instinctive" behaviors were puzzling in part because they often required more effort than the conditioned behaviors, thus violating "the so-called 'law of least effort.' " The Brelands concluded that "these animals are trapped by strong instinctive behaviors, and clearly we have here a demonstration of the prepotency of such behavior patterns over those which have been conditioned. . . . In a very boiled-down, simplified form, [the general principle] might be stated as 'learned behavior drifts toward instinctive behavior.' " The Brelands termed this phenomenon "instinctive drift." In all training, we are working both with and against our dogs' instincts, and must understand those instincts in order to train and problem solve effectively.

Jackpot (jackpotting): In Gary Wilkes's felicitous phrase, "extras for excellence." Jackpotting is simply giving the dog an extra dose of the primary reinforcer when the dog gives you an extra dose of effort to get it.

Latency: Bob Bailey of Animal Behavior Enterprises taught me the extreme importance of this concept. Latency refers to response or reaction time or the gap between stimulus (cue) and performance. The ideal latency in any behavior is zero.

Left-side walking: The informal walking method used as the first step in shaping heeling and for the pet owner. Dog walks at handler's left side within a "control area" consisting of an arc from a point at the handler's left to a point in front of the handler, with approximately an eighteen-inch radius.

Leg: A qualifying score toward a title, earned at a sanctioned AKC (or other registry) member or licensed trial. You need three legs under three different judges to attain the CD, CDX, or UD titles.

Limited hold: The technique for reducing *latency* in a behavior. Give the dog X amount of time to perform a behavior. Usually you will start with the existing response time. If the dog does not do the behavior in that time, terminate the exercise, wait a few moments and try again. When the dog is performing within that time period, reduce the allowed time further.

Long down: In obedience competition, the three- and five-minute "down/stay" group exercise. The dog must not move from the down position for the period required. See also *long sit.*

Long-duration behavior: Any behavior in which the dog must do a single thing, but over an extended distance (e.g., heeling) or period of time (e.g., the long sit).

Long sit: In obedience competition, the one- and three-minute "sit/stay" group exercise. The dog must not move from the sit position for the period required. See also *long down.*

Marking: Not the dog imparting his liquid scent to something, but the handler's action of using a hand signal to direct the dog to go forward on his own to a specific place or in a specific direction.

Negative reinforcement: Strengthening a behavior by the consequence of something undesirable being removed due to the behavior. If you are thirsty and drink water, the act of drinking water to slake thirst is negatively reinforced because the thirst goes away.

Non-qualifying score (NQ): Failure of dog and handler to achieve a leg, either because they did not score at least 170 points or because they did not achieve at least 50% of the possible points in each exercise.

Obedience Trial Championship (OTCh): The highest rung of the obedience title ladder. To obtain an OTCh the dog and handler must have obtained a UD. They must then achieve at least three first-place finishes in Open B and Utility B, with at least one in each. In addition, they must achieve 100 points, earned by finishing first or second in Open B or Utility B, and calculated by the number of dogs actually defeated in those classes at any given trial. In a typical year there are only between eighty and ninety OTChs awarded.

Offer (offering) behavior (also, "throwing" behaviors): The dog produces (emits) the behavior voluntarily in expectation of reinforcement.

Operant conditioning: Broadly, the process of shaping behaviors that operate on the environment to generate consequences, and which in turn are controlled by those consequences. All behaviors have consequences; the distinguishing feature of operant behavior is that the subject engages in the behavior in order to cause a result. That is, operant behavior works in the field of intended, as opposed to incidental, causation.

Overtraining: Simply, the process of training for a greater level of behavior than you can expect to face in competition. For example, train sits to eight or ten minutes rather than just the three minutes you will face in Open. Or, have the dog jump two to four inches higher than the regulations require.

Positive reinforcement: Strengthening a behavior by presenting a desirable consequence. If you want a drink of water, and press the lever on a drinking fountain and water comes out, the emergence of water positively reinforces your behavior of pressing on the lever.

Proofing: The process of confirming a learned behavior by exposing the dog to different environments and stimuli in the training process. I use the term *generalization* in this book because "proofing" has become associated with "setting the dog up to make a mistake" rather than as an application of positive reinforcement (giving the dog a realistic chance to succeed in a variety of situations).

Premack Principle: David Premack articulated this in 1959. A behavior with a high probability of occurrence may be used to reinforce a behavior with a lower probability of occurrence. In trainer's terms, you can use something the dog really likes (such as jumping) as a reinforcer for something the dog does not like so well (such as heeling).

Primary reinforcer (PR): Something the dog *naturally* likes, as opposed to something the dog is *taught or conditioned* to like through association. PRs include such things as food, sex, play, and physical interaction.

Punishment and punisher: Traditionally defined as a response to a behavior intended to stop (or which has the effect of stopping) the behavior. I consider that definition abstract and incorrect. I use "punishment" to describe a response to a behavior that is purely punitive in that it comes too late to stop the behavior and only inflicts a reprisal, and that may or may not affect whether the behavior occurs in future. A *punisher* is any response which inflicts punishment. Contrast this to *aversives.*

Random reinforcement: Similar to variable reinforcement, except that you are not delivering reinforcement on any set schedule. A variable schedule might look like this: bbrbbbbbrbrbbbrbbbbbbbrbr. A random schedule might look like this: brbbbbbbrbbrbbbbbrbbbbbbbbbbrbbbr.

Ratio of reinforcement: See *variable reinforcement.* Refers to number of behaviors demanded before delivering reinforcement. A 1 to 1 (1 : 1) ratio is *continuous reinforcement* (you are reinforcing for each behavior). A ratio of 2 to 1 (2 : 1—"two-fer") or higher is *variable* or *random reinforcement* (depending on how you structure it). Whether on a variable or random schedule, you are requiring that the subject produce multiples of a behavior before receiving reinforcement.

Recall (front and finish): In Novice, the dog comes from across the ring to sit in front of the handler ("front"). On cue, the dog then goes to heel position ("finish"). In Open the recall concludes four exercises: the drop on recall, the retrieve on flat, the retrieve over high and the broad jump. In Utility the recall concludes six exercises: signals, scent discrimination (2), directed retrieve, and directed jumping (2). In the Utility moving stand the dog goes directly to heel from the stand/stay position.

Reinforcement: Any consequence of a behavior that serves to strengthen the behavior, that is, make it increasingly likely that the actor will perform the same behavior in the future under the same or similar circumstances. See *positive reinforcement* and *negative reinforcement.*

Repertoire: The whole package of behaviors that a dog has.

Repertoire reinforcement and repertoire cuing: Repertoire reinforcement refers to the dynamic in any behavior chain where a behavior comes to serve as a reinforcer for the behavior that precedes it. In the basic Novice recall, the behavior of coming to you is a reinforcer for the "sit/stay." In a more complex behavior chain such as Utility directed jumping, getting to take the jump is a reinforcer for a correct go-out. *Repertoire cuing* is the same phenomenon, in reverse. In some chains the dog must do a series of behaviors on a single cue. For example, in the Open retrieve the dog must run to the dumbbell, pick it up, return to front, and hold the dumbbell, all on the single "fetch" cue. In any such chain, each behavior acts as a cue for the next behavior: going away from you is a cue to get the dumbbell, picking up the dumbbell is a cue to return to you, returning to you is a cue to sit in front, etc.

Respondent conditioning: Also referred to as "classical" or "Pavlovian" conditioning, this term generally refers to conditioning of reflex responses to otherwise neutral stimuli (e.g., Pavlov's dog learns to salivate at sound of bell, or your dog learns to associate the clicker with food).

Retrieve (Open): Dog must retrieve a wooden dumbbell twice, once going out on the flat (retrieve on flat, ROF) and once over a high jump (retrieve over high, ROH). On the retrieve over high jump the dog must go out and come back over the jump.

Scent discrimination (Utility): Consists of two retrieves of articles scented by the handler from a pile of unscented articles. One article is of metal and one of leather.

Selective reinforcement: Reinforcing elements in a behavior chain or single complex behavior, it is intended to prevent the deterioriation of elements of a chain or behavior that normally are not directly reinforced (e.g., C/T the "down" portion of the drop on recall).

Shaping: (or Successive approximation) The process of developing a behavior from a zero frequency of occurrence to a highly probable frequency of occurrence by selectively reinforcing closer and closer approximations of the goal behavior.

Signals exercise (Utility): Performed entirely without any verbal cues from the handler. Consists of a heeling pattern at the end of which the handler leaves the dog on a stand/stay. The handler goes to the other side of the ring and on cue from the judge gives the dog signals (in order) to lie down, sit, come, and finish.

Stand for examination and moving stand: Novice and Utility. In Novice the handler places the dog on a stand and leaves to a distance of six feet; the judge touches the dog's head, back, and hindquarters. The handler then returns around the dog to heel position. In Utility the dog is left on a moving stand (as dog and handler are walking forward the handler gives the dog a command and signal to "stand/stay" while handler continues forward to a distance of ten feet). The judge goes over the dog more thoroughly than in Novice. When the exam is complete the handler calls the dog to heel.

Stimulus: Any event that triggers a behavior. A rabbit running by is a stimulus for a dog to give chase. A conditioned (trained) cue is a discriminative stimulus, that is, a statement to the dog that a given behavior, and no other, is required regardless of any other stimuli that may be present, or other behaviors that may appear possible or desirable. See **discriminative stimulus.**

Stimulus control: The criteria for determining whether an exercise is truly trained. Stimulus control consists of four elements: (1) the dog does X behavior on X cue (sits when you say "sit"); (2) the dog does not do Y behavior on X cue (does not lie down when you say "sit"); (3) the dog does not do X behavior on Y cue (does not sit when you say "down"); and (4) the dog does not do X behavior except on cue (avoiding what we commonly refer to in obedience as "anticipation.")

Superstitious behavior: Behavior which the subject associates with a result without there being a clear causal relationship. In the movie *Bull Durham,* the rookie pitcher went on a winning streak and decided that to keep his streak alive he couldn't have sex.

Topography: What a given exercise looks like, or the structural components to an exercise, or what the dog has to do to perform the exercise. Different from criteria in that *criteria* refer to the performance requirements at any given stage in the training curve as well as the "next step"; topography refers to the overall "look" of the finished product.

United Kennel Club (UKC): A registry historically dedicated to working and hunting dogs, it is older than the AKC and recognizes more breeds. In recent years the UKC has become more active in obedience. In 1995 it merged with the American Mixed Breed Origin Registry (AMBOR), creating national recognition for obedience work with neutered, nonpurebred dogs. The UKC awards the same titles as the AKC. UKC titles have the letter "U" before the title, so the CD (AKC) is a UCD. UKC titles also precede the dog's name (e.g., UCD Pollyanna's Lucky Dog). The obedience exercises in all UKC classes are modeled on the AKC exercises but are modified in various ways. For example, in UKC Novice the recall is over a high jump. UKC jump heights are lower than AKC jump heights, even with the recent AKC rules changes. The UKC will set the jumps at the nearest two inches, rounded down. The AKC sets the jumps at the nearest two inches, rounding down or up. So, in UKC a seventeen and a half inch dog will jump sixteen inches; in AKC that same dog will jump eighteen inches.

Utility Dog (UD): Earned after you have earned your CD and CDX titles, with the same general qualifying criteria. There are typically about 850 UD titles awarded annually.

Utility Dog Excellent (UDX): New to the AKC in 1995. Earned after obtaining the UD. You earn this title by achieving qualifying scores in both Open B and Utility B in ten trials. Unlike the OTCh, placements and numbers of dogs competing are immaterial as long as the event is one in which a dog can earn a leg.

Variable reinforcement: Putting reinforcement on a schedule in which you require multiple behaviors before reinforcing. In the case of long-duration behaviors, you require increasingly extended times of performance before reinforcing. Variable reinforcement is on a preset schedule, which distinguishes it from *random reinforcement,* in which reinforcement comes unpredictably.

Suggested Readings

As with anything else, you can get as deep into this field as you want. The more you learn, the more you'll know; the more you know, the better you'll be. What I am listing here are books and periodicals that I have found particularly helpful to me in learning the fundamentals of canine behavior, training with operant conditioning and opening my mind generally to a holistic approach to dog training.

Benjamin, Carol	*Mother Knows Best (The Natural Way to Train Your Dog)*, Howell Book House, Macmillan Publishing Company (1985)
Burnham, Patricia	*Playtraining Your Dog*, St. Martin's Press (1980)
Burmaster, Corally (Editor)	*The Clicker Journal (bimonthly publication)*, 20146 Gleedsville Rd., Leesburg, VA 20175
Donaldson, Jean	*The Culture Clash*, James & Kenneth Publishers (1996)
Dunbar, Ian	*Dog Behavior*, T.F.H. Publications, Inc. (1979)
Johnson, Glen	*Tracking Dog Theory and Method*, Arner Publications, Inc. (1977)
Martin, Garry and Joseph Pear	*Behavior Modification: What It Is and How to Do It (5th Ed.)*, Prentice-Hall (1996)
McCaig, Donald	*Eminent Dogs, Dangerous Men*, Edward Burlingame Books (1991)
Pffaffenberger, Clarence	*The New Knowledge of Dog Behavior*, Howell Book House, Inc. (1963)
Pryor, Karen	*Don't Shoot the Dog*, Bantam Books (1985)
Pryor, Karen	*Lads Before the Wind (2nd Ed.)*, Sunshine Books (1991)
Pryor, Karen	*On Behavior*, Sunshine Books (1995)
Rugaas, Turid	*On Talking Terms with Dogs: Calming Signals*, Legacy by Mail, Inc. (1997)
Savoie, Jane	*That Winning Feeling!* Trafalgar Square Publishing (1992)
Sidman, Murray	*Coercion and Its Fallout*, Authors Cooperative, Inc. (1991)
Skinner, B. F.	*Science and Human Behavior*, The Free Press (1965)
Skinner, B. F.	*About Behaviorism*, Vintage Books (1976)
Tellington-Jones, Linda and Ursula Bruns	*An Introduction to the Tellington-Jones Equine Awareness Method*, Breakthrough Publications, Inc. (1988)
Wilkes, Gary	*A Behavior Sampler*, Sunshine Books (1994)
Woodhouse, Barbara	*Talking to Animals*, Berkley Books (1983)
Zink, Christine & Julie Daniels	*Jumping From A to Z—Teach Your Dog to Soar*, Canine Sports Productions (1996)

Acknowledgments

Writing a book is not easy. Had I known what I was in for, I doubt I would have tried it. What is in these pages is the product of everything I have done with dogs and their trainers in the last nine years—I cannot believe that it has not been longer than that. My wife tells me that she cannot imagine me living without dogs, and neither can I, although I did for forty years. I have a lot to make up for.

I must first of all acknowledge and thank Debra, my wife, partner and best friend, who first encouraged me to get dogs (I once preferred cats) and who has enjoyed, indulged, encouraged and at times been dumbfounded by my fascination with the training game ever since.

To Woody (UCD Rose City Woodland Dream, CDX CGC), my first obedience dog. He taught me how much I didn't know, and performed wonders despite me. He's been gone almost six years, and I miss him still. Someone once said that a dog trainer's life is all regrets; I don't know that I quite believe that, but loss is certainly part of the game—as is picking up and going on. And for that part of it, thank you Sam and Dylan.

Sam (UCD Rose City Sam-I-Am CDX, CGC) taught me many things, including how dogs can help you get through awful times, the benefits of Agility training and the mysteries of the crossover dog. Dylan (Rose City It's Your Call CDX, CGC— sometimes affectionately known as "brat") was my first completely clicker-trained dog; he taught me that it is all possible.

Special thanks to Karen Pryor who, after reading several of my e-mail posts to the click-l list told me "you're writing a book here, you know." Nearly four years later it's done, and someday I may forgive her for making the suggestion. Karen is the godmother of our "movement," and everyone who picks up a clicker owes her an undying debt of gratitude. More than that, she has been a mentor, a friend, and a very present help in trouble.

Thank you also to Marian and Bob Bailey, giants on whose shoulders we all stand. At some point in my development, for reasons I still do not fully understand, they became correspondents, then friends and mentors. They have opened doors and horizons to me that were unimaginable not long ago. I have benefited more than I can say from their company, Marian's genius and Bob's driving energy. I suppose in this same vein I must acknowledge a debt to Keller Breland as well, for if he had not had the gumption to launch the commercial training venture known as Animal Behavior Enterprises, who knows where any of us would be today?

Thanks to Corally Burmaster and Anita Fahrenwald. To Corally, for starting *The Clicker Journal* and giving me my first opportunity to write full-blown articles. Corally started the *Journal* at a time when there was very little by way of resources out there for the new clicker trainer and has been instrumental in helping build the wealth of resources that now exist. To Anita, for opening up the pages of NADOI News to "The Clicker Corner," giving me not only an audience but a forum in which to develop my writing ability (such as it is).

Thank you to Gary Wilkes for his ideas, his provocative wit, his seemingly boundless energy and for Megan the wonder dog.

Thank you to Kathleen Weaver for starting and maintaining the click-l list. With all its ups and downs it has been and remains a most significant forum for clicker trainers of all species. And in that same vein, thanks to Mike Richman and all the contributors, debaters and occasional flame artists on the obed-comp lists. Early in my clicker-training career I found myself on the list, forced to clarify and expand my ideas in the face of articulate challenges to both the theory and the method from people such as Janet Lewis and Judy Byron. I doubt that I would have become the trainer and writer that I have had I not had that experience.

I also want to thank my friend Laurel Hahn who brought Baron, her GSP to me and became my first student. My work with Laurel and Baron not only convinced me that this technology works, but gave me an opportunity to prove it with a dog that had defied traditional methods, to the point of needing a tie-out stake to hold a "sit/stay." As I had a few months earlier, Laurel had come to a point where she was ready to quit rather than listen to one more person tell her to "get tough with that dog." Thankfully, she did not quit, and Baron has his CD to show for it.

Thank you also to Karla Spitzer (Harpo UD), Scott Spitzer (Cleo and Helio), Linda D'Allesandro (Mace CDX), Ethel Mercer (Angel and Halo), Jamie Meyer (Nico), and Christy Hill (Rubi), students who let me use their dogs, pictures and names in this book, and who put up with my weird schedules and odd requests as I put this all together. Indeed, thank you to all my students. I hope you all have learned half as much from me as I have from you.

Thanks especially to Karla Spitzer for taking all the pictures of me with Sam and Dylan, as well as all the pictures of Scott with Cleo and Helio.

About the Author

Morgan Spector is a practicing attorney and respected obedience competitor, trainer and teacher in Southern California. In 1993 he came in contact with Karen Pryor and has been a dedicated clicker trainer since. He is well known in dog-training circles as an advocate and expositor of operant conditioning techniques through his participation on clicker e-mail lists and his regular columns in the NADOI News and the Clicker Journal. His own competition dogs are Shetland Sheepdogs, but his students come with all breeds, including many "non-obedience breeds" such as Weimaraners, Boxers, Greater Swiss Mountain Dogs, Miniature Pinschers, Wheaten Terriers and Caucasian Ovtcharkas. In the latter part of 1998 Morgan began consulting with Canine Companions for Independence together with Bob and Marian Bailey to help CCI incorporate operant conditioning into their service dog training program. Morgan can be reached via e-mail at *mslawdog@compuserve.com*.

Index